A New Economics for Modern Dynamic Economies

It is becoming increasingly clear that a new economics is required for investigating modern dynamic economies and the coming social world. Important features of those economies, such as innovation, uncertainty and entrepreneurship, are usually considered capitalist features. This may have been true historically, but this book argues that the contrary will be true for the future: the full and efficient operation of those supposed capitalist features will increasingly require the overcoming of capitalist civilization.

In this book, Angelo Fusari constructs a theoretical framework for the interpretation and management of modern dynamic economies which demonstrates that institutional transformations are essential if we are to move beyond the consumer-capitalist age and the age of the domination of financial capital. *A New Economics for Modern Dynamic Economies* opens with a consideration of the basic aspects of modern dynamic economies and proceeds to develop a representation of the whole economic system centered on the interrelationships between entrepreneurship, innovation and radical uncertainty in a 'dynamic competition' process. This model provides an explanation of business cycles that largely differs from current explanations as it derives from the notion of dynamic competition. The book is then extended from the sectoral to the micro level and then to the level of the firm. The second half of the book is concerned with operational problems and in particular with the integration of this analysis of cycles with the notion of historical phases of development. The final chapter explores the route of the transition from capitalism to a new economic and social order – a transition of vital importance, both for the contemporary world and for the coming world.

This volume is of great interest to those who study political economy, macroeconomics and economic theory and philosophy. The book shows the possibility of a scientific explanation of important ethical principles as indispensable to the organizational efficiency of the social system: for instance, the necessity and the way to conciliate productive efficiency, social justice and individual freedom.

Angelo Fusari was Director of Research at ISAE (Institute for Studies and Economic Analyses), where he dedicated attention to the performance of Business Tendency Surveys harmonized at the European level, was in charge of ISAE for Italy and investigated innovation, uncertainty and entrepreneurship with the connected forms of dynamic competition and business cycles.

Routledge Frontiers of Political Economy

For a full list of titles in this series please visit www.routledge.com/books/series/SE0345.

210 **Economics and Power**
A Marxist critique
Giulio Palermo

211 **Neoliberalism and the Moral Economy of Fraud**
Edited by David Whyte and Jörg Wiegratz

212 **Theoretical Foundations of Macroeconomic Policy**
Growth, productivity and public finance
Edited by Giovanni Di Bartolomeo and Enrico Saltari

213 **Heterodox Islamic Economics**
The Emergence of an Ethico-Economic Theory
Ishaq Bhatti and Masudul Alam Choudhury

214 **Intimate Economies of Immigration Detention**
Critical perspectives
Edited by Deirdre Conlon and Nancy Hiemstra

215 **Qualitative Methods in Economics**
Mirjana Radović-Marković and Beatrice Avolio Alecchi

216 **Quantum Macroeconomics**
The legacy of Bernard Schmitt
Edited by Jean-Luc Bailly, Alvaro Cencini and Sergio Rossi

217 **Creative Research in Economics**
Arnold Wentzel

218 **The Economic Ideas of Marx's Capital**
Steps towards post-Keynesian economics
Ludo Cuyvers

219 **A New Economics for Modern Dynamic Economies**
Innovation, uncertainty and entrepreneurship
Angelo Fusari

A New Economics for Modern Dynamic Economies

Innovation, uncertainty
and entrepreneurship

Angelo Fusari

LONDON AND NEW YORK

First published 2017
by Routledge
2 Park Square, Milton Park, Abingdon, Oxon OX14 4RN

and by Routledge
711 Third Avenue, New York, NY 10017

Routledge is an imprint of the Taylor & Francis Group, an informa business

© 2017 Angelo Fusari

The right of Angelo Fusari to be identified as author of this work has been asserted by him in accordance with sections 77 and 78 of the Copyright, Designs and Patents Act 1988.

All rights reserved. No part of this book may be reprinted or reproduced or utilised in any form or by any electronic, mechanical, or other means, now known or hereafter invented, including photocopying and recording, or in any information storage or retrieval system, without permission in writing from the publishers.

Trademark notice: Product or corporate names may be trademarks or registered trademarks, and are used only for identification and explanation without intent to infringe.

British Library Cataloguing in Publication Data
A catalogue record for this book is available from the British Library

Library of Congress Cataloging-in-Publication Data
Names: Fusari, Angelo, author.
Title: A new economics for modern dynamic economies : innovation, uncertainty and entrepreneurship / Angelo Fusari.
Description: 1 Edition. | New York : Routledge, 2016.
Identifiers: LCCN 2016021375 | ISBN 9781138208483 (hardback) | ISBN 9781315459134 (ebook)
Subjects: LCSH: Economics. | Entrepreneurship. | Business enterprises—Technological innovations. | Organizational change. | Economic policy. | Finance.
Classification: LCC HB171 .F87 2016 | DDC 330—dc23
LC record available at https://lccn.loc.gov/2016021375

ISBN: 978-1-138-20848-3 (hbk)
ISBN: 978-1-315-45913-4 (ebk)

Typeset in Times New Roman
by Apex CoVantage, LLC

Printed and bound by CPI Group (UK) Ltd, Croydon, CR0 4YY

In memory of my dear friend Angelo Reati, an important student of economics; and to a very important living student, Clifford R. Wymer, for his invaluable teachings on modelling, simulations and econometric applications.

Contents

List of figures	xv
List of tables	xvii
Preface	xviii

PART I
Theoretical frame   1

1 Innovation, uncertainty, entrepreneurship: modeling the dynamic process of the economy   3

2 Mainstream economics and heterodox economics: a misleading controversy – necessary system versus natural system   33

3 An explanation of economic change and development   51

4 A micro representation of the innovation-adaptation mechanism driving economic dynamics   97

5 An analysis on the theory of the firm: organizational forms and dimensions   137

6 Radical uncertainty, dynamic competition and a model of the business cycle: the implications of a measure and an explanation of what is supposed immeasurable and unexplainable   157

PART II
Problems of political economy: the need for reformations 191

7 An overview of the economic process 193

8 The role of demand in contemporary economics: theoretical and operational ambiguities and misunderstandings 201

9 Economic dualism: a model concerning Italy 216

10 Money, interest rate and financial markets 232

11 The ethical dimension: creativity and social justice 245

12 Toward a noncapitalist market system: spontaneous order and organization 253

Index of names 271
Subject index 274

Detailed contents

List of figures xv
List of tables xvii
Preface xviii

PART I
Theoretical frame 1

1 **Innovation, uncertainty, entrepreneurship: modeling the dynamic process of the economy** 3

   1.1 Introduction 3
   1.2 The theoretical foundations of our economic analysis 4
      1.2.1 Some consideration on method: a clarifying example 4
      1.2.2 Dynamic competition and economic development 5
      1.2.3 Radical uncertainty – the mistaken postulate of the impossibility of its explanation and measurability: the difference between uncertainty and expectations 8
      1.2.4 The problem of fixed capital 10
      1.2.5 Innovation, endogenous time and the dynamic motion of the economy: the cycles of process and product 12
   1.3 A critical review 14
      1.3.1 Some equivocations and omissions of general economics 14
      1.3.2 Important advancement, but damaged by the missing link between the two faces of dynamic competition: adaptation and innovation 19
      1.3.3 The exaggerated success of the notion of bounded rationality and the associated attack on optimization 22

    1.3.4 An ambivalence afflicting the potentialities of economic and institutional evolutionary thought: entrepreneurial skills and decisional routines 24
    1.3.5 Some limitations of econometrics and the definition of a measure of uncertainty 26
1.4 Conclusion 28

2 Mainstream economics and heterodox economics: a misleading controversy – necessary system versus natural system   33

2.1 Introduction 33
2.2 Some considerations on the method of the social sciences 35
2.3 Limits and omissions of classical natural systems and their similarity with those of neoclassical general equilibrium models 39
2.4 Indispensable extensions of the analysis 42
2.5 Necessity and choice possibility in the organization of the economy: the necessary system 43
2.6 For a new institutionalism, and a last note on the separation principle 46
2.7 Conclusion 47

3 An explanation of economic change and development   51

3.1 Introduction 51
3.2 The main factors of economic change and development 53
    3.2.1 Premise 53
    3.2.2 Entrepreneurship 53
    3.2.3 Radical uncertainty 54
    3.2.4 Innovation 55
    3.2.5 Profit and profit rate: necessity and choice possibility in the organization of the economy 56
    3.2.6 Dynamic competition 57
    3.2.7 Long waves 59
3.3 The model 61
    3.3.1 General features 62
        The conventional duration of the long wave 62
        The structure: the reduction of the model to only necessary variables 62
        The process of adaptation 63
        The diffusion process 63
        Market structures 63
        Rate of profit 64
        Inequality 64

3.3.2 Notations 64
　　　3.3.3 The equations 66
　　　　　Production, productivity and employment 66
　　　　　Uncertainty, entrepreneurship, time 70
　　　　　Wages, prices and profits 72
　　　　　Consumption and demand 76
　　　　　Capital and investment 77
　3.4 Numerical simulations 78
　　　3.4.1 General features 78
　　　3.4.2 Main results 79
　3.5 A micro version of the model 87
　3.6 Conclusion 87
　Appendix 89

4 **A micro representation of the innovation-adaptation mechanism driving economic dynamics**　　97

　4.1 Introduction 97
　4.2 Entrepreneurship and its endogenization 98
　　　4.2.1 The entrepreneur: role and definition 98
　　　4.2.2 Entrepreneurship and uncertainty 99
　　　4.2.3 Entrepreneurial skill: its formation, use and excess 100
　4.3 The adaptive model and its convergence to a stationary state 104
　　　4.3.1 The search for better techniques and prices 104
　　　4.3.2 The model 107
　　　4.3.3 The 'suicide' of entrepreneurship, the steady
　　　　　state solution and its stability 109
　　　4.3.4 Simulations of the adaptive model 110
　4.4 The model with innovation and adaptation: a currently
　　　disregarded cyclical interaction 114
　　　4.4.1 The cycle described by the model: differences from
　　　　　other theories of cycle 118
　　　4.4.2 Simulation of the model with innovation and adaptation 119
　4.5 An extension of the model to multiple goods and
　　　oligopolistic markets 126
　4.6 Conclusion 127
　Appendix 129

5 **An analysis on the theory of the firm: organizational forms and dimensions**　　137

　5.1 Introduction 137
　5.2 Some significant aspects of the debate on the firm 138
　5.3 Ambivalence in the theory of the firm 141

5.4 Optimization in the presence of true uncertainty 143
5.5 From individual firms to large-scale managerial firms:
    stimulants and boundaries to their dimensional growth 146
5.6 Some details on the factors counteracting the boundaries
    to the dimensions: the objective or institutional nature of
    the boundaries 151
5.7 Conclusion 153

6 **Radical uncertainty, dynamic competition and a model
  of the business cycle: the implications of a measure
  and an explanation of what is supposed immeasurable
  and unexplainable**   157

6.1 Introduction 157
6.2 Clarification of notions: uncertainty versus expectations 158
6.3 An analytical framework for the study of survey answers
    and the measurement of radical uncertainty 159
    6.3.1 Theoretical tool 159
    6.3.2 Indicators of radical uncertainty 160
6.4 Evidence from the business surveys 162
    6.4.1 Uncertainty and the size of the firm 162
    6.4.2 Business confidence indicator corrected for uncertainty 168
    6.4.3 Some applications concerning the permanence indicator
        and the correction of up, same and down by giving a double
        weight to R_{ii} (the repeated answers) 170
6.5 Uncertainty, innovation and business cycle 178
    6.5.1 Dynamic competition: the crucial role of uncertainty 178
    6.5.2 A formal model 179
    6.5.3 Econometric estimation 180
    6.3.1 Italy 181
    6.3.2 United Kingdom 182
    6.3.3 France 182
    6.3.4 Germany 183
6.6 Conclusion 185

**PART II
Problems of political economy: the need for reformations**   191

7 **An overview of the economic process**   193

7.1 Premise 193
7.2 A fundamental misunderstanding 193
7.3 Cycles and phases of development 195

7.4 On the process of social and historical development: the time arrow 197
7.5 Conclusion 199

8 The role of demand in contemporary economics: theoretical and operational ambiguities and misunderstandings — 201

8.1 Introduction 201
8.2 Formulation of the problem 202
8.3 The foundation of demand-led models on an important hypothesis about the labor market 203
8.4 Consequences and meanings, for demand models, of the nonoperation of the postulate of residuality of real wages 206
8.5 Ambiguities of the current analyses centered on demand: a scheme devoted to better considering previous arguments and some clarification on inflation 209
8.6 Conclusion 212

9 Economic dualism: a model concerning Italy — 216

9.1 Introduction 216
9.2 The bitter fate of economic planning and the phenomenon of dualism 216
9.3 Formulation of the model 220
   9.3.1 Variables of the model 222
   9.3.2 Equations of the model 223
9.4 Results of estimation 225
9.5 Stability and sensitivity analysis 227
9.6 Predictive performance of the model 228
9.7 Conclusion 229

10 Money, interest rate and financial markets — 232

10.1 Introduction 232
10.2 A brief review on the role and operation of money from the 1930s to the present time 232
10.3 The implications on financial activities of endogenous money variations 234
10.4 What about the present? 236
10.5 The rate of interest 238
   10.5.1 Is this the case? 239
10.6 A proposal on the organization of financial markets 240
   10.6.1 What new institutional and ethical-ideological forms are required by these passages? 240
10.7 Conclusion 242

11 The ethical dimension: creativity and social justice 245

11.1 Introduction 245
11.2 Diversity and equality: a fundamental proposition 245
11.3 Equality and diversity in ancient civilizations 247
11.4 The advent of capitalism 248
11.5 Some useful teachings: Keynes and Schumpeter 249
11.6 Entrepreneurship, innovation and effective demand 250
  11.6.1 What about cycle? 250
11.7 Conclusion 251

12 Toward a noncapitalist market system: spontaneous order and organization 253

12.1 Introduction 253
12.2 Historical sketch of the market 254
12.3 The capitalist market 257
12.4 Some other basic organizational needs of the present and coming economic systems 260
  12.4.1 Entrepreneurial role and profit rate: the public and private spheres within the working of the market 260
  12.4.2 Production and distribution within the market operating as a pure mechanism of imputation of costs and efficiency 262
12.5 Conclusion 266

Index of names 271
Subject index 274

Figures

3.1	Production of consumer goods	80
3.2	Production of new capital goods	80
3.3	Productivity of radical process innovation for the individual innovator: consumer goods	81
3.4	Employment (demand for labor): consumer goods	81
3.5	Diffusion of radical process innovations: consumer goods	81
3.6	Productivity of labor: consumer goods	82
3.7	Labor productivity from incremental innovations: new consumer goods	82
3.8	Radical uncertainty: consumer goods	83
3.9	Excess of entrepreneurship: consumer goods	83
3.10	Excess of entrepreneurship: new consumer goods	84
3.11	Price of consumer goods	84
3.12	Price of new consumer goods	85
3.13	Rate of profit: consumer goods	86
3.14	Markup: consumer goods	86
4.1	Total available and excess of entrepreneurial skill; variance of profit rates across firms	112
4.2	Labor productivity by firm, in natural logarithms	112
4.3	Total output and employment, in natural logarithms	113
4.4	Profit rates by firm	113
4.5	Sensitivity of convergence	114
4.6	Total available and excess of entrepreneurial skill; variance of profit rates across firms	120
4.7	Labor productivity by firms, in natural logarithms	121
4.8	Output and employment of all firms and of innovative firms, in natural logarithms	122
4.9	Profit rates by firm	122
4.10	Labor productivity by firm, in natural logarithms ($\eta_2 - 6\%$)	124
4.11	Profit rates by firm ($\eta_2 - 6\%$)	124
4.12	Labor productivity by firm, in natural logarithms ($\eta_2 + 6\%$)	125
4.13	Profit rates by firm ($\eta_2 + 6\%$)	125
6.1	First indicator of uncertainty by classes of business size	165

xvi *Figures*

6.2	Second indicator of uncertainty by classes of business size	165
6.3	Expectations and realizations differences	166
6.4	Radical uncertainty and confidence indicator	168
6.5	Usual confidence indicator and that corrected by radical uncertainty	169
6.6	Current overall order books, up	171
6.7	Current overall order books, same	172
6.8	Current overall order books, down	172
6.9	Current overall order books, balance	173
6.10	Current stock of finished products, up	173
6.11	Current stock of finished products, same	174
6.12	Current stock of finished products, down	174
6.13	Current stock of finished products, balance	175
6.14	Production expectations, up	175
6.15	Production expectations, same	176
6.16	Production expectations, down	176
6.17	Production expectations, balance	177

Tables

3.1	Propensity to innovate during the phases of the long wave	59
3.2	The main features of the long wave	61
A.1	Initial values of the endogenous and of exogenous variables by sectors	89
A.2	Parameters	90
A.3	Hypotheses underlying the simulations	90
A.4	First appearance of radical process and product innovations	91
4.1	Parameters identical across firms	111
4.2	Other data used by simulations	111
4.3	Parameters	120
4.4	Sensitivity of the indicated variables with respect to 6% positive and negative variation of η_2	123
6.1	Survey answers of two periods	160
6.2	Uncertainty on production	163
6.3	Uncertainty on delivery orders and demand	163
6.4	Uncertainty on prices	163
6.5	Uncertainty on cost of financing	164
6.6	Uncertainty on liquidity assets	164
6.7	General level of uncertainty, derived by the aggregation of the previous series	164
6.8	Model in Volterra's form	181
6.9	Model in Volterra's form	182
6.10	Model in Volterra's form	182
6.11	Model with the term PA in equation 2 instead of PA*u	183
6.12	Model in Volterra's form	183
6.13	Model with the term PA in equation 2 instead of PA*u	183
9.1	Estimated adjustment parameters	225
9.2	Estimated elasticities and growth rates	226
9.3	Stability and sensitivity analysis	227
9.4	*Ex post* root mean square errors of dynamic forecasts	229

Preface

This book arises out of a sustained critical reflection on (and dissatisfaction with) the current state of economic thought – a reflection based upon the systematic confrontation of current economics with the content of economic reality. The book attempts to construct a theoretical framework more adequate than current formulations for the interpretation and management of the economy.

Part I considers basic aspects of modern dynamic economies that are largely ignored by the dominant schools of economic thought, or are at best mentioned merely for the sake of the appearance of completeness, and which, in addition, are largely misunderstood by the dissenters from the dominant doctrines. Chapter 1 is an introductory chapter. It discusses some of the most important variables of modern dynamic economies and the explanatory power of their interactions and directs some criticisms at past economic thought for completely or partially ignoring these variables. Chapter 2 deepens those criticisms by turning to the method of economic and social science; we show that the analysis of social reality needs a third method that is in addition to and distinct from those of the natural sciences and the logic-formal sciences – a method that is founded on completely different postulates, rules and classifications. On such a basis, this chapter discusses some contemporary conflicts among schools of thought, particularly the opposition between mainstream and heterodox economics, which troubles current economic theory and even the teaching of eminent scholars. Chapter 3 offers a representation of the whole economic system centered on the interrelationships between entrepreneurship, various kinds of innovations and radical uncertainty in a 'dynamic competition' process. The devised model has been formalized at the maximum level of sectoral disaggregation (one sector for each specific good) and simulated with a restricted number of sectors. It provides an explanation of business cycles that largely differs from current explanations, as it derives from the notion of dynamic competition and shows that the duration of cycles, especially the long waves, is shortened by the intensity of dynamic competition as a result of the values of some parameters. Chapter 4 extends the analysis and formalization from the sectoral to the micro level. Chapter 5 develops the micro analysis with regard to the firm. Finally, Chapter 6 presents a substantial broadening of our understanding of radical uncertainty, the most typical and the most embarrassing element of economic dynamics, and probably, notwithstanding its

Preface xix

growing importance, the most misunderstood. The final section of this chapter presents the formalization and estimate of a model of the (intermediate) business cycle based on the interaction between innovation and radical uncertainty. This cycle and those considered in Chapter 3 are expressions of the theorized dynamic competition process – that is, they are implied by the exposition of the mechanism of this process; as such, they differ from the various types of cycles considered by current economics.

Part II is mainly concerned with operational problems. It commences with Chapter 7, which gives an overview of the economic process that integrates our analysis of cycles with the notion of historical phases of development. This integration is aimed at allowing an exploration of economic and social processes capable of improving our understanding of the course of history, in particular, of the direction of the ever-changing economic world in the wake of the emergence of new basic structures that will require new policies and organizational forms. Precisely, the changes of organizational procedures (as required by the new general conditions of development generated by economic dynamics), which mark the passage from one historical phase to another, will facilitate understanding of the advent of new features of cycles that develop over the course of history, as well as the content and administration of future economic order and development. This introductory chapter guides the development of the whole of Part II. It seems to us that the absence in economics and social studies of a grafting of cycles on historical phases and of an explanation of cycles based on the phenomenon of dynamic competition constitute two fundamental lacunae of economic theory; this is indeed a great drawback if we wish to be able to understand the changing content of cycles over the course of history and also the variable institutional (and ethical) needs of societies over time to manage their coming into being.

Chapters 8 and 9 are concerned with the role of demand and the question of economic-social and territorial dualism. Chapter 10 discusses money and financial variables, which play very important roles in any characterization of the globalization process; the analysis of money also offers a continuation of key themes treated in the earlier discussion of demand. Chapter 11 concerns the ethical dimension in economics on which the globalization process today confers a growing importance. The final chapter explores the content of a possible transition from capitalism to some new economic and social order (building on some anticipations of this matter set out in the two previous chapters); such a transition would appear of vital importance, both for the contemporary world and the coming world.

A number of chapters make substantial use of mathematical formalization and modeling. The intention is to make their content stringent and to clarify how mathematical specification is able to act as an important tool in representing and explaining economic processes; it is to be hoped that this clarification will contribute to overcoming the growing mistrust for mathematics by many economists and students of the social sciences, a mistrust caused by frequent oversimplification through mathematics and the resulting distortions, mainly in the work of neoclassical economists. In particular, Chapter 3 and, even more so, Chapter 4 should not be read as affected displays of mathematical virtuosity but taken, rather, as providing a demonstration of the flexibility of mathematical formalization in representing with realism important aspects of economic dynamics. Moreover, we set out some considerations on the appropriate use and limitations of econometrics in the study of modern dynamic economies and societies as characterized by growing nonrepetitiveness of events.

However, mathematical formalization is not a dominant feature of the book; history, sociology and political science are not passed over, but rather they play an important role in the proposed theoretical development of economics.

The chapters in Part I theorize on the present, but in doing so take care that the foundations of the theory rest on solid ground and, as such, are able to illuminate the future. But the past is not ignored, especially in Chapter 2, which criticizes previous theoretical approaches. Chapters 8 and 9 in Part II are, for the most part, concerned with the past, while the three chapters that follow move from important traits of the past and the present economic situation to set out, as just alluded to, some proposals envisaging necessary organizational forms concerning the future.

I first began to intensify my meditation on economic problems at the beginning of the 1970s as a result of my professional work on Italian economic programming at ISPE (Institute of Studies for Economic Programming), which was then the main Italian research institution on this subject. A real theoretical and operational enthusiasm then operated within the programming circles; it was an enthusiasm fueled by the participation of renowned Italian and foreign economists and sociologists in the preparation of the national economic plans and by frequent erudite debates, meetings and conferences enlivened by the charisma of important students and Nobel laureates.

My growing doubts as to the validity of various celebrated theories first arose by way of comparison between factual reality and the enunciated programmatic principles. Subsequent experience in macro and sectorial planning instilled in my mind the conviction that great misunderstandings were caused by profound equivocations on method. The upsetting evidence of those equivocations and misunderstandings has driven me to a laborious process of reflection and inquiry into the methods of economics and the social sciences, a work that has ultimately come to constitute the core of my scientific production and publications.

This book is intended to offer some basic lines of a new economics that are appropriate for investigating modern dynamic economies and the coming social world. Important features of those economies, such as innovation, uncertainty and entrepreneurship, are usually considered as essentially capitalist features. This is true from a historical perspective, capitalism having been the parent of the modern dynamic economies and societies. Nevertheless, we shall see that the contrary is true for the future: the full and efficient operation of those supposed capitalist features will increasingly require the overcoming of capitalist civilization. At any rate, it is impossible, or, at the very least, it will be extremely troublesome, to proceed without building up the institutional transformations (functional imperatives) caused by the transitions through the historical age of conflictual-consumeristic capitalism and the present age of financial (global) capitalism, as explained in the last three chapters of this book.

Some repetitions that occur over the course of the chapters should be met with patience on behalf of the reader, for they reinforce appreciation for, as well as deepen understanding of, crucial aspects of our analysis in addition to allowing an independent reading of each chapter.

Part I
Theoretical frame

1 Innovation, uncertainty, entrepreneurship

Modeling the dynamic process of the economy

1.1 Introduction

This chapter discusses some misunderstandings that afflict economic thought in an attempt to contribute to their clarification. They concern three important aspects of the economy tightly linked to each other: innovation, uncertainty and entrepreneurship. Their interaction will be represented here through the notion of *dynamic competition*.

This feature of the economy is inconsistent with the analytical apparatus of mainstream economics that, as a consequence, has yielded completely delusive results despite the use of sophisticated techniques and procedures. The situation is made worse by the fact that the various branches of heterodox economics, even if animated by an acute and growing dissatisfaction toward mainstream economics, have not offered a satisfactory treatment of the three aspects but only a fragmented analytical panorama. A study of the matter must meet a complex and encroaching intellectual apparatus that has been built over time on methodological bases that, although fashionable, are substantially misleading. This will oblige us to start from some consideration on method but is limited here to what is absolutely indispensable. The chapter is articulated as follows.

Section 1.2 sets out at first some brief considerations on method, mainly addressed to economics. Then it presents a simple and concise representation of the productive process that is mainly centered on the phenomenon of dynamic competition. It follows an analysis of uncertainty and innovation and a treatment of fixed capital, which is a protagonist of dynamic motion and is deeply concerned with innovation and uncertainty. The section ends up with a brief description of the dynamic and cyclical motion of the economy. These analyses will provide the foundations of subsequent development. Section 1.3 expounds a critical review, starting with some main omissions and equivocations of general economics. Afterward, we discuss two enlightening approaches that provide the premises for a satisfactory treatment of dynamic competition; this allows showing a missing ring, represented by the postulate of immeasurability of radical uncertainty and the impossibility of its explanation, a postulate that strongly opposes the necessary theoretical clarifications and advancement. We then suggest that the current insistence on bounded rationality, polemically with the neoclassical theory of perfect knowledge, has accentuated the difficulty of formalizing dynamic competition and caused various equivocations on decision making. Some consideration on institutions, with reference to the theory of the firm, will follow. The hope of these analyses is to stimulate some implementation of the economic research along lines that have been insufficiently deepened until now.

1.2 The theoretical foundations of our economic analysis

1.2.1 Some consideration on method: a clarifying example

The reader of this chapter may ask why, if our focalization on the importance of dynamic competition – and specifically a measure and explanation of radical (endogenous) uncertainty – is right, economists have dedicated so little attention to the matter. To answer this, a brief treatment on method, specifically referred to economics, is required. This important subject will be better analyzed in Chapter 2.[1]

The persistent acceleration of social change has determined a growing consciousness of economists and other social students of both the erroneousness of the postulate of repetition (and mere acceptance of the given situation) typical of the method of natural sciences and of the importance to consider appropriately the investigated reality. Unfortunately, this realization has led to an excess of analytical fragmentation and hence a lack of comparability among theories; a main cause of that is the frequent denial of the feasibility of *shared* methodological rules that make possible the confrontation among students and the control of theoretical hypotheses. As a consequence, many economists proceed freely; so an inconclusive and sterile pluralism is born, consisting in a variety of incompatible positions unable to interact.

An important aspect of the situation is economists' disregard for the explanation and measurability of uncertainty. Proper (or radical) uncertainty contradicts the postulate of the repetition of phenomena, implied by observational method, thus making itself unacceptable to the followers of that method. A frequent and easy way to set aside radical uncertainty is using 'abstract rationality' criterion and/or referring uncertainty to known subjective or objective distributions of probability, as is typical of the economics of perfect knowledge. Unfortunately, heterodox economics (and its criticism of mainstream economics), which strongly insists on radical uncertainty, the implied limits of knowledge and the connected notion of bounded rationality, has been conquered by the ideas of the immeasurability and nonexplanation of uncertainty.

To complete this analysis, it is necessary to remember the main methodological considerations that induce us to insist on some current misunderstandings on uncertainty, innovation and entrepreneurship. Unlike the natural sciences, social sciences concern a reality that is generated by man. This is obvious. What is not so obvious is the implication that social sciences, in order to properly investigate this reality, must focus on the better ways to organize social relations, that is, the institutional pillars of these.

The investigation on the organizational form of society may usefully start from some basic aspects of the considered reality (the character of the existing general conditions of development) and deduce their implications. In fact, those basic aspects require some organizational forms of the economic system coherent with them, the absence of which would weaken the competitiveness and sustainability of economic order. Uncertainty and the connected phenomena of innovation and entrepreneurship represent some of those organizational features and premises.

Keynesian economics clarifies this question well, but such clarification has not been pointed out by the numerous debates on Keynesian teaching. The core of such teaching can be outlined as follows:

- A main aspect of the general conditions of development of modern age is endogenous radical uncertainty caused by innovation.
- Uncertainty and the state of expectations imply, mainly through their influence on investment, that effective demand be either insufficient or in excess relative to production and hence reduce output or stimulate inflation.
- It follows that the control of effective demand is a main 'organizational requirement' or *necessity* of modern economies.
- This implies some important programmatic, normative and institutional prescriptions, such as redistributive policies, welfare state, fiscal and monetary policies and deficit spending.

As we can see, Keynesian theory starts from an important feature of the modern general conditions of development, that is, radical uncertainty and the possible deficiency of effective demand, and deduces some crucial implications or organizational *necessities*. Unfortunately, Keynesian teaching limits itself to such an aspect. Moreover, it concerns macroeconomics, thus omitting the microeconomic aspects of modern economies linked to uncertainty, mainly entrepreneurship and the explanation of innovation.

Let us reassert that the analysis that will follow emphasizes the relationship among entrepreneurship, innovation and uncertainty and their implications. The functional and organizational requirements implied by these phenomena are not deterministic entities that are automatically engendered by the economic process; they may be absent or badly reflected within the social system. Specific attention may be needed to remedy this deficiency.

1.2.2 Dynamic competition and economic development

Let's give now a schematic representation of economic process.

In a market economy, production is a way to get profit in the context of dynamic competition. This statement is referable to private and public entrepreneurship since, in any case, profit rate matters for accountability purposes, that is, to measure an entrepreneur's degree of success.

Economic phenomena, as resulting from some actions and decisions taken independently by a plurality of agents, generally assume different and even opposite contents from expected results. It is mistaken to think this fracture (between actions and results) may be remedied through a centralized system of decision making. Centralization only makes sense in a stationary society; it cannot face creative and innovative events, as these imply a qualitative leap with respect to the previous situation. In fact, the centralization of decision making is inconsistent with a world of beings endowed with limited capabilities but who are able to evolve. It tends to suppress novelties as it is almost impotent toward them and hence suffocates innovation and creativity, pushing economic systems toward a stationary state.

Advancement in knowledge, as well as in material and spiritual conditions, proceeds by trial and error, through a plurality of intuitions, decisions and initiatives in competition with each other. This requires the building of institutions able to stimulate personal qualities, especially creativity, to evaluate the achieved results and to facilitate coordination among the plurality of decisions. At the basis of these organizational requirements there is the limitation of knowledge, that is, uncertainty.

A qualitative and decisive leap in human history took place when the economy began to display an extraordinary ability to stimulate and govern innovation and took central stage in the social system. The modern age started at that point. All seems to indicate that the economic system will preserve this strategic position, even if flanked in the future by some other social subsystems. In fact, the economy is well equipped to operate in the presence of uncertainty and to stimulate exploration; in other words, it is well equipped to govern and feed the dynamism of social process. In particular, the economy has developed an efficient mechanism of the coordination of individual initiatives that, in addition, strongly stimulates innovation, gets information on tendencies at work and is clever in evaluating the degree of appropriateness of decision making and can adjust this as needed. Such a mechanism of production is represented by the competition in the market and the search for profit; it is a mechanism that warrants the adjustment to unpredictable events and attributes with inflexibility the merit and responsibility for success and failure in the entrepreneur's main function, that is, in meeting unpredictable events. The economy has also developed the key agent of such a mechanism, the entrepreneur, who meets and, through innovation, stimulates uncertainty with the purpose of making profit.

It is our hope that this brief description has shown some key elements for the representation of the dynamic competition process: the market warrants the coordination over time and space of individual initiatives, in particular demand and supply, while the entrepreneurial *arbitrage*, aimed at getting profit from market disequilibria, tends to erase profit opportunities deriving from 'errors' and market disequilibria. If entrepreneurs limited themselves to arbitrage, very low profit would result. But the entrepreneur can recreate disequilibria, uncertainty and the connected profit opportunities through innovation; thus even scarcely creative entrepreneurs can profit both through imitation of innovations and because these recreate spaces for arbitrage.

The described innovation-adaptation mechanism is not limited to the economy but constitutes a basic expression of social-historical processes and hence is an important analytical tool for the interpretation of those processes.[2] But it is the economy that exhibits the best and more efficient innovation-adaptation mechanism that, in addition, can be formalized and investigated in quantitative terms. The starting point of the dynamic process is innovation; but the entrepreneurial arbitrage and imitation of innovations push toward a stationary state, thus reducing uncertainty and the opportunities of arbitrage and imitation of innovations; this stimulates the introduction of novelties and hence a new rise of disequilibria and uncertainty that discourages further innovation, both directly and due to the advent of new profit opportunities through arbitrage. So, we have an incessant disequilibrating-equilibrating economic process pushed by the adaptive and innovative search, discovery and creation of profit opportunities.

We call this form of competition, which strongly characterizes economic action and production in modern age, the notion of *dynamic competition*; it is hinged on entrepreneurial innovative and adaptive action directed to take advantage of existing opportunities and create new ones, and it results from the interaction between entrepreneurship, innovation and uncertainty. One main task of economics should be the combination of those components in a unitary process that is able to explain innovation, uncertainty and entrepreneurship.

This dynamic competition is the basic mechanism of economic development and would be impossible in the absence both of uncertainty and the connected limitation of knowledge. Moreover, we shall see later that uncertainty is the crucial variable explaining both the demand and supply of entrepreneurship, and, in fact, this is inseparable from the phenomenon of radical uncertainty. Therefore, an accurate treatment of uncertainty is of central importance, and we will soon show that some misunderstandings in this regard are a main impediment to an acceptable specification of the notion of dynamic competition.

The current omission or fragmentation of the analysis of dynamic competition is a great lack of economics. This competition completely differs from that usually represented through the inclination of demand and supply curves: in fact, it causes day-by-day changes in those curves, creates new ones and influences costs, quality of products and so forth. The usual theoretical treatment of production based on the notion of production function well expresses the dimensions and the seriousness of the analytical lack of (and disregard for) dynamic competition. In fact, the production function approach is only apparent in accordance with evidence; in effect, that accordance is warranted only in a stationary economy. In incorporating a production function in dynamic analysis, various and sophisticated modifications of that function have been developed, mainly the inclusion of human capital and exogenous or endogenous technical progress. But no satisfactory results have been achieved along this line. A production function is useful if it is limited to cost specification. But other elements, in addition to cost, influence production. These elements can be taken into account only through the help of the notion of dynamic competition. We hope that the previous considerations on the importance of such phenomena will stimulate the production of statistical data on innovation, entrepreneurship and radical uncertainty – the basic components of the process of dynamic competition – so as to remedy a quite incredible lacuna of statistical economics in the field.

1.2.3 Radical uncertainty – the mistaken postulate of the impossibility of its explanation and measurability: the difference between uncertainty and expectations

This subsection specifically considers the question of uncertainty. The probability that, in the throwing of a well-balanced die, a determined face appears is undoubtedly one in six and expresses probabilistic certainty. This objective probability does not involve capabilities and does not express uncertainty; it is the same for everybody. On the contrary, uncertainty involves capabilities. Some people have better knowledge than others, some are cleverer, and some can adapt themselves to new events. Subjective distributions of probability are not identical for everybody, and they involve capability. But the subjective probabilistic approach presumes that the decision-maker knows the probabilities of the considered events; instead, true uncertainty is an expression of the degree of ignorance. Speaking of expectations, we shall see better that subjective probability has nothing to do with true (or radical) uncertainty, even if an eventual measure of this uncertainty should help to define subjective probability or expectations. Radical (or true) uncertainty simply expresses the lack of knowledge.

A growing number of students define uncertainty as each aleatory phenomenon that cannot be included in the notion of probability. They also maintain that uncertainty is impossible to measure and hence impossible to insure. This notion of uncertainty, apparently simple and clear, implies serious errors and confusions on measurability and insurability. Some clarifications are, therefore, indispensable.

In deciding on future events, an entrepreneur must formulate expectations. Some of the corresponding probability distribution will be well defined and the properties of the distribution either known or able to be specified to sufficiently good accuracy; others will not and will be more or even highly subjective. It is very important to measure the degree of reliability of the expectations, which does not correspond to a well-defined probability distribution and hence probabilistic certainty. The degree of variability, or the dispersion, of expectations expresses radical uncertainty. It is senseless to deny the possibility of measuring and explaining such uncertainty; as a matter of fact, entrepreneurs must pay great attention to get that measure. Expectations lacking in a measure of their reliability may be very deceitful.

It is important to underline that the question of insurability has no relevance in discussing uncertainty. Probably all possible events are insurable at a price; whether insurance is used depends on the cost and the assessment of the effect of having or not having it. Insurance companies may dislike treating very high degrees of uncertainty, but this has nothing to do with the impossibility of measuring uncertainty that, in fact, is supposed to be very high. It is well known that various hazardous events are insured even though they cannot be expressed through probability distributions allowing a precise measure of the risk corresponding to them. Insurance does not strictly need probability calculus; in fact, it was practiced much before such calculus was invented. Fire risks or theft and shipwreck risks are roughly classified to make possible their consolidation. Their insurance is not based on some accurate probability calculation; nevertheless, it is made convenient by its low cost relative to the damages that the occurrence of those events would cause.

On the contrary, it does not make sense to insure the casual events concerning dynamic competition among firms; nevertheless, the entrepreneur takes great care to measure the variability of expectations (or uncertainty), as just seen. The imposition by law of insurance for the benefit of creditors of bankrupt firms may be imagined, but not insurance aimed at avoiding bankruptcy; that contradicts dynamic competition, as we shall see soon. The insurance of firms' losses is made senseless not by the impossibility of measuring business uncertainty but by the peculiar content of the dynamic competition process. As we know, this process is made active by the search for profit opportunities, that is, the tendency to use entrepreneurial skills to get profits. But insurance against firms' losses tends to erase profit and implies the renunciation of the entrepreneurial role, making the entrepreneur similar to a foolhardy gambler; to cover insurance costs, he would look for ill-considered opportunities of profit and this would cause the rise of insurance costs, distort entrepreneurial function and hence push the gambler out of the market.

In conclusion, the uninsurability of firms' results is not a consequence of the impossibility of measuring uncertainty, but of the fact that businesses need the competence – that is, the judgment, intuition and responsibility – of decision-makers when facing uncertainty. The insurance of firms' losses would distort the role and use of those indispensable skills, so that these false entrepreneurs would be defeated by the competition of more genuine entrepreneurship.

Radical uncertainty is a result of innovation in the context of the dynamic competition process.[3] This is the key of its explanation that, in turn (and as we shall see), allows the explanation of entrepreneurship and its role, use and formation. More precisely, uncertainty is explained by radical process innovations and their diffusion, radical product innovations and incremental innovations.

Economics and empirical research attempt to remedy the supposed immeasurability of uncertainty through the estimation of expectations. But, even if uncertainty implies expectations, their estimation is a completely different matter from the measure of the degree of uncertainty. Expectation, and the notion of subjective probability (i.e. the degree of confidence that an agent attributes to the fact that some event may happen), expresses hope that is more or less well founded, while uncertainty simply indicates a limitation of knowledge so that its measure simply gives the degree of ignorance. Expectation is, in a certain sense, a pretension of knowledge, while uncertainty is an expression of cognitive impotence. Due to these differences, the effects of uncertainty on economic variables are different from those of expectations; the two take different roles in the economic process.

Economics has proposed some analytical expressions to estimate expectations: static expectations, adaptive expectations and rational expectations. These expressions give some arbitrary and oversimplified formalization. The study of their accuracy, for instance a sensitivity analysis of the effect of changes or errors in the parameters of those expressions, is referable to uncertainty. Expectations probably

10 *Theoretical frame*

represent the most important aspect of entrepreneurship; their content results in entrepreneurial *coup d'oeil*, intuition, talent and experience, so that each entrepreneur has his proper expectations. Uncertainty is another thing; it has to do with the variability of results and it can (and must) be explained and measured. We shall see that the postulate of the immeasurability and unexplainability of uncertainty causes great equivocations and deprives economists of an indispensable variable to represent the economic process with realism.

1.2.4 The problem of fixed capital

The stock of fixed capital is heavily influenced by innovation and by radical uncertainty, and it therefore deserves special treatment in a study focused specifically on these two phenomena – all the more so as present-day analyses of fixed capital mostly ignore them. In particular, the disregard of both those crucial aspects is complete in the formalized general models of the economy hinged upon the accumulation process, such as the Walrasian model with capital accumulation and Leontief's input-output dynamic model.

To make evident this limitation (and disregard), it may be useful to dedicate some detail to one of the most sophisticated analyses of the subject. Piero Sraffa and John von Neumann have inculcated the conviction that the problem of fixed capital can be adequately treated only by recourse of joint production models. But it seems that despite their formal, mathematical elegance and complications, these models offer no advantage in the treatment of fixed capital.

The claim that joint production models (i.e. the expedient of including capital goods inherited from the past among the products of the current year) permit the exact solution of the problem of depreciation is unfounded. It would be so only if technique were immutable. But this is not so. The desperate battle of the neo-Ricardian economists, with their command of linear algebra, against the difficulties of joint production in the name of the theory of capital resembles an attempt, with daring architectonical solutions, to construct an elegant building with foundations laid on clay. The clay that destabilizes the foundations of the neo-Ricardian analysis is the fact of technical progress, because when there is technical progress, the rate of obsolescence has a decisive impact on the depreciation table.[4] In this case, the neo-Ricardian method of calculating depreciation and the economic life of machinery by taking the technical coefficients, the physical life of machines and the distribution quotas of income as givens is incapable of yielding correct and reliable results.

Treating fixed capital through the joint production model is, in principle, no way superior to the Leontief method of defining a matrix each year of the amounts to depreciate alongside those of fixed and circulating capital. Indeed, this second method is simpler and corresponds better to real-world practice.

On the connected theme of the choice of technique, the neo-Ricardian school again seems to err on the side of excessive virtuosity. That is, the criteria of technological choice that it develops are solidly grounded only insofar as they deal with the problem of 'truncation', that is, determining the economic life of machinery (but here too they fall into the difficulties set out previously). The neo-Ricardian school posits that the technology considered has already been introduced (and the only question is to determine how to depreciate it) and that it is perfectly known. But when the question is whether or not to adopt a new technology, a number of complications arise that severely diminish the significance of the criteria for choice that the neo-Ricardians set out. Precisely, once a technology has been introduced there is no turning back, even if the circumstances that induced the choice cease, wholly or in part, and the technology to be introduced is almost never perfectly known, given that the proportions between its input ratios generally develop and evolve in the course of its creation and depend on a large number of circumstances that are variable from case to case and with which the businessman must grapple.

The foregoing means that technological choices cannot be made on the basis of the analysis of the 'factor price frontier,' since that frontier is unknown. This implies that it is unadvisable to base decisions on small variations in profitability. The decision to introduce a new technology will be made only if the prospective benefits are sufficiently great. In particular, these decisions will be made according to much more empirical criteria of valuation than the neo-Ricardians would maintain.[5]

In the presence of radical uncertainty (in this case, due to technical progress), the prices that are set necessarily rest on fragile bases, given the hypothetical nature of the costs for amortization. In these conditions, one way of dealing with uncertainty (if the entrepreneur is endowed with a good nose for business and common sense) is to set a period for recovering the capital invested and to distribute over that period the depreciation/amortization quotas, either rigidly or flexibly, depending on the circumstances, the policies adopted and so on. Competition will ensure that this calculation by businessmen will approximate reality fairly closely over the entire period considered when, naturally, the extra profits from innovation (i.e. from successfully dealing with the sort of uncertainty posited by Knight or Schumpeter) are considered as components of price.[6]

Our formulation, in Chapter 3, of a model of dynamic competition that is mainly based on the interaction of innovation, uncertainty and entrepreneurship presents a simple specification in considering the impact of innovation and uncertainty on the stock of fixed capital. We express this through an adjustment equation to production, corrected with a term representing the negative impact of radical uncertainty on that adjustment. If we substitute for the term production in this equation its explanatory variables, we can see the crucial effect on the variation of the capital stock of entrepreneurship, profit rate, and hence innovation, and again radical uncertainty. Thus we obtain a notion of fixed capital plainly linked to the critical phenomena that influence it in a dynamic economy that is powerfully affected by innovation and uncertainty.

For its part, gross investment, considered as a component of demand, is explained in the model in Chapter 3 by the variation of net capital stock, plus the replacement of the worn capital, plus obsolescence (of existing equipment) due to the diffusion of radical innovations concerning capital goods.

1.2.5 Innovation, endogenous time and the dynamic motion of the economy: the cycles of process and product

The exposition that follows is an anticipation of treatment in Chapter 3.

Economic dynamics is primed by innovation, that is, the introduction into practice of inventions that can be the result of discoveries sometimes made many decades before. But at the present time, invention and innovation are, for the most part, tightly linked to each other in the context of the research and development practiced by modern firms. Of course, many kinds of innovation may come to light. Here we limit ourselves to a main distinction which is of a great analytical importance: *radical innovation*, from time to time, gives rise to completely new products as well as to radically new organizational and technical processes and hence to an economic and behavioral revolution; *incremental innovations* improve existing products and processes that accompany the diffusion of the main innovations.[7] It may be useful to underline that here the new processes are intended both with reference to technical and organizational aspects (that Schumpeter considered separately); for its part, the concept of a new product can be extended to include the Schumpeterian discovery of new markets. The explanation of innovation must focus on entrepreneurship and uncertainty, as previously shown in the treatment of dynamic competition process.

Innovation implies a notion of *endogenous time*. This differs both from time intended as an absolute exogenous variable, in the Kantian sense, and a relative variable in the sense of Einstein/Minkowski or thermodynamics (Prigogine, Georgescu-Roegen). Our endogenous time also differs from the Darwinian evolutionary perspective, this being an extremely slow natural mutation-selection process that does not show true leaps. The endogeneity of time in this analysis may be interpreted as stating that a new time starts when radical innovation appears. In the formalized and simulated model of Chapter 3, endogenous time will appear in the diffusion, through a logistic (or a Gompertz function) of radical product innovation, while in the diffusion of radical process innovation, endogenous time is implicit in the 'memory' of a Gamma distribution. The leaps caused by the apparition of innovations are formalized through switch functions.

As we noted in the subsections on dynamic competition and uncertainty, the entrepreneur's search for profit is at the heart of the innovative process. In particular, the push to innovate depends on the persistence of negative profit rates (innovate or perish),[8] a low degree of radical uncertainty, the excess of entrepreneurship and the improvements stimulated by radical innovations; while product innovations are also stimulated by the difficulty of selling the existing products and the inequalities in income distribution. This will be formalized in Chapter 3. An important consequence of innovation, that is, breaking the existing equilibrium, is a push of radical uncertainty (to be distinguished by probabilistic certainty) that reinforces the entrepreneur's role. The development process is obliged to be an entrepreneurial one, both because it cannot do without innovation, its prime mover, and because it is obscured by the clouds of radical uncertainty.

The interaction between innovation, uncertainty and entrepreneurship, in the context of the dynamic competition process previously discussed, generates a cyclical behavior promoted by the advent of new processes and new products. The cycle can be described as follows.

Let us start from a cyclical phase characterized by the stagnation of production, low innovation and low uncertainty (since there is no variability of expectations and opinions, they are diffusely and firmly negative), and hence a high excess of entrepreneurship (depression). This situation and the associated decline in profit rates will favor the use of radical innovations (innovate or perish) and hence the beginning of a recovery of production and profit rates. During the depression, innovation operates both in the field of process and product; it privileges existing industries which can benefit from a more immediate push. But recovery sees a fall in the main process innovations in existing industries, while the advent of product innovation persists. The diffusion of radical innovation and the advent of incremental innovations following the radical ones will favor expansion, thus opening the door to a phase of prosperity. The associated economic expansion markedly reduces the excess of entrepreneurship and innovation, leading toward a break point: recession. The consequent decrease in profit rates opens the door to a new phase of depression and the excess of entrepreneurship. Such a mechanism is at the heart of the so called *long waves*.[9]

This cyclical motion is twofold, as distinguished by the adoption of new productive forms and techniques, with the associated increases in productivity, and the advent of new products, mainly new consumer goods. In parallel, the advent of new capital goods will strengthen the achievement of productivity increases.

There exists an important nexus between both kinds of innovations: precisely, the advent of new products is pushed and *made necessary* by the increase in productivity due to process innovation; in fact, sooner or later, the demand for the existing goods will become insufficient to absorb the productivity increase. Pyka and Saviotti[10] have pointed out this aspect. But their modeling is partial since it does not contemplate process innovations, notwithstanding these are indispensable to cause, through the productivity rise and the deficiency in the demand for existing goods, product innovation.

The advent of a new product and its diffusion according to a sigmoid function (the logistic or Gompertz curve) explain the product cycle that goes through the following phases: introduction of the new product in the market; acceleration of its demand; maturity, when demand stops growth; decline, when consumers' preferences for the product start to decrease. New products cause the increase of uncertainty in the existing sectors of consumer and capital goods. This interferes with the process innovations that precede, in some sense, the cycle of consumer products and, as previously seen, are promoted by the search for productivity increases.

The formal model expressed in Chapter 3 will provide a more stringent description of the development process in the modern dynamic economies; a main purpose is to give some substantial push to the research in this field afflicted by too many misunderstandings.

1.3 A critical review

1.3.1 *Some equivocations and omissions of general economics*

Economics has usually disregarded uncertainty. In particular, mainstream economics has grown as a theory of perfect knowledge. Coherently with this assumption, it has taken care to include only casual events expressing probabilistic certainty (i.e. well-specified probability distributions), while it does not consider uncertainty, entrepreneurship, innovation or, in other words, *dynamic competition*.

F.H. Knight was the first economist that insisted on the notion of uncertainty; with this term, he intended to imply chance rather than a known probability distribution and, therefore, something uninsurable and for which cost cannot be provided. This author insistently underlines that both profit and entrepreneurial function are the result of immeasurable uncertainty. That immeasurability is the leitmotif of his main work. He writes: "We restrict the use of the term 'uncertainty' to non quantitative cases. It is this 'effective' uncertainty, not risk, as we said, that constitutes the base for a correct theory of profit and gives account of the divergences between effective and theoretical competition. . . . The essential principle of perfect competition that warrants, in principle, the results toward which effective competition 'tends', is the absence of uncertainty (in the true sense of non measurable uncertainty)".[11]

We have seen that one main task of economics and businessmen is to get a measure (and explanation) of the degree of uncertainty of expectations. Moreover, we shall see in Chapter 6 that it is generally quite easy to measure uncertainty by industry and size of firms.[12] Knight insists on the uniqueness of the events representing uncertainty. As we said, a lot of events that are normally insured are unique. A theft and a fire are unique events; their grouping by homogeneous classes is always rather forced. A road accident is unique as connected to the ability of the driver. Notwithstanding, those events are, as a rule, insured.

Knight writes in a note: "If in a particular case uncertainty is measurable, it can be substantially eliminated by grouping and consolidating a number of cases large enough to warrant certainty with respect to the all group".[13] But we have previously seen that firms' results are not insured because the entrepreneur must be charged with the final responsibility of decision making to be induced to decide accurately. It seems important to insist on the falsity of Knight's postulate of immeasurability of uncertainty since it has caused great equivocations in economic thought, mainly a diffused hostility to (and a denial of) the possibility of explaining radical uncertainty, as we shall see later more in detail. For this point to be clarified, it must be connected to the notion of dynamic competition that, as we know, has uncertainty at center stage. More precisely, it is necessary to assert that it is not the immeasurability of uncertainty that causes dynamic competition and prevents insurance; the opposite is true: dynamic competition is the central feature of the economic process and the engine of economic growth and development, which stimulates uncertainty and makes senseless the insurance of firms' results.

Knight does not discuss the phenomenon of dynamic competition. At the basis of this omission there is a methodological misunderstanding, which is surprising in an author who dedicated great attention to method. Precisely, he confuses abstraction, necessary to any theoretical development, with the method of abstract rationality typical of logical-formal sciences that use postulates abstracted from reality; as such, they may upset the content of reality and lead to absurd formulations. Knight treats the theory of perfect knowledge (pure economics) without seeing that the idea of perfect knowledge implies a total distortion of reality. He introduces the notion of uncertainty only to mitigate the hypothesis of omniscience, while accurately ignoring the crucial phenomenon of dynamic competition as this is inconsistent with the neoclassical approach. He states that the removal of the hypothesis of perfect knowledge implies only some insubstantial difference with respect to the neoclassical model of omniscience, and that such difference is expressed by the appearance of profit and losses. In sum, he limits himself to operating in a neoclassical context. His insistence on uncertainty represents an analytical advancement, but he refuses to see the irremediable fracture that uncertainty introduces with respect to neoclassical theory, mainly through the correlated phenomenon of dynamic competition. In effect, Knight's contribution is aimed at conferring a realistic look to neoclassical economics; in this way, he gets honors and avoids being considered a heretic. In effect, the ability to confer to their strongly unrealistic approach a realistic look through some superficial manipulations is frequent among neoclassical students.

But reality cannot be suppressed. In fact, the phenomenon of uncertainty soon regained a first order position in economics with Keynes's macroeconomic analysis. Keynes concentrated on the links among uncertainty, money, long-term expectations and the connected volatility of investment and proved, on this basis, the phenomenon of the deficiency or excess of effective demand. This led him to show the importance of managing demand in facing the ghost of uncertainty. The Second World War, which caused an enormous expansion of public expenditure, offered a precious opportunity to prove the usefulness of that theory and the associated economic policies.

Neoclassical students quickly integrated Keynes' teaching into their theories, in particular through the Hicksian IS-LM approach that accepts the idea of the non-neutrality of money. But at the micro level persisted the hegemony of the Walrasian theory of general equilibrium, with its pretension to represent the whole economic system rigorously and in all details. That persistence was strongly supported by Knight's teaching on uncertainty. Precisely, the exclusion from microeconomics of all the crucial features of modern economies represented by uncertainty, entrepreneurship and innovation was considered, on the basis of Knight's teaching, as an admissible simplification instead of an unacceptable distortion of reality. The confusion afflicting the method of social thought preserved by substantial criticism the majestic futility of the Walrasian theoretical approach. As far as we know, nobody has insisted with the due energy (as H. Ekstedt does[14]) on the basic mistake of general equilibrium models, that is, their inspiration to the method of abstract rationality, typical of logical-formal sciences: a method that leads to deduce, from purely nominalist postulates, some precise but useless and totally misleading consequences.

Neo-Ricardian criticism has limited itself to show the inconsistency of the neoclassical aggregate function of production, but this has not affected the substance of Walrasian microeconomics. Indeed, neo-Ricardian animosity against neoclassical economics could not do more since it shared with the basic neoclassical methodology the method of abstract rationality, thus purging theory from uncertainty, entrepreneurship, innovation and hence dynamic competition, exactly like mainstream economics does. In effect, neo-Ricardian students have formalized nothing more than a simple linear system of prices by industry. This, together with its dual counterpart represented by output equations, gives a general equilibrium model specified at the industry level and hence is much more limited than the neoclassical one. Its usefulness only concerns the statistical field.

The previous reference to general equilibrium models cannot omit a consideration on von Neumann's system, representing another largely appreciated application of the abstract rationality method. Von Neumann substitutes, to neoclassical unreal hypotheses, some others no less unreal (the absence of scarce resources, strictly subsistence wages, equal rates of growth by industry); on this basis and using the duality relation between output and prices, he calculates a vector of prices that, being associated to the highest possible rate of growth, are considered to be some of the best efficiency parameters.

All these general models of the economy share a basic lack: the absence of dynamic competition and the corresponding triad, that is, uncertainty, innovation and entrepreneurship. Their attraction only depends on them being some brilliant mathematical toys. The fact that the models of perfect knowledge and stationary motion are coherent both with the prevailing method based on observation (and the connected hypothesis of repetition of events) and the method of abstract rationality has helped their acceptance. But both methods are inappropriate to social reality. The acceptance, by the main economic schools, of the previously mentioned senseless methodologies has impeded a fruitful debate and the necessary revision.

As is well known, the controversies between classical and neoclassical schools of thought were mainly centered on the problem of economic value and exploitation, and precisely the relations between prices and income distribution. But they did not achieve some important advancement in knowledge. What is worse, in such a field dominated by resentments and class conflicts, theoretical equivocations have caused dramatic consequences in practice. In particular, Marxism has associated with the fight against exploitation an extreme struggle against the entrepreneur and the market made plausible by the diffuse misconception of the phenomenon of uncertainty. Let us insist on this vicissitude constituting an important example of the absurdities that may be generated by human minds, even the sharpest ones, if deviated by methodological misunderstandings.

The Marxist interpretation of social and historical process offers, notwithstanding some serious errors,[15] a superb theoretical monument if confronted with the analytical poverty of the models sketched previously. Marx draws an analysis of capitalism magnifying the role of the market and the bourgeoisie in the building of the modern world. Such interpretation could have favored the development of a realistic and fecund economic theory, but, on the contrary, it has propitiated a real theoretical and operational disaster. What are the reasons for that?

Marx, as an economist, was strongly influenced by classical thought, but much more by Ricardian than Smithian thought. In particular, Marx insisted on the value-labor theory and hence indicated the market and entrepreneur as major causes of the troubles of society and exploitation. He concluded, therefore, that it is necessary to erase those institutions, as a condition of erasing exploitation.[16] Marx's *Das Kapital* presents some traits of the superb Marxian interpretation of history, particularly in the second and third books where, as a consequence, the sterility of Ricardian influence becomes evident. He ignores the problem of the concrete organization of socialist systems that commit to the 'imagination of history', with his method swinging between naturalism and Hegel's teaching. But a social order deprived by the entrepreneur and the market is obliged to be a centralized social system, like 'real socialism', and hence only suitable to a stationary society, that is, antecedent to the stage of a modern dynamic society.

If Marx's economics had been more influenced by his historical analysis of capitalism than by the specifications of classical economists, probably he would have perceived the necessity, in modern dynamic societies, of the market and the entrepreneurial role (even if not necessarily in the form of the capitalist entrepreneur). All that should have appeared obvious to a student of historical process of Marx's stature. What is the reason for his misunderstandings on the matter? Certainly the arid Ricardo's teaching was not enough to confuse Marx. The roots of his mistakes are in his method that blends Darwin's and Hegel's teachings, a mixture which is disastrous for the analysis of social reality mainly because both these authors associate real with rational, for different reasons, despite the importance of reducing, in social reality, the distance between real and rational. Marx considered society in Darwinian terms, that is, as resulting from spontaneous evolution; at the same time, he considered, like Hegel, evolution to be able to proceed with rationality and evolve toward paradise on earth. This position forbade Marx to think in terms of the organization of social systems, that is, to investigate the institutional pillars requested by the general conditions of development typical of each historical age.[17] In particular, this prevented him from understanding the importance of the entrepreneur and the institutional implications of uncertainty.

Mainstream economics, which has not been concerned with the Marxian-Darwinian-Hegelian methodological wave, has largely used, as previously seen, the methods of abstract rationality and observation. Sometimes those methodologies operate simultaneously, as it is witnessed by the neo-Ricardian mixtures between Marxism and abstract rationalism, as well as by the mixture between naturalism and abstract rationality frequent in neoclassical thought.

In this theoretical landscape, the hypothesis of perfect knowledge and neoclassical economics could consolidate their hegemony without difficulty. As a consequence, even the controversy on market socialism that occurred between the two world wars was almost naturally based on the neoclassical theoretical paradigm. But the versatility of the neoclassical theoretical approach to incorporating both centralization, as in E. Barone's essay 'The ministry of production in collectivist state', and decentralization, as in Lange-Lerner-Taylor's decentralized socialism, where a simple rule for decision making substitutes for the entrepreneurial role and reveals the total unrealism of the approach. In fact, such a surprising possibility of generalization of the model derives from the fact that it ignores the crucial phenomena of entrepreneurship, uncertainty and innovation that make up the dynamic competition process, so it has nothing to do with reality. It is, therefore, not surprising that the debate on market socialism gave up in favor of the more realistic and useful Keynesian policies that made possible 'social democratic compromise'. But some posthumous resurrection of Barone's teaching took place in the 1960s and fed the Soviet Union's illusion to warrant the efficiency of its centralized economy simply using optimization models.

Finally, the total failure of real socialism made clear that its main vice consisted in the denial of some crucial *necessities* of modern dynamic economies, mainly the entrepreneur and the market; it became clear that it was improper and foolish to oppose the two in the name of social justice and that such opposition had given rise to a system of domination worse than the capitalist one. Unfortunately, the roots of wrong institutions and theories cannot be rapidly extirpated; dominating interests always act as fierce defenders of them.

The analyses on market forms, mainly perfect and monopolistic competition and monopoly, added no clarification on the omissions and misunderstandings discussed, in particular on the triad of uncertainty, entrepreneurship and innovation and the notion of dynamic competition. Those static analyses were based on the shape of supply-demand curves, with some exception in the studies of oligopoly. But it is easy to see that the earthquake caused by dynamic competition destroys the graphical bases of those theories on market forms. Dynamic competition implies, among other things, different prices for identical goods or, more precisely, that one source of profit is the skill to get advantageous prices. Besides, dynamic competition implies monopoly prices on new goods for the duration of the degree of the monopoly deriving from novelties.

Of course, price variations in a competitive market are caused by the disequilibria between supply and demand that drive to the coordination of both. But what factors cause the variation of the supply and demand curves? This is the true problem, and it is impossible to solve if the notion of dynamic competition and its components – uncertainty, entrepreneurship and innovation – are ignored.

Post-Keynesian economics has extended Keynesian macroeconomics to industry level, thus driving economic theory to a higher degree of realism. But it does not consider microeconomic level and dynamic competition. The post-Keynesian attempts to combine Keynes's, Marx's and Ricardo's teachings have caused some strong equivocations as a result of that omission.

The vivacious criticism addressed to the Walrasian notion of equilibrium[18] has not offered some formulation able to remedy what is lacking in mainstream economics. Today, the fragmentation of economics in a variety of schools of thought that are unable to interact dominates the scene. Such a fragmented and confused theoretical context has prevented some important intuitions (that we shall consider in next paragraphs) to express useful synergies. In this theoretical landscape, neoclassical economics has been able to preserve the fascination deriving from its pretension to give a detailed and coherent representation of the economic system. Various students of this school of thought have been clever to mask its unrealism, both at the macro level (e.g. through the models of endogenous growth and the IS-LM approach) and at the micro level (e.g. R. W. Clower's removal of the Walrasian hypothesis that transactions take place at equilibrium prices, which has stimulated a proliferation of studies on the so-called non-Walrasian equilibrium). A development even more elegant and innocuous was provided by D. Patinkin by introducing money in the Walrasian model of general equilibrium, eliminating (but only apparently) the breakage between the monetary and real aspects without violating the idea of the neutrality of money. For their part, A. Wald, J. von Neumann and S. Zeuthen's contributions warranted the existence of economically meaningful solutions (non-negative output and prices) of equilibrium models. Finally, the theorists of rational expectations have managed to specify a surreptitious form of perfect knowledge in spite of radical uncertainty.

So, the neoclassical theory of omniscience, even if based on some absurd postulates and methods, has succeeded in reinforcing its hegemony through astute patchworks and with the help of the errors of opponents. It must be recognized, however, that among all schools of economic thought, the neoclassical one is distinguished by an admirable coherence. It has been a gymnasium of theoretical skills that may offer some important contribution, as soon as a methodology more appropriate to economic reality will be defined.

Now consider some formulations that may offer useful elements to build an economic theory that is able to bring on to the scene the great absent: dynamic competition, to be placed at the center stage of economics.

1.3.2 Important advancement, but damaged by the missing link between the two faces of dynamic competition: adaptation and innovation

As previously seen, Keynes provided, at the macro level, a precious deepening on the question of uncertainty. But, in other aspects, this phenomenon has been misunderstood or neglected, mainly due to the influence of Knight's analysis that held the consideration of uncertainty just as a refinement of the economics of perfect knowledge. Nevertheless, the problem of uncertainty was not long in returning to the fore and was subject to considerable deepening by G.L.S Shackle and P. Davidson. They insisted on crucial decisions and experiments, the world of order and inspiration, essential novelties and creative events, ergodicity and nonergodicity of processes, and subjective and objective uncertainty. But the attribution of decisive importance to the limits of knowledge and to trial and error processes is to the merit of neo-Austrian economics. The students of this school of thought have insistently underlined the links between entrepreneurship and uncertainty and the role of the market as a mechanism of information and discovery. In particular, they have insisted on representing economic competition as a result of entrepreneurial activity directed at benefiting from the profit opportunities engendered by disequilibria, errors in decision making and the accidents which make economic life uneven. But neo-Austrians are responsible for some unilateral exaggerations, in particular Hayek, who based an apologia of spontaneous order on the limits of knowledge. He forgets that the condemnation of man to advance by trial and error implies that it is important to find ways of reducing as much as possible the number of errors, mainly through interventionism and the building of some organizational forms suitable to dynamic reality.

Probably the most enlightening teachings on uncertainty in neo-Austrian economics are due to I. Kirzner's work, mainly his development on 'market process'. He delineates a realistic and effective, even if incomplete, representation of the process of economic production and competition based on entrepreneurial alertness in taking profit from the opportunities offered by economic reality and the inevitable failures of forecasting. Unfortunately, Kirzner's analysis explains only one half of the process of dynamic competition, the one concerning adaptive entrepreneurial action directed to take advantage of the existing profit opportunities, which, as we saw, tends to erase profit. Kirzner neglects entrepreneurship directed at creating new profit opportunities through innovation. Indeed, he makes some attempts to remedy this lack by dividing entrepreneurial process in two components: entrepreneurial short-run competition and entrepreneurial discovery in the long run. But Kirzner limits himself to emphasizing the discovery of the existing opportunities, not the creation of new opportunities.[19] He substantially ignores entrepreneurial action that engenders uncertainty and disequilibria, thus giving rise to arbitrage and market process. In sum, Kirzner disregards specifying radical innovation or, more generally, the dynamic aspect of the competition process, and hence 'endogenous' uncertainty.

A promising way to remedy this shortcoming and try to complete the representation of the dynamic competition process may consist of marrying Kirzner's market process to the Schumpeterian 'creative destruction'. Unfortunately, neo-Austrian and Schumpeterian teachings remain two separated branches of investigation, notwithstanding their strong complementarity. They make two opposite errors: the substantial absence of consideration of innovation, which is typical of neo-Austrians, and the substantial Schumpeterian absence of consideration of uncertainty.[20] In particular, Schumpeter does not attribute any importance to endogenous uncertainty that is produced by the economic system, notwithstanding that such endogeneity clearly springs off his notion of 'creative destruction'. This omission has determined the most surprising Schumpeterian error: the forecasting of the exhaustion of entrepreneurial function[21] and the advent of socialism through big business. The error was repeated by J. K. Galbraith in *The New Industrial State*, which diagnosed the convergence between capitalism and socialism through the managerial firm.[22] A superficial consideration of uncertainty would have been sufficient to show the authors the great obstacle that such a phenomenon poses to the centralization of decision making.

It is surprising that these two approaches have not been unified so as to supply a proper theoretical analysis of the great absent: dynamic competition. The missing ring that has prevented an effective and persuasive representation of a dynamic competition process, starting from the above neo-Austrian and Schumpeterian contributions, is represented by the exclusion from economics of a variable expressing the dimension of true or radical uncertainty and the explanation of this. In fact, the representation of the interaction between innovation and adaptation requires the expression of the endogenous variations of the level of uncertainty. Those variations cause: (a) the rise of entrepreneurial adaptive action when uncertainty (and disequilibria) grow together with the connected profit opportunities; and (b) the rise of innovation when uncertainty (and disequilibria) decrease due to adaptation process, since this decrease will make easier to innovate and will oblige to create profit opportunities through innovation. The explanation of the level of uncertainty is necessary, and it may allow for unification of neo-Austrian and Schumpeterian competition and, in this way, give a more complete and coherent formulation of the dynamic competition process and of the explanation of entrepreneurship. The mistaken Knight's postulate of the immeasurability of uncertainty, retained by economists with a surprising superficiality, and the connected diffusion of the idea that radical uncertainty cannot (and must not) be explained, have obstructed such a development. For better evidence of the persistent separation in economics of the two branches of dynamic competition, innovation and adaptation, it may be useful to quote the opinion that Kirzner expressed to us on the matter.[23] He said:

> I realize, of course (and this was one of the purposes of my 'Creativity and/ or alertness' paper) that there are differences between the kinds of innovation Schumpeter had in mind, and the entrepreneurial 'discoveries' which I had insisted were the steps in the process by which Schumpeter's 'imitators' tend to bring about equilibrium. ... I am reminded of Samuelson's imagery of the Schumpeterian process as similar to a violin string that has been plucked into vibration (by innovation), subsequently returning to its quiescent state (through the imitators) – except that you postulate that the very quiescence of this state stimulates further innovation, etc. ... You imply that a reduction of uncertainty stimulates the rate of Schumpeterian innovation. I have not yet seen any reasoning firmly leading to this conclusion. You seem to take it as obvious.

Yes, it simply is an expression of the search for profit and it is crucial for the specification of dynamic competition as given by the interaction of innovation

22 Theoretical frame

and adaptation: when uncertainty and the adaptive opportunities of profit are low, there will be a stimulus to create opportunities of profit through innovation, which is easier to introduce in the presence of low uncertainty.

The persistent lack of consideration of dynamic competition is surprising. This seems to be a result of the absence of a method of social theory appropriate to the basic character of social reality. Such a lack condemns economics to offer confusing teachings. These darken even the most obvious and elementary problems through complicated and misleading formulations, with everybody claiming to be right in their own way. The next subsection will consider some equivocations that affect the strong opposition of heterodox economics to the economics of perfect knowledge.

1.3.3 *The exaggerated success of the notion of bounded rationality and the associated attack on optimization*

The aversion to the economics of perfect knowledge has grown with the acceleration of economic dynamics and hence the rise of uncertainty. In such an intellectual climate, the notion of 'bounded rationality' has come to light and has enjoyed rapid success due to its usefulness in opposing neoclassical perfect rationality. Unfortunately, that notion is undermined by numerous equivocations that need to be clarified.

In every field of life, man is forced to go ahead by trial and error. The understanding of nature is made difficult by the fact that such reality is not the work of man. On the contrary, the understanding of social reality is made difficult by the fact that it is a result of the interaction of a lot of human actions and creative events. But this difficulty is better expressed by the terms *uncertainty* or *limited knowledge* than by the expression 'bounded rationality'. In effect, human skills and rationality are always bound, by definition, to the limits of human knowledge.

An interesting definition may consist in the notion of 'cognitive rationality' that underlines the learning process connected to the use of human rationality.[24] This process requires a measure of the degree of uncertainty to express the formation and use of entrepreneurial skills and to define the constraints of the cognitive process, as we shall soon see.

It must be recognized that the notion of bounded rationality has promoted some useful deepening of cognitive processes, in conjunction with M. Polanyi's research on 'tacit knowledge'. Unfortunately, that notion almost neglects the dynamic competition process although this represents the backbone of the economic process in the presence of limited knowledge. What is more surprising in the economics of bounded rationality is that it does not seem to understand the crucial importance of considering the level (and hence a measure) of the factor on which the limits of rationality depend, that is, the degree of radical uncertainty. This omission has implied the denial or the darkening of the possibility to explain uncertainty and suffocates the potentiality of this branch of heterodox economics; it prevents, as just seen with reference to neo-Austrian and Schumpeterian teachings, the formalization of the phenomenon of dynamic competition. It seems, therefore, sensible to ask to the growing number of students insisting on the notion of bounded rationality: what prevents you from seeing the importance of a measure and an explanation of the factor expressing the limitation of rationality, that is, the level of uncertainty? The economists who insist on bounded rationality disregard the question of the accuracy of expectations. But their negligence in producing a measure and an explanation of the volatility or variability of expectations is a surprising omission. This volatility is, at the same time, perfectly coherent with the notion of bounded rationality and gives a possible measure of the degree of uncertainty.

The galaxy of theories constituting the so-called heterodox economics testifies to an enormous analytical fragmentation that prevents the unification of efforts and results. One of the few aspects shared by heterodox students is the disputation with mainstream economics. But this convergence is afflicted by exaggerations and equivocations. In particular, the disputation has obscured, mainly through some abuse of the expression 'bounded rationality', the important fact that man is obliged, by his interests and competition, to use his rational skills, just like the optimization procedure maintains. It has been erroneously assumed that optimization presumes omniscience, an assumption that indeed would imply that Pontryagin's and Kantorovich's works are pointless. Kirzner wrote: "Where the circumstances of decision are believed to be certainly known to the decision-maker, we can 'predict' what form that decision will take merely by identifying the optimum course of action relevant to the known circumstances. Now this 'mechanical' interpretation of decision-making would be entirely acceptable for a world of perfect knowledge and prediction".[25] This assimilation of optimization to neoclassical economics is mistaken. Optimization does not require perfect knowledge; it is only a tool for decision making that often is more rational than others. Perhaps it would be much more enlightening to hinge the polemics against neoclassical thought on the notion of uncertainty than on that of bounded rationality.

The father of bounded rationality, H. Simon, opposed to optimization the principle of 'satisfying behavior'. But this principle is vague and can be variously interpreted, mainly with reference to the levels of aspiration and satisfaction.

All seems to show that the hostility against optimization is mainly due to two prejudices: (1) the habit of connecting the optimization principle to the hypothesis of omniscience, that is, perfect knowledge, thus forgetting that such a principle is simply a mathematical tool that does not need that hypothesis; and (2) the postulate of immeasurability and unexplainability of uncertainty, that is, the denial of the possibility of defining an endogenous variable expressing the degree of limitation of knowledge; this denial prevents the possibility of formalizing an optimization model including both uncertainty and the availability of entrepreneurial skills and hence the tension in the use of these. In fact, to define availability and tension, a measure and an explanation of the degree of uncertainty are needed.

Firms are forced by competition, more than other subjects, to act rationally as much as possible. This implies that firms' competition drives them to optimization; but this only means that optimization gives better solution than other procedures. In sum, an aprioristic refusal of optimization is not wise, this being able to supply a

24 Theoretical frame

better rationality criterion than other decision-making tools. All that is quite simple and evident. The main reason obscuring this banal evidence is (let us repeat) the conviction that uncertainty is something impalpable and, as such, is inconsistent with optimization; this conviction leads to intend optimization as only referable to the absurd hypothesis of perfect information. The result is that, while neoclassical economists tend to strongly exaggerate human knowledge on the basis of the hypothesis of perfect knowledge, their opponents make an opposite exaggeration: the postulate of immeasurability and unexplainability of uncertainty that prevents obtaining important knowledge and urgent analytical development.

1.3.4 An ambivalence afflicting the potentialities of economic and institutional evolutionary thought: entrepreneurial skills and decisional routines

The notion of evolution strongly influences the modern economic thought and the analysis of institutions, in connection with the insistence on the limits of knowledge or radical uncertainty. Unfortunately, the use by economics of the evolutionary metaphor is afflicted by ambivalence. From the one side, Hayek and neo-Austrians underline the limitation of knowledge as a support to the idea that economic processes and the evolution of institutions are the result of spontaneous behavior; as a consequence, they strongly dislike the organizational view of method, to which they oppose 'spontaneous order', and hence they are inclined to neglect the problem of the firm. On the contrary, institutional students emphasize organization and utilize the notion of uncertainty to explain institutions and, hence, the firm.

To understand these aspects, some consideration of Nelson and Winter's contribution may be useful.[26] The development of these authors is mainly based on Schumpeterian work; this has prevented, for the reasons indicated previously, the adequate representation of the dynamic competition process, which should be at the center stage of heterodox economics. Nelson and Winter's analysis shows, however, some differences with respect to Schumpeter that must be noted.

Evolutionary economics does not neglect uncertainty, but it incorporates it in the notion of bounded rationality and considers unquestionable the postulate of immeasurability of (and the impossibility to explain) uncertainty. Unfortunately, this postulate, and the consequent setting aside of the optimization principle, engender a vague theoretic atmosphere. Evolutionary economics' main remedy to that vagueness is the notion of 'decisional routines', which are intended to provide a solid conceptual basis to decision making; some evolutionary economists have assimilated decisional routines to biological genes. Here appears again the methodological inappropriateness of the postulate of immeasurability of uncertainty. In fact, it is mainly due to that postulate that this branch of economics separates entrepreneurial function from uncertainty in the context of the notion of *routine*. But the various developments on routines do not provide stringent empirical and conceptual formulations;[27] they presume some very simple decisional rules emphasizing the automaticity of decision making, but this is inconsistent with the entrepreneurial role and hence does not allow the explanation of entrepreneurship.

Nelson and Winter intend routines as organizational memories, as forms of tacit knowledge, in M. Polanyi's sense. They consider routines to be the most important storage of organizational knowledge. The firm's behavior should be explained through the used routines, and it should be expected that in the future the firm will behave similarly to the past, the change in routines being obstructed by the consequent fracture of equilibrium and organizational compromises. However, innovation in the rules of decision making is considered possible and important. But entrepreneurship is inconceivable and inexplicable if separated by radical uncertainty. It must be stressed that the notion of routine has nothing to do with entrepreneurship. Entrepreneurship is mainly a skill to meet uncertainty, while *routine* means repetition and hence implies bureaucratic skills. Heterodox analyses have dedicated a good deal of work to organizational skills, but they say very little on entrepreneurship. Entrepreneurial decisions, at least the most important of them, do not follow any precise rules. The various branches of heterodox economics, in trying to reduce, through the notion of routine, the indeterminacy deriving from the notion of bounded rationality and from the postulate of immeasurability of uncertainty, forget the flexibility and versatility of entrepreneurship. M. Egidi and A. Narduzzo have empirically shown that the use of routines that were effective in the past may cause systematic decisional errors.[28] It is our opinion that the analytical indeterminacy of entrepreneurial decisions cannot be faced through the reference to some precise decisional rules; it requires ventures in uncertainty, where entrepreneurship acts. More precisely, it is important to define some criteria that allow for measuring and explaining the level of radical uncertainty and its variations, so as to provide both a more solid basis to decision making and some analytical developments on the formation and the use of entrepreneurial skills; on innovation, disequilibria and adaptation, in brief, on the dynamic competition process.

It must be noted, however, that the growing attention dedicated to uncertainty and to the limits of knowledge has stimulated, among evolutionary students and in opposition to spontaneous evolutionism, some interesting developments on organization, mainly in the field of the firm. We saw that uncertainty requires some peculiar institutional forms. In this light, it is relevant that the firm has been indicated, by the economists of 'transaction costs', as an organizational necessity since it reduces uncertainty due to those costs by introducing hierarchical command mechanisms to the market. This theory is important, but it explains less than supposed, mainly on the firm dimension. In fact, the increase in the sizes of firms reduces the market transactions and hence the uncertainty caused by the incompleteness of corresponding contracts. Moreover, the bureaucratization of decision making in large firms reduces the capabilities to face the unknown. Of course, it is possible to remedy that inconvenience through decentralized organizational forms, but this possibility is opposed by the centralization of last instance responsibility. Besides, the strategies devoted to reducing uncertainty are weakened and opposed by the fact that entrepreneurial innovation engenders uncertainty.

The dimensions of the firm seem mainly influenced by the quality and quantity of available entrepreneurial skills and uncertainty, which determine the potentialities of those skills and their demand. In conclusion, the best way to treat radical or true uncertainty seems to be introducing explicitly it into the models for decision making so as to estimate its impact on strategic choices and some other important variables, rather than setting uncertainty aside on the basis of the hypothesis that it cannot be measured and explained.

Neoclassical students, with the purpose to improve the realism of their theories, have suggested introducing into optimization models the skill to face uncertainty. But this idea and the others concerning uncertainty need a variable expressing their levels, a possibility denied by the postulate of immeasurability (and nonexplanation) of radical uncertainty. Such a postulate seems to represent a principal obstacle to the building of an economic theory that is able to conjugate uncertainty, entrepreneurship and innovation and an obstacle to defining the way uncertainty influences (and is influenced by) entrepreneurship and innovation. The representation of the dynamic competition process and economic development requires the abolition of that postulate. There exists a tight link between entrepreneurial skill and uncertainty; in fact, in the absence of radical uncertainty, there would be no need for (and no formation of) entrepreneurship. As the notion of dynamic competition shows, the entrepreneur meets uncertainty, but also generates uncertainty, through innovation.

Entrepreneurial capabilities are mainly a result of *tacit knowledge* (learning by doing, by watching and by using) and innate skills. These capabilities vary, therefore, with experience. It follows that, even if one main characteristic of them is versatility, the operational experience confers to skills some degree of specialization that restricts their field of competence. Darwinian evolution cannot be referred to the interpretation of economic and social events. Such interpretation needs an organizational view to consider the growing pace of economic and social change, while the extremely low change concerning the advent of new animal species allows, in biology, the use of the observational view. However, after the elimination of the misunderstandings considered in this section, the combination of institutional and evolutionary thought seems to offer a fecund methodological perspective for the study of social events. In fact, the institutional character of human societies decisively influences the pace of their evolutionary change and, for its part, the sedimentation of changes determines the necessity to edify, in the context of changing general conditions of development, new institutions. So the importance of the institutional aspect side by side with the evolutionary motion appears evident and concerns also the ethical aspect. In this regard, see Section 2.2 on the role of ontological imperatives (often of ethical content) in pushing the evolutionary motion, and the role of functional imperatives in providing the institutions required by the changing general conditions of development.

1.3.5 *Some limitations of econometrics and the definition of a measure of uncertainty*

In the last 50 years, sophisticated econometric methods have been developed, sometimes using some impressive mathematical techniques. A dominating conviction is that those methodologies are able to express some universally valid results. But the opposite is true.

In general, econometric estimations may be referred only to the past or, more precisely, to the considered observation period, not to the future. Some limited and cautious application to the future may be justified if there exist reasons to think that the considered phenomena are long lasting. But how does one prove this property of phenomena? An important way to do that may be to determine if they result from the existing *general conditions of development*. In this case, the high durability characterizing those conditions should warrant a parallel durability of the corresponding phenomena, these being an expression of those conditions of development that impose corresponding organizational structures for reasons of coherence and efficiency. Well, dynamic competition and its constituent triad, that is, uncertainty, entrepreneurship and innovation, are basic durable aspects of modern dynamic economies. Even if the parameters resulting from the connected estimation may vary over time, those variations do not destroy the explanatory power of the estimated relations. But statistical data do not exist on these variables. This prevents us from making econometric estimations about them, as we shall see in the modeling outlined in Chapters 3 and 4, where we have been obliged to restrict our analysis to simulations, since econometric estimations are prevented by the absence of statistical data on entrepreneurship, innovation and radical uncertainty. In particular, the dominant conviction as to the impossibility of providing a measure of radical uncertainty completely voids the question of the availability of data on this variable. But we have seen in Section 1.2 that the idea of nonmeasurableness of radical uncertainty is completely wrong.

To get ahold of the ghost of uncertainty, more than one quantitative indicator of this variable must be defined. As we shall see extensively in Chapter 6, we have specified and tested three criteria of measure. One has been derived from the European Union-Institute of Studies for Economic Analysis (EU-ISAE) surveys on business tendency and consists of the measure of the variability over time of the answers, that is, the volatility of the opinions (concerning the expectations on delivery orders, production, prices and cost of financing and liquidity assets) *of each firm* of the utilized sample. Another indicator has been provided through the inclusion of an opposite question on uncertainty in an ISAE survey for some recent quarterlies starting from April 2004; another measure of uncertainty could be derived from the deviations between expectations and results in the EU-ISAE surveys. A peculiar indicator of uncertainty may be given by the standard deviation of profit rates across firms; in fact, in the absence of uncertainty and of institutional monopolies, profit (and hence its standard deviation across firms) would be zero. Differentials in capabilities and the associated profits are conceivable only in the presence of limits to knowledge (true uncertainty); for this reason, the variance of profit rates across firms may be intended as an expression of the limits of knowledge and hence of uncertainty.

Some other indicators of uncertainty may be the specification of a minimum-maximum range of expectations, with the distance between the minimum and maximum expectation that may be considered as an expression of the degree of uncertainty. Also the standard deviation (i.e. the distribution about the means) of foresights may be interpreted as a measure of uncertainty.

As is well known, uncertainty displays some very important effects on irrevocable choices and hence on investment. In order to improve the explanation of investment, some studies[29] have proposed specifying the laws (or costs) of learning in getting information on decisions that are postponed, so that they may estimate the convenience of postponing the decisions to invest. But the hypotheses concerning those laws and costs are, in general, scarcely realistic. Uncertainty discourages investment in a different and more direct way. Precisely, high uncertainty suggests the postponement of investment for at least two reasons: (1) waiting for a more serene atmosphere and (2) increase in the use of entrepreneurial skills in ordinary activities, requested by the increase in turbulences. This makes the degree of uncertainty an important explanatory variable of investment. Unfortunately, econometric estimations using some proper indicators of the degree of uncertainty are rare. We dedicate much attention to uncertainty in Chapter 6.

1.4 Conclusion

This chapter points out that one main deficiency of economic thought is the lack of consideration of dynamic competition processes that are hinged upon entrepreneurship, innovation and uncertainty. This aspect is completely neglected by mainstream economics. Only three schools of thought have dedicated some useful considerations to the phenomenon. Two of them, neo-Austrian and Schumpeterian, are strongly complementary: the first emphasizes uncertainty and entrepreneurship, but almost ignores innovation, while the second emphasizes the entrepreneurial role and innovation but neglects uncertainty. These omissions prevent the two schools of thought adequately developing the notion of dynamic competition. We have seen that the assumption of immeasurability of uncertainty and the associated denial of its explanation, which are explicit in neo-Austrians (Kirzner's 'fog of uncertainty') and implicit in Schumpeter, prevents an adequate treatment of the formation and use of entrepreneurship and the innovation-adaptation process, hence economic development. Moreover, the assumption of immeasurability of uncertainty and the emphasis on the limits of knowledge have diffused the mistaken conviction that the maximization principle is only applicable to the neoclassical economics of perfect knowledge.

The equivocations we are stressing are shared by heterodox economics, which insists on the notion of 'bounded rationality'. Indeed, this notion has amplified the misunderstandings provoked by the assumption of immeasurability and unexplanability of uncertainty. This is clearly evident in evolutionary economics, the third school of thought that embodies some aspects of dynamic competition. Such a school (following Schumpeterian thought) has, at its heart, innovation and emphasizes the limits of knowledge as expressed by the notion of bounded rationality. Unfortunately, this notion is rather ambiguous; human rationality is always bounded, but this does not deny that decision making must make an effort to use reason at its best, as the optimization approach attempts to do. Nevertheless, heterodox economics rejects optimization.

Evolutionary economics tries to remedy some theoretical vacuity arising from the limitations mentioned through the notion of 'decisional routines'. But this notion is far from clear. In particular, it refers to a kind of skill that has nothing to do with entrepreneurship since it postulates repetitive, bureaucratic decision making, while a main characteristic of entrepreneurial skills is versatility and flexibility. Evolutionary economics is also afflicted by various misunderstandings on dynamic competition, even if for theoretical reasons partly different from neo-Austrian and Schumpeterian thought.

In sum, the crucial phenomenon represented by dynamic competition, when it is not disregarded altogether, is treated in a partial and misleading way without properly considering entrepreneurship, uncertainty and innovation. This chapter has tried to remedy these drawbacks.

Notes

1 It has been fully developed in A. Fusari, *Methodological Misconceptions in the Social Sciences* (Springer, 2014).
2 See A. Fusari (1996a).
3 With the exception of its exogenous part depending, for instance, on natural events.
4 When a better technology is invented, the old production processes must adapt to the prices imposed by the new one. At this point, if those prices no longer enable old producers to amortize the costs of their plants and the latter cannot be fully depreciated, the businesses with obsolete technology will have losses. There will also be losses if the new prices only permit, for the remaining physical life of the equipment, amortization rates lower than would be necessary to fully recoup the investment.
5 Thus their analysis is not particularly suitable for explaining the efficiency of choices made in different social and institutional contexts.
6 If depreciation was systematically overestimated (and thus overcharged), this would introduce an arbitrary element of extra profit. If, on the other hand, depreciation was systematically underestimated, it would introduce a systematic factor of loss. But this cannot happen, due to competition.
7 The distinction between radical and incremental innovations, frequent in economics, is for the most part not rigorous. It needs a precise expression of the degree of importance of innovations.

The degree of importance of a new consumer product can be represented by the quantity of its production (the conquered market as expressed by the superior asymptote of the logistic) at the end of the diffusion period and by the substitution and complementary effects of the new product on the existing consumer goods.

The degree of importance of a capital product innovation may be expressed by the superior asymptote of the logistic and the parameters indicating the stimulating effects of the new capital products on process innovation.

Finally, the degree of importance of process innovations is represented by the leap in productivity that they cause.
8 See Mensch (1979).
9 See Fusari and Reati (2013).
10 See Pyka and Saviotti (2004).
11 See F. H. Knight (1950), pp. 18 and 19.
12 See A. Fusari (2006).
13 See F. H. Knight (1950), p. 165.
14 See Ekstedt and Fusari (2010).
15 See A. Fusari (1996a).
16 The generic attribution of production to labor is pointless since production largely results from human creativity. Another thing is the statement that the fruits of the natural

lottery of talents must be for the benefit of the whole society, but paying attention to not obstruct creativeness, as we shall see in Chapter 11.
17 See (Fusari 2014).
18 Kaldor wrote: "In effect, the theory of (general) equilibrium has reached a stage of development characterized by the fact that pure theorists have succeeded (even if unconsciously) to prove the impossibility that the implications of that theory are empirically true" (cited in D'Antonio 1975, p. 77).
19 Kirzner writes: "To understand development it is necessary to understand the entrepreneurial process whereby opportunities that were hitherto existent but unseen become opportunities seen and exploited" (Kirzner 1985, p. 74).
20 Schumpeter very much admired the Walrasian model of general equilibrium: "Magna Carta of economics . . . enormous research program . . . the base of the best work of our time". See Schumpeter (1972), pp. 482 and 556.
21 Schumpeter writes: "The giant industrial unit, perfectly bureaucratised . . . supplants the entrepreneur" (Schumpeter 1977, p. 130).
22 Galbraith says: "Nothing is today more interesting than to see that the entity previously known as capitalist firm and that previously known as socialist firm begin to resemble under the oligarchic direction of technostructure" (Galbraith 1968, p. 343).
23 Private correspondence dated 7 December 2006.
24 See Morroni (2005).
25 See Kirzner (1973), pp. 33 and 37.
26 See Nelson and Winter (1982).
27 See Becker (2001).
28 See Egidi and Narduzzo (1997).
29 See Pindyck (1991) and Ulph and Ulph (1994).

References

Alchian, A. A. & Demsetz, H. (1972), Production, information costs, and economic organization, *American Economic Review*, vol. 62, pp. 777–795.
Barone, E. (1971), Il ministro della produzione nello stato collettivista, in G. Lunghini (a cura di), *Valore, prezzi ed equilibrio generale*, Il Mulino, Bologna, p. 76.
Becker, M. C. (2001), *Empirical research on routines: The state of the art and its integration into the routines debate*, EAEPE Conference of Siena, November 8–11.
Berardi, G. G. (1969), *Saggi sullo sviluppo economico e sociale dei paesi arretrati*, Giuffrè, Milan.
Calcagnini, G. & Saltari, E. (1997), Un'analisi del principio dell'acceleratore in condizioni di incertezza, *Rassegna dei Lavori dell'ISCO*, vol. 1, pp. 183–212.
Cantner, U., Hanusch, H. & Pyka, A. (1998), Routinized innovations: Dynamic capabilities in a simulation study, in O. Eliasson & C. Green (eds), *The microfoundations of economic growth*, University of Michigan Press, Ann Arbor, pp. 131–155.
Coase, H. (1937), The nature of the firm, *Economica*, vol. 4, pp. 386–405.
D'Antonio, M. (a cura di). (1975), *La crisi post-keynesiana*, Boringhieri, Torino.
Davidson, P. (1994), *Post Keynesian macroeconomic theory*, Edward Elgar, Aldershot.
Dosi, G., Nelson, R. R. & Winter, S. G. (2000), *Introduction: The nature and dynamics of organizational capabilities*, Oxford University Press, Oxford.
Dosi, G. & Teece, D. J. (1998), Organizational competences and the boundaries of the firm, in R. A. Arena & C. Longhi (eds), *Market and organization*, Springer, Berlin, pp. 281–302.
Egidi, M. & Narduzzo, A. (1997), The emergence of path-dependent behaviors in cooperative contexts, *International Journal of Industrial Organization*, vol. 15, no. 6, pp. 677–709.
Ekstedt, H. (2006), *Homo economicus versus homo politicus: A note on rationality*, EAEPE International Conference of Istanbul.

Ekstedt, H. & Fusari, A. (2010), *Economic Theory and Social Change*, Routledge, London, New York.
Fusari, A. (1996a), Sviluppo e organizzazione dei sistemi sociali. Una teoria interpretativa dei processi storici. *Sociologia*, vol. 1, no. 1, pp. 125–178.
Fusari, A. (1996b), Paths of economic development: Modelling factors of endogenous growth, *International Journal of Social Economics*, vol. 23, no. 10/11, pp. 164–191.
Fusari, A. (2004), A reconsideration on the method of economic and social sciences: Procedure, rules, classifications, *International Journal of Social Economics*, vol. 31, no. 5/6, pp. 501–535.
Fusari, A. (2005a), Toward a non-capitalist market system: Practical suggestions for curing the ills of our economic system, *American Review of Political Economy*, vol. 3, no. 1, pp. 85–125. www.arpejournal.com.
Fusari, A. (2005b), A model of the innovation-adaptation mechanism driving economic dynamics: A micro representation, *Journal of Evolutionary Economics*, vol. 15, no. 3, pp. 297–333.
Fusari, A. (2006), *Radical uncertainty indicators: Quantitative specifications and applications*, 28th CIRET Conference, Rome, on "Cyclical Indicators and Economic Policy Decisions".
Fusari A. (2014), *Methodological Misconceptions in the Social Sciences. Rethinking social thought and social processes*, Springer, Dordrecht, Heidelberg, New York, London.
Fusari, A. & Reati, A. (2013), Endogenizing technical change: Uncertainty, profits, entrepreneurship. A long-term view of sectoral dynamics, *Structural Change and Economic Dynamics (SCED)*, vol. 24, 76–100.
Galbraith, J. K. (1968), *Il nuovo stato industriale*, Einaudi, Torino.
Grebel, T., Hanusch, H. & Pyka, A. (2001), *An evolutionary approach to the theory of entrepreneurship*, EAEPE Conference of Siena.
Hanusch, H. & Pyka, A. (2007), *Elgar companion to neo-schumpeterian economics*, E. Elgar, Cheltenham.
Hodgson, G. M. (1999), *Evolution and institutions*, Edward Elgar Cheltenham, UK and Northampton, MA.
Kirzner, I. M. (1973), *Competition and entrepreneurship*, The University of Chicago Press, Chicago and London.
Kirzner, I. M. (1985), *Discovery and the capitalist process*, The University of Chicago Press, Chicago and London.
Knight, F. H. (1950), *Risk, uncertainty and profit*, La Nuova Italia, Firenze.
Lange, O. & Taylor, F. M. (1938), *On the economic theory of socialism*, edited by B. Lippincot, University of Minnesota Press, Minneapolis.
Langlois, R. N. & Foss, N. J. (1999), Capabilities and governance: The rebirth of production in the theory of economic organization, *Kyklos*, vol. 52, pp. 201–218.
Lerner, A. P. (1938), Theory and practice in socialist economics, *The Review of Economic Studies*, vol. 6, no. 1, pp. 71–77.
Mensch, G. (1979), *Stalemate in Technology. Innovations Overcome the Depression*, Ballinger, Cambridge, MA.
Mises von, L. (1946), Economic calculus in the socialist state, in F. A. Hayek (ed), *Collectivist economic planning*, University of Chicago Press, Chicago.
Morroni, M. (2005), *Knowledge, scale and transactions in the theory of the firm*, Cambridge University Press, Cambridge.
Nelson, R. R. & Winter, S. G. (1982), *An evolutionary theory of economic change*, The Belknap Press of Harvard University Press, Cambridge, MA.
Neumann von, J. (1952), *Un modello di equilibrio economico generale*, L'Industria, Il Mulino, Bologna.

Odagiri, H. (1994), *Growth through competition, competition through growth*, Clarendon Press, Oxford.

Pasinetti, L. L. (1981), *Structural change and economic growth: A theoretical essay on the dynamics of the wealth of nations*, Cambridge University Press, Cambridge.

Pindyck, R. S. (1991), Irreversibility, uncertainty, and investment, *Journal of Economic Literature*, vol. XXIX, no. 3, pp. 1110–1148.

Polanyi, M. (1966), *The tacit dimension*, Doubleday, Garden City, NY.

Pyka, A. & Saviotti, P. P. (2004), Economic development by the creation of new sector, *Journal of Evolutionary Economics*, vol. 14, no. 1, February, pp. 1–35.

Reati, A. (1998), Technological revolutions in Pasinetti's model of structural change, productivity and prices, *Structural Change and Economic Dynamics*, vol. 9, no. 2, pp. 245–262.

Richardson, G. B. (1972), The organization of industry, *The Economic Journal*, vol. 82, pp. 883–896.

Saviotti, P. P. (1996), *Technological evolution, variety and the economy*, E. Elgar, Cheltenham.

Saviotti, P. P. (2001), Variety, growth and demand, *Journal of Evolutionary Economics*, vol. 11, no. 1, pp. 119–142.

Saviotti, P. P. & Metcalfe, J. S. (Eds.). (1991), *Evolutionary theories of economic and technological change*, Harwood Academic Publishers, Reading.

Schumpeter, J. A. (1934), *The theory of economic development*, Harvard University Press, Cambridge, MA.

Schumpeter, J. A. (1954), *Capitalism, socialism and democracy*, Allin and Unwin, London, Italian edition by Etas Libri, Milan, 1977.

Schumpeter, J. A. (1972), *History of economic analysis*, Boringhieri, Torino.

Scott, M. F. (1989), *A new view of economic growth*, Clarendon Press, Oxford.

Shackle, G. L. S. (1990), *Time, expectations and uncertainty in economics: Selected essays*, edited by J. L. Ford, Edward Elgar, Aldershot.

Stoneman, P. (2007), *Technological diffusion: Aspects of self-propagation as a neo-Schumpeterian characteristic*, in Hansuch & Pyka (eds), pp. 377–387.

Ulph, A. & Ulph, D. (1994), *The irreversibility effect revisited*, Department of Economics, University of Southampton, Southampton.

Walras, L. (1926), *Elements d'économie politique pure ou theorie de la richesse sociale*, R. Penchon et R. Durand-Auxia, Parigi.

Williamson, O. E. (1981), The modern corporation: Origins, evolution, attributes, *Journal of Economic Literature*, vol. XIX, December, pp. 1537–1568.

Wymer, C. R., WYSEA package for system estimation. Mimeograph.

Wymer, C. R. & Knight, M. D. (1978), A Macroeconomic Model of the United Kingdom, *International Monetary Fund Staff Papers*, vol. 25, no. 4, pp. 742–778.

2 Mainstream economics and heterodox economics

A misleading controversy – necessary system versus natural system[1]

2.1 Introduction

This chapter amplifies the deepening of economic thought in Chapter 1 by considering more extensively some contemporary economic theories that are currently considered important examples of scientific procedure. We refer to so-called mainstream economics and also to some important theoretical developments that have strongly opposed it. The analysis will be hinged on an accurate and peculiar treatment of the method of social sciences. Curiously, both the dominant economic teaching and its opponents will be seen to suffer from the same, crucial shortcoming: a disregard for basic aspects of economic reality and the consequent implications that often render misleading the works and teaching of economists.

The chapter sets out some reference to the famous controversy between the two Cambridges: Cambridge, UK, and Cambridge, Massachusetts (US); a controversy that for some while animated economic debate but which has now been confined to the history of economic thought. From here we will be led to aspects of other important theories: those of the post-Keynesians, Schumpeterians and the neo-Austrians, and institutionalism and the fragmented positions that make up modern heterodox economics. Notwithstanding the vigorous attack directed from Cambridge, UK, the neoclassical school associated with Cambridge, Massachusetts, and its recent developments, which opposes to its opponents a substantial cohesiveness and the use of prestigious and consolidated methodologies giving a strict scientific appearance, remains the dominant orthodoxy of the present. We must ask the reason for this continual dominance of the neoclassical tradition, and this chapter will attempt to clarify the primary reasons for the substantial failure of the attacks upon this neoclassical mainstream[2] and specify some possibly crucial points that have been omitted from the debate.

An efficient way of performing the required analysis will be to focus primarily upon L. Pasinetti's attempt to complete the post-Keynesian revolution and remedy the theoretical fragmentation that has by now arisen from the multiplicity of those post-Keynesian contributions that have recently become a part of heterodox economics.

Pasinetti's analysis establishes two important methodological principles: the realism of postulates and the so-called separation theorem. These two principles are strictly linked to each other in that, while the first generates a substantial methodological impasse, the second provides a means of overcoming that impasse. More precisely, the first principle (realism of postulates) prohibits the 'abstract rationality' implied by the method of the logical-formal sciences and, at the same time, collides with the use in social science of the method based on observation because this method is contradicted by the nonrepetitiveness of the large part of social phenomena. So, the statement concerning the realism of postulates is inconsistent with the operation in social studies of current methods (abstract rationality and observation-verification).

The idea of 'separation' between, so to speak, fundamental and nonfundamental variables provides the means of overcoming such a methodological dead end. Pasinetti and I share the analytical importance and necessity of separation, even if we have different opinions on how and where to lay down the demarcation line between 'necessity' and 'choice possibility'. As we shall see, to profit from the idea of separation, a deep revision of the method of the social sciences is needed. Pasinetti does not seem to perceive this exigency. He uses the 'separation' principle in the context of the 'natural' system of classical economists. But unfortunately, such a system omits crucial aspects of modern dynamic economies, an omission that contradicts the principle concerning the realism of postulates. In sum, the separation that the natural system implies has no real methodological relevance (i.e. one aimed at avoiding the methodological dead end previously mentioned). The use by Pasinetti of 'separation' with regard to the natural system acts merely as a simplification,[3] and we shall see that it contradicts his emphasis on the realism of postulates.

It seems to us that the failure of the attack of heterodox economics and, more particularly, of Cambridge, UK, against mainstream economics, must be attributed to the omission of a basic problem of social sciences, *viz.* the difficulties inflicted upon the method of social thought by the nonrepetitiveness of observed events. In fact, further developing such methodological difficulty and consideration seems to be the only way to show the weakness of mainstream microeconomics, which is indeed very clever and accurate in using the current methodologies.

Let us immediately proceed to clarify, in Section 2.2, the methodological issues sketched previously. Then, Section 2.3 will show that both the classical natural system and Walrasian economics omit the same crucial economic variables, thus falling in what we call the 'abstract rationality' standard. In Section 2.4, we shall insert in the representation some indispensable variables of dynamic economies, and in Section 2.5, a 'necessary' system will be set out together with a distinction between 'necessity' and 'choice-possibility-creativeness' able to provide a more fecund and reliable separation between production and distribution of income, as suggested by the proposal on method presented in Section 2.2. Finally, Section 2.6 draws some implication of our theoretical construction.

2.2 Some considerations on the method of the social sciences[4]

In order to make clear the foundation of what follows, a preliminary and basic distinction is indispensable, that is, the distinction between the method of the logical-formal sciences (a) and the method based on the observation of reality (b):

a The method of the logical-formal sciences (that we refer to as the *abstract rationality method*) consists of the deduction of logical implications of postulates that abstract from the given reality. The theoretical results yielded by this method may seem logical fictions or even jokes but, as a consequence of such intense abstraction, this method can lead to explanations of great generality and the solution of unexpected problems. Boolean algebra and non-Euclidean geometries offer important examples in this regard; born as mere logical abstractions, they subsequently showed their value in computational technology and the exploration of extraterrestrial space.
b The method based on the observation of the considered reality can be represented by the series O-H-O_c (initial observation - theoretical hypotheses - new control observations intended to verify the validity of the formulated theory), but Popper's falsification limits the procedure to the series H-O_c (from an initial theoretical hypothesis, which may be derived even by chance, an observation-verification is established in the process of submitting the theory to an extremely rigorous experimental procedure that may lead to its falsification even as a result of the presence of a single contradictory fact).

We can see that in both procedures (O-H-O_c and H-O_c), the control-verification of the theories under consideration is based on a strict confrontation with reality. But such a verification method implies the hypothesis that events (in our case, social events) are repetitive, thus allowing the derivation of laws of motion from the accurate observation of facts (or experiments). This method is appropriate to the study of natural phenomena, even if these demonstrate rare and random innovations, as is the case in biology (Darwinian evolutionism); but it is useless and misleading if the hypothesis of repetitiveness is violated by the frequent and substantial innovations typical of social phenomena, particularly in the economy, where innovation is fostered by competition (based on innovation). In sum, with regard to the social world, the second method (b) can be referred only to the quasistationary societies that dominated human history prior to the modern age.

It must be underlined, however, that a large part of those studies that are based on the accurate observation of social reality reject the hypothesis of repetitiveness of the considered phenomena and events. But this observational attitude, to make sense, is obliged to intend reality as 'necessity' (what happened had to happen). This 'weak' observational standard (i.e. excluding repetitiveness) has driven the work of the major students of human societies (Marx and Weber, among others). Statistical and observational data are, however, useful in studies concerning the historical period of time to which they refer and with regard to long-lasting

36 *Theoretical frame*

phenomena expressing organizational necessity, such as functional imperatives. But if things change due to constructive and innovative human work, statistical data will prove misleading.

A primary expression of the prevalent observation-experimental attitude of economic thought is the current distinction between economics, which as so conceived defines the observational discovery of the laws of motion of the economy and political economy, the latter of which concerns intervention in the economy on the basis of those laws. In fact, such a distinction is substantially absent in Keynesian thought, which has a basic organizational (much more than observational) feature, so that Keynesian diagnosis implies the requisite therapies for the overcoming of the crisis even if, being the diagnosis simply centered on the principle of effective demand, this makes Keynesian teaching unilateral (as we shall see). In the present book, as based on the organizational view, Part II on therapies is just a lengthening and continuation of Part I.

It must be frankly recognized that the method of social thought exists within a great confusion that has grown over time. There is no space here to present a critical review on method.[5] Pareto's work provides one of the main examples of the analytical ambiguities generated by this methodological confusion. Pareto, as an economist, founded the model of general equilibrium on the method of abstract rationality (a), but he uses the method of observation-verification (b) in stating the invariance of his alpha coefficient concerning income distribution. Moreover, his sociological inquiry uses a third methodology, based upon the notions of *residual* and *derivation,* in an attempt to capture the irrational content of human behaviors. This third method amounts to an impressive illustration of *observational blindness:* even such a great rationalist as Pareto could forget that a main task of social science is to unmask and prevent the effects of behavioral irrationalities in the organization and functioning of human societies and instead accept those irrationalities as inescapable, as Pareto's sociological inquiry in fact does.

An important part of social thought that disapproves methods (a) and (b) opposes to them a *constructivist* approach based on *doing,* but largely disregarding *being.* This approach, mainly distinguished by a programmatic feature, was considered from the beginning of the second half of last century with attention from important students[6] and was largely characterized as economic and social planning. But this constructivist methodological proposal has been discredited by its tendency to supplant being in the name of doing.

Methodological confusions and ambiguities are so diffuse and well-rooted that some important social students (primarily P. Feyerabend) have even denied the relevance of method (methodological anarchism). But some different attitude of heterodoxy is at work. J. B. Davis emphasizes the alternance in social thought between pluralism and dominance.[7] This alternance expresses indeed a physiological feature of the process of knowledge. But the pathology of social thought is different; it consists in some well-rooted methodological misconceptions that afflict the whole history of social theories and that, to be reversed, need real methodological rebuilding that is able, among other things, to meet two main peculiarities of social reality that Davis underlines: the difficulty of experimentation and the value-ladenness in economics. This need of rebuilding is not achieved by the multiplicity of recent methodological developments (behavioral and experimental economics, neuroeconomics, happiness and subjective well being research, agent-based modeling, evolutionary thinking, computational economics, etc.) to which Davis refers.[8] For its part, the Salanti and Screpanti's reference to methodological pluralism, sociological understanding, the complementary of methods and the distinction between pluralism of academy and of methods by one researcher[9] is no less insufficient with regard to the need of defining some methodological procedures and rules that are shaped around the basic features of social reality; that is, a method (c) that replaces, in social studies, both the methods (a) and (b) and remedies the drawbacks of methodological pluralism expressed by some dominant practices of modern heterodoxy, a veritable methodological Babel that obstructs interaction and communication among students and consequently injures the same fruitfulness of pluralism and the cumulative advance of scientific knowledge.

We shall attempt to propose a method (procedure, rules and classification criteria) appropriate to an inquiry into nonrepetitive reality. In attempting to do so, we are obliged to begin from a basic consideration: as we said in Chapter 1, social reality is a product of humanity, in contrast to natural reality, which is preexisting to humanity and on which humanity merely exerts an interactive action based on the knowledge of the contents of the natural world and its laws of motion. This means that a method of inquiry into social reality cannot confine itself to *being* but must be able to consider and represent also the constructive and organizational activity of humanity (*doing*). So, if we are to arrive at an understanding of *becoming*, our sought-after method must combine being and doing. It follows that the extensive use of econometrics by empirical economists is exaggerated and misleading, with the exception of reference to highly aggregated variables. Moreover, it follows that Hume's statement on the logical impossibility of moving from being to doing cannot be referred to social inquiry; it concerns only natural reality, but simply because in this case doing is meaningless.

The first step of the method that we are going to propose is that – just as Pasinetti recommends – we start from *realistic postulates* (i.e. postulates expressing relevant aspects of the considered reality) and that we derive all implications from them. It is evident that such a procedure combines being and doing. The real and basic problem concerns the selection of postulates. In fact, the impossibility, due to the nonrepetitiveness of social reality, of verifying and corroborating with the help of statistical inference the theories deducted negates the usefulness of a hypothetical generation of theories (that Popper's observational falsification even suggests to propose by chance). In sum, the impossibility of verifying theories (via observation) points to a decisive role, in warranting reliability and fruitfulness to theoretical deductions, for the definition of rules concerning the formulation and classification of 'realistic postulates' in order to replace the unreliable role at present pertaining (in economic modeling) to the econometric control of hypotheses. Those rules and classifications express the core of our proposal on method.

At least four possible classifications of realistic postulates (with the implied rules) can be set forth:

1 *Postulates directed to the deduction of general principles demanded for pressing reasons of organizational efficiency.* These principles will act as strong attraction and gravitational points of social processes. The postulates must express very significant features of the 'general conditions of development'; therefore, they are long-lasting, a product of the path of history, and they exclude specific ideological, technological and naturalistic aspects and innovations. We denominate *functional imperatives* the general organizational principles deduced from assumptions and postulates listed here.[10]

2 *Postulates expressing conditions of nature that have important institutional and organizational implications.* These conditions are local and were decisive in characterizing the societies of the past (e.g. desert, steppe, agricultural or seafaring peoples). Technological development has greatly reduced their influence (and hence importance), mainly through the increasing role of artifacts and the tremendous speed of communications.

3 *Postulates that specify aspects indispensable to the unfolding of human evolutionary potentialities (i.e. of the natural human ability to develop).* They are decisive for the operation and development of those potentialities, and they have a very general character, more general and more enduring than those of point 1; but they can also be violated over very long periods of time (and often have been in closed societies, not only in primitive age but, even more, in the best structured and advanced empires of the past) since their violation does not affect organizational coherence and can even enforce this. These postulates express the true dynamic principle and engine of social development. In a sense, they are halfway between the postulates 1 and 4, and we denominate their implications onto logical imperatives. These imperatives mainly express important ethical values that, as such, assume an objective (not relativistic) content. For instance, the tolerance principle and pluralism (i.e. the free confrontation of ideas and inspirations), the role and dignity of the individual and the respect for his initiative are principles indispensable to the efflorescence of creativity and the valorization of human diversified skills and evolutionary potential. With regard to the economy, a fundamental ontological imperative is entrepreneurship. It is important to underline that, in the modern dynamic society, ontological imperatives also become functional imperatives, that is, in such a society they are demanded by pressing reasons of coherence and efficiency. It may be useful to make a distinction relating to two very important aspects of this postulate about human evolutionary capabilities:

- *Human rational skills.* An excess of rational drive with respect to creative drive may hasten scientific progress and social development.
- *Human creative skills.* The excess of creative drive with respect to rational drive may cause social disintegration.

The realistic postulates sub 1 and sub 2 with their implications give the field of 'necessity' in the organization of social systems (but, of course, not with regard to individual decisions, where what is necessity under some circumstances may be choice under others). In modern dynamic society (which is the object of this essay), also the postulates sub 3 with their implications must be added as a component of the field of necessity, that is, indispensable to such dynamism.

4 *Postulates concerning ideological aspects and choices and creative events.* The organizational and institutional forms deriving from them define the field of 'choice-possibility-creativity'. They do not pertain, therefore, to the field of necessity, even if the most important of them (i.e. the choices of *civilization*) are characterized by long duration and pervasiveness. This makes it clear that the usual identification of durability with necessity is erroneous.

So we have the methodological succession and procedure CRP-TD (classification of realistic postulates - theoretical deductions), instead of $O-H-O_c$ (observation – hypotheses - control observation) typical of the observational inductive and deductive methods, or $H-O_c$ typical of the Popperian hypothesis falsification. The previous rules and classifications show the methodological features and importance of the separation between necessity and choice possibility in social sciences. These summary rules alone, however, cannot guarantee the appropriate selection of postulates. The fruitfulness of the selection depends also on the scholar's own intellect and sense of reality.

The sections that will follow go beyond this great abstraction and give, with reference to economics, various examples of necessity and choice possibility and, in general, applications of the methodological procedure that we have briefly set out.

It might be shown that the interaction between ontological imperatives, functional imperatives and civilizations is precious for the interpretation of social-historic development: the degree of satisfaction, by each civilization, of ontological imperatives (i.e. concerning the unfolding of human evolutionary potentialities) determines the degree of variation over time of the general conditions of development and the consequent advent of new functional imperatives that will imply a tormented change of the civilizations inconsistent with them.

The variation of functional imperatives can be taken as expressing an objective criterion of distinction of historical ages. Capitalism is a civilization consistent with the functional imperatives of the present age and will be forced to disappear by the advent, with the variation of the general conditions of development, of new functional imperatives inconsistent with capitalist civilization.

2.3 Limits and omissions of classical natural systems and their similarity with those of neoclassical general equilibrium models

We come back now more specifically to economics, primarily to Pasinetti's theoretical approach aimed at challenging the orthodoxy dominating economics. Following the tradition of classical thought, he opposes the production paradigm to the exchange paradigm, the latter of which he takes as the basic feature of neoclassical thinking and which he criticizes for its multitude of unrealistic assumptions and implications. Coherently with such reproach, he underlines that a main task of economic theory is to found itself on initially realistic hypotheses. More precisely, Pasinetti opposes the neoclassical scheme with one that combines Sraffa's equations of prices (and production equations) and the Keynesian principle of effective demand.[11] In developing this opposition, he points out the basic relations that are treated as 'natural' by classical economists (the natural system), distinguishing them from the contingent ones (for instance, natural from market prices). Pasinetti's modeling intends, in this way, to make evident the objective and fundamental variables of an industrial economy that logically precede every institutional asset. This natural system is taken as expressing optimal positions, both in terms of efficiency and social equity.

According to Pasinetti, the exponents of the school of Cambridge (UK) have failed to separate the fundamental relations from the institutional side of economic life, and this is a main cause of their failure to formulate a comprehensive and unified theoretical system able to prevail against the neoclassical mainstream. Pasinetti's formalization incorporates, in the system of equations, both exogenous technical progress and the long-run dynamics of consumptions, thereby deriving prices, production and employment. The institutional side, as well as the policy decisions of political economy, should be derived in compliance with this natural system. A comparison between effective results and natural configurations would provide a criterion by which to judge the actually existing institutional mechanisms of a society. Unfortunately, this approach forgets Pasinetti's emphasis upon the need for realistic postulates and thereby falls into the trap of what we denominate 'abstract rationality'. A comparison between the Walrasian model of general equilibrium and Pasinetti's natural system will help to clarify the point.

Contrary to the claim of Pasinetti (and objection to Langlois, that the neoclassical model is very demanding and exclusive with regard to institutions),[12] Walras's general equilibrium model does not necessarily need free market (and capitalist) institutions. This is clearly proved by two well-known applications of Walras's model mentioned in Chapter 1: that of E. Barone in his essay 'The ministry of production in the collectivist state'; the other by Lange, Lerner and Taylor in the course of a debate on market socialism in the 1930s. Barone demonstrated that the problem of prices and optimal allocation of resources is identical in both socialist and capitalist economies and can be solved by a ministry of production operating through trial and error. For their part, Lange, Lerner and Taylor showed that the simple decisional rule of marginal cost equals price allows the entrepreneur's role to be eliminated. Both approaches postulate a stationary-repetitive economy, with something similar to the market but in which the entrepreneur does not exist by definition. In fact, the manager of a socialist economy responsible for implementing the rule of marginal cost equals price has nothing to do with the role of the entrepreneur in meeting (as we shall see) radical uncertainty and introducing innovation.

As with Walrasian economic theory, Pasinetti's pure and preinstitutional economics is intended to be applicable to both capitalism and socialism. In fact,

Pasinetti suggests that the reader who entertains some doubt about the very idea of a natural system should "think first in terms of a centrally planned economy . . . then extend the results to the case of a market economy".[13] Indeed, the natural system has immediate reference to a centralized economy: the profit, exogenous innovation and accumulation abstracted from the innovative entrepreneur in Pasinetti's natural model make sense with reference to central planning and, more generally, to the extended reproduction of a stationary economy in which there is no place for the entrepreneur and profit properly understood. Put another way, this natural system can explain growth, not development.

One point to take from all this is that serious shortcomings may affect excessively pure theories. If a pure model can be reconciled with institutional and organizational forms inconsistent with the modern world (as socialist centralization certainly is), then clearly it lacks something indispensable that would exclude those absurdities from its application. To avoid those implications, which obscure and damage the usefulness of the idea of separation, we must integrate into the marriage of Keynes and the neo-Ricardians some further indispensable additions or, more precisely, some basic aspects ignored by both Walrasian and natural systems that the principle of realism of postulates requires.

In order to better explore this subject, a brief consideration of the 'less pure' content of Pasinetti's proposal may be useful, specifically: the Keynesian demand-led approach and the classical notion of natural prices. We shall see in Part II that the idea that demand is the cause of production subtends (i.e. requires) the hypothesis of a 'residual character to real wages' (i.e. trade union bargaining concerns only nominal wages, while real wages result from price variations) that avoids persistent pressures deriving from the side of distribution and a money supply that follows the demand for money; moreover, such an idea of demand-led production does not apply in the presence of diffused territorial and social dualisms (and, in the short run, in the presence of structural bottlenecks) obstructing the demand impulse to production. Therefore, the hypothesis of a demand-led system (shared by Keynesians, post-Keynesians and Leontievians) suffers from a remarkable lack of generality. Also Sraffa's system of prices, which supposes an exogenous profit rate or exogenous money wage rate, implies the previously mentioned residual character of real wages, as these depend on the solution of price system.

Some objection must also be made against the classical notion of natural prices.[14] The reproducibility of goods is essential to such a notion, but reproducibility is made largely evanescent by innovation. In fact, goods resulting from innovation become reproducible not immediately after their appearance, but only after the diffusion of the innovation; before that, the new goods can only be reproduced by the respective innovator. In the meantime, some other innovation can be introduced that may substitute for the previous innovation. So, what about the hypothesis of reproducibility? The classical price of production, based on the hypothesis of reproducibility, does not indeed contain much sense in the presence of considerable flows of innovation. The natural system of prices (and production) is plainly applicable only to stationary economies or, let us repeat, to economic growth, not development.

42   Theoretical frame

In sum, Pasinetti's post-Keynesian and neoclassical models are consistent only with the introduction of exogenous technical progress and/or a merely accumulation process, that is, excluding innovation. The two models ignore or treat expeditiously some crucial and distinguishing features of modern dynamic economies, namely endogenous innovation and radical (i.e. nonprobabilistic) uncertainty. As a consequence, they also ignore the real substance of both the entrepreneurial role and the profit rate. Pasinetti maintains that only the financing of accumulation justifies profits. But as a matter of fact, accumulation could be fueled by the banking system on some such basis as the degree of an entrepreneur's success as expressed by the actual (and/or expected) profit rate, that is, intended not as a mere surplus (or interest rate), but precisely as an accountability (not necessarily a distributive) variable.

2.4   Indispensable extensions of the analysis

We now extend the natural system by attempting to incorporate some basic realistic premises that are also ignored by Walras's general equilibrium model. Schumpeter's notion of competition based on the introduction of innovations (creative destruction) will provide us with a helpful start. Schumpeter's idea of 'dynamic competition' implies the existence of temporary monopolies and corresponding profits due to the possible success of innovation. Moreover, the notion of competition based on innovation underlines the importance of radical (i.e. nonprobabilistic) uncertainty, a variable that is both the product of innovation and inseparable from innovation, although this was neglected by Schumpeter (as it had been before by classical economists). In Chapter 1, we saw that radical uncertainty, together with the connected idea of expectations, plays a crucial role in Keynes's macro explanation of the deficiency of effective demand and that the implications at the micro level have been emphasized by members of the neo-Austrian school, primarily Kirzner and Hayek, but in a way that violates scientific objectivity, as we shall see.

We also saw that there can be no doubt as to the theoretical value of combining the Schumpeterian idea of innovative entrepreneurship and the neo-Austrian idea of what may be called 'adaptive entrepreneurship' aimed at taking advantage of profit opportunities offered by market disequilibria (neo-Austrian adaptive competition). Such an analytical combination provides a full representation, so to speak, of dynamic processes and dynamic competition centered on the interaction between innovative entrepreneurship, which causes disequilibria and uncertainty, and adaptive entrepreneurship that, in the effort to take profit from disequilibria, implicitly tends to eliminate such disequilibria and reduce uncertainty, thus preparing the conditions for a new innovative wave.[15] Such a theoretical context illustrates the importance of rethinking the phenomenon of radical uncertainty in a way that avoids framing it simply as a fog (as many heterodox economists do) but instead makes evident the possibility of measuring it.[16] Again, this measurement would be of incalculable value to understand and govern the process of innovation-adaptation previously described and the business cycle, as this process and cycle are characterized by radical uncertainty.

We can see, therefore, that the entrepreneur, uncertainty and profit must take on central and *essential* roles in a dynamic representation of economic processes (where dynamics means more than simply the introduction of time).[17] Moreover, the analytical value of the *accountability* role of the profit rate becomes clear, that is, the rate of profit is intended as a measure of the degree of success of entrepreneurial decision making. It is easy to show that such a role cannot be replaced by other quantitative indicators.

Our extension is indispensable if we are to derive any real profit from Pasinetti's separation idea and, in particular, to supply clarifications regarding the institutional side. The entrepreneur and profit, being necessary and irrefutable elements of a dynamic economy (with innovation, uncertainty etc.), must pertain to the left (or natural) side of the separation. But it is not necessary that they take a capitalist form; they can also be related to public firms operating in the market and directed by managers endowed with entrepreneurial responsibilities. This means that the choice between public and private entrepreneurship pertains to the right-hand institutional side of the separation.

The questions considered in this section also clarify some serious and frequent equivocations that mar the teaching of important economists, for example, the previously remembered Schumpeter's forecast of a convergence upon socialism by way of the great managerial firm, an idea resumed by J. K. Galbraith; let us restate that the appeal of this forecast was premised upon ignoring the phenomenon of radical uncertainty that allowed Schumpeter and Galbraith to negate the necessity of the entrepreneurial function ("innovation is reducing to a *routine*"[18]). For their part, neo-Austrians based the legitimization of capitalism on the necessary role of the entrepreneur in the presence of radical uncertainty, ignoring the possibility that the entrepreneur partake of a noncapitalist substance.

2.5 Necessity and choice possibility in the organization of the economy: the necessary system

We acknowledge that an important merit of Pasinetti's idea of separation is to provide a precious analytical tool for distinguishing necessity from choice possibility in the organization and management of social systems. Here we shall try to provide, in line with our considerations on method set out in Section 2.2, a better expression of Pasinetti's ideas of separation. The building of any social system always involves institutions; therefore, speaking of a preinstitutional nucleus can be inappropriate. Classical economists asserted the natural character of the market (intending the capitalist market). But history teaches us that in the past, the market has often been but a very minor institution, and it was harshly opposed in the most advanced societies of the ancient world, represented by the great bureaucratic-centralized empires. Today, in our modern dynamic societies, in which competition based on the introduction of innovations prevails, along with the associated forms of radical uncertainty and entrepreneurship, the market has become an 'organizational necessity'.

At this point, the methodological procedure, classifications and rules set out in Section 2.2 can be recalled to exemplify and profit of their usefulness for a clear and rigorous solution to the problems that we are facing, mainly with regard to separation. The existence, in the present historical epoch, of economies (general conditions of development) that have moved far beyond the quasistationary state necessitates and/or implies the presence and action of the market, the entrepreneur, profit, innovation and radical uncertainty. These phenomena first became necessary aspects of economic and social life in medieval Italian and Flemish communes. They imply a number of ethical values that henceforth assume an objective as opposed to a relative character.[19] In the modern world, the negation of these values and the institutions that stand behind them lead to social disaster, as demonstrated by the 20th-century experiments of 'real socialism'; this clearly states the necessity of those values and institutions.

These institutions and values can be called *functional imperatives* of modern dynamic economies, and some of the mentioned ethical values are also *ontological imperatives* (i.e. requested by the expression and operation of the evolutionary potential of humanity and also become functional imperatives in the present age, see Section 2.2). They constitute the aspect of necessity, together with some basic characteristics of modern dynamic economies, such as radical uncertainty.

Substituting the term *fundamental* for *natural* in Pasinetti's system improves clearness very little. In fact, the necessities (or fundamental elements) considered previously are, for the most part, institutional elements, and hence they concern that side of Pasinetti's division opposed to the natural-fundamental. In sum, fundamental (necessary) and institutional aspects are tightly mixed. Therefore, the separation needed is different from that which Pasinetti proposes; it requires some accurate analyses and, as we saw in Section 2.2, can be expressed through the terms *necessity* and *choice possibility creativity*.

We just recounted some examples of necessity; here, then, are some elements relating to choice possibility. Almost the whole income distribution pertains to choice possibility, starting from interest rate. J. S. Mill was the first economist that insisted on the independence of income distribution from production, but he did not prove his assertion and it was strongly denied by neoclassical thinking. Mainstream economics maintains that the interest rate is indispensable to the equilibrium between saving and investment. But it is not. Indeed, saving depends on the amount of income gained and therefore on the level of production; while entrepreneurs' demand for capital depends on levels of entrepreneurship in relation to the state of business, which is mainly expressed by profit expectations. The supposed role of interest rate as necessary in order to prevent waste of capital is fulfilled by the profit rate, that is, entrepreneurs' tendencies (at least imposed by accountability reasons) to derive profit from investment. Therefore, the interest rate could be abolished, but only in real terms, which means that nominal interest rate should equate the rate of inflation as is necessary to preserve the incentive to save and to preserve the real value of saving. We shall analyze the point more specifically in Chapter 10. Of course, such abolition would require overcoming the current financial systems toward a deep reformation at the international level of the role of the banking system.

For its part (and as we saw), the profit rate is necessary for accountability reasons, that is, as a measure of the success of entrepreneurial decision making but not as a distributive variable in public firms. Finally, wages represent a necessary variable only for a modest part required by reasons of incentive and an accountability variable expressing the imputation on prices of the demand and supply of various kinds of labor. We can see, therefore, that a very large part of the distribution of income pertains to the side of choice possibility. The composition of final demand, *specific* innovations, the sectoral division of investment, types of entrepreneurship (public, private, cooperative, individual, etc.) also pertain to this side. A crucial kind of choice possibility is represented by civilization forms, which constitute long enduring yet mighty options since they are well integrated in the social system and provide its physiognomy. Capitalism is a civilization expressed by a dynamic society born through long-lasting processes of trial and error. But civilizations other than capitalism are consistent with modern dynamic society, for instance, civilizations with (a) the market operating as a pure mechanism for imputing costs and efficiency, that is, without affecting income distribution that therefore becomes exogenous, except for the provision of material incentives in the case of alienating activities; and (b) the financial system operating as the *servant* as opposed to the *master* of production, that is, in the service of production.[20]

Pasinetti's formalization places important institutional necessities on the right-hand side of the separation, as they are intended as nonfundamental. But, as just seen, institutions are to be seen as appearing in both the field of necessity and that of choice possibility. The distinction between necessity and choice possibility leads to the specification of a necessary system being substituted to the natural one; this necessary system includes all the variables that, as previously seen, are required for (and implied by) the existence and performance of a dynamic economy: the entrepreneur, the market (also the noncompetitive forms of dynamic competition, but excluding institutional monopolies, i.e. monopolies not determined by genuine scarcity but artificially created by law), uncertainty, Schumpeterian innovation and profit intended as excluding interests on capital. Clearly, some of these necessary variables represent important institutions. A formalization and simulation of a model very near to this necessary standard will be given in Chapter 3. The model includes elements the absence of which, in both natural and Walrasian systems, makes these systems misleading and consistent with both centralized and decentralized systems, as previously seen. Indeed, the absence of some of these elements also mars Keynesian, post-Keynesian, Schumpeterian, neo-Austrian and other heterodox theories, rendering them all partial and unilateral in their almost haphazard consideration of some important elements and simultaneous disregard for others that are no less important.

It seems to us that, if we are to speak of 'pure theory' in a sense that is not misleading, then we must consider a necessary system, that is, a system that includes basic and unavoidable elements that are required by the reality considered (specifically, the elements previously considered as required by the existence and performance of a dynamic economy), among which will be found various elements constituting institutional and organizational necessities.

2.6 For a new institutionalism, and a last note on the separation principle

The institutional question is often afflicted by some basic (and sometimes selfish) misunderstandings. Many neoclassical economists, some of whom are quoted by Pasinetti, have attempted, with great bravery and by way of various stratagems, to conciliate pure neoclassical theory with important institutional and noninstitutional elements of reality. Many of these – often acute – attempts to extend validity of the pure neoclassical model fall into what Pasinetti highlights as the trap of loyalty to tradition. A primary example of stumbling into such a trap is Knight's pioneering analysis on uncertainty,[21] the ultimate message of which is that uncertainty is only a cause of deviation around a neoclassical equilibrium.

If properly included in (and referred to as) our necessary system, thereby better expressing both their implications and potential, uncertainty and also the content of various neo-institutional analyses (Coase, Solow, Williamson) critically considered by Pasinetti, lose the equivocal limitations that derived from their reference to the neoclassical model. In sum, institutionalism needs a basic model that, as with our necessary system, also includes important institutional necessities rather than concentrating all of them on the institutional as opposed to the natural side. Such a necessary model grants theoretical and formal coherence in the specification of the institutional side, thereby saving (just as Pasinetti had hoped) institutionalism from a mere subjection to a general model (the neoclassical one) that reduces its breath. Therefore, the necessary system may be greatly attractive to institutional analysts.

Pasinetti writes: "The *separation theorem* suggests separating the investigation of those characteristics that lie at the foundation of the production economies . . . from the investigation of the institutions. . . . Economic science has proceeded for too long to mix up the two stages of investigation".[22] But such a mixing is in part inevitable. The very problem is that the natural system erases some necessary aspects in representing a dynamic economy; the substantial feature of this (innovation, uncertainty, entrepreneurship etc.) cannot be reduced to exogenous technical progress. The natural system does not include those necessary variables, similarly to the Walrasian system (as Section 2.3 shows), thus falling in the abstract rationality standard, in contradiction with the principle of the realism of postulates. This consideration comes before Pasinetti's discussion in his book *Keynes and the Cambridge Keynesians* (pp. 323–327); it makes, in some sense, such a discussion (objections and counterobjections) not properly relevant. Pasinetti says: "If we really want a theoretical framework able to integrate institutional and economic analysis, this theoretical framework must be solid and comprehensive enough to be used as an *alternative* to the neoclassical one and to be able to support *all* institutional investigations: those of the old, or if we like 'true' institutionalism, as well as those of the so called 'new' institutionalism".[23] We plainly agree with this statement, but with the proviso that some completely different specification (from Pasinetti) of the separation theorem is needed.[24]

2.7 Conclusion

The neoclassical school of thought has demonstrated great versatility and also a far greater propensity to generalize than has its opponents. We saw in Chapter 1 that it has notched up a number of achievements with regard to the remedying of its original Walrasian purity: Don Patinkin's theory of money, the Hicksian IS-LM model, endogenous growth models, extensions to the analysis of the phenomena of reproduction and accumulation, some aspects of the thought of Schumpeter (facilitated by this economist's great admiration for Walras), even equilibria with unemployment and noncompetitive equilibria[25] and, last but not least, a number of down institutional analyses. These extensions and some more recent ones have allowed neoclassical theory to achieve and preserve its mainstream character.

The success has been strengthened by the accurate and extensive use of both the well-developed and indeed dominating scientific methods: the methods of logical-formal sciences and of natural sciences. The resulting system of thought does not fear the criticisms of heterodox economics, with its large variety of explanatory approaches that often harshly fight each other.

For challenging orthodox economics (as modern heterodoxy is aimed at doing), it needs to set forth the foundations of a methodology more appropriate to social reality than those of logical-formal and natural sciences and offer an equally wider perspective – that is, a methodology that conjugates a constructivist organizational substance (as required by a reality which is a result of men's work and genius) to realism and that conjugates being and doing (see Section 2.2) and, on this basis, tries to understand becoming. Pasinetti's idea of separation and his principle of the 'realism of postulates' can be precious in this regard, particularly in deriving, from the general conditions of development typical of the considered historical era, the organizational necessities that must be fulfilled, to which the optional and creative aspects (of the separation) should be combined. Those necessities are not a mere observational matter and hence cannot be captured through the method of natural sciences based on observation and verification; in fact, they are often disregarded and trampled across history. Also the logical-formal abstraction typical of mathematics and logic is unable to capture those necessities.

Pasinetti admonishes that formal coherence is indispensable if a new institutionalism is to avoid ending up a merely descriptive useless formulation, as was the older institutionalism of Veblen, Commons and the like. Our necessary model (like the one that will be specified in Chapter 3) is intended to provide, among other things, a solution to this advocated exigency of a new institutionalism.

Notes

1 An article very similar to the content of this chapter was deposited in the RePEc archive in 2014 on behalf and with the assent of the *Journal of Business and Economics*.
2 Of course, this does not intend to deny, for instance, the successful criticism against the neoclassical aggregate function of production and the aggregate notion (and hence measurement) of capital.
3 It acts as "an analytical device to face complexity" (see Pasinetti 2007, p. 322).

4 Parts of this section reproduce methodological propositions that were expressed in another book (Fusari, *Methodological Misconceptions in the Social Sciences*, Springer, 2014); their strict scientific content sometimes suggests a precise reproposition of them.
5 A critical review of this kind can be found in Fusari (2004 and 2014).
6 R. Frish, J. Tinbergen, L. Johansen and, in a sense, V. Leontief, among the others.
7 This author writes: "it might not be too much to argue that dominant research programs create conditions for their subsequent fragmentation, whereas periods of pluralism create conditions for the re-emergence of new dominant approaches" (see Davis 2008, p. 32).
8 See Davis and Wade Hands (2011).
9 See Salanti and Screpanti (1997).
10 Note that those functional imperatives have a completely different meaning from T. Parsons's notion of functional imperative.
11 Something similar was performed by using the Leontief's dynamic model to determine sectoral quantities and prices in the preparation, at the end of the 1960s, of the reference framework of the second Italian Economic and Social Plan.
12 Pasinetti states: "The [neoclassical] model is – with regard to institutions – very demanding; or, we may say, from another point of view, very constraining and exclusive" (see Delorme and Dopfer 1994, p. 37).
13 See Pasinetti (1981), p. 25.
14 P. Garegnani has denominated 'core system' as the Sraffian system of these prices and the 'outside variables' as the variables concerning surplus; this is analogous to Pasinetti's separation between natural system and institutional side and hence shares the limitations of such a separation.
15 This mechanism of interaction, also mentioned in Chapter 1, will be plainly drawn in Chapters 3 and 4.
16 For a discussion of this topic, see Chapter 6.
17 This representation does not necessarily require a micro specification but can be represented at the sectoral level, as in Chapter 3.
18 See Schumpeter (1977), p. 128.
19 We insist on this in Chapters 11 and 12.
20 The basic lines of an organizational model satisfying these points are set out in Chapters 10 and 12. We show there that the statement insisted upon by adherents of the neoclassical school (*viz.* that efficiency is in collision with social justice and which implies distributional inequalities) is a mistaken one, with the exception of the material incentives required by alienating jobs.
21 See Knight (1950).
22 See Pasinetti (2007), pp. 322–323.
23 See Delorme and Dopfer (1994), p. 40 (emphasis in original).
24 Moreover, Pasinetti trusts in evolutionary economics. This is important. But sometimes evolutionary economics is afflicted by serious limitations that follow mainly from its drawing inspiration from a natural science (i.e. biology). Darwinian innovation takes a very long time to occur since it depends on casual and very slow processes of selection by trial and error. Social change is a very different thing; it is not casual but is caused by systematic factors, mainly by competition based on the introduction of innovations. This implies the need for a completely different methodological base from evolutionary economics.
25 See Zaghini (1974), Clower and others.

References

Barone, E. (1971), The ministry of production in collectivist state, in G. Lunghini II (ed), *Valore, prezzi ed equilibrio generale*, Mulino, Bologna, p. 76.
Davis, J. B. (2008), The turn in recent economics and return of orthodoxy, *Cambridge Journal of Economics*, vol. 32, no. 3, pp. 349–366.

Davis, J. B. & Wade Hands, D. (Eds.). (2011), *The Elgar companion to recent economic methodology*, Edward Elgar, Cheltenham.

Delorme, R. & Dopfer, K. (Eds.). (1994), *The political economy of diversity*, Edward Elgar, Cheltenham.

Dow, S. C. (2011), Heterodox economics: History and prospects, *Cambridge Journal of Economics*, vol. 35, pp. 1151–1165.

Ekstedt, H. & Fusari, A. (2010), *Economic theory and social change*, Routledge, London and New York.

Feyerabend, P. K. (1975), *Against method: Outline of an anarchistic theory of knowledge*, NBL and Feltrinelli, Milan 2002.

Friedman, M. (2002), *Capitalism and freedom*, University of Chicago Press, Chicago.

Frisch, R. (1976), *Economic planning studies*, Selected and introduced by Frank Long, Reidel, Dordrecht.

Fusari, A. (2004), A reconsideration on the method of economic and social sciences: Procedures, rules, classifications, *International Journal of Social Economics*, vol. 31, no. 5/6, pp. 501–535.

Fusari, A. (2005a), A model of the innovation-adaptation mechanism driving economic dynamics: A micro representation, *Journal of Evolutionary Economics*, vol. 15, no. 3, pp. 297–335.

Fusari, A. (2005b), Toward a non-capitalist market economy: Spontaneous order and organization, *American Review of Political Economy*, vol. 3, no. 1, pp. 85–125. www.arpejournal.com.

Fusari, A. (2012), *Economics and society: Freedom, creativity and social justice*, WEA Online Conference, on "Economics in Society: The Ethical Dimension".

Fusari, A. (2013), Radical uncertainty, dynamic competition and a model of business cycle: The implications of a measure and explanation of what is supposed non-measurable and non-explainable, *International Journal of Business and Management*, vol. 8, no. 12, pp. 8–28.

Fusari, A. (2014), The contrast between mainstream and heterodox economics: A misleading controversy – "necessary" system versus "natural" system, *Journal of Business and Economics*, vol. 5, no. 7, pp. 1077–1091.

Fusari, A. & Reati, A. (2013), Endogenizing technical change: Uncertainty, profits, entrepreneurship – A long-term view of sectoral dynamics, *Structural Change and Economic Dynamics*, vol. 24, pp. 76–100.

Garegnani, P. (1984), Value and distribution in the classical economists and Marx, *Oxford Economic Papers*, vol. 36, no. 2, pp. 291–325.

Hicks, J. R. (1974), *The crisis in Keynesian economics*, Basil Blackwell, Oxford.

Homer, S. (1996), *History of interest rates*, Rutgers University Press, New Brunswick, NJ.

Kaldor, N. (1960), Alternative theories of distribution, in *Essays on value and distribution*, Gerald Duckworth & Co. Ltd, London, pp. 83–100.

Kirzner, I. M. (1973), *Competition and entrepreneurship*, The University of Chicago Press, Chicago and London.

Kirzner, I. M. (1985), *Discovery and the capitalist process*, The University of Chicago Press, Chicago and London.

Knight, F. (1950), *Risk, uncertainty and profit*, La Nuova Italia edition, Florence.

Lange, O. & Taylor, F. M. (1938), *On the economic theory of socialism*, edited by B. Lippincot, Minneapolis.

Lawson, T. (2006), The nature of heterodox economics, *Cambridge Journal of Economics*, vol. 30, no. 4, pp. 483–505.

Lee, F. S. (2009), *A history of heterodox economics: Challenging the mainstream in the twentieth century*, Routledge, London.

Lerner, A. P. (1938), Theory and practice in socialist economics, *The Review of Economic Studies*, vol. 6, no. 1, pp. 71–75.

Mäki, U. (Ed.). (2001), *The economic world view: Studies in the ontology of economics*, Cambridge University Press, Cambridge.

Pasinetti, L. L. (1981), *Structural change and economic growth: A theoretical essay on the dynamics of wealth of nations*, Cambridge University Press, Cambridge.

Pasinetti, L. L. (2007), *Keynes and the Cambridge Keynesians*, Cambridge University Press, Cambridge.

Robinson, J. (1965), *The accumulation of capital*, Macmillan, London.

Salanti, A. & Screpanti, E. (Eds.). (1997), *Pluralism in economics: New perspective in history and methodology*, Edward Elgar, Aldershot.

Schumpeter, J. A. (1977), *Capitalism, socialism and democracy*, Universale Etas, Milan.

Sraffa, P. (1960), *Production of commodities by means of commodities*, Cambridge University Press, Cambridge.

Stiglitz, J. E. (2002), *Globalization and its discontents*, Einaudi, Turin.

Tinbergen, J. (1964), *Central planning*, Yale University Press, New Haven.

Zaghini, E. (1974), On the existence of equilibria with un-voluntary unemployment, *Rassegna Economica*, no. 5, pp. 1195–1211.

3 An explanation of economic change and development

3.1 Introduction

This chapter puts into effect the developments in Chapters 1 and 2. In particular, we resume here some basic analytical categories set out in Chapter 1 in order to provide (and formalize) a model of dynamic competition based on their interactions. Precisely, the contribution to the explanation of economic change that this chapter sets out is centered on a core of interconnected endogenous variables, mainly innovation, radical uncertainty and entrepreneurship, which current economic analyses consider only in part and separately, sometimes as endogenous but for the most as exogenous. The chapter (and the formalized model) suppose that the functioning of the economy is not disturbed by the operation of pathological factors mainly concerning the public sector, as happens significantly in the present moment, for instance: excessive public debt and public deficit; great inefficiencies and waste in the public sector and administration, and hence high taxation; inefficiencies, slowness and arbitrariness of judicial power; diffused organized criminality; financial capital operating, mainly at the international level, as master instead of servant of production, that is, largely devoted to speculation. A proper and efficient operation of the economy requires that such anomalies are absent. We attempt to explain economic change and development with regard to modern dynamic economies where these pathologies have been removed. This supposition would be strengthened by the reduction of the model to only necessary variables, as devised in Section 3.3.1.

The theoretical frame of the proposed explanation is a dynamic competitive process, that is, a competition based not merely on prices but also put into action by entrepreneurs' searches for opportunities for profit attached to successful innovations, which generate profits through temporary monopolies and also engender disequilibria and radical uncertainty that will provide additional opportunities for profit.

This dynamic competitive process is a great agent of economic change and evolutionary motion. As a first stage approximation, it can be thought of as a combination of Schumpeterian innovative entrepreneurship and action with the neo-Austrian market process and entrepreneurship: a combination mentioned in Chapter 1 and describing the advent of innovations and the subsequent adaptive push enacted by the imitative diffusion of innovations and the search for other opportunities of profit allowed by rising disequilibria and uncertainty; a push that leads toward the reduction of the inconsistencies and radical uncertainty caused by innovation and (hence) toward a reorganization and re-equilibration of the economy on new structural bases. The understanding of the process of change and development is greatly obscured by the current separation of the two theoretical perspectives mentioned. But it must be added that the explanation of such processes requires more than the simple combination of the two perspectives.

The notion of profit relevant with regard to the envisaged dynamic competition process does not include interest on the employed capital; it concerns only true profits, the so-called extra profits resulting from entrepreneurial gains from successful innovations and the profit opportunities attached to the consequent disequilibria and uncertain perspectives. Let us remember that the ratio between those profits and the capital employed, expressed as the profit rate, is relevant mainly in that it is the only reliable indicator of the degree of success of an entrepreneur's decision making, primarily in introducing innovations and meeting disequilibria and uncertainty. However, here we are not interested in the distribution of profits, that is, whether profit takes on a capitalist nature or is yielded by public or self-managed firms, and so on. Such distributive characteristics express simply a choice of civilization, which is incidental to the mere question of economic change and development.

Our model is not limited to the explanation of the core variables (that is, various kinds of innovation, such as radical and incremental process innovations and innovations of product, the demand and supply of entrepreneurship, and radical uncertainty) crucial in the representation of the whole process of change and the inherent disequilibrating and re-equilibrating evolutionary motion. The specified model also includes (and explains) other important variables such as output, employment, investment, prices and wages. It refers to the maximum level of sectoral disaggregation, a sector for each specific good, and describes long waves. A specification with a restricted number of sectors is used for simulations.

The structure of the chapter is as follows: the first section presents the introduction, and a second section is dedicated to a literary presentation of the theoretical construction concerned mainly with the main variables enacting dynamic competition (entrepreneurship, radical uncertainty, innovation, profit) and long waves. A third section presents the formal specification of the model. This section is divided into five blocks. Block I concerns the explanation of radical process innovations and the advent of new products (that occur as soon as their explanatory equations reach some specified trigger values) and incremental innovations, while some Gamma distributions describe the diffusion of the radical process innovations across the economy, that is, the adaptive process following the innovative breakthroughs. Block II includes the equations explaining uncertainty and the availability of entrepreneurship and its demand, and hence the excess of entrepreneurial skills. Block III, which includes the equations of prices, wages and profits, has a conventional content, with the exception of some explanations of markup and the definition of the rate of true profit, which excludes interests on capital. Block IV concerns consumption and, in particular, the diffusion of new consumer goods. Block V concerns capital and investment. A fourth section presents three simulations of the model that suppose different degrees of intensity of dynamic competition. Section 3.5, which exposes some reference to a microspecification of the model at the level of the firm, opens the door to Chapter 4.

3.2 The main factors of economic change and development

3.2.1 Premise

Explanation of economic change is one of the most deficient components of modern economics. It is also one of the most embarrassing, for the ever more important competition based on innovations fuels that intense and growing dynamism that has become one of the primary characteristics of modern economies. The poverty of the treatment of the primary sources of economic change is striking: in economic modeling, dynamic motion is often expressed merely by the inclusion of time in equations.

Any serious analysis of economic change and development is obliged to pay attention to entrepreneurship and its counterpart, profit, as well as to radical uncertainty and innovation along with the associated process of dynamic competition and the implied long waves. But, even if not ignored by economists, these variables and processes are usually represented in a fragmented and incomplete way. This implies, among other things, a scarcity of available data on those variables; hopefully the emphasis of economics on their importance should remedy this.

3.2.2 Entrepreneurship

The entrepreneur is a primary dynamic force within the economy and the main agent of economic change. In the absence of the entrepreneur, technological inventions would remain useless from an economic point of view, as happened in ancient (and also recent) bureaucratic-centralized empires.[1] The transformation of inventions into innovations and its acceleration through R&D are the work of entrepreneurship. A dynamic economy, that is, one with technological change and innovation, cannot do without the entrepreneur for promoting innovation, meeting the resulting radical uncertainty and, in sum, governing the whole process of disequilibration and re-equilibration expressing change.

However, it may be useful to underline that the capitalist character of both entrepreneurship and economic dynamics must be considered, from a scientific point of view, a contingency resulting from the operation across history of specific kinds of spontaneous forces. More generally, the social sciences should consider capitalism as but one particular choice of civilization. But the figure of the entrepreneur as innovator and manager of uncertain perspectives cannot be erased by modern societies (be they capitalist or not) without destroying their dynamic content. The entrepreneur represents an organizational necessity, who both legitimates and strengthens this necessity through innovative actions generating true or radical uncertainty and, therefore, also the need of an agent able to face it.

Economics has largely disregarded the entrepreneur and has too readily opted to conceive of entrepreneurship simply as an expression of animal spirits, thereby avoiding the question of the demand and supply of this important agent. In particular, growth economics substantially neglects entrepreneurship. As a consequence, quantitative data on entrepreneurship are lacking.[2]

Our model will explain the supply of entrepreneurship as a function of the degree of radical uncertainty multiplied by the level of production and the dynamics of innovations, these expressing proxies of entrepreneurial learning by doing; eventually some sociological explanatory factor should be added. The demand for entrepreneurship will be explained by the same variables but with different adjustment speeds, that is, as a function of the level of production weighted with the degree of radical uncertainty and the intensity of innovative action. For zero uncertainty and innovation, there will be no learning by doing of entrepreneurship and no need for entrepreneurship; indeed there will not be entrepreneurship at all.

So, entrepreneurship generated and absorbed by business activity is directly correlated to the degree of uncertainty. Entrepreneurial skills increase when deep uncertainty compels entrepreneurs to put into motion all their capabilities and deteriorate when the economic situation does not require such an effort as happens, for instance, in equilibrium. But the demand for entrepreneurial skills varies with a shorter lag than the supply, with respect to the same independent variables of both equations. The result is the variation of the 'excess' of entrepreneurial skills, the difference between the supply and demand of entrepreneurship, a variable that, as we shall see, is crucial for the explanation of innovation and the representation of the dynamic competition process.

3.2.3 Radical uncertainty

This is the uncertainty in regard to which "there is no scientific basis on which to form any calculable probability whatever".[3] Radical (or true) uncertainty just expresses a lack of knowledge. In this respect, such uncertainty is completely different from expectations that allow reaction to the uncertainty of perspectives and, as we have seen, constitute an attempt to penetrate the future; expectations constitute an expression of hope, which is quite different from the expression of the limitation of knowledge proper of radical uncertainty. As such, radical uncertainty has to do with the violation of expectations, their variability and dispersion; in a sense, it expresses the degree of unreliability of expectations.

As we saw, F. H. Knight, who may be considered the father of the notion of uncertainty, has insisted on its immeasurability; and economics, while proposing various ways of estimating expectations (sometimes implausible – think, for instance, of the notion of rational expectations), follows Knight in denying the measurability of radical uncertainty, effectively designating this a fog. Such a denial can be accepted with reference to many specific events that the entrepreneur encounters; after all, the measurement of the degree of uncertainty of these specific events would imply the erasing of uncertainty and its transformation into insurable risk, and hence would expunge entrepreneurship. But the sectoral degree of uncertainty is quite another thing: the denial of the measurability of sectoral uncertainty constitutes a substantial and unwarranted limitation.

In the first chapter, we saw that various measures of radical uncertainty by sector can be proposed, for example, the *volatility* of opinions as expressed by the EU surveys on business tendency and concerning firms' expectations on delivery orders, production, prices, cost of financing and liquidity assets. Another indicator of uncertainty may be represented by the sectoral standard deviation of profit rates across firms; in the absence of institutional monopolies, these standard deviations are the consequence of different abilities to meet uncertainty and hence increase with uncertainty, becoming zero in its absence. Again, sectoral uncertainty may be measured by a minimum-maximum range of expectations, with the distance between the minimum and the maximum expressing the degree of uncertainty. Yet another potential measure is provided by the standard deviation of foresights. But statistical data for these measures are unfortunately lacking.

Radical uncertainty is strictly linked to the figure of the entrepreneur. As previously seen, it implies the necessity of the entrepreneur and, at the same time, it is largely the result of entrepreneurial innovative action. In the absence of this action, only exogenous uncertainty would survive, that is, a very limited portion of uncertainty.

Our model explains the variations of radical uncertainty as a function of innovation: radical process and product innovations, as well as the diffusion of radical and incremental process innovations; an exogenous term is added in the explanation, meaning that in the absence of innovations, uncertainty would tend to decrease toward the operation of exogenous factors.

3.2.4 Innovation

The explanation of innovation is a central aspect of the model that we are going to specify. Innovations can be radical, that is, concerning completely new processes and products, or they can be incremental if they simply improve existing processes. As is well known, Schumpeter distinguished five kinds of innovations: (1) the production of new goods, (2) the introduction of a new method of production, (3) the opening of a market, (4) the conquest of a new source of supply of raw materials and of semi-finished products and (5) industrial reorganization. With some approximation and useful simplification, our model will put together Schumpeterian innovations of types 1, 3 and 4 under the category *new products*, while types 2 and 5 may be considered under the category *new processes*. Of course, the introduction of innovations is delayed with respect to the corresponding inventions and discoveries. The delay is shortened by the combination of the two aspects in the firms' strategy of R&D.

The explanation of innovation is one of the most unsatisfactory aspects of economics. Often the need for such explanation is simply ignored, with innovations treated as exogenous. Attempts to explain them operate, for the most part, in the context of the function of production, adding into this function some additional factors such as human capital (Lucas), the operation of an innovative sector producing knowledge (Shell and Romer) and the advent of new intermediate products and quality based innovation (Grossman and Helpman and Aghion and Howitt). But these explanations ignore the role of entrepreneurship and its availability, radical uncertainty, and the distinction between radical and incremental innovations and between new products and new processes (in the context of the dynamic competition process that we are going to discuss). A different and distinctly better landscape is offered by some micro models, for instance the model of Saviotti and Pyka that, unfortunately, only concerns the advent of new products and "does not contemplate process innovations, notwithstanding the insistence of both the authors on their indispensability to cause, through the productivity rise, the deficiency in the demand for the existing goods, a deficiency that pushes product innovation".[4]

Innovation constitutes a main component of entrepreneurial action and is stimulated by the excess (difference between supply and demand) of entrepreneurship. A crucial aspect, from an explanatory point of view, is the relation between innovation and radical uncertainty: while the first tends to stimulate uncertainty (as just seen), the second discourages innovation since, if uncertainty is high, a large part of entrepreneurship is absorbed by ordinary activity and hence is deflected from innovation. Moreover, innovations are negatively influenced by the profit rate: when this is negative, the firm is forced to innovate (Mensh's 'innovate or perish'). Innovations of process are also stimulated by the apparition of new capital goods, which imply changes of processes. For its part, the explanation of innovations of product, while excluding (of course) the role of new capital goods, adds (to the factors considered previously) both the stimulus due to the saturation of the demand of existing goods (emphasized by Saviotti and Pyka) and the degree of inequality in income distribution, since such inequality generates market niches that are inclined to buy new products.

Radical innovations constitute important discontinuities. In our model, they materialize as soon as their explanatory equations reach a value equal to some established threshold. Moreover, we specify the diffusion of radical product and process innovations through, respectively, a Gamma distribution and a logistic. For their part, incremental innovations are negatively influenced by uncertainty and positively influenced by the excess of entrepreneurship. They are also stimulated by the diffusion of radical process innovations weighted by the excess of entrepreneurship; in fact, many incremental innovations are a result of entrepreneurs' attempts to achieve the best performance of radical innovations; as a consequence, incremental innovations become dominant features of the dynamic motion after the complete diffusion of radical innovations.

3.2.5 *Profit and profit rate: necessity and choice possibility in the organization of the economy*

Profit is a counterpoint of entrepreneurship; it does not make sense to conceive of entrepreneurship independently of profit. In fact, the profit rate is economically essential in that it is the only reliable and overall measure of the degree of success of the entrepreneur's decision making; it represents an organizational necessity.

However, it is important to restate that what is relevant in measuring such a degree of success is the rate of the so-called extra (or true) profit on used capital – that is, not including the interest rate on the capital employed.

Our very general reference to the profit rate should not be thought of as establishing a category of income distribution. The kind of attribution of profit simply expresses a choice of civilization; for instance, the capitalist character of social organization. This feature of our analysis must be strongly underlined in order to avoid the frequent prejudices that arise concerning the organization of the economic systems – an emphasis that constitutes not a subversive assessment, but a scientific assertion.[5] The problem that arises here is part of a more general question: the distinction between necessity and choice possibility creativeness in the organization of social systems. In order to better clarify this point, we shall delineate at the beginning of Section 3.3 (dedicated to the formal model), some transformations of the model directed so as to express only necessities, that is, to reduce the model to *necessary institutions* which vary only in the long run, across historical ages, as scanned by the variation of the general conditions of development.[6]

3.2.6 Dynamic competition

Now we unify the previous treatments in the notion of dynamic competition. This should provide a much more articulated and comprehensive explanatory model of economic change and development than those based on the notion of the production function. Our approach joins together all the factors considered in the previous four subsections, that is, entrepreneurship, the various kinds of innovations and their diffusion, radical uncertainty and the role of the profit rate. Economic change is practically impossible, at least as an enduring feature, in the absence of competition of such a kind.

The dynamic competitive process is a result of the entrepreneurial search for profit. As previously seen, description of some of the main contents of such a process has been provided both by the Schumpeterian theory of entrepreneurship, innovation and development and the neo-Austrian market process centered on the entrepreneur's alertness to the existence of price differences between inputs and outputs, to new goals, new available resources and other unnoticed opportunities. One of the most surprising aspects of current economics is that the two approaches remain separated as products of two different and opposing schools of thought, notwithstanding their strong and stimulating complementariness, mainly in explaining economic change. Probably, the history of economic thought will consider, from an analytical point of view, such an opposition one of the strangest and most senseless phenomena in the development of economics.[7]

It is indubitable that the entrepreneurial search for profit through the various kinds of innovations previously considered constitutes a main engine of economic change and development. But this is not enough. Innovation is a powerful source of radical uncertainty and disequilibria, which represent further crucial challenges for the entrepreneur and provide additional opportunities to put into effect the business's ability to obtain profits. This adaptive search for profits gives rise to a phase of re-equilibration and organizational structuring that follow the initial innovative dash. Excuse us for repeating that, in the envisaged process, the neo-Austrian entrepreneur acts as an equilibrating force, while the Schumpeterian entrepreneur acts as a disequilibrating one. In this respect, the combination of Schumpeterian and neo-Austrian theoretical perspectives is precious from an analytical point of view. It is very instructive to analyze the dynamic competitive process of change and development in the light of such a combination. Let us so proceed.

Approaching the equilibrium of the economy as a consequence of the action of the neo-Austrian adaptive entrepreneur tends to erase radical uncertainty (with the exception of that caused by exogenous factors, such as natural disasters) and also to erase economic change and profit. But low uncertainty makes it easy to invest and innovate and increases the excess of entrepreneurship to be dedicated to innovation; moreover, innovation is powerfully stimulated by the fact that the neo-Austrian push toward equilibrium makes innovation the main effective way to make profits. The rise, with the consequent innovation dash, of disequilibria and radical uncertainty recreates new adaptive opportunities for profit, as implied by the neo-Austrian arbitrage and market process, and hence a renewed push toward equilibrium, and so forth in a cyclical process of innovation and subsequent reorganization that gives rise to a more advanced structural base of the economy.

It may be useful to insist on a description of the process, notwithstanding the risk of some repetition. As we can see, variations in the degree of radical uncertainty and of the excess of entrepreneurship are crucial for representing the working of the dynamic competition process: adaptive equilibrating competition implied by the market process causes the reduction of disequilibria and uncertainty and, therefore, reduces both the need for entrepreneurship and the existing opportunities of profit; but, in this way, adaptive equilibrating competition increases the excess of entrepreneurship and, hence, the entrepreneurship available to introduce innovations aimed at creating new opportunities of profit, so that the reduction in radical uncertainty generates a favorable climate for the introduction of innovations and vice versa. In sum, the variations of radical uncertainty determine the way an entrepreneur's alertness is oriented toward the two complementary kinds of entrepreneurial competition (the Schumpeterian and the neo-Austrian one) and, more generally, the way the disequilibrating/re-equilibrating process of dynamic competition operates.

Innovation by itself would result in a paralyzing confusion, while adaptive structural organization leads toward equilibrium, thus erasing innovation, change and entrepreneurship. To avoid those inconveniences, the combination of the two theoretical perspectives, the Schumpeterian and neo-Austrian, is needed. But this combination is insufficient for the adequate representation of the whole process of change and development; some further variables implied by the process relating to radical uncertainty and entrepreneurship must be considered and explained. In fact, and as just seen, it is the rise of radical uncertainty caused by innovation that generates the push toward adaptation and structural organization, while the consequent decrease in radical uncertainty opens the door to the subsequent new rise of innovation. The whole process is the work of entrepreneurship and hence depends on its availability.

Unfortunately, and as we saw, radical uncertainty is not specified but only implied by the Schumpeterian theory of development; and although it is emphasized by neo-Austrians, it is nevertheless treated simply as a fog and an exogenous variable. Moreover, the explanation of the availability (demand and supply, and hence the excess) of entrepreneurship is disregarded by both theories. Probably, the lack of such a theoretical deepening is the main reason behind the surprising persistence of the separation of the two theoretical perspectives. Our model will attempt to give a rigorous formal specification of all the aspects of dynamic competition specified in Sections 3.2.2 to 3.2.5. This will enable us to provide a representation and an explanation of economic change and business cycles that is more complete than that offered by the current models.

3.2.7   Long waves[8]

It may be interesting to say something about the long waves attached to innovation and economic change in the context of the dynamic competition process described previously and as part of the explanation of economic change.

The cyclical interaction between innovation and adaptation and disequilibrating and re-equilibrating motion implies long waves. Table 3.1 shows the intensity of the various kinds of innovation during the phases of the long wave.

As we can see (and as A. Reati writes),

> during the depression phase of the long-wave major innovations tend to appear in existing industries and concern processes as well as products. In the latter case, a radical product innovation concerns the satisfaction of an already existing need by a completely new product (the PC replaces the mechanical typewriter; the photocopying machine is a substitute for carbon paper, etc.). During the recovery, the number of major process innovations in existing industries falls sharply while the flow of product innovations continues. However, the dominant feature of this phase is the appearance of radical product innovations leading to the creation of new industries, which means that there is the creation of a new need. This is summarised next in Table 3.1.[9]

Table 3.1 Propensity to innovate during the phases of the long wave (Van Duijn 1983, p. 137)

	Stagnation		Expansion	
	Depression	Recovery	Prosperity	Recession
1. Product innovations (new industries)	*	****	**	*
2. Product innovations (existing industries)	***	***	*	*
3. Process innovations (existing industries)	***	*	**	**
4. Process innovations (basic sectors)	*	**	***	**

The more stars, the greater the propensity to innovate.

60 Theoretical frame

Now we come to the process of diffusion of innovations, which has much to do with waves. A. Reati writes:

> In order to understand the dynamics of *product* innovations, let us recall that new (final) *products* pass through four stages life cycle: *(i)* market development (introduction), when the product is first brought to the market; *(ii)* growth, when demand begins to accelerate and the size of the total market expands rapidly; *(iii)* maturity, when demand levels off and grows, for the most part, only at the replacement and new family-formation rate; *(iv)* decline, when the product begins to lose consumer appeal and sales drift downwards.
>
> The reasons underlying consumer behaviour in the first and second stages are primarily due to the gradual spread among consumers of information on the existence of the new commodity, its characteristics and its appropriateness in satisfying a particular need: it is the 'epidemic' model. Next we turn to prices. Very often, the introduction of a new product requires heavy investment in research and development as well as considerable marketing expenditure. In such circumstances, the price at the initial stage in the product life-cycle will be set at a high level to allow the innovator to recoup his costs before too many imitators enter the market. The ensuing high profits will attract imitators while the decrease in inequality occurring when the economy enters into the recovery and the prosperity phases will gradually enlarge the potential market for the new product. Diffusion is also facilitated by the fact that the initial price level, which 'skims the cream of the demand', will be progressively abandoned during the later stages of the product life cycle so as to stimulate demand from other segments of the market. Further price reductions of this kind will be engendered by the growing competition from newcomers as well as by process innovations in the sector concerned and in the corresponding capital goods sector.
>
> The pattern of diffusion of *process* innovations is explained by the fact that, for instance, the enterprises in the sector do not have the necessary information to perceive immediately the advantage of imitating the first innovator or, if they are fully aware of the new opportunities, they prefer to wait so as to avoid the cost of accelerated scrapping or they are unable to adopt the new technology for organizational or institutional reasons (they do not know how to master the new technology or do not have the necessary skills; managers are reluctant to change radically the organization of the company).
>
> Product and process innovations can also be favoured by organizational factors. "As the S-curve matures . . . , the business becomes bigger and more bureaucratic. That's where 'creative destruction' comes in because the more something becomes bureaucratized, the more room it leaves at the bottom for individuals and small teams of heretics to redefine the game in new ways" (Stefik and Stefik 2006, p. 4). The number of years it takes to reach a complete

Table 3.2 The main features of the long wave

	Stagnation		Expansion	
	Depression	Recovery	Prosperity	Recession
Rate of profit	Decreasing and very low	Increasing	High and stable	Decreasing
Degree of inequality	High	High	Decreasing to low	Low but increasing
Unused entrepreneurial skills (excess)	High	High but decreasing	Low	Low but (slightly) increasing
Degree of radical uncertainty	Low then increasing	High	Low	Low
Expectations	Negative	Slightly improving	Favorable	Favorable but deteriorating

diffusion of radical innovations differs substantially according to the type of innovation.

For *process* innovations, we assume that diffusion is almost complete by the end of the phase of the long-wave in which the technological revolution started off.

For *product* innovations, the length of the diffusion period varies a great deal from one product to another, but in general, the maturity stage is reached much later than in the case of process innovations. Empirical research by Gort and Klepper (1982) based on a sample of 'basic' product innovations first commercially introduced between 1887 and 1960 shows that, on average, the maturity stage was reached within 37 years. However, the interval required for successful imitation has systematically declined over time. While the overall average length of the first stage (introduction) is 14.4 years, for products introduced before 1930 this interval was 23.1 years; it was 9.6 years for those introduced in the period 1930–39 and only 4.9 years for products introduced in 1940 or later (Gort and Klepper 1982, p. 640; see also Stefik and Stefik 2006, pp. 203–204 for further evidence concerning the USA).[10]

A. Reati has also set forth Table 3.2 concerning the relation between some variables and the various phases of the waves.

3.3 The model

Our model has a double purpose: first, to deepen the mechanism of economic change and evolution by complementing the theory of Section 3.2 with analytical details; and second, to prepare the ground for ascertaining the overall consistency of the model through numerical simulations.

62 Theoretical frame

3.3.1 General features

The conventional duration of the long wave

In our model we conventionally assume that a long wave lasts 50 years, long expansion and stagnation 25 years each, and individual phases last 20 years (prosperity), 5 years (recession), 15 years (depression) and 10 years (recovery).[11]

The structure: the reduction of the model to only necessary variables

Initially, our model is composed of two sectors: (1) the consumer (final) goods sector, grouping n industries, and (2) the capital goods sector, grouping m industries. Radical product innovations are taken into account by adding new industries to the sector in which they appear, which means that the structure of the economy is made up of two 'big' capital goods and consumer goods sectors operating with the traditional technology, to which are now added the new sectors.

We generalize this by supposing that we have h new capital goods industries and g new consumer goods industries. Therefore, our model formalizes, for each endogenous variable, four groups of n, m, g and h equations expressing a complete disaggregation of the economy – one industry for each commodity.

The discontinuities represented by radical innovations are introduced into the model through a 'switch' binary variable similar to a Dirac function δ. Value 1 of the switch opens the door to the innovation, while value 0 precludes it. To see how this operates in practice, consider a function z (e.g. the level or the rate of change of productivity of an enterprise) and posit that a radical innovation materializes when z exceeds or is equal to a given threshold k ($z \geq k$). Then, defining a variable y as the difference between z and its threshold ($y = z - k$), our switch function δ is such that

$$\delta(y) = 1 \text{ if } y \geq 0, \text{ otherwise } \delta(y) = 0.$$

Alternatively, when a radical innovation appears when z is below the threshold, we change the direction of δ by a new switch ω, which is

$$\omega = 1 - \delta.$$

In this case, $\omega(y) = 1$ if $y < 0$, otherwise $\omega(y) = 0$.

By way of an example, let us consider depression and put z = rate of profit – the variable that, as we have seen, represents one of the main triggering factors for radical innovations. If, for a given time span (e.g. three years), the rate of profit is on average less than a certain threshold level (e.g. 1.5%) and we fix the threshold $k = 1.5$, the diffusion of the innovation will start the fourth year.

We indicate now, as promised in Section 3.2.5, some modifications intended to reduce the formal model to only necessary variables. The modifications are as follows: (a) the real interest rate should be null, so that the nominal interest rate equates with inflation; (b) money wages should be expressed as a function of only the demand and supply of labor, so as to represent just an element of cost charged on prices and not a component of income distribution; (c) the degree of inequality of income distribution should be erased in the equation for new products in its role as a variable stimulating product innovation, such a stimulus being relevant only in a particular social system, capitalism; and (d) in the equation of consumption, total money wages should be replaced by some other component of income distribution, wages being excluded from income distribution and only intended as an element of cost (see item b).[12]

The process of adaptation

For the sake of realism, we posit that the theoretical ('normal') level of some variables does not fully materialize immediately but instead determines the actual level within a temporal lag. The rationale for this adjustment process – which applies to entrepreneurship, wages, prices, markup and consumption – will be set out next when illustrating the relevant equations.

The diffusion process

The diffusion process of radical *product* innovations is represented by a logistic function for which rates of change are decreasing and the derivative is bell shaped. For *process* innovations, we instead use a Gamma distribution in order to formalize more efficiently the successive appearance of new radical innovations[13] and also to take into consideration the fact that some improvements of a previous process innovation can be considered as an additional radical innovation. By choosing the appropriate parameters for the Gamma distribution, it is possible to approximate the sigmoid pattern of diffusion, with its bell-shaped derivative.

Market structures

We assume the ubiquitous presence of economic power and 'domination effect' (Perroux 1964). This means, among other things, that in every industry there is either monopolistic competition or an oligopoly in its various forms.

Competitive sectors are defined on the basis of 'workable competition', that is, the rivalry that is possible within the prevailing market structures. Thus, monopolistic competition implies that each firm has a certain market power resulting from product differentiation; concerning oligopolistic market structures, we assume that there are no agreements restricting competition and also that rivalry entails that selling prices roughly follow the evolution of productivity.

Market power evolves over time in relation to the changing structures of the economy which characterizes the long wave. The stylized facts are:

- During the depression phase of long stagnation, competition strongly intensifies, and this reduces the market power of existing firms; this phenomenon is exacerbated by the low level of demand.

64 Theoretical frame

- Pressures on the market power of firms are slightly reduced during the recovery phase as demand begins to recover.
- During the long expansion phase, enterprises can fully exploit the potentialities offered by buoyant demand, charging prices that fully reflect their potential market power. In the final phase of the long expansion, the market power of firms tends to remain stable.

Rate of profit

The rate of profit is determined with respect to the net fixed capital stock at current replacement prices. To quantify the 'true' appropriation for entrepreneurship (i.e. the part of surplus exceeding the imputed wage), we deduct the rate of interest from the rate of profit. This adjustment of the profit rate is based on the fact that the owner of capital has to decide either to buy securities (obtaining an interest) or to invest his capital in a productive activity, thereby becoming an entrepreneur.

Inequality

The best way to take into consideration the degree of inequality would be to introduce exogenously into the model a Gini index. However, considering that we want to limit the number of exogenous variables, as a proxy for inequality we consider the share of wages with respect to net output at current prices. In this way, we assume a negative correlation between the two variables: when the wage share is low, inequality is high, and vice versa. At present, this global indicator is reinforced by the fact that the current technological revolution in information technologies has strongly increased the wage dispersion. Thus, we have a rather low wage share and strong inequality among wage earners.

3.3.2 Notations

Endogenous variables

CON = Consumption
CT = Average consumption level over a specified number of recent years
Ec = Unused entrepreneurial skills ('excess' of entrepreneurship)
Ed = Demand for entrepreneurship
Es = Supply of entrepreneurship
I = Gross investment (at constant prices)
K = Net fixed capital stock (at constant prices)
KD = Demand of existing capital goods
KDT = Demand of existing capital goods: average level over a specified number of recent years
L = Employment (demand for labor), economy as a whole; variable with subscript refers to specific industries

Explanation of economic change

M	= Variable that singles out the advent of a new sector
MKP	= Markup
ND	= Demand for new goods
NDT	= Demand for new goods: average level over a specified number of recent years
Pr	= Labor productivity (VA/L); subscript (av) means that productivity refers to the average of the economy ($Pr_{(av)}$)
PRE	= Prices
PrI	= Labor productivity of incremental innovations
$PrR_{(f)}$	= Labor productivity of radical process innovations for the individual innovator
r	= Rate of profit
R	= Rate of profit: average level over a specified number of recent years
SW	= Variable that singles out the appearance of radical process innovations
u	= Radical uncertainty
VA	= Value added at constant prices
$VA_{(nom)}$	= Value added at current prices
w	= Nominal wage rate
X	= Production at constant prices
XT	= Average level of output over a specified number of recent years
Γ	= Gamma distribution for the diffusion of radical process innovations
γ	= Variable to reduce the second order derivative concerning Γ to a first order one

Exogenous variables

i_r	= Interest rate
Ls	= Supply of labor
t	= Time

Other notations

a	= constant term
D	= Derivative with respect to time
e	= Unit column vector
I	= Column vector ($i + j + (n)i + (n)j$ components) of investments in existing capital goods
$k_{(M)}$	= Threshold level for the advent of radical product innovation
$k_{(PrR)}$	= Threshold level for the advent of radical process innovation
$K^{(d)}$	= Diagonal matrix (of order $i + j$) of net fixed capital stock (constant prices)
KD	= Column vector (j components) of demand of existing capital goods
ln	= Natural logarithm
PRE	= Row vector (j components) of the prices of capital goods
Q	= Percentage increase in the productivity level of the individual innovator resulting from a radical process innovation

66 *Theoretical frame*

TI	= Transition matrix $[j \times (i + j + (n)i + (n)j)]$ of investment from sectors of utilization to sectors of origin
TK	= Transition matrix $[j \times (i + j + (n)i + (n)j)]$ of capital from sectors of utilization to sectors of origin
α	= Adjustment parameter
β	= Other parameters
δ	= Switch variable (Dirac function)
η	= Obsolescence as a percentage of new capital goods
λ	= Scaling parameter
μ_1	= Depreciation rate of capital (worn-out capacity)
v	= Technical coefficient linking VA to X
ω	= Complement to one of the switch variable ($\omega = 1 - \delta$)

Indexes and subscripts

'	= Symbol indicating partial equilibrium variables in adjustment equations
i	= Subscript indicating consumer goods
j	= Subscript indicating capital goods
(n)i	= Subscript indicating new consumer goods
(n)j	= Subscript indicating new capital goods

3.3.3 *The equations*

Our model is structured around five blocks of equations. Block I concerns the production side of the economy, including employment; Block II introduces uncertainty and the behavioral hypotheses relating to entrepreneurship; Block III sets out the distributive variables; and Blocks IV and V refer to the demand side of the system.

We usually take the natural logarithms of the variables for the sake of convenience, as the derivative of the logarithm indicates the rate of change and the coefficient of the logarithm the elasticity.

Where the equations for sectors $i, j, (n)i$ and $(n)j$ are similar, they will be specified only for sector i and, to simplify matters, the parameters of each explanatory variable are almost always identical for every i.

Production, productivity and employment

GROSS OUTPUT

$$DlnX_i = \beta_1 r_i + \beta_2 \ln(Es_i/Ed_i) + \beta_3 \ln CON_i \quad i = 1, 2, 3 \ldots n \quad (I.1)$$

$$DlnX_j = \beta_1 r_j + \beta_2 \ln(Es_j/Ed_j) + \beta_4 \ln KD_j \quad j = 1, 2, 3 \ldots m \quad (I.2)$$

$$DlnX_{(n)i} = \omega(-M_{(n)i}) \beta_5 D(ND_{(n)i}) \quad (n)i = 1, 2, 3 \ldots g \quad (I.3)$$

$$DlnX_{(n)j} = \omega(-M_{(n)j}) \beta_6 D(ND_{(n)j}) \quad (n)j = 1, 2, 3 \ldots h \quad (I.4)$$

Behavioral equations I.1 and I.2 explain the changes in output of consumer and capital goods in existing industries in terms of three factors: the current rate of profit, the entrepreneurial skills and demand.[14] Profitability and demand indicators should be seen as *proxies* for the *expected* values of these variables (firms extrapolate the present situation).

For new consumer and capital goods (equations I.3 and I.4), production is fundamentally driven by demand.

OUTPUT LEVEL IN RECENT YEARS

$$D\ln XT_i = \alpha_1 \ln(X_i / XT_i) \tag{I.5}$$

This equation is derived from the expression for distributed lags, with a weight of 0.63 for X_i for the last $1/\alpha_1$ years.

The equation concerning sectors j is similar.

VALUE ADDED

(a) Constant prices

$$VA_i = v_1 X_i \tag{I.6}$$

(b) Current prices

$$VA_{(nom)i} = v_2 X_i PRE_i \tag{I.7}$$

For the sake of convenience, we posit that value added is linked to gross output through the technical coefficients v that are supposed to be constant.

TRIGGER FUNCTIONS EXPRESSING THE ADVENT OF NEW PRODUCTS

$$D(M_{(n)i}) = \delta\{[-\beta_7 u_i + \beta_8 \ln(Es_i/Ed_i) - \beta_9 R_i - \beta_{10}\ln(CT_i/XT_i) + \beta_{11} \ln Es_i - \beta_{12}\ln(w\,L\,/VA_{nom})\,] - k_{(M)i}\} \tag{I.8}$$

$$D(M_{(n)j}) = \delta\{[-\beta_7 u_j + \beta_8 \ln(Es_j/Ed_j) - \beta_9 R_j - \beta_{13}\ln(KDT_j/XT_j) + \beta_{14}\ln Es_j] - k_{(M)j}\} \tag{I.9}$$

Equations I.8 and I.9 summarize our previous analysis of the endogenous factors that generate a radical product innovation in consumer goods (eq. I.8) as well as in capital goods (eq. I.9). These innovations materialize when the expression in square brackets is higher than or equal to the trigger value $k_{(M)}$.

Some terms within the square brackets (such as uncertainty or 'excess' entrepreneurship [Es_i/Ed_i]) do not require specific comments. We just note the following:

68 Theoretical frame

- R represents the profit motive for innovation: if profitability is persistently negative, this will stimulate the radical change represented by the innovation.[15]
- Terms CT_j/XT_i and KDT_j/XT_j express the saturation effect of the demand for existing products, which is inversely related to the propensity to innovate. CT_j/XT_i or KDT_j/XT_j less than one means stagnating demand, which is a positive incentive to innovate.
- Terms Es mean that the higher the supply of entrepreneurship the more likely innovation will occur.
- The last term in square brackets in formula I.8 – that is, the inverse of the wage share – is a *proxy* for the degree of inequality in income distribution, inequality being directly related to the propensity to innovate.[16]
- In equation I.9, the term representing the degree of inequality does not appear because it is not relevant for launching new plant and equipment onto the market.

LABOR PRODUCTIVITY OF THE INDIVIDUAL INNOVATOR RESULTING
FROM RADICAL PROCESS INNOVATIONS

As already noted, radical process innovation entails a leap in the productivity level of the innovator. We explain the process of adoption of such innovations and the subsequent change in productivity in two steps. First, we define the factors that determine the occurrence of the innovation in question. Then we derive the productivity function for the individual innovator.

The switch function that marks the presence of the radical innovation is

$$D(SW_i) = \delta\{[-\beta_7 u_i + \beta_8 \ln(Es_i/Ed_i) - \beta_9 R_i + \beta_{15}\, \omega(-M_{(n)j})] - k_{(PrR)i}\} \quad (I.10)$$

$SW = 1$ if $k_{(PrR)i}$ is lower than or equal to the expression in square brackets, otherwise SW is zero. The equation expresses the constraint $D\ln PrR_{(f)i} \geq k_{(PrR)i}$.

$k_{(PrR)i}$ is the minimum productivity increase that a radical process innovation must yield, that is, a trigger for the advent of radical process innovation.

Term $\omega(-M_{(n)j})$ refers to the fact that the appearance of a new capital goods (product innovation in the capital goods sector) could produce a process innovation in another industry.

$\beta_{15} = 0$ if the new capital goods in question do not materialize

From this we derive the individual innovator's productivity function

$$D\ln PrR_{(f)i} = \omega(-SW_i)\, \beta_{16}\, (Q - PrR_{(f)i}) \quad (I.11)$$

Q may take different values for radical process innovations in consumer and capital goods (respectively Q_1 and Q_2).

Explanation of economic change 69

The equations for sectors j are similar, as are those for $(n)i$ and $(n)j$ provided that they are multiplied by $\omega(-M_{(n)i})$ and $\omega(-M_{(n)j})$, that mark the advent of new sectors (see eq. II.8 and II.9). This proviso must be extended to all other following groups.

GAMMA DISTRIBUTION FOR THE DIFFUSION OF
RADICAL PROCESS INNOVATIONS

$$D^2\Gamma_i = \beta_{17}\beta_{18}(D\ln PrR_{(f)i} - \Gamma_i) - (\beta_{17} + \beta_{18})D\Gamma_i \tag{I.12}$$

The Gamma function aggregates the productivity of the individual innovators of industry i, thus showing how the productivity of this industry evolves under the effect of the diffusion of innovation.[17]

Equation I.12 can be reduced to a first-order derivative (and hence the model to a first-order one) by adding a first order identity $D\Gamma_i = \gamma_i$, thus obtaining

$$D\gamma_i = f(x) \tag{I.12bis}$$

where $f(x)$ is the right-hand side of equation I.12.

Substituting $D\Gamma_i$ in γ, we come back to the second order derivative of equation I.12.

The endogenous time does not appear explicitly because it is embodied in the 'memory' of the Gamma function.

The Gamma distribution is the device we adopt to obtain the evolution of productivity of a given sector – something that occurs at the end of the process of the progressive adoption of radical technical change by individual innovators. As explained in Section 3.2, there is a first innovator who is then followed by others. This process of imitation/diffusion follows a sigmoid path that in turn shapes the curve of the sector's productivity.

LABOR PRODUCTIVITY YIELDED BY INCREMENTAL INNOVATIONS

$$D\ln PrI_i = -\beta_{19}u_i + \beta_{20}\ln(Es_i/Ed_i) + \beta_{21}\Gamma_i \ln(Es_i/Ed_i)$$
with the positivity constraint $D\ln PrI_i > 0$ \hfill (I.13)

This equation formalizes the two sources of incremental innovations, the endogenous ones, that is, uncertainty $(-\beta_{19}u_i)$ and the excess of entrepreneurship (the term $\beta_{20}\ln(Es_i/Ed_i)$), as well as the "imported" innovations, that is, the incremental productivity promoted by the diffusion of radical process innovation (the third term on the right) weighted by the excess of entrepreneurship that favors the diffusion of the incremental innovations in question.

LABOR PRODUCTIVITY IN EACH INDUSTRY

$$D\ln Pr_i = \Gamma_i + D\ln PrI_i \tag{I.14}$$

Theoretical frame

The productivity of the industry is the sum total of radical and incremental innovations.

EMPLOYMENT

(a) Demand for labor

$$L_i \equiv VA_i/Pr_i \tag{I.15}$$

(b) Supply of labor

$$Ls = (Ls_0\, e^{\beta_{22}t}) \tag{I.16}$$

The supply of labor is exogenously determined on the basis of an exponential trend with respect to an initial level Ls_0.

Uncertainty, entrepreneurship, time

RADICAL UNCERTAINTY

$$Du_i = \beta_{23}\Gamma + \beta_{24}DlnPrI_i + \beta_{25}DlnPrR_{(f)i} + \beta_{26}\Sigma D(ND_i) - a_1 \tag{II.1}$$

The third and fourth terms on the right-hand side are the result of the fact already referred to that radical uncertainty is increased when radical process and product innovations jeopardize the industry's equilibrium. By the same token, the diffusion of radical and incremental process innovations produces supplementary uncertainty, which is taken into account by the first and second terms on the right of the equation. The constant term a_1 means that, in the absence of innovations, uncertainty tends to decrease to the level caused by the exogenous factors.

ENTREPRENEURSHIP

(a) Availability of entrepreneurship

As already noted, we start by defining the theoretical ('normal') specification of the variable in order to show the adjustment process leading to the actual value.
Considering first the existing sectors we have:

$$lnEs'_i = \beta_{27}ln(u_i\, X_i) + \beta_{28}\, DlnPr_i + \beta_{29}\, u_i\, t \tag{II.2}$$

Equation II.2 shows that entrepreneurial skills vary in relation to three factors:

1. Learning by doing that is proportional to the quantity produced, to be weighted by the degree of uncertainty associated to the entrepreneurial activity. As already noted, strong uncertainty obliges entrepreneurs to

Explanation of economic change 71

mobilize all their potentialities, thus improving their skills. Conversely, where uncertainty vanishes, no entrepreneurial capabilities are required.
2   The learning by doing that is also influenced by innovation, expressed here by the percentage change in productivity.
3   The third term on the right-hand side is a trend element capturing the changes in entrepreneurship not resulting from learning.

Considering that the process of learning takes time, the actual supply of entrepreneurial skills appears after some delay with respect to the factors described in equation II.2. Thus, we have:

$$D\ln Es_i = \alpha_2 \ln(Es'_i/Es_i) \qquad (II.3)$$

where $1/\alpha_2$ refers to the length of the adjustment process.

As usual, for the existing capital goods sector, the equation is similar.

Entrepreneurship in the new sectors (both consumer and capital goods) evolves in a more complex way. For the new consumer goods we have:

$$\ln Es'_{(n)i} = \beta_{30} D\ln X_{(n)i} + \beta_{31} \ln(u\, X_{(n)i}) + \beta_{32} D\ln Pr_{n(i)} + \beta_{33}\, r_{(n)i} \qquad (II.4)$$

The learning component appears here in three ways. Looking at the right-hand side of equation II.4 we see that it depends on:

1   the percentage rate of change in output (the first term); considering that output follows a logistic path, this implies a substantial entry into the sector
2   the quantity produced, weighted by uncertainty (the second term)
3   the innovation, as before (the third term).

In addition, the supply of entrepreneurship is also positively influenced by the rate of profit of the sector, an element which can stimulate new initiatives.

As in the previous case, we have a process of adaptation:

$$D\ln Es_{(n)i} = \alpha_3 \ln(Es'_{(n)i}/Es_{(n)i})$$

For the new capital goods sector the equation is analogous.

(b) Demand of entrepreneurship

$$\ln Ed'_i = \beta_{34} \ln(u_i\, X_i) + \beta_{35} D\ln Pr_i \qquad (II.5)$$

Equation II.5 shows that the demand of entrepreneurship is:

1   positively related to the quantity of output, weighted by the degree of uncertainty, since without uncertainty no entrepreneurial skills are requested (see Section 3.2)

72 *Theoretical frame*

2   positively related to the degree of innovation, represented by the increase in productivity.

In this case, too, the actual demand for entrepreneurship follows its theoretical level with some time lag, which is nevertheless smaller than in the case of the creation of skills.

$$D\ln Ed_i = \alpha_4 \ln(Ed'_i/Ed_i) \tag{II.6}$$

(c) Unused entrepreneurial skills (excess of entrepreneurship)

Excess of entrepreneurship is the difference between the supply of and the demand for entrepreneurial skills.

$$\ln E_c = \ln(E_s/E_d) \tag{II.7}$$

The adjustment process for the excess of entrepreneurship is the result of the different speed of adjustment of supply and demand, as reflected by parameters α_2 and α_4 of II.3 and II.6.

TIME

$$Dt_i = \omega(-M_{(n)i}) \quad (n)i = 1,2,3,\ldots g \tag{II.8}$$
$$Dt_j = \omega(-M_{(n)j}) \quad (n)j = 1,2,3,\ldots h \tag{II.9}$$

These equations mark the advent of radically new products in final sector *i* as well as in capital sector *j* (when M is positive). For radical process innovations, as indicated previously, time is embodied into the memory of the Gamma function.

Wages, prices and profits

NOMINAL WAGE RATE

As before, we first define the normal wage rate as resulting from the wage bargaining which occurs periodically; then we consider the adjustment process of the actual wage rate with respect to its normal level.

$$\ln w' = \beta_{36} \ln Pr_{(av)} + \beta_{37} \ln(\text{index } PRE_i) + \beta_{38} \ln L - \beta_{38} \ln Ls \tag{III.1}$$

Formula III.1 shows that the normal wage rate depends on three factors:

1   the productivity of the economy as a whole
2   the rate of inflation.
3   the relative strength of the unions; as a *proxy* of this element, we take the difference between the demand for (L) and the supply of labor (Ls).[18]

The linkage between wages and the productivity of the system (instead of the sectoral productivity) means that workers in all industries (including the least progressive) benefit from technical progress. This criterion is suggested as a measure of social fairness. In addition, if competition works effectively, the proposed link between wages and productivity results in the stability of the general price level. In fact, the industries with a percentage increase in their productivity higher than the average of the system will decrease their prices and vice versa for the industries whose productivity increases less than the average.[19]

A uniform wage rate can be interpreted either as a normative criterion which is at odds with the prevailing trends in our societies, or, as it is done in Sraffa,[20] by assuming that any differences in the quality of labor "have been previously reduced to equivalent differences in quantity so that each unit of labour receives the same wage".

The fact that wage bargaining occurs only at discrete intervals of time (every few years) implies that current wages follow prices and productivity evolution with considerable delay. Thus, actual wage rate (w) does not coincide all the time with the normal one (w'), to which is nevertheless supposed to converge. Equation III.2 describes this adjustment process, where parameter α_5 quantifies the speed of the adjustment ($1/\alpha_5$ being the time lag)

$$D\ln w = \alpha_5 \ln(w'/w) \tag{III.2}$$

PRICES

Contrary to what is generally done here – where the formulae for capital goods as well as new consumer and capital goods correspond *mutatis mutandis* to the formulae concerning consumer goods (the only differences being the subscripts) – for prices it is preferable to write *in extenso* the formulae for the individual sectors.

Similarly to what has been done for the wage rate, the price equations express the adjustment process of market prices in relation to the normal prices defined later. We thus suppose that market prices can differ from the normal prices because of temporary disequilibria between supply and demand.

(a) Prices of consumer goods

$$\ln PRE_i' = \beta_{39} \ln(w/Pr_i) + \beta_{39} \ln(1 + MKP_i) + \beta_{40} \ln(CON_i/X_i) \tag{III.3}$$

and

$$D\ln PRE_i = \alpha_6 \ln(PRE_i'/PRE_i) \tag{III.4}$$

The first term on the right-hand side of formula III.3 means that prices are directly related to the unit wage costs (wage rate divided by productivity) that are taken here as a *proxy* for total unit costs. Parameter β_{39} refers to the relative importance of the set of enterprises of the sector adopting administered prices

74 Theoretical frame

(the oligopolistic industries), while β_{40} gives the weight of the other enterprises. For the first group of enterprises, prices are relatively sticky because they reflect the evolution of the markup; on the contrary, for the second group of enterprises, prices are more subject to pressures from competition and, consequently, reflect more closely temporary fluctuations of demand as formalized by the last term of equation III.3. Market power is reflected in the magnitude of the markup over costs. Thus, if the enterprises detain an important monopolistic power β_{39} will be high. The evolution over time of the market power is defined in equations III.8 to III.11.

(b) Prices of capital goods

$$\ln PRE'_j = \beta_{39} \ln(w/Pr_j) + \beta_{39} \ln(1 + MKP_j) + \beta_{41} \ln(KD_j/X_j)$$

and

$$D\ln PRE_j = \alpha_6 \ln(PRE'_j / PRE_j) \qquad (III.5)$$

(c) Prices of new consumer goods

$$\ln PRE'_{(n)i} = \beta_{42} \ln(w/Pr_{(n)i}) + \beta_{42} \ln(1 + MKP_{(n)i}) - \beta_{43} D\ln(ND)$$

and

$$D\ln PRE_{(n)i} = \omega(-M_{(n)i}) \, [\alpha_6 \ln(PRE'_{(n)i}/PRE_{(n)i})] \qquad (III.6)$$

The minus sign of Dln(ND) in the first equation is the result of the fact that where the demand for radically new commodities gains momentum, enterprises reduce the price in order to capture new segments of demand.

(d) Prices of new capital goods

$$\ln PRE'_{(n)j} = \beta_{42} \ln(w/Pr_{(n)j}) + \beta_{42} \ln(1 + MKP_{(n)j})$$

$\beta_{42} > \beta_{39}$, since the degree of monopoly and hence the markup are higher on new goods than the existing ones.

Thus we posit that, in the sectors of the new consumer and capital goods, prices are administered instead of being fully determined by competition.

As in the other cases, the adjustment process is

$$D\ln PRE_{(n)j} = \omega(-M_{(n)j}) \, [\alpha_6 \ln(PRE'_{(n)j}/PRE_{(n)j})] \qquad (III.7)$$

MARKUP

Bearing in mind that markup is relevant for concentrated (oligopolistic) industries, we have here two patterns of evolution, one referring to the existing consumer and capital goods and the other to the new commodities.

(a) Existing industries

For these industries, empirical evidence shows that markup fluctuates procyclically, in relation to changes in demand.[21] During the long stagnation phase, whereby the demand for existing products is sluggish, the markup is low. During the long expansion phase, the buoyant demand gives the possibility to charge an increasing markup which in turn declines when the cycle approaches maturity.[22]

In our model the stepwise evolution of markup is approached by taking the moving average of demand in equations III.8 and III.10 and, subsequently, by introducing a time lag between the actual and the theoretical evolution of the markup (equations III.9 and III.11).

$$MKP'_i = \beta_{44} DlnCT_i + \lambda_i \tag{III.8}$$
$$DMKP_i = \alpha_7(MKP'_i - MKP_i) \tag{III.9}$$
$$MKP'_j = \beta_{44} DlnKDT_j + \lambda_j \tag{III.10}$$
$$DMKP_j = \alpha_7(MKP'_j - MKP_j)] \tag{III.11}$$

(b) New commodities

The evolution of markup for (radically) new consumer goods is explained on the basis of the pattern of demand and on the triggering factor for innovation. On the one hand, demand follows a logistic path (equation IV.4). On the other hand, the unequal income distribution characterizing the long stagnation offers the possibility to exploit a niche in the market and to charge high prices (i.e. high markup). As diffusion proceeds, prices are gradually reduced to stimulate demand, thereby entailing a corresponding decline in the markup that reaches its minimum at the end of the long wave. In equation III.12, this constant decline of the markup results from the percentage rate of change of demand.

$$KP'_{(n)i} = \beta_{45} Dln(ND_{(n)i}) + \lambda_{(n)i} \tag{III.12}$$

Equation III.13 refers to the adaptation process between theoretical and actual markups.

$$DMKP_{(n)i} = (\omega)(-M_{(n)i})\{\alpha_7(MKP'_{(n)i} - MKP_{(n)i})\} \tag{III.13}$$

For the new capital goods, positing the same pattern of demand (logistically shaped), we obtain a similar evolution of the markup with a corresponding adaptation process.

$$MKP'_{(n)j} = \beta_{46} Dln(ND_{(n)j}) + \lambda_{(n)j} \tag{III.14}$$
$$DMKP_{(n)j} = (\omega)(-M_{(n)j})\{\alpha_7(MKP'_{(n)j} - MKP_{(n)j})\} \tag{III.15}$$

PROFIT RATE

$$r_i = \frac{VA_{(nom)i} - L_i w}{PRE\ TK\ K^{(d)} e_i} - i_r \tag{III.16}$$

76 *Theoretical frame*

In our simulations with only five sectors, vector PRE and the matrices become scalars.

PROFIT RATES IN RECENT YEARS

$$DR_i = \alpha_8(r_i - R_i) \tag{III.17}$$

This equation, and equations IV.3 and V.4, are derived from the expression for distributed lags, attributing a weight of 0.63 to r_i of the last $1/\alpha_8$ years.

Consumption and demand

CONSUMPTION

$$\ln CON'_i = \beta_{47}\ln(w\,L) - \beta_{48}\ln PRE_i - \beta_{49}\ln(CT_i/XT_i) + \lambda_i \tag{IV.1}$$

and

$$D\ln CON_i = \alpha_9 \ln(CON'_i / CON_i) \tag{IV.2}$$

In equation IV.1, the first two terms on the right-hand side are self-explanatory. The third term refers to the saturation of demand occurring when for a number of years the share of consumption with respect to output rises beyond its 'physiological' level. Equation IV.2 expresses the adjustment of normal consumption CON'_i with respect to the current consumption.

CONSUMPTION IN RECENT YEARS

$$D\ln CT_i = \alpha_{10}\ln(CON_i / CT_i) \tag{IV.3}$$

CON of the last $1/\alpha_{10}$ years has a weight of 0.63.

DEMAND FOR NEW GOODS

This variable evolves according to the derivative of a logistic which, obviously, starts at the moment of the first innovation.

$$D(ND_{(n)i}) = (\omega)(-M_{(n)i})\,\frac{ND_{as}\,\beta_{50}\,\beta_{51}\,e^{-\beta_{51}(t_i - t_c)}}{\left(1+\beta_{50}\,e^{-\beta_{51}(t_i - t_c)}\right)^2} \tag{IV.4}$$

The first term on the right-hand side marks the advent of a new commodity, something that happens when M is positive and consequently the switch is 1. When the switch is zero (i.e. M negative), there is no demand for the new goods. The second term is the derivative of a logistic, where ND_{as} is the asymptote of ND

Explanation of economic change 77

(the saturation level) and t_c is the midpoint of the period considered. In the present simulation $t_c = 14$ and $ND_{as} = 800$ for new consumer goods.

The demand for new capital goods corresponds to formula (IV.4) *mutatis mutandis*, that is, attributing to ND the values 50 and 40 for the two sectors of new capital goods.

Capital and investment

STOCK OF FIXED CAPITAL

For the existing sectors (*i* and *j*) changes in the capital stock are determined by the desired output/capital ratio corrected by the importance of radical uncertainty. Considering sector *i*, we have:

$$D \ln K_i = [\beta_{52}(X_i/K_i) - a_2] - \beta_{53} u_i \qquad (V.1)$$

Constant a_2 results from the adjustment (in continuous time) of capital stock.

The formula for sector *j* is similar.

However, for the new sectors (consumer goods *n(i)* and capital goods *n(j)*) the capital stock is driven by the change in output of the sector concerned; radical uncertainty appears on the scene in this case too. For the new consumer goods sector we have:

$$D \ln K_{n(i)} = \omega(-M_{n(i)}) [D \ln X_{n(i)}] - \beta_{54} D u_{n(i)} \qquad (V.2)$$

For the new capital goods sectors the equations are similar.

GROSS INVESTMENT

$$I_i = (D \ln K_i) K_i + \mu_1 K_i + \eta_i \Sigma X_{(n)j} \qquad (V.3)$$

Gross investment is the sum total of three components:

1 the enlargement of existing productive capacity, or net investment (the first term on the right-hand side)
2 the replacement of worn-up capacity (the second term)
3 the obsolescence of existing plants and equipment resulting from the adoption of radical and incremental innovations (the third term).

In our simulation with only five sectors, obsolescence is expressed as a percentage (η) of the amount of new capital goods, and total gross investment (I) is the sum of investment in the five sectors, that is, $I = \sum_{i=1}^{5}(D \ln K)K_i + \mu_1 \sum_{i=1}^{5} K_i + \eta_i \Sigma X_{(n)j}$.

DEMAND FOR EXISTING CAPITAL GOODS

$$KD = TI \ I \qquad (V.4)$$

78 *Theoretical frame*

Let us recall that the dimensions of matrix TI and vector I are respectively:

$$[j \times (i+j+(n)i+(n)j)] \text{ and } [(i+j+(n)i+(n)j \times 1]$$

The transition matrix TI from sector of utilization to sectors of origin is held constant over time, something that represents an important drawback for a model centered on innovation. This inconvenience could be almost eliminated by introducing in the elements of TI some changes proportional to the obsolescence of capital as expressed by equation V.3. However, we deemed that this would have complicated the model unnecessarily and in the absence of anything better we preferred to stick to the simplification in question.

In any case, in our numerical simulations this matrix does not appear since only one sector of existing capital goods is considered. Therefore we have the following scalars:

$$KD = I - \Sigma ND_j \qquad (j = 1, 2)$$

The same considerations hold for matrix TK.

DEMAND FOR EXISTING CAPITAL GOODS IN RECENT YEARS

$$D \ln KDT_j = \alpha_{11} \ln(KD_j/KDT_j) \qquad (V.5)$$

KD_j is weighted by 0.63 for the last $1/\alpha_{11}$ years.

3.4 Numerical simulations

3.4.1 General features

The best way to check the plausibility of our model would be an econometric test on the basis of long-term statistical series for a sufficient number of countries. Unfortunately, in our case, such an inquiry is not possible owing to a lack of data. Some data – which in theory could exist – are not available in practice at the necessary level of detail (sectoral data at 4 or 5 statistical digits). Some other data, concerning for instance the productivity level for individual innovators, could perhaps be obtained from industrial surveys; however, this could create a problem of coherence with respect to the source of data for the other variables of the model.

For this reason, we were obliged to adopt a weaker notion of plausibility, in that we test the consistency of results through numerical simulations. Thus, relying on realistic hypotheses on the structure of the economy and on 'reasonable' values for the parameters, it is possible to check whether the dynamic path of the variables resulting from our system of equations conforms to or contradicts our theory.

The numerical simulations were performed using the software WYSEA: System estimation analysis, developed by Clifford R. Wymer.[23] We considered a period of 50 years, starting from the depression phase of the long wave.

Explanation of economic change 79

To have something manageable, we relied on a simplified model of just five sectors – one for the existing consumer goods ($i = 1$), another for the existing capital goods ($j = 1$) and three additional sectors for new commodities: one for consumer goods ($n(i) = 1$) and two sectors for capital goods ($n(j) = 2$). For radical product innovations in consumer goods, the additional sector covers both the case of innovations occurring in existing industries and the case in which they give birth to a new industry. Radical process innovations materialize first of all in existing consumer and capital goods sectors but in order to see the combined effects of process and product innovations, we assumed that in the additional sector of consumer goods, radical process innovation also occurs.

The initial values of the variables are arbitrary although, in order to have plausible levels, we referred to the Italian national accounts whenever possible.[24]

We performed three simulations (A, B and C) that differ according to:

- the importance of the leap in the productivity level of the individual firm adopting radical process innovation
- the intensity of dynamic competition, that is, the relative importance of innovations and the speed of their diffusion within the sector
- the period in which the innovation first materializes in the various sectors.

This last aspect is quantified by attributing alternative values to some β parameters, to parameter Q referring to the productivity leap and to the threshold levels for the appearance of radical product and process innovations (parameters $k_{(M)}$ and $k_{(PrR)}$). Simulation B refers to a high level of dynamic competition, simulation C to a low level of such competition while simulation A represents an intermediate case.

Tables A.1 and A.2 in the appendix provide the initial values of the endogenous and exogenous variables, the values of the parameters common to the three simulations; Table A.3 shows the elements that differ in the three simulations; and Table A.4 shows the periods of appearance of radical innovations.

The present model can be extended to include successive long waves by simply taking the outcome of the previous simulation as initial values; what were previously new sectors are now incorporated into the existing ones and the model can be specified as in the first run. However, the character, length and content of each long wave are influenced by the historical phase of development in course, as resulting from the process of dynamic competition. This interaction between cycles and phases of development will be emphasized at the beginning of Part II of this book.

3.4.2 *Main results*

Figures 3.1 through 3.14 provide a selection of the results of our simulations. We have limited the number of figures to a bare minimum in order to save space, although we shall be pleased to communicate the entire set on request. For the sake of brevity, we usually focus on the consumer goods sector; this means that where we add no comments on the peculiarities of the other sectors, their evolution is quite similar to the consumer goods sector.

80 Theoretical frame

The main aggregates such as total output, value added, consumption, employment and investment display the typical long-wave (S-shaped) pattern. Figures 3.1, 3.2 and 3.4 provide examples. Figure 3.2, on the output of new capital goods, has been chosen to illustrate our hypotheses regarding this sector. As a general feature, simulation B – based on the assumption of stronger dynamic competition – shows higher values than the other two simulations.

Referring to consumer goods, Figure 3.3 depicts the productivity function for the individual innovator resulting from radical process innovations, while Figure 3.5 gives the percentage rate of productivity change of the whole sector. Figure 3.5 conforms to the results of historical analysis summarized in Table 3.1, as the pace of innovation is stronger at the beginning of the period, when the system is in the phase of long stagnation.

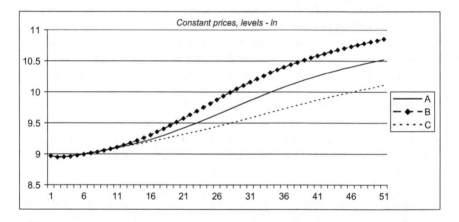

Figure 3.1 Production of consumer goods

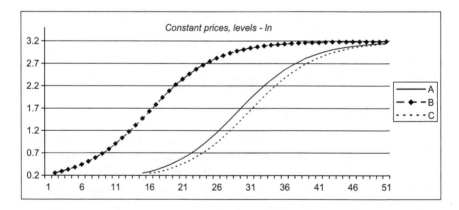

Figure 3.2 Production of new capital goods

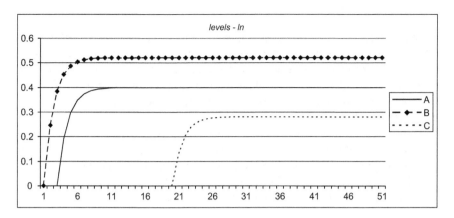

Figure 3.3 Productivity of radical process innovation for the individual innovator: consumer goods

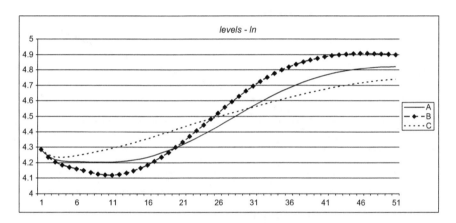

Figure 3.4 Employment (demand for labor): consumer goods

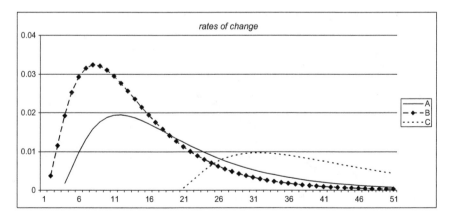

Figure 3.5 Diffusion of radical process innovations: consumer goods

82 *Theoretical frame*

The productivity level of the consumer goods industry – summing up the effects of radical and incremental innovations – appears in Figure 3.6. For the new consumer goods, productivity grows faster because we posit that in this case the interaction between radical and incremental innovations exerts a strong stimulus for the adoption of incremental technical change (Figure 3.7 shows the level of productivity determined by this kind of technical change).

In the two sectors of new capital goods (not reported) – where there are no radical process innovations (see Section 3.4.1) – the pace of productivity is driven by incremental innovations. However, we assume here that incremental innovations entail a productivity growth higher than in the other sectors because of the wider scope for improvements inherent to new commodities.

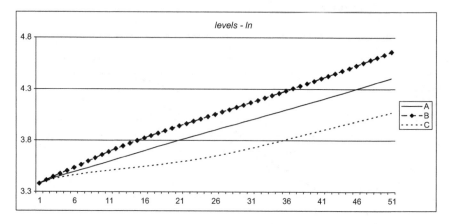

Figure 3.6 Productivity of labor: consumer goods

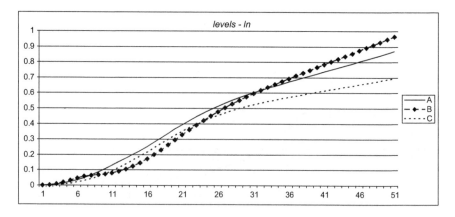

Figure 3.7 Labor productivity from incremental innovations: new consumer goods

Radical uncertainty (Figure 3.8) behaves as expected under the theory: it increases substantially during long stagnation – when the 'creative destruction' of the innovation activity is stronger and destabilizes the system – and slows down when the pace of radical technical change normalizes. In the sector of new consumer goods (not reported), the increase in uncertainty during the first two decades is even more prominent as a result of the combined effect of process and product innovations.

Unused entrepreneurial skills (excess of entrepreneurship) in the existing sectors (Figure 3.9) mirror the process of diffusion of radical technical change (see Figure 3.5). When the pace of innovation is strong, entrepreneurs must make full use of their capabilities to cope with the turbulent environment. During the second

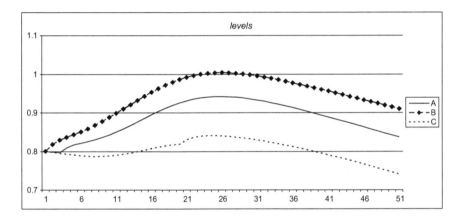

Figure 3.8 Radical uncertainty: consumer goods

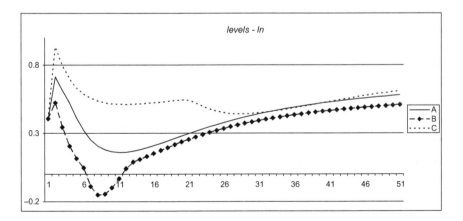

Figure 3.9 Excess of entrepreneurship: consumer goods

84 *Theoretical frame*

half of the long wave, when the system is on a steady state growth path, the general environment is less demanding and this can justify an increase in unused entrepreneurial skills.

The characteristics of the new sectors (both consumer and capital goods) entail completely different dynamics (Figure 3.10). In fact, when a new sector appears, unused entrepreneurial skills are very low, but as the new product progresses and new competitors enter the market, this increases the supply of entrepreneurship and correspondingly increases excess entrepreneurship. When the sector reaches maturity, the available skills are fully mobilized while the excess tends to vanish.

Consumer goods prices (Figure 3.11) are strongly influenced by the evolution of productivity. In simulations A and B, during the depression phase of the

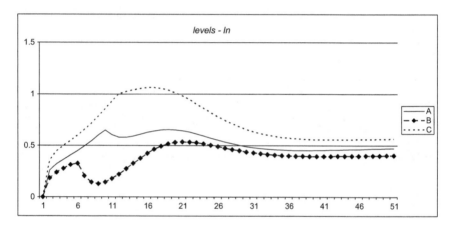

Figure 3.10 Excess of entrepreneurship: new consumer goods

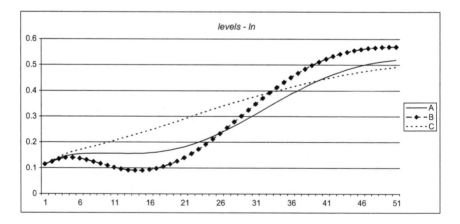

Figure 3.11 Price of consumer goods

wave – when the long-run trajectory of radical innovations and productivity is incipient – they remain stationary or decline until about the beginning of the long expansion, following the dynamics of productivity; the following ascending trend is produced by the buoyant demand which characterizes the long expansion phase.

The different level and dynamics of prices in simulation C constitute the obvious effect of less dynamic productivity.

The price evolution of the capital goods sector (not reported) is quite similar.

The new consumer goods sector displays quite different price dynamics (Figure 3.12). As noted previously, the main reason for the first successful launching on the market of radically new products is the inequality in income distribution that marks the depression phase of the wave and the possibility for the innovating firms to exploit a niche in the market. This justifies the relative high level of prices at the beginning of the period and, also, explains why, as far as the long-wave displays of its potentialities, such prices decline. In fact, when the income distribution becomes less unequal, firms can attract new layers of demand by reducing their prices. This strategy is also reinforced by the fact that the period of high prices gives enterprises the possibility to recover part of the money invested in the new product during the launching period. The ascending trend in the second half of the long wave is caused by cost increases because, during that period, wages tend to increase more than productivity.

The prices of new capital goods (omitted here) show a shorter decline at the beginning of the wave and a longer growing trend rooted in cost increases.

With regard to the profit rate, Figure 3.13 shows, for the consumer goods sector, a strong increase until the end of the long stagnation, then stability followed by decline. The markup displays a similar path (Figure 3.14).

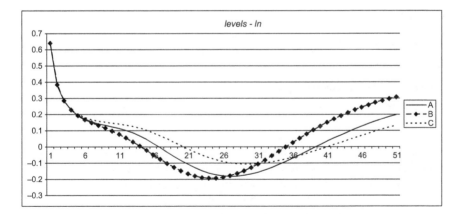

Figure 3.12 Price of new consumer goods

Note: Considering that prices are expressed in natural logarithms, the negative values mean that the natural levels are positive and less than 1.

86 *Theoretical frame*

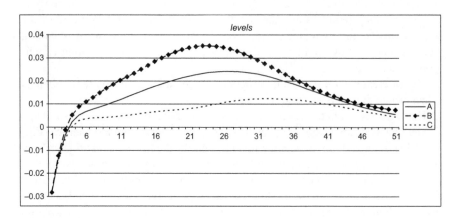

Figure 3.13 Rate of profit: consumer goods

Note: See the above footnote concerning the negative logarithms. Here profit rates of the first three periods, expressed in level, are true negative numbers.

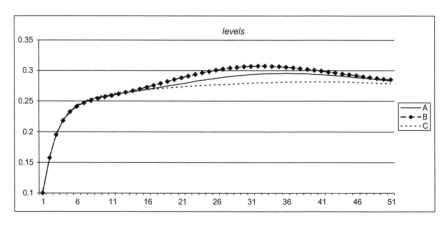

Figure 3.14 Markup: consumer goods

Conversely, in the new sectors (both consumer and capital goods) the markup (not represented here) follows a decreasing trend that is justified by the price policy for these commodities: starting from a high level, the markup progressively reaches its minimum level towards the end of the wave.

We notice an almost identical evolution for the rate of profit of the new consumer goods, while in the case of the new capital goods, profitability shows a growing trend since the beginning of the recovery phase of the wave.

3.5 A micro version of the model

Chapter 4 provides a micro (firm-level) version of the model here discussed, but it refers only to one sector and to process innovations. The model considers n firms, m of which display both innovation and adaptation, while $n-m$ only practice adaptation. Moreover $h \leq m$ firms display both radical and incremental innovations.

The model with only adaptive entrepreneurship (i.e. without innovation) converges toward a stationary equilibrium. In fact, in the absence of innovation, the search for profits implies the convergence to uniform technique as well as the annulment of (endogenous) radical uncertainty and, hence, of the need for entrepreneurship. In sum, in this merely adaptive case, the entrepreneurial convergence, through imitation, toward the best available technology would imply a 'suicide' of entrepreneurship, a steady state solution of the model and its stability. More precisely, the simulation of the model for a long period of time after the above convergence shows a limit cycle about the steady state solution.

A micro model with innovation, imitation and adaptation is then considered, and hence simulated. In this model, the stationary state is impossible in that it fades away before the system converges. In fact (and as we know), the reduction in radical uncertainty and the progressive increase in the excess of entrepreneurial skills will stimulate both radical and incremental innovation. But the rise in innovation will cause, in turn, a parallel rise in radical uncertainty and a reduction in the excess of entrepreneurship, that is, the rise in the need of entrepreneurship, in opposition to the suicide of this (both directly and through the increase of uncertainty) that will provoke the reduction in innovation and a recovery of adaptation.

Innovation of products, and hence a variety of products (i.e. more than one sector), can be included in the micro model. In this regard, our one good micro model, which only considers process innovation, may obtain some inspiration from Pyka and Saviotti's micro model, which only considers product innovation.[25]

3.6 Conclusion

In this research we pursue an ambitious objective that, if successful, should advance the frontier of our knowledge regarding the long-term dynamics of the economy. In fact, in Section 3.2, we try to provide a fully endogenous explanation of the factors that trigger the technological revolutions underlying a new long upswing. More particularly, we emphasize the role of the profit rate in explaining the appearance of radical process and product innovations and also the impact of inequality and the stagnation of demand on the adoption of radical product innovations.

The framework, which implies an analysis at macro and meso levels, marries Schumpeter with the neo-Austrian market process; moreover, it is enriched by some microeconomic components such as entrepreneurship and radical uncertainty and is open to a full micro specification. The introduction of radical uncertainty also implies some reference to Keynes. But we make a step forward with respect to the current Keynesian (and Hayekian) approach, which conceives radical uncertainty as something that by its very nature escapes measurement. Indeed, we show that such a measure is possible at sectoral level and establishes a link between radical uncertainty and the behavior of innovation. The incipient diffusion of radical process and product innovations in existing industries destabilizes the incumbents' positions and creates fundamental (or radical) uncertainty, which we identify with the volatility of expectations. The depression phase is thus characterized by the coexistence of diffuse negative expectations and hence low (volatility of these) but increasing radical uncertainty. During the recovery phase, radical uncertainty persists because the diffusion of product innovations in existing industries gains momentum while the same occurs for product innovations that create new needs. The dominant traits of long expansion are favorable expectations and relatively low radical uncertainty because the process of diffusion of radical process and product innovations is very advanced and the innovative activity concerns mainly incremental innovations – the kind of innovations that are less destabilizing for the system.

Continuing our effort to quantify what is usually deemed to be unquantifiable, we put into evidence how the innovation process is also shaped by unused entrepreneurial skills (the 'excess of entrepreneurship') – a notion that compares the available skills with the skills required to run the enterprise at a specific moment in time. If the current level of activity and the low uncertainty do not imply full utilization of the available skills, there is an excess of entrepreneurial skills that could be mobilized for innovations.

Our theoretical analysis is enhanced by further analytical details in the multi-sectoral dynamic model presented in Section 3.3. One aim of this model is to test the overall consistency of our theoretical construction. For this purpose, we have numerically simulated a reduced version of the model with only five big sectors: one for the existing consumer goods, another for the existing capital goods and three additional sectors for new commodities: one for consumer goods and two sectors for capital goods. Radical process innovations materialize first of all in the existing consumer and capital goods sectors, but in order to see the combined effects of process and product innovations, we assumed that in the additional sector of new consumer goods radical process innovation also occurs. We performed three simulations that differ essentially according to the characteristics and the importance of radical technical change. The selection of results presented at the end of the chapter confirms the robustness of our approach.

Appendix

Table A.1 Initial values of the endogenous and of exogenous variables by sectors (natural logarithms, except for SW, Γ, γ, M, MKP, ND, u, R, r, i_r)

Endogenous variables	Sectors				
	i	j	(n)i	(n)j1	(n)j2
X	8.9628	6.47383	0.42	0.3	0.25
PrR	0.0	0.0	0.0		
SW	0.0	0.0	0.0		
K	8.7008	6.5028	0.5	0.4	0.33
PrI	0.0	0.0	0.0	0.0	0.0
γ	0.0	0.0	0.0		
Γ	0.0	0.0	0.0		
ND			1.0	1.0	1.0
M			0.0	0.0	0.0
Pr	3.38	3.38	3.6	3.6	3.68
W*	3.435				
PRE	0.0115	0.065	0.64	0.51	0.51
u	0.8	0.8	1.0	1.0	1.0
CON*	8.9748				
t			0.0	00	0.0
CT	8.94				
XT	8.95				
XT2		6.36			
KDT		6.35			
R	−0.03	−0.018	0.09	0.028	0.028
Es	5.858	3.367	0.0	0.0	0.0
Ed	5.452	3.063	0.0	0.0	0.0
MKP	0.1	0.1	0.34	0.34	0.34
Exogenous variables					
L_{s0}	4.367				
i_r	0.05				

* Whole economy

Table A.2 Parameters

$\alpha_1 = 0.166$	$\alpha_2 = 0.52$	$\alpha_3 = 0.7$	$\alpha_4 = 2.8$
$\alpha_5 = 0.57$	$\alpha_6 = 0.53$	$\alpha_7 = 0.43$	$\alpha_8 = 0.25$
$\alpha_9 = 0.65$	$\alpha_{10} = 0.166$	$\alpha_{11} = 0.166$	
$\beta_1 = 1.5$	$\beta_2 = 0.02$	$\beta_3 = 0.00017$	$\beta_4 = 0.0044$
$\beta_5 = 0.00828$	$\beta_6 = 0.078$	$\beta_7 = 0.095$	$\beta_8 = 0.35$
$\beta_9 = 2.3$	$\beta_{10} = 0.87$	$\beta_{11} = 0.0025$	$\beta_{12} = 0.008$
$\beta_{13} = 1.17$	$\beta_{14} = 0.0035$	$\beta_{15} = 0.161$	$\beta_{16} = 0.7$[a]
			$\beta_{16} = 4.0$[b]
$\beta_{17} = 0.1$	$\beta_{18} = 0.2$	$\beta_{19} = 0.093$	$\beta_{20} = 0.049$
$\beta_{21} = 0.5$	$\beta_{22} = 0.001$	$\beta_{23} = 0.34$	$\beta_{24} = 0.17$[c]
$\beta_{25} = 0.075$	$\beta_{26} = 0.000293$[d]	$\beta_{27} = 0.4$	$\beta_{28} = 30.5$
$\beta_{29} = 0.01$	$\beta_{30} = 6.0$	$\beta_{31} = 0.48$	$\beta_{32} = 20.5$
$\beta_{33} = 2.5$	$\beta_{34} = 0.33$	$\beta_{35} = 55.7$	$\beta_{36} = 0.99$
$\beta_{37} = 0.58$	$\beta_{38} = 0.43$	$\beta_{39} = 0.79$	$\beta_{40} = 0.27$
$\beta_{41} = 0.1$	$\beta_{42} = 1.2$	$\beta_{43} = 0.1$	$\beta_{44} = 0.9$
$\beta_{45} = 0.17$	$\beta_{46} = 0.18$	$\beta_{47} = 0.983$	$\beta_{48} = 1.02$
$\beta_{49} = 0.56$	$\beta_{50} = 1.0$	$\beta_{51} = 0.2$	$\beta_{52} = 0.03$[e]
$\beta_{53} = 0.01$	$\beta_{54} = 2.6$		
$a_1 = 0.0091$	$a_2 = 0.026$		
$\mu_1 = 0.08$	$\eta_1 = 0.19$	$v_1 = -1.298$	$v_2 = -1.298$

Scaling parameters λ: 1.01 in the consumption equation; 0.11 in all markup equations

a Existing consumer and capital goods
b New goods
c 0.41 for new goods
d 0.0022 for new goods
e 0.0215 for capital goods

Table A.3 Hypotheses underlying the simulations

Parameters and constants

	Intermediate case	High dynamic competition	Low dynamic competition
	Simulation A	Simulation B	Simulation C
β_{19}	0.0093	0.0065	0.0121
β_{20}	0.049	0.0637	0.0343
β_{21}	0.5	0.65	0.35
β_{17}	0.1	0.13	0.07
β_{18}	0.2	0.26	0.14
Q_1	0.40	0.52	0.28
Q_2	0.50	0.65	0.35
$k_{(PrR)1}$	0.32	0.192	0.42
$k_{(PrR)2}$	0.21	0.13	0.31

Parameters and constants

	Intermediate case	High dynamic competition	Low dynamic competition
	Simulation A	Simulation B	Simulation C
$k_{(PrR)3}$	0.23	0.2	0.38
$k_{(M)1}$	0.11	0.13	0.11
$k_{(M)2}$	0.175	0.127	0.218
$k_{(M)3}$	0.195	0.13	0.285

Table A.4 First appearance of radical process and product innovations

Sector	Simulation	Period
Process innovations		
Consumer goods *(i)*	A	4
	B	2
	C	21
Capital goods *(j)*	A	4
	B	2
	C	4
New consumer goods *(n)i*	A	10
	B	6
	C	12
Product innovations		
New consumer goods *(n)i*	A	2
	B	2
	C	2
New capital goods I *(n)j$_1$*	A	4
	B	2
	C	4
New capital goods II *(n)j$_2$*	A	16
	B	3
	C	17

Notes

1 Think, for instance, of some important inventions of ancient China and of the Alexandrian academicians (an institution financed by Ptolemaic absolute state of Egypt), such as the piston, the connecting rod and the aeolipile. These important mechanical and steam power inventions, which two millennia later would spur industrial revolutions, remained confined to the condition of toys. For their part, the modern systems of 'real socialism' excelled only in innovations pushed by the military system. For a detailed treatment of this subject, see A. Fusari, *Human Adventure: An Inquiry on the Ways of People and Civilizations* (SEAM, Roma, 2000).
2 It is significant that in Italy the best statistical data on entrepreneurship are not provided by ISTAT but by CERVED. Elsewhere the situation is not better.
3 See Keynes (1937), p. 214.
4 See Fusari, p. 144, in H. Ekstedt and A. Fusari (2010).
5 Israel Kirzner, who is not a subversive but certainly is a serious student, has insisted on the fact that ownership and entrepreneurship are completely separate functions.
6 In this regard and, in particular, on the definition of the notion of historical phase, see A. Fusari, *Methodological Misconceptions in the Social Sciences*, Chapter 4, "Social Development and Historical Processes".
7 An opposition strongly influenced by ideological reasons that, however, disappear if we consider the notion of the entrepreneur only with reference to decision making and not also to the appropriation of profit (i.e. independently of the public or private character of entrepreneurship).
8 This subsection offers a synthesis of some development by A. Reati in the article by Fusari and Reati (2013).
9 By A. Reati. See Fusari and Reati (2013) p. 78.
10 By A. Reati. See Fusari and Reati (2013) p. 79.
11 In our numerical simulations reported later, changes in the parameters (particularly those concerning the degree of dynamic competition) produce slight changes in this periodization.
12 For a broad exposition of this matter, see Ekstedt and Fusari (2010), Chapter 8.
13 This is because the Gamma distribution has a 'memory', in such a way that the new radical innovations are grafted on the events of the past.
14 In equations I.1 and I.2, we take the level of demand instead of its rate of change just to reduce the number of derivatives entering the model that complicates the simulations. The resulting inconvenience is minor because the importance of such factors within the equations is low. In equations I.3 and I.4, the rate of change in demand is expressed by the rate of change of the logistics formalizing the diffusion of these products, a derivative that in any case exists in the model.
15 Considering that during the depression phase R is supposed to be negative, $-\beta_6 R_i$ becomes positive. We shall see later that we define the rate of profit in a particular way, by deducting the rate of interest from the profits. Thus, when actual profits are below the threshold level represented by the rate of interest, R becomes negative.
16 The sign minus could give the wrong impression of an inverse relation between inequality and innovation instead of a direct one. This is because we take the logarithm of the wage share, that is, $\ln(w L) - \ln(VA_{nom})$, which is negative, instead of its inverse.
17 What we do here on the basis of the Gamma function is not to describe the microeconomic process of diffusion but just to consider its final effect on the productivity of the sector.
18 One could observe that, in order to obtain percentage rates of change, formula III.1 should be $D\ln w'$ and the symbol of derivative should also be inserted in the right-hand side of III.1. In fact, the percentage rate of change in wages results from the structure of the adjustment of equation III.2.
19 For a detailed analysis of this last point, see Pasinetti (1981).
20 See Sraffa (1960) p. 10.

21 See Goldstein (1986).
22 The evidence presented by Goldstein (1986) refers to the business cycle, although his analysis can be extended to the long wave. See, however, Oliveira Martins and Scarpetta (2002) for contrasting findings.
23 See Wymer (2006).
24 See ISTAT (2007).
25 See Saviotti and Pyka (2004).

References

Aghion, P. & Howitt, P. (1992), A model of growth through creative destruction. *NBER Working Paper*, no. 3223, January, pp. 1–48.
Andersen, E. S. (2001), Satiation in an evolutionary model of structural economic dynamics, *Journal of Evolutionary Economics*, vol. 11, no. 1, pp. 143–164.
Anderson, P. & Tushman, M. L. (1990), Technological discontinuities and dominant designs: A cyclical model of technological change, *Administrative Science Quarterly*, vol. 35, pp. 604–633.
Atkinson, A. B. & Bourguignon, F. (Eds.). (2000), *Handbook of income distribution*, North-Holland, Amsterdam.
Clark, J., Freeman, C. & Soete, L. (1981), Long-waves and technological development in the 20th century, *Konjunktur, Krise, Gesellschaft*, vol. 25, no. 2, pp. 132–169.
Ekstedt, H. & Fusari, A. (2010), *Economic theory and social change: Problems and revisions*, Routledge, London.
Erixon, L. (2007), Even the bad times are good: A behavioural theory of transformation pressure, *Cambridge Journal of Economics*, vol. 31, no. 3, May, pp. 327–348.
European Commission. (2006), *The Joint Harmonised EU Programme of Business and Consumer Surveys*, European Economy, Directorate-General for Economic and Financial Affairs, Special Report, no. 5.
Falkinger, J. & Zweimüller, J. (1997), The impact of income inequality on product diversity and economic growth, *Metroeconomica*, vol. 48, no. 3, pp. 211–237.
Fatás-Villafranca, F., Jarne, G. & Sánchez-Chóliz, J. (2012), Innovation, cycles and growth, *Journal of Evolutionary Economics*, vol. 22, no. 2, April, pp. 207–233.
Foellmi, R. & Zweimüller, J. (2006), Income distribution and demand-induced innovations, *The Review of Economic Studies*, vol. 73, pp. 941–960.
Freeman, C. (Ed.). (1996), *Long wave theory*, E. Elgar, Cheltenham.
Freeman, C. & Louçã, F. (2001), *As time goes by: From the industrial revolutions to the information revolution*, Oxford University Press, Oxford.
Fusari, A. (2005), A model of the innovation-adaptation mechanism driving economic dynamics: A micro presentation, *Journal of Evolutionary Economics*, vol. 15, no. 3, August, pp. 297–333.
Fusari, A. (2007), *Uncertainty, entrepreneurship, innovation: Some almost neglected features of the economic process*, Paper Presented at the 2007 EAEPE Conference, Porto, November 1–3.
Fusari, A. (2013), Radical uncertainty, dynamic competition and a model of business cycle: The implications of a measure and an explanation of what is supposed non-measurable and non-explainable, *International Journal of Business and Management*, vol. 8, no. 12, June, pp. 8–28.
Fusari, A. & Reati, A. (2013), Endogenizing technical change: Uncertainty, profits, entrepreneurship. A long term view of sectoral dynamics, *Structural Change and Economic Dynamics*, vol. 24, pp. 76–100.

Gandolfo, G. (1980), *Economic dynamics: Methods and models*, North-Holland, Amsterdam.
Gandolfo, G., Martinengo, G. & Padoan, P. C. (1981), *Qualitative analysis and econometric estimation of continuous time dynamic models*, North-Holland, Amsterdam.
Goldstein, J. (1986), Markup variability and flexibility: Theory and empirical evidence, *Journal of Business*, vol. 59, no. 4, pp. 599–621.
Gort, M. & Klepper, S. (1982), Time paths in the diffusion of product innovations, *Economic Journal*, vol. 92, no. 367, pp. 630–653.
Grossman, G. M. & Helpman, E. (1991), Quality ladders in the theory of growth. *Review of Economic Studies*, vol. 58, pp. 43–61.
Hanusch, H. & Pyka, A. (Eds.). (2007), *Elgar companion to neo-schumpeterian economics*, E. Elgar, Cheltenham.
Hatipoglu, O. (2008), *An empirical analysis of the relationship between inequality and innovation in a schumpeterian framework*, MPRA Paper No. 7856, March 20.
Hayek, F. A. (1945), The knowledge in society, *American Economic Review*, no. 4, September, pp. 519–530.
Howitt, P. (1997), Expectations and uncertainty in contemporary Keynesian models, in G. C. Harcourt & P. A. Riach (eds), *A 'second edition' of the general theory*, Routledge, London, vol. 1, pp. 238–260.
ISTAT (Italian Statistical Office). (2007), *Contabilità nazionale: Conti economici nazionali. Anni 1970–2005*, Istat, Rome.
Jarne, G., Sánchez-Chóliz, J. & Fatás-Villafranca, F. (2005), "S-shaped" economic dynamics: The logistic and Gompertz curves generalized, *The Electronic Journal of Evolutionary Modeling and Economic Dynamics*, no. 1048. www.e-jemed.org/1048/index.php.
Keynes, J. M. (1937), The general theory of employment, *The Quarterly Journal of Economics*, vol. 51, no. 2, February, pp. 209–223.
Keynes, J. M. (2007 [1936]), *The general theory of employment, interest and money*, Palgrave MacMillan, London.
Kirzner, I. M. (1973), *Competition and entrepreneurship*, The University of Chicago Press, Chicago and London.
Kirzner, I. M. (1985), *Discovery and the capitalist process*, The University of Chicago Press, Chicago, IL and London.
Kleinknecht, A. (1990), Are there Schumpeterian waves of innovations? *Cambridge Journal of Economics*, vol. 14, no. 1, pp. 81–92.
Li, M., Xiao, F. & Zhu, A. (2007), Long waves, institutional changes, and historical trends: A study of the long-term movement of the profit rate in the capitalist world-economy, *Journal of World-Systems Research*, vol. XIII, no. 1, pp. 33–54.
Louçã, F. & Reijnders, J. (Eds.). (1999), *The foundations of long wave theory: Models and methodology*, E. Elgar, Cheltenham.
Lucas, R. E. (1988), On the mechanics of economic development, *Journal of Monetary Economics*, vol. 22, pp. 3–42.
Lunghini, G. (1996), *L'età dello spreco: Disoccupazione e bisogni sociali*, Bollati Boringhieri, Turin.
Mensch, G. O. (1979), *Stalemate in technology: Innovations overcome the depression*, Ballinger, Cambridge, MA.
Mensch, G. O. (1981), Long-waves and technological development in the 20th century: Comment, *Konjunktur, Krise, Gesellschaft*, vol. 25, no. 2, pp. 170–179.
Nelson, R. R. (2008), Economic development from the perspective of evolutionary economic theory, *Oxford Development Studies*, vol. 36, no. 1, pp. 9–21.

Nelson, R. R. & Winter, S. G. (1983), *An evolutionary theory of economic change*, Belknap, Harvard University Press, Cambridge, MA and London.
Oliveira Martins, J. & Scarpetta, S. (2002), Estimation of the cyclical behaviour of mark-ups: A technical note, *OECD Economic Studies*, vol. 34, pp. 173–188.
Pasinetti, L. L. (1981), *Structural change and economic growth: A theoretical essay on the dynamics of the wealth of nations*, Cambridge University Press, Cambridge.
Pasinetti, L. L. (1987), *Growth theory and its future*, 7th Latin American Meeting of the Econometric Society.
Perez, C. (2010), Technological revolutions and techno-economic paradigms, *Cambridge Journal of Economics*, vol. 34, no. 1, January, pp. 185–202.
Perroux, F. (1964), *L'économie du XXème siecle*, PUF, Paris.
Piketty, T. & Saez, E. (2003), Income inequality in the United States, 1913–1998, *The Quarterly Journal of Economics*, vol. CXVII, no. 1, February, pp. 1–39.
Reati, A. (1990), *Taux de profit et accumulation de capital dans l'onde longue de l'après guerre: Le cas de l'industrie au Royaume-Uni, en France, en Italie et en Allemagne*, Editions de l'Université de Bruxelles, Bruxelles.
Reati, A. (1998a), A long-wave pattern for output and employment in Pasinetti's model of structural change, *Economie Appliquée*, tome LI, no. 2, pp. 27–75.
Reati, A. (1998b), Technological revolutions in Pasinetti's model of structural change: Productivity and prices, *Structural Change and Economic Dynamics*, vol. 9, no. 2, pp. 245–262.
Romer, P. M. (1990), Endogenous technological change, *Journal of Political Economy*, vol. 98, no. 5, pp. 71–102.
Saviotti, P. (2001), Variety, growth and demand, *Journal of Evolutionary Economics*, vol. 11, no. 1, pp. 119–142.
Saviotti, P. & Pyka, A. (2004), Economic development by the creation of new sectors, *Journal of Evolutionary Economics*, vol. 14, no. 1, February, pp. 1–35.
Saviotti, P. & Pyka, A. (2008), Micro and macro dynamics: Industry life cycles, inter-sector coordination and aggregate growth, *Journal of Evolutionary Economics*, vol. 18, no. 2, April, pp. 167–182.
Schumpeter, J. A. (1934), *The theory of economic development*, Harvard University Press, Cambridge, MA.
Schumpeter, J. A. (1939), *Business cycles: A theoretical, historical, and statistical analysis of the capitalist process*, McGraw-Hill, New York.
Schumpeter, J. A. (1954), *Capitalism, socialism and democracy*, Allen & Unwin, London.
Shell, K. (1967), *A model of inventive activity and capital accumulation: Essays on the theory of optimal economic growth*, MIT Press, Cambridge, MA.
Silverberg, G. (2007), Long waves: Conceptual, empirical and modelling issues, in H. Hanusch & A. Pyka (eds), *Elgar companion to neo-schumpeterian economics*, E. Elgar, Cheltenham, pp. 800–819.
Solomou, S. (1987), *Phases of economic growth, 1850–1973: Kondratieff waves and Kuznets swings*, Cambridge University Press, Cambridge.
Sraffa, P. (1960), *Production of Commodities by Means of Commodities*, Cambridge University Press, Cambridge.
Stefik, M. & Stefik, B. (2006), *Breakthrough: Stories and strategies of radical innovation*, MIT Press, Cambridge, MA.
Stoneman, P. (2007), Technological diffusion: Aspects of self-propagation as a neo-schumpeterian characteristic, in Hanusch & Pyka (eds), E. Elgar, Cheltenham, pp. 377–385.

Van Duijn, J. J. (1983), *The long wave in economic life*, Allen and Unwin, London.

Wymer, C. R. (2006), *Wysea system estimation analysis*, Package Developed by Clifford R. Wymer (wymer@mail.com).

Yin, X. & Zuscovitch, E. (2001), Interaction of drastic and incremental innovations: Economic development through schumpeterian waves, *Economie Appliquée*, tome LIII, no. 2, pp. 7–35.

Zweimüller, J. (2000), Schumpeterian entrepreneurs meet Engel's law: The impact of inequality on innovation-driven growth, *Journal of Economic Growth*, vol. 5, no. 5, June, pp. 185–206.

Zweimüller, J. & Brunner, J. K. (2005), Innovation and growth with rich and poor consumers, *Metroeconomica*, vol. 56, no. 2, pp. 233–262.

4 A micro representation of the innovation-adaptation mechanism driving economic dynamics[1]

4.1 Introduction

This chapter extends the analysis and formalization from the sectoral level considered in Chapter 3 to the micro level.

A major weakness of mainstream economics is that it largely ignores entrepreneurship, considers innovation to be exogenous[2] and disregards uncertainty properly understood. As a consequence, it precludes a proper study of the true engine of competition and economic process in modern dynamic economies.

The firm without entrepreneurship is pointless. Probably the lack of consideration for entrepreneurial capabilities in economics depends on the difficulty of quantifying the entrepreneur's and firm's skills from outside. They are known only to the firm, and always in a highly approximate manner. But this inconvenience does not warrant relegating capabilities to a secondary role as an evanescent entity. In fact, one of the most important prerequisites for the firm's success is the knowledge of its capabilities, even if approximate, which allows one to consider available opportunities accurately. Our research shows that, in the absence of a clear formalization of capabilities, it is impossible to model a realistic theory of the firm, and such formalization needs a gauge of the degree of uncertainty; in fact, one characteristic of the firm is the daily confrontation with uncertainty, understood as lack of knowledge.

Truth to tell, uncertainty permeates every aspect of human life; but with respect to the firm's activity the situation is special, not only because the level of uncertainty is particularly high but also because firms professionally and insistently generate uncertainty through innovation. This implies the existence of an unbreakable link between capabilities and uncertainty. They simply cannot be treated separately.

As we saw in Chapter 1, one micro approach to overcome these limitations is that of the neo-Austrian economists, mainly Kirzner, who have centered their theoretical work on the crucial link between competition and entrepreneurship. Kirzner writes: "the competitive market process is essentially entrepreneurial",[3] being driven by entrepreneurs' alertness in taking advantage of opportunities for profit arising from disequilibria caused by poor decisions and forecasts. Kirzner's notion of entrepreneurship and alertness explicitly includes competition based on the introduction of new techniques and products. But in his later work, he almost ignores innovation; he considers profit as the result of an arbitrage and his 'market process' is a purely adaptive one devoted to coordination.

We also saw that the Schumpeterian treatment of innovative competition (the so-called creative destruction) makes innovation endogenous and so remedies these shortcomings, but it neglects the neo-Austrian's perspective on entrepreneurial alertness, coordination and the learning and discovery process in the presence of uncertainty. Therefore, a combination of neo-Austrian and Schumpeterian ideas may greatly contribute to a better understanding of the role of dynamic competition in modern economies.

This study also shows the erroneousness of the conviction, largely diffused among neo-Austrians and Schumpeterian economists, that their insights become relevant only at the point at which formal methods reach the boundaries of their usefulness.

Section 4.2 discusses entrepreneurship and its endogenization, while Section 4.3 gives a formal representation of the adaptive model, the core of which consists of the search procedure for better techniques among those existing; its steady state solution is discussed. Section 4.4 presents the complete model, one that links innovation to adaptation giving an explanation of the innovative process at the micro level. Section 4.5 extends the theory to multiple goods and oligopolistic markets. Quantitative simulations of both the adaptive and innovative behaviors illustrate, in Sections 4.3 and 4.4, respectively, the overall behavior of the model.

As this is a study of the endogeneity of entrepreneurship and innovation in general economics, it limits itself to a consideration of those variables in broad outline. But the formulated model is flexible enough to incorporate various kinds of entrepreneurial skills and more specific strategies and behavior of innovation and knowledge creation and utilization.

4.2 Entrepreneurship and its endogenization

4.2.1 The entrepreneur: role and definition

More than two centuries have not been sufficient to allow economics to converge to a unitary and unambiguous definition of the entrepreneur and his role. At the beginning of the story, R. Cantillon indicated, as a main feature of the entrepreneur, foresight and the ability to face uncertainty. J. B. Say insisted on the entrepreneur's task to coordinate the factors of production and the description of some other indispensable qualities to successful entrepreneurial action. Both the authors consider uncertainty (which remained a confused notion until Knight) as only one particular aspect of the entrepreneur's activity, instead of something that penetrates the whole entrepreneurial action. Surprisingly, this misunderstanding preserves a diffuse presence in our time.

Cantillon's and Say's entrepreneurs are main actors of market process and disequilibrium dynamics. This aspect has received an acute deepening by neo-Austrian economics, which suggests that the entrepreneur's search for profit is the engine of market competition in the presence of limited knowledge and information. In neo-Austrian thought, uncertainty appears to be the basic and distinguishing feature of entrepreneurship, which is the protagonist of an adjustment process toward a perpetually elusive equilibrium. But such elusiveness comes from outside the model. This represents the main limitation of the neo-Austrian entrepreneur, being inconsistent with economic development.

J. A. Schumpeter presented a different dimension, one which was first pointed out by Badeau in the 18th century: the notion of the entrepreneur as innovator and hence as disequilibrium maker. Surprisingly, he neglected uncertainty that nevertheless is behind the scene, his entrepreneur being an uncertainty maker and a main uncertainty bearer. Schumpeter insisted on the discontinuous character of entrepreneurial action. He writes: "Whatever the type, everyone is an entrepreneur only when he actually carries out new combinations and loses that character as soon as he has built his business".[4] This definition of the entrepreneur is too restrictive. If we consider some other entrepreneurial dimension, mainly that emphasized by neo-Austrians, it appears that the businessman is engaged in a continuous entrepreneurial action in a world dominated by disequilibria and uncertainty.

H. Leibenstein attempted to give a more complete and equilibrated definition of the entrepreneur. He recognized that the Knight's "achievement in trying to ascribe to the entrepreneur the unique capacity to undertake uncertainty is still the best description of the entrepreneur's role".[5] But he immediately added the proviso that many individuals meet uncertainty without being entrepreneurs. To give a more satisfactory definition, he described entrepreneurial activity as a spectrum with "at one pole . . . routine entrepreneurship, which is really a type of management, and at the other end of the spectrum the Schumpeterian or 'innovational' entrepreneurship".[6] This definition is too inclusive. It incorporates the idea that uncertainty simply is one possible aspect of entrepreneurship. But routine and well-established activities have nothing to do with entrepreneurship. Leibenstein attributed, as J. B. Say did, an excessive importance to factors coordination, so that he forgot that an entrepreneurial role must be recognized, for instance, for the banker who finances an innovation and hence is obliged to evaluate its perspective profitableness to avoid losses.

A close inspection shows that uncertainty is a recurrent aspect of all the theories of entrepreneurship and a dominating feature of this one. In the absence of uncertainty, only administrative nonentrepreneurial decisions would occur and the economy could be efficiently managed as a centralized one, that is excluding any entrepreneurial role. But uncertainty characterizes every aspect of human life, and therefore, a definition of the entrepreneur must be something more specific. It seems to us that a fusion of the Schumpeterian and the neo-Austrian entrepreneur gives a general and complete representation of this figure and his role.[7]

A more complete discussion on entrepreneurship must concentrate on entrepreneurial skills and their demand and supply, which are key influences on economic development. But some previous deepening on the problem of uncertainty is necessary.

4.2.2 *Entrepreneurship and uncertainty*

Since Knight, economists have much discussed the links between entrepreneurship, uncertainty and profit. In particular, they have underlined the fact that the *proprium* of uncertainty is the impossibility to express it through a probability distribution and, more broadly, to measure and endogenize it, being a result of incomplete knowledge (true uncertainty). But this assumption on the immeasurableness of uncertainty is referable at most to single (entrepreneurial) decisions, not to the sectoral or global degree of uncertainty. Nevertheless, the 'postulate' that uncertainty is an unknown quantity, an indeterminate value, has so deeply penetrated economic thought that even the greatest economists of uncertainty (Keynes, Davidson, the hypersubjectivist Shackle and the neo-Austrians) have not perceived the importance of a measure of the sectoral, territorial and global degree of uncertainty and its variation over time for the endogenization of entrepreneurial function and capabilities, the explanation of innovation and, more broadly, of the economic process.

A 'natural' proxy of the degree of uncertainty by industry and at the aggregate level, and as an endogenous variable of the systems, seems to be represented by the variance of profit rates across firms. This is suggested by the fact that profit rates and their interfirm differentials are the result of uncertainty, that is, of the incompleteness of knowledge and information. In the absence of uncertainty (complete knowledge), profit would be zero and the entrepreneurial function erased. The interfirm differentials of profit rates grow with uncertainty and the associated incompleteness of knowledge and allow entrepreneurs to take advantage of their differentials in ability and knowledge, so as to make profits. So, the variance of profit rates across firms offers a reliable measure (and an endogenous expression) of the degree of uncertainty by sectors and relative to the whole economy,[8] and hence of the difficulties that, on the whole, entrepreneurial activity has to meet. Moreover, it gives a plausible measure of disequilibria across the economy and hence of the disequilibrating-equilibrating movements that represent a main feature of economic development. Of course, the calculation of the variance of profit rates across firms as expressive of uncertainty has to consider the whole market of the relative commodity: for instance, with reference to the auto industry, every oligopoly operating in the world market should be considered.

Some objections may be addressed to the use of the variance of profit rates across firms as a proxy of uncertainty. But that variance, notwithstanding its limitations, is particularly fecund in representing the succession innovation-adaptation and the corresponding disequilibrating-equilibrating motion. A more reliable indicator of uncertainty may be obtained through some survey for a sample of firms asking information on the degree of uncertainty. This indicator should be substituted to the variance of profit rates across firms in the model formulation. The substitution would imply, in Section 4.4, some equation directed to explain the endogenous part of uncertainty taking, for instance, innovation as explanatory variable. Other suggestions can be derived in Chapter 6 on uncertainty.

4.2.3 Entrepreneurial skill: its formation, use and excess

Entrepreneurial skill is the capability to act as an entrepreneur, that is, to take decisions in the presence of uncertainty.[9] It is, in one sense, an elusive entity, like uncertainty, and has no market price, for otherwise it could be hired, in the same way as labor, and would correspond to a specific productivity but not profit rate. For estimation purposes, its measure may be specified in various ways, but this is not relevant from a theoretical point of view; it is important, instead, to be cognizant of an entrepreneur's awareness (even if necessarily rough) of the dimension and potentiality of his shill, as its overvaluation may cause the firm's disaster.

An insistence on entrepreneurial capabilities, in particular their demand and supply, was set out by H. Leibenstein, but the importance of such a contribution has been hidden until now by the absence of a measure of the degree of uncertainty, necessary to remedy to the elusivity of the notion of entrepreneurial skill. A different treatment of this skill is presented by Drucker. He dislikes creative destruction and considers innovation to be the answer to external changes, which are aimed at taking advantage of the opportunities for profit that change offers. This allows him to show that entrepreneurial capabilities may be the object of teaching, mainly by stimulating the ability to perceive those opportunities and their sources.

A more promising insistence on skills has accompanied some developments on the theory of the firm, since the seminal contribution of E. Penrose in her 'Theory of the growth of the firm' largely hinges on entrepreneurial competence. It must be recognized that the reference to the firm provides a rather solid ground to the analysis of capabilities, as entrepreneurial action takes place, for the most, inside the firm. Nowadays some intensive and stimulating treatment of entrepreneurial skills is in progress in evolutionary economics, mainly with reference to the revision of the theory of the firm. But the notion of decisional routine represents an equivocal achievement in this regard, since routines do not imply entrepreneurship. Of major importance is the insistence of evolutionary economics on tacit knowledge and the learning process as the main source of entrepreneurial skill. This opens the road to the specification of an endogenous mechanism of the formation and use of capabilities. But a satisfactory specification in this regard has not appeared till now: the measure of the degree of uncertainty by industry, area and so forth specified previously through the variance of profit rates across firms is crucial for theorizing about that mechanism. High variance of profit rates across firms obliges the firm to use intensively its skill both to improve its opportunities for profit and to avoid being defeated by competitors. At the same time, that use of skills helps the formation of entrepreneurship through learning by doing and learning by watching. So the proposed proxy of uncertainty allows both the available entrepreneurial capabilities and those 'used' by the productive process to be endogenized.

The availability of entrepreneurial skills may be formalized as follows:

Let $E_{(t)}$ be current stock of entrepreneurial skill and $(e...)$ be a function defining the increase in entrepreneurial skill at time t. Let z be a decay factor (a function if required). Thus the loss in entrepreneurial skill at time t is $zE_{(t)}$. Then

$$E_{(t)} = \int_{-\infty}^{\infty} [e_{(s)} ds - z E_{(t)}]$$

or

$$DE_{(t)} = e_{(t)} - z$$

102 Theoretical frame

More specifically, the variation of entrepreneurial skill, intended as a knowledge process based on learning by doing, may be expressed as a function of ordinary activity and innovation

$$DE_{(t)} = g_{si} u X_i^{\eta_1} + \beta_{sA} D\pi_{Ai} + \beta_{sI} D\pi_{Ii} - \lambda_1/(\lambda_2 + u) - \beta_{ob} E_i$$

Where:
- E = Available entrepreneurial skill
- u = Variance of profit rates across firms, considered here as an indicator of disequilibria across the economy and of the sectoral or global degree of uncertainty (the lack of knowledge)
- X = Output level
- π = Labor productivity (its deponents A or I indicate productivity increases respectively due to imitation of innovation and innovation)
- g_s = Parameter of the relation between the formation of entrepreneurial skill and activity level as affected by a degree u of uncertainty and hence difficulty
- β_{sA} = Parameter of the relation between the formation of entrepreneurial skill and the imitative introduction of innovation
- β_{sI} = Parameter of the relation between the formation of entrepreneurial skill and the introduction of innovation
- β_{ob} = Proportional rate of obsolescence of entrepreneurial skill
- λ_1 and λ_2 = Parameters of the retirement and decay of unutilized skills
- D = Symbol of derivative (d/d_t)
- i = Indicates firm

This expression postulates a 'learning by doing' entrepreneurship in that the availability of entrepreneurial skills grows (a) with the product between uncertainty and output, but at a decreasing rate ($0 < \eta_1 < 1$) with respect to output owing to the physical organizational limits to the skills of the firm and the reduction, with the concentration process, of adaptive skills; and (b) with the increase in productivity, intended as an expression of the care required by innovation or imitation of innovations. A multiplicative relation has been postulated between u and X in the representation of the learning process so that, for $u = 0$ (and hence $D\pi = 0$), that is, in the absence of uncertainty (and innovation), no entrepreneurial learning by doing takes place simply because entrepreneurship is not required.

The loss in entrepreneurial skill is represented by the obsolescence of knowledge and the factor $\lambda_1/(\lambda_2 + u)$ expressing the retirement and the decay of unutilized skill that arises from a decrease in u (uncertainty). Parameters λ_1 and λ_2 must be such that the influence of this decay factor is strong for low values of u and is delayed with respect to the convergence of u to zero.

Of course, the equation for E may also include, as explanatory variables, some exogenous (political and sociological) factors influencing entrepreneurship and the birth of new firms. It may also include investment in human capital, providing the entrepreneur with a superior perceptive capability and alertness, major information and imagination, as P. Drucker has pointed out.

Now we come to the explanation of the entrepreneurship used in production. The demand for entrepreneurial skill is a positive function of the activity level and the degree of difficulty (expressed by uncertainty) to perform the considered activity. Similar to entrepreneurial learning by doing, entrepreneurial skill requested by production processes is a multiplicative function of u and X and a function of the increase in productivity due to innovation; therefore, in an absence of uncertainty and innovation, demand for entrepreneurial skill will be zero.[10]

Let the entrepreneurial skill required to produce X units of output in the presence of uncertainty be a function $g_d(u)X^{\eta 2}$ where $0 < \eta 2 < 1$; thus the use of entrepreneurial skill in production increases with X at a decreasing rate, owing to indivisibilities. Let $\beta_{dA}D\pi_A + \beta_{dI}D\pi_{Ii}$ be the entrepreneurial skill needed for both imitation of the existing innovations and innovation. Hence the excess of entrepreneurial skill is:

$$E_i^c = E_i - g_{di}uX_i^{\eta 2} + \beta_{dA}D\pi_{Ai} + \beta_{dI}D\pi_{Ii}$$

Where the function $g_d(u)$ is assumed linear and

E^c = Excess of entrepreneurial skill; of course, for new entrepreneurs $E_i^c = E_i$

g_d = Parameter of the relation between the entrepreneurial skill that the firm employs normally to produce an activity level as affected by a degree u of uncertainty (and hence of difficulty)

β_{dA} = Parameter of the relation between the use of entrepreneurial skill and the imitative introduction of innovation (The entrepreneurial skill required to introduce innovation is considered proportional to the productivity increase intended as expressive of the engagement requested to innovate.)

β_{dI} = Parameter of the relation between the use of entrepreneurial skill and the introduction of innovation.

i = Indicates firm

Hence, in this model, with $g_d > g_s$, $\beta_{dA} > \beta_{sA}$, $\beta_{dI} > \beta_{sI}$ and $\eta_2 > \eta_1$, the entrepreneurial skill requested in production is higher and grows more rapidly than its implementation stimulated by the corresponding learning by doing. When there is no uncertainty, $u = 0$ (and π is constant), both supply and demand of entrepreneurship disappear, and so $E^c = 0$. In a world without uncertainty, there would be no place for the entrepreneur, as in a world without land there would be no place for farmers.

We shall see in Sections 4.3 and 4.4 the paramount importance of the excess of entrepreneurial skill (E^c) for the theory that we are going to illustrate. That excess is a simple result of the fact that the available entrepreneurship (E) is different from that requested by production. Note that E^c may either be positive or negative. Its negative value indicates a deficiency of entrepreneurship or, in other words, shows that the available entrepreneurial skill is appended to a quantity of output larger

104 Theoretical frame

than that allowed by the given values of g_{di} (the entrepreneurial skill that the firm i employs normally to produce, in the presence of a given uncertainty, u).

Various kinds of entrepreneurial skill may be considered through additional equations for E^c and E.

A major distinction between the approach proposed in this chapter and some content of the standard theory of the firm needs to be emphasized. In a dynamic context, with innovation and uncertainty, production is not based simply on the availability of factors, but also on the entrepreneur's behavior, ability and aggressiveness. Of course, the availability of factors must be considered, as production is a transformation process of factors into output. But the point is that only in a stationary economy may production be simply seen as a transformation of factors (as production functions do). In a dynamic context, where the results achieved depend much more on the success of the discovery process performed by entrepreneurs[11] than on the availability of factors, production is a more complex instance; it involves some variables usually disregarded by general economics, mainly entrepreneurship, true uncertainty and innovation.

4.3 The adaptive model and its convergence to a stationary state

It may be useful to give at first a specification of the model with only adaptive competition (i.e. excluding innovation),[12] which is relevant both from a theoretical point of view and a historical perspective. It is assumed that the economy is initially in a state of disequilibrium (owing to previous innovations or exogenous disturbances); the initial point is assumed to be random. With only adaptive competition, the model tends to a stationary state, where entrepreneurship is unnecessary.

The model assumes that the economy produces only one good. This limitation offers two main advantages: first, it simplifies the analysis without losing sight of special features of the dynamic model; second, it allows an adaptive mechanism that is not necessarily based on the role of prices. This means that the different degree of importance attributed to prices by neo-Austrian and Schumpeterian economists is scarcely relevant and does not prevent the two schools of thought being unified. The one good assumption is merely a simplification; in Section 4.5, the model is extended to a plurality of commodities and incorporates various ways of price formation.

4.3.1 The search for better techniques and prices

The entrepreneurial search for profit considered here involves the prospective profit rate. Of course, the most important part of that search by the entrepreneur concerns technology.

Assume a set of production technologies with different degrees of profitableness and allow for the entrepreneur to be able to see the set of existing technologies but with varying knowledge and clarity. The distance between the best technology and that adopted is an increasing function of the variance of profit rates across firms, making the choice of technology more difficult and the propensity to invest lower; it is a decreasing function of the excess of entrepreneurship (E^c), that is, the effort the entrepreneur can dedicate to search. Each firm will choose the most profitable technologies among those considered.

The search process for profitable techniques allows available technologies to be ordered according to their profitableness. This ranking may be derived from the profit rate of each productive combination, that is, $r_i = (1 - w/p\pi_i)/v_i - i_r$, where r is the profit rate, π and v are, respectively, the average labor productivity and the capital/output ratio of each technique, w/p is the real wage and i_r is the real interest rate. As w/p and i_r are constant for all i, the ranking of prospective profitableness is given by $(1 - 1/\pi_i)/v_i$.

The exposition may be simplified by assuming that available technologies have an identical capital-output ratio (v), so that their degree of profitableness is given by labor productivity. Under this hypothesis, the adaptive search for profitable techniques by firm may be represented by the following equation:[13]

$$D\ln(\pi_{max}/\pi_i) = f(u, E_i^c)$$

where

$$\partial f/\partial E_i^c < 0$$

ln indicates natural logarithm. π is the average labor productivity and expresses the degree of profitableness of the considered technology, while π_{max} indicates the most profitable (the best practice) technique and is given in the absence of innovation. Therefore, the ratio π_{max}/π_I is the distance between the best technology and that adopted. $D = d/d_t$; i indicates the firm.

It is $\pi_{max} \geq \pi_i$, so that the profitableness of the discovered technology cannot exceed that of the best existing technology; it is $D\ln\pi_i > 0$ or k if $\pi_{max} > \pi_i$ otherwise 0, so that a new technique is introduced if its productivity is higher than that of the technique currently being used. Therefore, $D\log(\pi_{max}/\pi_i) \leq 0$ or k, where $k \geq 0$ indicates the losses for disinvestments implied by the introduction of the new technique.[14] This is a precautionary factor (if π_i is stochastic) to prevent the possibility that some error in estimating the profitability of new techniques would result in a lower value of their actual profitability than that of the technology previously used.[15]

π_{max}/π_i is the distance between the best technology and that adopted. As π_{max} is given in the economy without innovation, the previous equation determines π_i. Therefore, the efficiency (π_i) of the adopted technology is a decreasing function of the interfirm variance of profit rates u, expressing the uncertainty relative to the firm technological search and investment, and an increasing function of E^c, the entrepreneurial skill available for that search. Under the hypothesis of discrete techniques the firm will choose, in the set of technologies with $\pi \leq \pi_i$, the π nearest (possibly equal) to π_i.[16]

106 Theoretical frame

The use of π as an indicator of the profitableness of techniques assumes (as we have just seen) that there are identical capital/output ratios. A more general formalization for the search of profitable technologies may be provided as follows. Take the technology corresponding to the maximum profitableness, that is, $r^{\#}_{max} = \max(1 - /\pi_i)v_i$, where $r^{\#}$ refers to the profitableness of technology as opposed to actual profitability, which is also influenced by other factors. Hence, an equation may be written for $D(r^{\#}_{max} - r^{\#}_i)$, similar to the previous equation for $D\ln(\pi_{max}/\pi_i)$, subject to the constraints $r^{\#}_{max} \geq r^{\#}_i$ and $D\, r^{\#}_i > k$ if $r^{\#}_{max} > r^{\#}_i$ otherwise 0; $k \geq 0$. Under the hypothesis of discrete techniques, once we obtain $r^{\#}_i$ from the equation for $D(r^{\#}_{max} - r^{\#}_i)$, the technology with $r^{\#}$ nearest to $r^{\#}_i$ but not higher (i.e. the best technology that the firm is able to see) will be chosen, together with the corresponding π and v (see the Appendix).[17]

In the presence of more than one market for the considered commodity or, more specifically, of a multiplicity of prices for that commodity, the search for more convenient prices must be combined with that for profitable techniques; it may be specified in a similar way to the previous equation for the search of profitable techniques, but with p_{max} (the best price), and hence all prices, varying, for instance with the excess of demand.[18] The specified equations for adaptive search giving π_i (and p_i) may also include, as an independent variable, uncertainty caused by exogenous shocks or some disturbances.

Mainstream economics explains the choice of the best practice technology by combining the notions of an ex ante technological frontier and entrepreneurial expectations, but without explicitly considering entrepreneurial skill and the variation of endogenous uncertainty. It presumes that each entrepreneur clearly sees the blueprint of techniques and the *ex ante* technology frontier, and chooses according to his expectations. Such a theory based on expectations in this way is fragile. An additional and even more serious limitation of neoclassical theory is that the technology frontier is considered exogenous, thus precluding the explanation of innovation that will be the object of the next section.

The explanation of techniques is a central point of evolutionary economics. In modeling the firm's search for more profitable techniques, Nelson and Winter assume that "the actual probability of 'finding different techniques for a firm that is searching are ... a weighted average of the probabilities defined by 'local search' and the probabilities defined by 'imitation'. ... Probabilities for transition from a given technique to others are then determined as a decreasing linear function of distance among techniques; but for imitation the possibility that (the firm) will find a particular technique is proportional to the fraction of total industry output produced by that technique in the period in question"[19]. Further on, in modeling Schumpeterian competition, Nelson and Winter maintain that R&D costs generate productivity increases through a random process. U. Cantner and A. Pyka have provided a considerable advancement along this line by analyzing technological heterogeneity.[20] As far as we know on the matter, evolutionary economics has limited itself to those formulations. It seems that the sectoral degree of uncertainty and the excess of entrepreneurial skill strongly influence the ability to see the techniques to imitate and to make innovations (see next section) and the propensity toward the investment required by new techniques. It is a pity that evolutionary economics has neglected, until now, to insist on true uncertainty and the tension between the availability and use of entrepreneurial capabilities in different phases of economic process (as expressed by the notion of excess of entrepreneurial skill).

4.3.2 The model

In the model specified here, the adaptive search for profit refers only to technological opportunities, but that may also involve organization (for instance new decisional routines). The model may also include a search for other kinds of profit opportunities, such as the discovery of some better price opportunities or better sources of raw materials. For simplicity, the model preserves the hypothesis that the degree of profitableness of technique is expressed by the average labor productivity (π) so that available techniques have an identical capital/output ratio; thus, the introduction of new techniques implies neutral technological progress.[21] Given labor productivity (π) and output (X) we obtain labor employment (L), so that the stock of capital (K) may be derived; hence the identities of profit rates and their variance across firms may be specified, thus getting all the relevant variables of this theory.

The compact formalization of the model, assuming an economy of n firms producing one homogeneous commodity and with adaptation only, is:

(1) $D\ln X_i = \beta_1 r_i - \beta_2 g_i u + \beta_3 E_i^c$
(2) $D\ln K_i = \beta_4 D\log X_i - \beta_5 u$
(3) $D\ln(\pi_{max}/\pi_i) = \beta_6 u - \beta_7 E_i^c$ with $\pi_{max} \geq \pi_i$ and $D\ln\pi_i > k$ if $\pi_{max} > \pi_i$ otherwise 0; π_{max} is constant and $k \geq 0$
(4) $D\ln w = \alpha_1 \ln(\Sigma_i L_i / \omega L_S) + a_0$
(5) $D\ln p = \alpha_2 \ln(X^d / \Sigma_i X_i)$
(6) $X^d = \beta_8 \Sigma_i X_i^{n3}$
(7) $r_i = (1 - w/p\pi_i) X_i/K_i - i_r$
(8) $u = \Sigma_i(r_i - \Sigma_i r_i/n)^2/n$
(9) $L_i = X_i/\pi_i$
(10) $DE_i = \beta_9 g_i u X_i^{n1} + \beta_{10} D\pi_i - \beta_{11} E_i - \lambda_1/(\lambda_2 + u)$
       with $E_i \geq 0$
(11) $E_i^c = E_i - X^{n2}_i g_i u - \beta_{12} D\pi_i$
(12) $L_S = L_{S0} e^{\lambda_3 t}$

Of course, in case of a new entrepreneur, the initial value of output will be zero.[22] Firm is indicated by i, and D is a derivative sign (d/d_t).

Endogenous

X   = Output
K   = Stock of capital
π_{max}/π = Distance between the maximum of labor productivity and that yielded by the adopted technology

108 *Theoretical frame*

w = Nominal wage rate
p = Price level
π = Average labor productivity of the adopted technology
X^d = Global demand
r = Profit rate
u = Variance of profit rates across firms
L = Employment
E^e = Excess of entrepreneurial skill
L_s = Total available labor force
E = Available entrepreneurial skill

Exogenous

i_r = Real interest rate
π_{max} = Maximum of labor productivity
ω = Ratio (<1) between total labor employment and total labor supply
k = Indicator of the losses for disinvestments (and a precautionary factor)
g = Proportion of the entrepreneurial skill used (and learned) in the production of a unit of output in the presence of u uncertainty
e – Indicates exponential
i – Indicates firm
ln – Indicates natural logarithm

Equation 1 expresses the rate of change of output as an increasing function of the profit rate and of the excess of entrepreneurship and a negative function of $g_i u$ that gives the entrepreneurial skill used per unit of output.[23] The negative influence on output of the factor $g_i u$ is motivated by the fact that, owing to the increasing entrepreneurial skill required in the face of uncertainty, the constraint of available entrepreneurial skill becomes more stringent. The explanatory role of E^e is motivated by the opposite reason: a large positive value of E^e allows to expound production without subtracting entrepreneurship in the search for profit opportunities, while a deficit of entrepreneurial skill, expressed by the negativity of E^e, stimulates the contraction of activity level.

Equation 2 is the rate of change of the capital stock assuming that the capital stock is (in a competitive market) proportional to output with the capital/output ratio being determined by the chosen technique.[24] An important feature of this equation is that capital/stock adjustment is influenced negatively by the variance of profit rates across firms, this being a proxy of uncertainty. Equation 2 is, therefore, specified in such a way that, when the variance of profit rates rises, capital/output ratio decreases, but this itself increases in the presence of a low variance of profit rates but remains identical across firms. Therefore, the variation of the capital/output ratio does not invalidate the choice of technique simply based on their productivity.

Equation 3 defines the distance between the best technology (maximum labor productivity) and that adopted by firms. The adoption by the firm of the chosen technology is bounded by a superior and an inferior limit; in the absence of innovation, as presumed here, the adopted technique cannot be superior to the best technology existing on the market (as indicated by $\pi_{max} \geq \pi$), but it must be superior to the technology that the particular firm was using previously (as indicated by the constraint $D\log\pi > k$ if $\pi_{max} > \pi$ and 0 otherwise, with $k \geq 0$).[25]

Equation 4 gives the rate of change of the nominal wage rate as a result of the adjustment between demand and supply of labor. ω is a critical value of the ratio between total employment and total supply of labor (hence < 1); if this critical value is exceeded, competition for labor causes a positive variation in the wage rate, and vice versa if employment falls below that critical ratio. While wage formation may follow some other rule, the specification here has the advantage of explicitly incorporating natural limited resources and gives an efficient price of labor.

Equation 5 gives the rate of change of price as a result of the adjustment between global demand and supply. But the notion of dynamic competition at the center stage of this book goes beyond competition based on prices, so that some of the considered firms could have an oligopolistic character.

Equation 6 expresses global demand as a function of total output (η_3 should be less than one because of the absence of new goods, and $\beta_8 > 1$), while identity (eq. 7) defines the profit rate and identity (eq. 8) gives the variance of profit rates across firms.

Identity (eq. 9) expresses labor employed by each firm (the ratio between output and labor productivity). Equations 10 and 11 were fully discussed in Section 4.2. Finally, equation 12 assumes exponential growth of the supply of labor.

4.3.3 The 'suicide' of entrepreneurship, the steady state solution and its stability

The model converges to a stationary equilibrium. The technological search, in the absence of innovation, implies convergence to uniform technique and profit rates, hence the elimination of their variance and, therefore, of the need for entrepreneurship, that is, $\pi_i = \pi_{max}$; $r_i = r$; $u = 0$; $E_i^c = E_i = 0$. A steady state exists if these equalities are fulfilled. This requires that the $D\ln\pi_i$ is positive until π_{max} is reached. As $D\ln\pi_i = -\beta_6 u + \beta_7 E_i^c$, $D\ln\pi_i$ will be positive if $\beta_7 E_i^c > \beta_6 u$. The constraint $D\ln\pi_i > k$ if $\pi_{max} > \pi_i$ and 0 otherwise (meaning that a new technology is introduced if its productivity is higher than that of the technique currently being used) implies the non-negativity (but not necessarily the positivity) of $D\ln\pi_i$. So the condition (for convergence) $D\ln\pi_i > 0$ (or $\beta_7 E_i^c > \beta_6 u$) could be violated by some firm.

To see this convergence, suppose the extreme case that no firm satisfies the condition $\beta_7 E_i^c > \beta_6 u$. In this case, all techniques and u will remain unchanged.[26] But the increase, according to equation 10, in the availability of entrepreneurial skill (E) over time will imply a rise in the excess of entrepreneurial skills (E^c) and hence the fulfillment, sooner or later, of the condition $\beta_7 E_i^c > \beta_6 u$ by some firms, while firms with less clever entrepreneurs will be eliminated in due time. In consequence, u will fall. This leads to a progressive acceleration of the convergence to π_{max}, owing to the direct positive effect on $D\ln\pi_i$ (and hence on $\beta_7 E_i^c > \beta_6 u$) of

110 *Theoretical frame*

the reduction in u and its indirect positive effect on $D\ln\pi_i$, as a consequence of the increase in E^c caused by the decrease in u (see equation 11 of the model).[27]

A similar reasoning may be applied to show the convergence of p_i to p_{max} in a model with multiple prices for each commodity.

As soon as the model converges to π_{max} (and possibly p_{max}) with identical labor productivity (and prices) across firms, r_i (profit rates) become equal, so u = 0 and uncertainty disappears. In consequence, $E_i^c = E_i = 0$ as equations 10 and 11 show; entrepreneurship is no longer needed as the economic process is now a purely repetitive one.[28] The adaptive search for profit has caused the suicide of entrepreneurship.[29] But we shall see in the next section that entrepreneurs owe a powerful antidote against this mortal disease: innovation.

The calculation of the steady state is in the Appendix. Stability analysis has not been performed. But the model has been simulated for a long period after the convergence to $\pi_i = \pi_{max}$; $r_i = r$; u = 0; $E_i^c = E_i = 0$ and shows a cyclical behavior which appears to be a limit cycle about the steady state solution.

In a stochastic simulation of the model, where profit rates are subject to a random process, the consequent increase in u, indicating a variation in uncertainty, will prevent convergence to a stationary state.

The model without innovation considered here is significant from a historical point of view, as it may be compared to the quasistationary societies of ancient time. The consequence of disturbances was greater in turbulent societies, particularly in decentralized societies (such as the Phoenician and Greek poleis), as it stimulated their need for entrepreneurship. Conversely, the great centralized empires were driven by their institutions and civilizations to minimize the effect of outside disturbances and hence to allow a quasi-uniform reproduction of their existence for long periods that almost cancelled their need for entrepreneurship.

4.3.4 Simulations of the adaptive model

The model is simulated over an interval of 16 to 64 periods and assumes the existence of 18 firms. For simplicity, it supposes that demand and supply are equal by definition ($\beta_8 = 1.0$, $\eta_3 = 1.0$) so that price is constant over time and therefore w behaves as the real wage.

Parameter β_1 expresses a strong influence of the profit rate on output; in the steady state solution, it determines the profit rate required to stimulate a growth of output equal to the rate of growth of the labor supply λ_3 that is able to absorb the increase in the labor supply (see the steady state solution in the Appendix).

To reduce the number of parameters, the g_i are the same in both the expression for the use and supply of entrepreneurial skill; parameter $\beta_9 < 1$ ensures that the condition $g_s < g_d$ is satisfied.

In the equation explaining labor productivity (π) and the convergence to π_{max}, the parameter β_6 obstructs convergence to π_{max} and hence the stationary solution, while β_7 promotes the convergence. The speed of convergence is stimulated if β_7 rises with respect to β_6, and vice-versa. The values of β_6 and β_7 have been defined

Table 4.1 Parameters identical across firms

$\beta_1 = 0.6$	$\beta_2 = 100.0$	$\beta_3 = 0.2$	$\beta_4 = 1.06$	$\beta_5 = 0.004$	$\beta_6 = 0.023$	$\beta_7 = 3.3$	$\beta_8 = 1.0$
$\beta_9 = 0.4$	$\beta_{10} = 0.35$	$\beta_{11} = 0.015$	$\beta_{12} = 0.52$	$\alpha_1 = 0.4$	$\alpha_2 = 0.7$	$\eta_1 = 0.7$	$\eta_2 = 0.96$
$\eta_3 = 1.0$	$\lambda_1 = 0.0006$	$\lambda_2 = 0.00025$	$\lambda_3 = 0.006$	$k = 0$			

Table 4.2 Other data used by simulations

Reference number of firms	Initial values of variables					Parameters that differ across firms
	$\log X_i$	$\log(\pi_{max}/\pi_i)$	$\log K_i$	$\log \pi_i$	E_i	g_i
1	8.370	0.441	9.468	2.248	0.0707	0.000021
2	8.645	0.156	9.744	2.533	0.1105	0.000024
3	7.976	0.873	9.074	1.816	0.0764	0.000035
4	9.090	0.083	10.189	2.606	0.3528	0.000051
5	8.425	0.889	9.523	1.800	0.0310	0.000008
6	8.676	0.756	9.775	1.933	0.1591	0.000034
7	8.703	0.610	9.802	2.079	0.2925	0.000057
8	9.063	0.0	10.161	2.689	0.3975	0.000060
9	8.615	0.315	9.714	2.374	0.2925	0.000068
10	7.000	0.341	8.099	2.348	0.0599	0.000065
11	8.520	0.207	9.619	2.482	0.1706	0.000042
12	9.187	0.911	10.286	1.778	0.0595	0.000007
13	6.091	0.373	7.190	2.316	0.0208	0.000059
14	8.625	0.250	9.724	2.439	0.2029	0.000044
15	8.643	0.388	9.741	2.301	0.2593	0.000061
16	7.657	0.056	8.756	2.633	0.0308	0.000018
17	6.045	0.391	7.144	2.298	0.0230	0.000070
18	9.102	0.211	10.201	2.478	0.1930	0.000028

The initial value of $\ln p$ is 4.605, and that of $\ln w$ is 6.397 (ln indicates natural logarithm); $i_r = 0.05$; $\ln L_{S0} = 9.145$; $u° = 0.006$; $\omega = 0.97$; $a_0 = 0.0365$ (an intercept of equation 4). An initial capital/output ratio = 3 for all firms has been postulated. The initial values of X_i and π_i have been defined through a random uniform distribution

such that the condition for convergence $\beta_7 E_i^c > \beta_6 u$ is fulfilled at the beginning of the simulation interval for the major part of the firms, to make clear the tendency to converge; the simulations show that there is a region for ß₆ and ß₇ that delimits an area within which convergence takes place in a reasonable period, while for values outside the region, the time to converge grows in proportion to the distance from those boundary values.

Figures 4.1 through 4.5 show some simulation results. Figure 4.1 shows that, after a modest growth of the variance of profit rates across firms in the first five

112 *Theoretical frame*

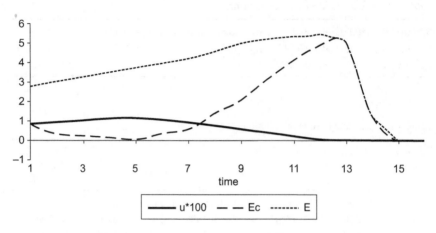

Figure 4.1 Total available and excess of entrepreneurial skill; variance of profit rates across firms

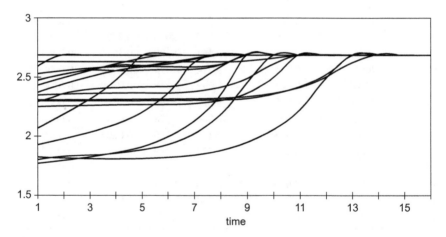

Figure 4.2 Labor productivity by firm, in natural logarithms

periods, this variable starts to decrease toward zero. E^c decreases initially, owing to the increase in u. After the 12th period, both E^c and E begin to decrease rapidly, reflecting the progressive decay and retirement of entrepreneurship because of a lack of utilization (for low u) over a long period of time. Of course, u = 0 implies E^c = E. The convergence E^c = E = 0 is attained about two periods later than u = 0, so entrepreneurial skill is no longer required. This expresses the suicide of entrepreneurship.

Figure 4.2 shows that the trajectories of the labor productivity of each firm converge toward the highest one, leading to a uniform technology and constant productivity. Some trajectories remain initially about constant; this is a consequence of the fact that the initial increase in the variance of profit rates across firms causes a

The innovation-adaptation mechanism 113

deficiency, or a severe shortage, of entrepreneurial skills in some firms so that they are unable to discover better techniques than those currently in use, and therefore they continue to utilize old techniques, representing an inferior technological bound.

The model has been simulated for 48 periods after convergence of u, E^c and E. The behavior of output and employment over the whole simulation period of 64 periods is shown in Figure 4.3.

The deviations between the curves represent labor productivity, which grows at the beginning, owing to the convergence of labor productivity of firms to the best technology, and then remains constant. Output and employment move along a stable cycle of about 25 periods and around an increasing trend, the rate of growth of which is given by $\lambda_3 = 0.006$ (the rate of growth of labor supply), in coherence with the steady state solution in the Appendix.

Figure 4.4 shows the profit rate associated to this behavior.

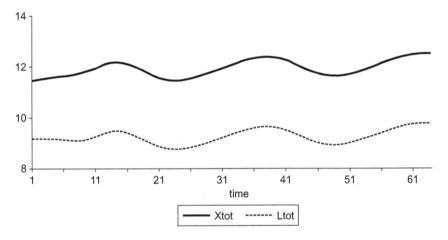

Figure 4.3 Total output and employment, in natural logarithms

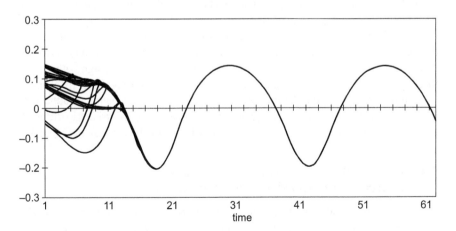

Figure 4.4 Profit rates by firm

114 *Theoretical frame*

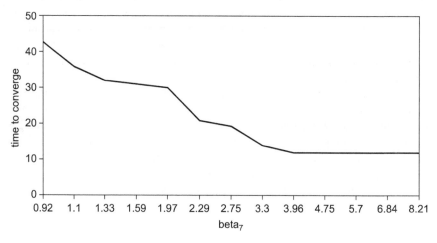

Figure 4.5 Sensitivity of convergence

Profit rates of the firm converge to a unique rate in about 15 periods, with convergence to a unique technology, as in Figure 4.2. This makes the variance of profit rates across firms, u, zero and eliminates the need for the entrepreneur. The profit rate then fluctuates about zero as a limit cycle.

It is of interest to investigate the behavior of the convergence to the stationary solution for alternative values of parameters $ß_6$ and $ß_7$, as it is the relative value of these parameters which is important for convergence.

Figure 4.5 shows the effect of change in $ß_7$: as $ß_7$ increases, the time to converge decreases with convergence obtained once $ß_7$ is greater than 4. Simulations with changes in $ß_6$ show corresponding results and rapid convergence for $ß_6 \leq 0.023$; higher values of $ß_6$ lead to show increasing time of convergence, with more irregularity than in Figure 4.5.

Further simulations representing the effects on variables of both an increase and a decrease of 6% of η_2 (the exponential parameter of output in the equation for the excess of entrepreneurial skill) have been performed that allow us to get information on the effect of this crucial variable on the behavior of the model. In general, the results consequent to a positive variation of 6% in η_2 have opposite sign with respect to a negative variation of 6% in η_2. In particular, the results are significantly changed from those for the base simulation. Convergence to the optimal technique appears to be much faster for $\eta_2 - 6\%$. For $\eta_2 + 6\%$, however, the results are strikingly different. Firms achieve convergence to the best technique (π_{max}) much later than in Figure 4.2.

4.4 The model with innovation and adaptation: a currently disregarded cyclical interaction

In the complete model herein, innovation can be viewed as a response to the disappearance of entrepreneurship, as implied by the adaptive convergence to a stationary state. Specifically, the explanation of innovation presented here

The innovation-adaptation mechanism   115

hinges on an ability to innovate to create alternative and additional opportunities of profit as the adaptive opportunities are eroded by competition. Thus, innovation and adaptation unify to become the basic engine of development and growth.

A model of this hypothesis considers n firms, m of which display both adaptation and innovation while the remaining $n-m$ firms only practice adaptation. $h \leq m$ firms display both basic and applied innovation, where basic innovations imply some substantial jump in knowledge. But the distinction in this model between applied and basic innovation is a schematic one, aimed only at exemplifying the manner of inclusion of various kinds of innovations and their effects. In the model in Chapter 3, the notion of radical and complementary innovations substitutes that of basic and applied innovations here.

The model formalization is:

(1) $D \ln X_i = \beta_1 r_i - \beta_2 g_i u + \beta_3 E_i^c$
(2) $D \ln K_i = \beta_4 D \ln X_i - \beta_5 u$
(3) $D\pi_{max} = \max(\pi^{IB}, \pi^I) - \pi_{max}$, if $\max(\pi^{IB}, \pi^I) > \pi_{max}$ and 0 otherwise
(4) $D(\pi_{max} - \pi^A_i) = e^{-\beta 6u} - \beta_7 E_i^c - \beta_{10}$ SL $+ \beta_{11} D\pi_{max}$
    but β_7 becomes β_8 for $i = 1 \ldots m$
    with $\pi_{max} \geq \pi^A_i$; $D\pi^A_i > k$ if $\pi_{max} > \pi^A_i$ and 0 otherwise, $k \geq 0$
(5) $DSL = \alpha_3\{\beta_9 \Sigma^m_i [\max(\pi^I, \pi^{IB}) - \pi^A_i] - SL\}$
    if $\max(\pi^I, \pi^{IB}) - \pi^A_i > 0$ and zero otherwise
(6) $D \ln w = \alpha_1 \ln(\Sigma_i L_i / \omega L_S) + a_0$
(7) $D \ln p = \alpha_2 \log(X_d / \Sigma_i X_i)$
(8) $D^2 S_i^B = \beta_{12} \beta_{13}(SF_i - S_i^B) - (\beta_{12} + \beta_{13}) DS_i^B$ $i = 1 \ldots h$
(9) $SF_i = \pi_i^{IB} - \max(\pi_i^I, \pi_i^A)$
    which is $= 1$ if $\pi_i^{IB} \geq \max(\pi_i^I, \pi_i^A)$ and 0 otherwise
(10) $D\pi_i^I = -\beta_{14} u + [\beta_{15} + \beta_{16} \Sigma^h_{i=1} DS_i^B] E_i^c + \beta_{17} D\Gamma\pi^{I,IB}_i$ $i = 1 \ldots m$
(11) $D\pi_i^{IB} = -\beta_{18} u + \beta_{19} E_i^c - \beta_{20}$ $i = 1 \ldots h$
(12) $D\pi_i = D\pi^A_i$ but, for $i = 1 \ldots h$, if $\max(\pi^I_i, \pi^{IB}_i) - \pi^A_i > q$ with $q \geq 0$
     $= \max(\pi^I_i, \pi^{IB}_i) - \pi^A_i$
     and for $i = 1 \ldots m - h$, if $\pi^I_i - \pi^A_i > q$ with $q \geq 0$
     $= \pi^I_i - \pi^A_i$
(13) $D^2\Gamma\pi^{I,IB}_i = \beta_{21}\beta_{22}[(\pi^{I,IB}_i - \pi^A_i) - \Gamma\pi^{I,IB}_i] - (\beta_{21}+\beta_{22})D\Gamma\pi^{I,IB}_i$
     if $\pi^{I,IB}_i > \pi^A_i + q$ and zero otherwise $i = 1 \ldots m$
(14) $X^d = \beta_{23} \Sigma_i X_i^{\eta 3}$
(15) $r_i = (1 - w/p\pi_i)X_i/K_i - i_r$
(16) $u = \Sigma_i(r_i - \Sigma_i r_i/n)^2 / n$
(17) $L_i = X_i / \pi_i$
(18) $DE_i = \beta_{24} u X_i^{\eta 1} + \beta_{25} D\Gamma\pi^{I,IB}_i + \beta_{26} D\Gamma\pi^A_i - \beta_{27} E_i$
(19) $E_i^c = E_i - g_i u X_i^{\eta 2} - \beta_{28} D\Gamma\pi^A_i - \beta_{29} D\Gamma\pi^{I,IB}_i$
(20) $L_S = L_{S\,0} e^{\lambda 3 t}$

i = indicates firm, goes from 1 to n unless differently specified
D = Derivative sign (d/d_t)
In addition to those of the adaptive model, the variables are as follows.

116 *Theoretical frame*

Endogenous

π^A	= Logarithm of labor productivity resulting from adaptive search
π^I	= Logarithm of labor productivity resulting from ordinary innovation
π^{IB}	= Logarithm of labor productivity resulting from basic innovation
$\pi^{I,IB}$	= Logarithm of labor productivity resulting from applied and basic innovation

Note: All the variables in π are expressed in natural logarithms, to economize notation, unless otherwise specified.

SL	= Stimuli of innovation to imitation
SF	= Seminal event, represented by the introduction of basic innovation
S^B	= Seminal effects of basic innovations
Γ	= Distribution over time of technological improvements and the skills caused and required by a gradual introduction of new techniques
q	= Difference between k (the factor concerning losses for disinvestment and precaution) relative to innovation and k relative to adaptation

The Appendix of this chapter gives the specification of constraints and the choice and substitution of variables as used by the computation of the model.

A generalization of the model relative to technological choice is possible by using the expression $(1 - 1/\pi_i)/v_i$ given in Section 4.3 (instead of π_i) as an indicator of the degree of profitableness of technology. Of course, this requires some equations explaining v^I and v^{IB}.[30] Both π and v may be stochastic so that the realized values may differ from those that arose in the search process.

To reduce the number of equations, productivity due to innovation is expressed as an increase in the productivity concerning the whole output.[31]

The output equations and some other equations similar to those of the adaptive model are not discussed here. The model in this section also includes:

- An equation (3) for the rate of change of maximum labor productivity, depending on the differential between the maximum productivity discovered through innovation and the previous maximum, providing this differential is positive. If k > 0 this equation is substituted by:

$D\pi_{max} = max\pi_i - \pi_{max}$, if $max\pi_i > \pi_{max}$ and 0 otherwise i = 1 ... m[32] (3 bis)

- A set of equations (4) for the adaptive search for profit (defining the rate of change of the distance $\pi_{max} - \pi^A_i$). The term $e^{-\beta 6u}$ in these equations expresses the fact that the positive effect of u on the distance $\pi_{max} - \pi^A_i$ decreases with the increase in u, since the growth of the variance of profit rates across firms causes an increase of the possibility of imitation. The explanatory variable $D\pi_{max}$ indicates that this variation opposes the reduction in the distance $\pi_{max} - \pi^A_i$. Of course, the condition $D\pi^A_i > 0$ now implies $D(\pi_{max} - \pi^A_i) \leq D\pi_{max}$ instead of ≤ 0.

- An equation (5) that specifies the stimulus to imitation caused by the appearance of new techniques; the adjustment lag α_3 refers to the obstacles to imitation due to patent rights, industrial secrecy, the non-immediate reception of the appearance of innovation and lack of clarity as to their contents.
- An equation (12) that chooses the highest value between innovative and adaptive labor productivity.

The main difference with respect to the adaptive model, however, is represented by equations 8 and 9, expressing, respectively, the seminal effects over time of basic innovation and seminal events (SF); and equations 10 and 11 concerning innovation.

The seminal effects of basic innovation are formalized using a Gamma distribution in equation 8.[33] The parameter values of this distribution are such that the seminal effects rise to a peak during the three periods following their appearance and then fall asymptotically to zero. Equation 9 shows the advent of seminal events: basic innovation arises once $\pi^{IB} > \pi^I$ (and $> \pi^A_i$), with its impact being memorized by a Gamma function that provides the continuing effects on applied innovation.

The hypothesis that the introduction of some innovation will stimulate improvements is also considered. It is specified in equation 10 through the term $D\Gamma\pi^{I,IB}_i$. Equation 13 specifies a Gamma distribution for those improvements and also used for distributing over time (in equations 18 and 19) the skill respectively caused (through learning) and required by a gradual introduction of the new technique, with the requested skill being considered proportional to productivity increases.

Equations 10 to 11 show the endogenization of innovation at the micro level. The equations for applied innovation express the growth in labor productivity as a decreasing function of the variance of profit rates across firms, an increasing function of the excess of entrepreneurial skill (since a large availability of these skills stimulates innovation) and of the seminal effects of basic innovation multiplied by the excess of entrepreneurial skill, indicating the strength with which the entrepreneur can implement applied innovations, as well as of the term $D\Gamma\pi^{I,IB}_i$ on improvements considered previously. The parameters of E^c are such that applied innovation dominates the adaptive search. This expresses the fact that: (a) when the excess of entrepreneurial skill is low, applied innovation is weak, since basic innovation (and hence also seminal effects) stagnate, and entrepreneurs concentrate their search for profit on adaptation; (b) but, if the excess of entrepreneurial skill is high, entrepreneurs concentrate both on basic and applied innovation.

Basic innovation (eq. 11) is inversely correlated with the variance of profit rates across firms and directly correlated with the excess of entrepreneurial skill with the parameters being higher than those in the equations for applied innovation. This reflects the fact that large disequilibria and uncertainty make planning difficult. Moreover, the fact that $\beta_{19} > \beta_{15}$ and the intercept β_{20} is negative mean that a large excess of entrepreneurial skill gives a stronger stimulus to basic innovation (with its requirement of more skills) than applied innovation.

The influence of basic innovation on the behavior of the model, mainly on the cycle, also depends on parameter β_{16}, while the parameters of the Gamma distribution only influence the duration over time of the effects of basic innovations. But the cyclical behavior of the model, primed by innovation, would be preserved also in the absence of the distinction between basic and applied innovations.

These tendencies would be strengthened if a rise in g_i (the entrepreneurial skill that the firm i employs normally per unit of output) with innovation were introduced.

Note that it is not necessary to weigh down the model with the constraint that $D\ln\pi_i$ is positive, since an innovation getting a negative increase in productivity is automatically excluded by equation 12 for the choice of technique, $D\ln \pi^A$ being constrained to be positive.

So innovation is a negative function of u and a positive function of E^c, as in equations 10 and 11;[34] it is also braked by k or q (concerning the loss for disinvestments and precaution), as in equation 12. Among other things, high uncertainty makes it difficult to act according to decisional routines, thus increasing the required entrepreneurial skills. More generally, a high u implies a high absorption of entrepreneurial skill in ordinary activity, which reduces skill to be used in innovation; moreover, it discourages investment and hence innovation. After all, innovation implies high uncertainty, so the introduction of innovations requires a low sectoral uncertainty and a large excess of entrepreneurial skills. It may appear surprising that there is an absence, among the explanatory equations of innovation, of the expenditure for research and development (R&D). But this expenditure may be intended to stimulate invention, not innovation, so that its impact may be considered expressed by the dimension of the parameter of E^c in equations 10 and 11.[35] The central point, however, is that the introduction of innovations needs a preliminary and accurate estimation of their profitableness; the correctness of that estimation depends on the excess of entrepreneurial skill and the degree of uncertainty, so that these are the ultimate explanatory variables of innovations.

4.4.1 The cycle described by the model: differences from other theories of cycle

The behavior of the model may be described as follows. Adaptive search for profit drives labor productivity and hence profit rates toward uniformity, thus implying the reduction in their variance. This causes the system to converge to a stationary state, so that there is a progressive increase in the excess of entrepreneurship. Of course, in the complete model (that is, with innovations) the stationary state is a mirage, in that it fades away before the system converges; the reduction in the variance of profit rates and the progressive increase in the excess of entrepreneurship will stimulate both applied innovation and basic innovation that eventually influences applied innovation. But the rise in innovation will cause, in turn, a parallel rise in the variance of profit rates across firms and a reduction in the excess of entrepreneurship (both directly and through the increase in the variance) that will provoke the reduction in innovation and a recovery of adaptation. This cycle is superimposed on a longer one determined by basic innovation, the seminal effects of which play a crucial role in this regard.

The model, therefore, shows a cyclical interaction between innovation and adaptation which forms the basic dynamics of the economy. It explains why economic systems neither fall into increasingly disequilibrating movements nor converge to a stationary state, but instead grow with an incessant disequilibrating-equilibrating movement.[36]

As is well known, empirical evidence does not give a clear proof of the cycle of innovations, mainly of long waves.[37] But this may be attributed to the impact of exogenous uncertainty, which presumably has a random distribution. The separation of endogenous from exogenous uncertainty should allow some contribution to the solution of the controversies in this field. These are also fueled by some theoretical arguments. N. Rosenberg underlines the possibility that the expectation of further innovations would cause a delay in the decisions to innovate, in order to reduce obsolescence.[38] This reasoning and some other theoretical reservations expressed by various economists on the cycle of innovation are vitiated by their lack of consideration for the counterpart of innovation, that is, adaptation. To prove such a cycle, it does not suffice to consider only innovation and one aspect of adaptive action: the imitation of innovations by pioneers. It is necessary to consider the whole adaptive action. Innovation may explain, by itself, the life cycle of product, not the business cycle. In fact, the cluster of innovations does not explain business cycle, as it may be followed by another one concerning other commodities, and so forth, that delete the cycle. Moreover, the explanation of cycle based on the strong resistance to change and the initiatives of pioneers in the presence of equilibrium is not convincing. In general, the contrary happens: innovation is stimulated by the approaching to equilibrium, which causes the squeeze of uncertainty and the increase in the excess of entrepreneurial skills.

The cycle innovation-adaptation began to emerge for the first time in Western European countries during the medieval period. Its presence became more and more relevant and more evident during the 16th and 17th centuries, mainly in consequence of the more stringent symbiosis between the economy and science made active by the entrepreneurial search for profit, and it appeared definitively and clearly established during the first industrial revolution.

4.4.2 Simulation of the model with innovation and adaptation

The full model with innovation and adaptation was simulated using the same initial values of variables and the g_i parameters (as given in Table 4.2), as well as the parameters given in Table 4.3. Parameters that are unchanged from the previous simulations are shown with an asterisk.

The simulated model considers 18 firms, the first eight of which perform both innovation and adaptation, but only two of which perform basic innovation; the remaining 10 firms only practice adaptation. The initial values of the seminal effects of basic innovation, as well as k and q, are assumed to be null.[39]

Within the innovation model, $ß_{10}$ expresses the positive effect on the adaptive search of the introduction of innovations that stimulates imitation.

Table 4.3 Parameters

*β_1 = 0.6	*β_2 = 100.0	β_3 = 0.5	*β_4 = 1.06	β_5 = 0.005	β_6 = 0.037	*β_7 = 3.3	β_8 = 2.0
β_9 = 0.58	β_{10} = 1.10	β_{11} = 0.87	β_{12} = 0.75	β_{13} = 0.99	β_{14} = 0.09	β_{15} = 2.8	β_{16} = 5.5
β_{17} = 5.0	β_{18} = 0.11	β_{19} = 7.8	β_{20} = –0.05	β_{21} = 0.6	β_{22} = 0.88	β_{23} = 1.0	
β_{24} = 0.000014	β_{25} = 0.9	β_{26} = 0.45	β_{27} = 0.03	β_{28} = 2.3	β_{29} = 6.8	*α_1 = 0.4	*α_2 = 0.7
α_3 = 0.5	*η_1 = 0.7	*η_2 = 0.96	*η_3 = 1.0	*λ_3 = 0.006	a_0 = 0.0265		

* is identical to that in Table 4.2 (0.97).

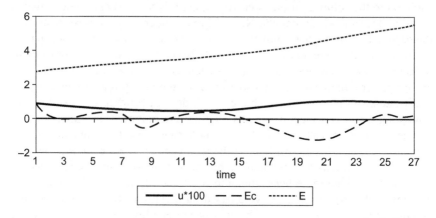

Figure 4.6 Total available and excess of entrepreneurial skill; variance of profit rates across firms

β_{12} and β_{13} are the parameters of the Gamma distribution relative to the seminal effects of basic innovation; as previously seen, their values are such that the seminal effects of basic innovations will rise in the three initial years and then decrease asymptotically to zero; β_{21} and β_{22} are the parameters of the Gamma distribution used to distribute over time technological improvements and the entrepreneurial skill required and utilized by innovation.

The simulation shows that firm 1 introduces a basic innovation in period 7, while firm 2 introduces two basic innovations, in periods 2 and 8. The considerable number of applied innovations is partly stimulated by the basic ones, and the simulations show a substantial diffusion of innovations toward adaptive firms. Of course, the share of innovative firms and, among them, of the firms performing basic innovations, influence the results.

We give some figures concerning simulations. Figure 4.6 shows excess of entrepreneurial skill and the variance of profit rates and may be compared to Figure 4.1. The total availability of entrepreneurial skills grows substantially. The variance of profit rates (u) shows a cyclical behavior due to innovation, as stated in the theoretical discussion of the model with innovation and adaptation. This causes a large deficiency of entrepreneurial skill between periods 16 and 23, while the moderate deficiency of this skill between periods 8 and 9 is due to the large absorption of

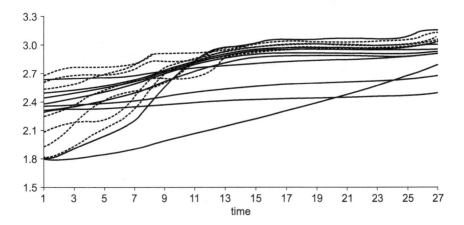

Figure 4.7 Labor productivity by firms, in natural logarithms

skill caused by the innovative dash (see Figure 4.7). In the figure, π_{max}, the productivity of the best practice technique, which was 2.689 (in natural logarithms) in the adaptive model, increases to 3.16 in the innovation-adaptation model.

> In this and the following figures of this chapter, dotted lines refer to innovative firms, while solid lines refer to adaptive firms.

Figure 4.7 shows a strong push to innovate (and hence imitate) in the first 10 periods. But the consequent growth in uncertainty and the associated deficiency of entrepreneurial skill obstruct later adaptation as well as further innovations. Only in the final periods does a new rise of productivity (i.e. of innovation and imitation) become evident, as a consequence of the reduction in uncertainty and the reappearance of an excess of entrepreneurial skill. So, the cycle of both uncertainty and the excess of entrepreneurial skill is reflected in the behavior of productivity.

Figure 4.8 shows that the initial higher increase in productivity (the deviation between the curves of output and employment) of innovative firms relative to all firms corresponds to a lower decrease in their employment. As a consequence, the growth of output of innovative firms is a little higher than that of the whole of firms. Output rises in the initial part of Figure 4.8, due to innovative push, but later starts to decrease in correspondence of the rise in uncertainty and a deficiency of entrepreneurial skill. Employment follows a similar but more moderate performance. The recovery of output after the 24th period appears to be insufficient to cause the recovery of employment.

Figure 4.9 shows that, for the most part, innovative firms (dotted lines) have higher profit rates than adaptive firms. More specifically, profit rates of innovative firms grow substantially in the initial periods, characterized by an innovative dash, and are followed, with some lag, by profits of adaptive firms owing to the increase in productivity derived, through imitation, from the innovative firms. But

122 *Theoretical frame*

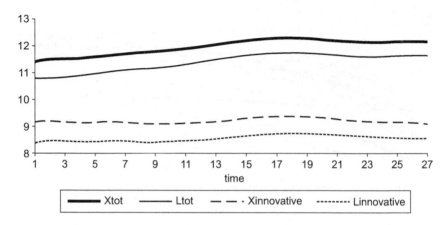

Figure 4.8 Output and employment of all firms and of innovative firms, in natural logarithms

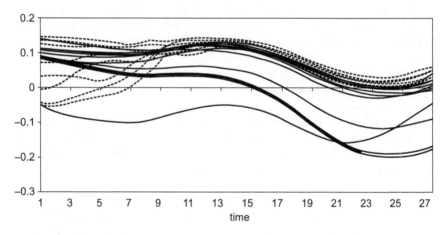

Figure 4.9 Profit rates by firm

the subsequent end of the innovative dash because of a deficiency of entrepreneurial skill and a high variance of profit rates across firms causes a reduction in profit rates that only in the final periods show a recovery. So, the cycle expressed by productivity and output is reproposed (with more clearness) by the behavior of profit rates. The figure shows that innovation opposes the reduction in the variance of profit rates across firms; it also shows the cyclical interaction between that variance and innovation. Adaptive firms experience a much more rapid decline in their profit rates than innovative ones. But the increase in productivity that adaptive firms may derive, by imitation, from the increase in the productivity of innovative firms helps adaptive firms defend their profitability. Profitability benefits from a recovery in the final part

Table 4.4 Sensitivity of the indicated variables with respect to 6% positive and negative variation of η_2 (difference of variables after and before the parameter change)

	$\eta_2 - 6\%$					$\eta_2 + 6\%$				
Periods	X_{tot}	L_{tot}	u	E	E^c	X_{tot}	L_{tot}	u	E	E^c
1	0.013	−0.040	−0.083	−0.002	−0.372	−0.043	−0.001	0.096	0.002	−1.084
5	0.016	−0.148	−0.171	−0.077	0.093	−0.313	−0.100	0.567	0.119	−1.530
9	0.356	0.047	−0.128	−0.143	0.060	−0.391	−0.081	0.031	0.197	0.944
13	0.354	−0.081	−0.204	−0.168	−0.589	−0.250	0.016	−0.260	0.071	0.957
17	0.695	0.069	−0.308	−0.241	0.998	−0.172	0.004	−0.282	−0.128	0.140
21	0.851	0.237	0.494	0.190	−4.225	−0.128	0.045	−0.355	−0.398	−0.373
25	0.556	−0.015	1.217	1.635	−2.586	−0.192	0.013	−0.324	−0.627	−0.050

of the graph: the beginning of a new phase of innovation. The negative value of some profit rates in the final periods must be attributed to the hypothesis of a quite large increase in u (the variance of profit rates across firms) consequent to innovation.

Further simulations provide a more extensive sensitivity analysis. Since the model is nonlinear, conventional sensitivity analysis is impossible, while a linearization of the model is not feasible owing to the important role played by inequality constraints. These simulations provide crude partial derivatives. Table 4.4 presents the deviations of variables from the base simulation; for variables in logarithms, these deviations are proportional. For space reasons, the results are expressed for every four years, although yearly data would not give different information. We suppose some positive and negative variations of the parameter η_2 concerning the demand of entrepreneurship in equation 19 (the excess of entrepreneurial skills), and hence show the effects of variations of such an excess.

A decrease in the parameter η_2 causes a progressive increase in output, except the initial years. Employment decreases slowly as an effect of the rise of labor productivity; but, starting from the 17th period, it begins to growth in consequence of the large increase in output. The behavior of u is interesting. The lower use of entrepreneurial skill caused by the reduction in η_2 initially causes an intensification of adaptation and hence a reduction in u. This stimulates a stronger and more prolonged innovative dash than in the base simulation, which gives a vigorous impulse to output. But later high innovation causes a rapid increase in the variance of profit rates across firms, which curbs innovation and output. The availability of skills (E) is influenced by the proceeding of u that largely determines the learning process. For its part, the behavior of the excess of entrepreneurial skill (E^c) is a cyclical one, mainly due to the different proceeding and dimension of innovative process, which is 'skill using'.

The effects of an increase in η_2, as shown on the right side of the previous table have, in general, an opposite sign with respect to a decrease in η_2, but with a different sensitivity owing to the nonlinearity of the model. Such an increase discourages adaptation, thus causing a substantial increase in u in the initial nine periods

124 *Theoretical frame*

with respect to the base simulation, which stimulates E. But later, the increasing excess of entrepreneurial skill promotes adaptation, which causes the reduction in u. The decrease in E caused by the compression of u and the parallel innovations determine an inversion in the behavior of the excess of entrepreneurial skill, which obstructs further innovations.

Figures 4.10 through 4.13, which show the effects of these parameter (η_2) changes on productivity and profit rates by firm, give a suggestive picture of the behavior of innovation and adaptation.

Compared to Figure 4.7, Figure 4.10 shows a much higher and more prolonged initial growth of innovation (hence imitation), followed by stationarity.

The initial growth of profit rates in Figure 4.11 is much higher than in the base simulation (Figure 4.9), as a consequence of the higher increase in productivity

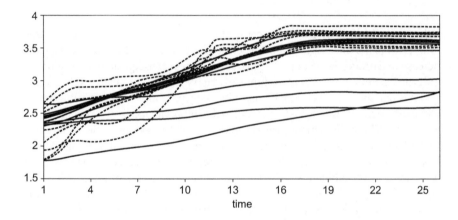

Figure 4.10 Labor productivity by firm, in natural logarithms ($\eta_2 - 6\%$)

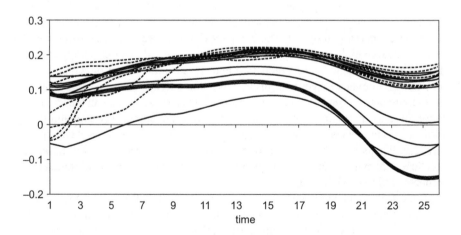

Figure 4.11 Profit rates by firm ($\eta_2 - 6\%$)

The innovation-adaptation mechanism 125

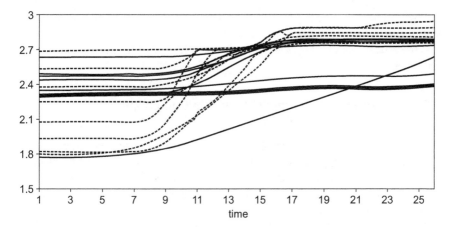

Figure 4.12 Labor productivity by firm, in natural logarithms ($\eta_2 + 6\%$)

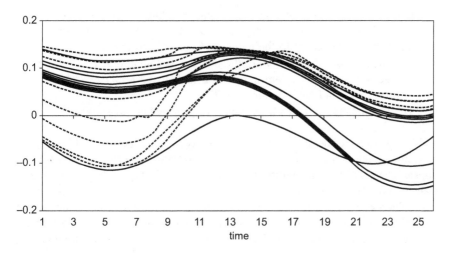

Figure 4.13 Profit rates by firm ($\eta_2 + 6\%$)

(shown by Figure 4.10 with respect to Figure 4.7). In the second part of the graph, the fall of profit rates appears to be lower than in Figure 4.9, as an effect of the more prolonged innovative dash.

The results of 6% increase in η_2, shown by Figures 4.12 and 4.13, are of course in the opposite direction. The main feature of this simulation is the disappearance of innovation (and adaptation) in the initial periods, as a consequence of high u and high deficiency of entrepreneurial skill. But later the recovery of the excess of entrepreneurial skill stimulates innovation in the central part of the graph. The consequent deficiency of entrepreneurial skill (negative E^e) curbs innovation, so productivity becomes almost stationary followed by a marked fall in profits.

126 Theoretical frame

The cycle appears here more distinctly than in the previous figures, showing that the cyclical impact of entrepreneurship is accentuated by the rise of η_2 that stimulates the use of entrepreneurial skills.

A 6% reduction in η_2 causes an increase in π_{max} from 3.16 (as in the base simulation) to 3.73.

4.5 An extension of the model to multiple goods and oligopolistic markets

The models specified in Sections 4.3 and 4.4 are open to various developments.

The use of some appropriate procedure of distribution over time of innovation (e.g. the use of a Gamma function, previously employed to specify the seminal effects of basic innovation) would allow a more realistic simulation of the introduction of new techniques.

The model can be extended to a plurality of commodities. This extension implies the following changes:

- Equations for output, capital stock, adaptive and innovative labor productivity, profit rate and labor employment have to be repeated, for each firm, a number of times equal to the number of goods it produces.
- A number of equations equal to the number of commodities must be given for each one of these variables: prices, wage rate, sectoral demand, variance of profit rates and labor supply.
- The parameters of each variable may vary by sectors of activity.

The equations for demand of each commodity must be specified differently for consumer goods and intermediate goods and a multiplicity of capital goods should appear, instead of K.[40] In a multisectoral model, the identity of profit rate needs a transition matrix of capital goods from sectors of origin to sectors of utilization, while the identity for the excess of entrepreneurship have to sum, in the second term of the identity's right-hand side, the entrepreneurship absorbed by each sector practiced by the considered firm. The profit rates of imitators may sometimes result higher than those of innovators, if imitators enjoy the availability of complementary resources or some lower labor or financial costs.

An important question is the way to introduce new products. Some functions may be specified to allow this to be simulated.[41] This aspect has been considered in the model of Chapter 3.

Another important question is the inclusion, in the multisectoral model with innovation, of oligopolistic markets. Such a generalization does not require a modification in the logic of the model and may be seen as follows: (a) replace the price equation based on the excess demand by one based on the markup principle, and (b) replace the capital equations by equations determining K/X (the relation between capital invested and output produced) as a function of excess demand. Thus, oligopolistic firms control prices by changing output (and hence the degree of utilization of plants); demand condition influences, therefore, profit rate (through variation of capital/output ratio) instead of prices.

In oligopolistic sectors, the variance of profit rates across firms is scarcely meaningful because of the low number of firms operating in the sector. This shortcoming affects the endogenization of entrepreneurial skill. But that may be overcome by making g a function of innovation, as innovation uses more entrepreneurial skills, and since competition based on innovation plays an important role in oligopolistic sectors.

4.6 Conclusion

The absence of data, mainly on entrepreneurship, has prevented econometric estimation of these micro models; it is to be hoped that the theory specified here will provide an incentive to redress that problem. Simulations have given, however, a fair confirmation of:

- The results of qualitative analysis on the steady state and, more precisely, on the tendency of neo-Austrian economics (intended as abstracting from innovation and limiting itself to adaptive search and discovery) towards a stationary state if exogenous shocks causing uncertainty are excluded, which implies the uselessness of entrepreneurship; this shows that innovation is not only a result of entrepreneurship, but is also a main condition for the existence of entrepreneurship.
- The importance of expressing uncertainty as an outcome of the economic process (mainly creative destruction) and of expressing its measure and the parallel importance of the notion of the excess of entrepreneurial skill (expressing the tension between demand and supply of entrepreneurial capabilities) to capture the impact of those capabilities on the economy. The sensitivity analysis with respect to a main parameter influencing the use of entrepreneurial skills confirms the strong effect of entrepreneurial action on the most important variables of the system.
- The cyclical behavior that confers to the whole model the core mechanism of economic dynamics as represented by the interaction between innovative and adaptive search for profit.

In a one good model, such as in this chapter, intermediate goods are absent and the role of prices greatly reduced, so that expectations are largely irrelevant except for the choice of techniques.

The crucial mechanism of innovation and adaptation, at the core of this book, goes well beyond economics and requires a study of the form of civilization and institutional frameworks that are decisive in determining the content and incidence of both innovation and adaptation in a broad sense.[42] The economic analysis in this chapter is an attempt to express such a mechanism in mathematical and quantitative terms.

Some developments of the theory, additional to those indicated in Section 4.5, are possible. For instance, a qualitative analysis rigorously specifying (and possibly improving) the properties of the complete model in Section 4.4, would help us to better understand the conditions determining the structural dynamics and the behavior over time of the development process. The model may also offer a useful tool for developing firms' strategies and a means to study the effect of entrepreneurship availability. Moreover, the nonlinearities in the innovation and adaptive process suggest a reason why social systems show nonperiodic dynamics and sometimes chaos in the mathematical sense.

The economy described here is inconsistent with an ideal world amended by disequilibria and conflicts; it shows that this ideal represents a vision achievement that requires the stationary state and stagnancy.

Appendix

Steady state solution of the adaptive model

If $\pi_i = \pi_{max}$; $r_i = r$; $u = 0$; $E_i^c = E_i = 0$, owing to the convergent motion discussed in Section 4.3, the reduction of the model in Section 4.3 to its fundamental dynamic system gives:

(1) $D\ln X_i = \beta_1 r$

Equation 2 is identical to equation 1 as, with a unique technology ($\pi_i = \pi_{max}$) and $u = 0$, $\beta_4 = 1$ and the rates of change of X and K are equal, so that is

(2) $D\ln K_i = \beta_1 r$
(3) $D\ln \pi_i = 0$
(4) $D\ln w = \alpha_1 [\ln(\Sigma_i X_i / \pi_{max}) - \ln L_{So} - \lambda_3 - \ln\omega]$ (4)+(9)+(11)
(5) $D\ln p = \alpha_2 (\eta_3 - 1)\ln\Sigma_i X_i + \alpha_2 \ln\beta_g$ (5)+(6)

To calculate the steady state solution, let's put:

$X_i = X_i^* e^{\rho_1 t}$; $K_i = K_i^* e^{\rho_2 t}$; $w = w^* e^{\rho_3 t}$; $p = p^* e^{\rho_4 t}$

Note that both ρ_1 and ρ_2 are identical by firms being identical equations 1 and 2.

The substitution of these exponential expressions and of the identity of profit rate in the above fundamental dynamic system gives:

(1') $\rho_1 = \beta_1[(1 - e^{(\rho_3-\rho_4)t} w^*/p^*\pi_{max}) e^{(\rho_1-\rho_2)t} X^*/K^* - i_r]$
(2') $\rho_2 = \beta_1[(1 - e^{(\rho_3-\rho_4)} w^*/p^*\pi_{max}) e^{(\rho_1-\rho_2)t} X^*/K^* - i_r]$
(3') $\rho_3 = \alpha_1 \ln \Sigma_i X_i^* + \rho_{1t} - \ln\pi_{max} - \ln L^*_S - \lambda_{3t} - \log\omega)$
(4') $\rho_4 = \alpha_2 (\eta_3 - 1)\ln\Sigma_i X^*_i + \alpha_2 (\eta_3 - 1)\rho_{1t} + \alpha_2 \ln\beta_g$

The first two equations are peculiar in that the dynamic model collapses to identical steady state equations, so that one or more of the steady state 'parameters' (X^*, K^*, w^*, or p^*) become indeterminate and it is possible to solve for their ratio only.

$\rho_1 = \rho_2$ (being identical equations 1 and 2); therefore, the exponential $e^{(\rho_1-\rho_2)t}$ disappears. Also ρ_3 and ρ_4 have to be equal (thus implying the constancy of the real

130 Theoretical frame

wage rate), otherwise equations 1 and 2 would not be verified with constant values of ρ_1 and ρ_2. Since the steady state values of 3' and 4' are identical, by subtracting 4' from 3' and collecting the terms in t, we have the following:

(5') $(\alpha_1\rho_1 - \alpha_2\rho_1\eta_3 + \alpha_2\rho_1 - \alpha_1\lambda_3)t + [\alpha_1 - \alpha_2(\eta_3 - 1)]\ln\Sigma_i X_i^* - \alpha_1(\ln\pi_{max} + \ln L^*_s + \ln\omega) - \alpha_2\ln\beta_g = 0$

This equation is verified if the coefficients of t are null and if the sum of the remaining terms is null too. Equating to zero the coefficients of t, gives:

$$\rho_1 = \alpha_1\lambda_3/[\alpha_1 - \alpha_2(\eta_3 - 1)]$$

If η_3 (the elasticity of demand with respect to X) = 1, is $\rho_1 = \lambda_3$, i.e. the variation rate of output is equal to the variation rate of labor force. If $\eta_3 < 1$, $\rho_1 < \lambda_3$ and vice versa; if η_3 is such that $(\eta_3 - 1) > \alpha_1/\alpha_2$, ρ_1 becomes negative.

Equating to zero the remaining part of 5', gives:

$$\ln\Sigma_i X_i^* = [\alpha_1(\ln\pi_{max} + \ln L^*_s + \ln\omega) + \alpha_2\ln\beta_g]/[\alpha_1 - \alpha_2(\eta_3 - 1)]$$

while the proportions among X_i^* may be freely determined.

If $\eta_3 = 1$ and $\beta_g = 1$ (i.e. demand and supply of goods are always in equilibrium), is $\Sigma_i X_i^*/\pi_{max} = L^*_s\omega$, that is total demand and supply for labor are equal; ρ_4 (and hence ρ_3) = 0, as equation 4' shows, so that w behaves as real wage.

The substitution in 3' of the above values of ρ_1 and $\ln\Sigma_i X_i^*$ gives the value of ρ_3 (and hence ρ_4).

The profit rate necessary to obtain a growth rate of output equal to λ_3 is λ_3/β_1 (resulting from the substitution of λ_3 to ρ_1 in equation 1'). Putting equation 1' in the form $\rho_1/\beta_1 = (1 - w^*/p^*\pi_{max}) X^*/K^* - i_r$, (as $\rho_3 - \rho_4 = 0$ and $\rho_1 - \rho_2 = 0$) results, after some transformation, in the real wage $w^*/p^* = \pi_{max}[1 - (\rho_1 K^*/X^*)/\beta_1 - i_r]$. It emerges, therefore, that the real wage adjusts to the labor productivity, with the share of labor productivity that goes to labor depending on the term $1 - (\rho_1 K^*/X^*)/\beta_1 - i_r$, so that such a share decreases with the increase in K^*/X^*, i_r and ρ_1. In effect, it is immediately evident that the increase in the interest rate and capital/output ratio (as well as in the profit rate ρ_1/β_1) causes the increase in the income share of capital, while the income of labor grows with the increase in β_1 (the elasticity of output with respect to r), that causes the reduction in the profit rate $(r = \rho_1/\beta_1)$.

Specification of inequality conditions and choice and substitution of variables

These operations extensively use the Dirac function δ, which is such that $\delta(y) = 1$ if $y \geq 0$, otherwise = 0. Alternatively $1 - \delta(y) = 1$ if $y < 0$, otherwise = 0

Specification of constraints

Constraint $\pi_{max} \geq \pi_i$, in equation 3 (in Chapter 4) of the adaptive model and in equation 4 (in Chapter 4) of the model with innovation and adaptation, may be specified as follows:

$$D\ln(\pi_{max}/\pi_i) = \delta[\ln(\pi_{max}/\pi_i)]f(x)$$

Where f(x) is a function explaining the rate of change of π_{max}/π_i.

$D\ln(\pi_{max}/\pi_i)$ will be zero as soon as $\ln(\pi_{max}/\pi_i) < 0$. Any tendency for $\ln(\pi_{max}/\pi_i)$ to be negative would cause $\delta[\ln(\pi_{max}/\pi_i)]$ to be zero.

Convergence of π to π_{max} may imply (due to rounding errors) that $D\ln(\pi_{max}/\pi_i)$ becomes negative, thus continuing to be reset to zero even if it should be positive. To avoid this inconvenience, this constraint has been specified as follows:

$D\ln(\pi_{max}/\pi_i) = \{1 - \delta[\ln(\pi_{max}/\pi_i)]\}f(x) \, \delta[f(x) + \delta[\ln(\pi_{max}/\pi_i)] \, f(x)$. If $\delta[\ln(\pi_{max}/\pi_i)] = 1$ then $1 - \delta[\ln(\pi_{max}/\pi_i)] = 0$ and vice versa, so only one term will be non-zero at any moment. If $\delta\ln(\pi_{max}/\pi_i) = 0$ because $\ln(\pi_{max}/\pi_i) < 0$ (perhaps due to rounding errors), then $D\ln(\pi_{max}/\pi_i)$ will be zero only if $f(x) < 0$ and otherwise will be f(x).

Another way to specify constraints (for instance, y < h) used by equation 3 of the model in Section 4.3 and by equation 4 of the model in Section 4.4 to specify the inferior limit of technology, that is, $D\ln\pi_i > 0$ if $\pi_{max} > \pi$ and 0 otherwise is:

$$\delta(y - h)y + (1 - \delta)(y - h)h \quad \text{where h is the new technology and y is the old one.}$$

This expression chooses y if $y - h \geq 0$ (that is the old technique is retained if it is better or equally profitable than the new technique) and h if $y - h < 0$ (the new technique is introduced, as it is more profitable than the old one), since $\delta = 1$ if $y - h \geq 0$ and 0 otherwise, while $1 - \delta = 1$ if $y - h < 0$, and 0 otherwise.

More precisely, the expression used in equation 4 of the model in Section 4.4 is:
$D\ln(\pi_{max}/\pi_i) = \delta[D\ln(\pi_{max}/\pi_i) - D\ln\pi_{max}]D\ln\pi_{max} + (1 - \delta)[D\ln(\pi_{max}/\pi_i) - D\ln\pi_{max}]$
$D\ln(\pi_{max}/\pi_i)$. It says that the distance between π_{max} and π cannot grow more than $D\ln\pi_{max}$, as the firm is not interested in introducing a worse technique than the one used. A similar expression has been employed in equation 3 of the model in Section 4.3, but with $D\ln\pi_{max} = 0$, π_{max} being a constant.

Choice and substitution of variables

To choose the maximum of a set of numbers (for instance π^a_i, indicating the profitableness of existing technologies), the following procedure has been used.

Assume i = 4 and let $V_1 = \delta[(\pi^a_1 - \pi^a_2)\pi^a_1 + (1 - \delta)(\pi^a_1 - \pi^a_2)\pi^a_2$ or, more simply, $V_1 = \pi^a_2 + \delta(\pi^a_1 - \pi^a_2)(\pi^a_1 - \pi^a_2)$. If $\pi^a_1 \geq \pi^a_2$ the terms in π^a_2 cancel, otherwise the second term is zero. Then $V_2 = \pi^a_3 + \delta(V_1 - \pi^a_3)(V_1 - \pi^a_3)$ and $V_3 = \pi^a_4 + \delta(V_2 - \pi^a_4)(V_2 - \pi^a_4)$. Thus V_3 is the maximum of $\pi^a_1 \ldots \pi^a_4$. This can be extended to as many π^a_i as required.

This procedure has been used in equations 3 and 11 of the model in Section 4.4 to find π_{max} and to perform the choice of the best technique by firms practicing both innovation and adaptation.

It is easy to define, on these bases, a choice procedure for the case of discrete techniques.

Notes

1 We are indebted to C. R. Wymer for his advice and for the computer programs that have permitted the simulations of the model in this chapter, including choice and substitutions of variables and specification of inequality conditions. These programs form part of the WYSEA (Wymer's System Estimation and Analysis) package. Some substantial parts of this chapter have been taken from Fusari (2005).
2 As mentioned in Chapter 3, some attempts to endogenize innovation have been made in macroeconomics. The failure of microeconomics in this regard implies a substantial failure of the aim of deriving macro theory from solid microfoundations. A proper answer to this shortcoming cannot be found in Shell's (1967) inventive sector devoted to produce knowledge and its enrichment by Romer (1990), Grossman and Helpman (1991) and Aghion and Howitt (1992), which link the accumulation of knowledge to the emergence of new intermediate products and quality based innovation, or in the role of human capital, as in Lucas (1988). In fact, all these explanations are simply based on the addition of some particular factor in the production function. The exogenous treatment of innovation is widely diffused in economics, however, so that Pasinetti's analysis, for instance, considers technological progress exogenous notwithstanding the prominent importance the author attributes to such a phenomenon (see Pasinetti 1981).
3 See Kirzner (1973), p. 15.
4 See Schumpeter (1934), p. 78.
5 See Leibenstein (1978), p. 40.
6 Ibid., p. 40.
7 Blink and Vale (1990) have set out a classification of entrepreneurial events (catalytic, allocating and refining) aimed at synthesizing Schumpeterian, neo-Austrian and Leibensteinian theories on entrepreneurship. But the refining events, coming from Leibenstein, if uncertain, form part of neo-Austrian entrepreneurship; otherwise, they are nonentrepreneurial events.
8 But we do not deny that a more refined indicator of uncertainty may be proposed, for instance: $u_t = \int_{t0} e^{-\lambda(t-s)} \sigma_{(s)} ds$, that is $Du_{(t)} = \sigma_{(t)}$, where u indicates uncertainty, σ is the standard deviation of profit rates across firms and the term $e^{-\lambda t}$ is a discount factor of the above standard deviation over time. Profit differentials due to institutional or natural monopoly (and hence not expressive of differences in knowledge) should be eliminated (for instance, through some sort of normalization) from the calculation of the variance of profit rates across firms intended as an indicator of uncertainty; but this model excludes the presence of such a monopoly.
9 Of course, entrepreneurial skills have a different content in managerial and individual firms. Nelson and Winter's notion of decisional routines gives an important representation of some of them, especially with reference to big organizations (see Nelson and Winter, 1982).
10 In a hypothetical economy where entrepreneurs produce identical goods utilizing an identical and unvarying technology and where market disequilibria are absent and economic process is a repetitive one (so that it may operate as an automaton), no entrepreneurship would be required and profit rates would be constant, so that their variance would be zero. High variance of profit rates across firms obliges the firm to intensively use its skill both to get better opportunities for profit and to avoid to be defeated by competitors.
11 R. P. Rumelt has calculated the variance of profit rates both across firms and by sectors of a sample of 1292 American firms covering 20 years. He shows that the

variance across firms is about five times higher than by sectors (see Rumelt 1982). This expresses the crucial role that entrepreneurship plays for the results achieved by firms and that, basically, profit is attributable to the differentials of entrepreneurial skills among firms.

12 Various economists (for instance, M. F. Scott 1992) maintain the impossibility of distinguishing innovation from adaptation. In effect, each innovation takes advantage from existing knowledge and even some very important innovations represent only a small addition to such knowledge. But even small additions may imply enormous changes.

13 A more appropriate formulation should include, as explanatory variables, two variances: that of profit rates, u, and the variance across firms of labor productivity (with the productivity weighted with the degree of 'visibility' of each firm that may be represented by the activity level). This variance of productivity is devoted to express the intensity of imitation that stimulates the decrease in $\log(\pi_{max}/\pi_i)$, that is, in the distance from π_{max}.

14 For instance, k may be determined in such a way that the discounted revenue due to the productivity increase compensates the loss for disinvestments.

15 In the presence of high uncertainty, $D\log\pi$ may be negative, as a consequence of erroneous expectations and inefficient combination of productive factors; therefore, $D\log\pi$ should be constrained to be higher than a modest negative value.

16 The choice procedure is explained in the Appendix.

17 This chapter does not specify any kind of production function; it is enough for our purposes to know, for each technique, average labor productivity and average capital productivity (hence capital/output ratio). But production function may be introduced as follows:

Let a production function be $X = f(L,K)$. Given the technology resulting from the search, say $X = f^i(L,K)$, it is possible to find the employment of capital (K) and labor (L) simply by maximizing profit rate constrained by the selected production function, that is, $\text{Max}[(1 - Lw/pX) X/K - i_r]$ subject to $f^i(L,K) \geq X$, where X is output and w/p is the real wage.

The solution of this problem yields L and K, and hence X/L and K/L. Note that the production functions selected in the search for profit do not determine output directly but affect profit rate and consequently output.

18 Littlechild and Owen (1980) have dedicated a rather complicated essay to proving the convergence of the neo-Austrian market process to a uniform price. See S. C. Littlechild and G. Owen (1980). But they make some limiting assumptions, for example, the exogeneity of (innate) alertness, following M. I. Kirzner (1973 and 1985), which in this paper is endogenous and is expressed by E^c. Besides, the procedure envisaged in this chapter with reference to price formation seems more natural and easier to use than that in Littlechild and Owen.

19 See Nelson and Winter (1982), p. 212.

20 See Cantner and Pyka (1997).

21 This hypothesis of neutral technological progress differs from the Kaldorian approach in this field (see Kaldor 1960), both because it considers the micro level instead of the macro one and it is only a simplification, not a theoretical result.

22 An interesting model of the foundation of new firm is in Grebel, Hanusch and Pyka (2001). But it ignores some factors influencing the birth of new firms such as, for small firms, the level of dependent employment that, if low, stimulates independent employment and hence the foundation of new firms. Besides, the death of firms should also be considered, and hence mergers and takeovers.

The entry of new firms could be expressed as a function of the average profit rate, the variance of profit rates across firms and some sociological and political variables stimulating entrepreneurship. The available entrepreneurship of new firms might be expressed as a function of some random variable. Entry will take place, through a switch procedure, as soon as the above entry function makes switch = 1.

23 Some econometric estimates of this equation at the aggregate level are in Fusari (1992 and 1996).

134 Theoretical frame

24 The hypothesis of neutral technological progress, allowing expressing the degree of profitableness of technique through labor productivity, implies that capital/output ratio is constant over time.
25 As previously seen, under the hypothesis of discrete techniques, the choice procedure in the Appendix should be used.
26 Note that in an entrepreneurial economy the possible constancy over time of the techniques will raise the probability that a better technology will be discovered among the existing ones, but this effect is not incorporated in the specified model.
27 In some special case, u, hence the difficulty to search, could rise (instead of diminishing) as a consequence of the increase in some π_i; this may happen if a π_i near the average grows rapidly, approaching π_{max} and this increasing effect on variance is not compensated by variations of other techniques. However, it is extremely unlikely that such an effect is not compensated in the considered period. If it is not, the increase in u will compress technology toward its inferior bound (i.e. its constancy), while in subsequent periods the convergent motion will again become operative.
28 The convergence to a stationary equilibrium is warranted, for any initial values of the variables, by the constraint $Dlog\pi_1 > k$ that prevents technology from diverging. It may seem that an exaggerated evaluation by the entrepreneur of the profitableness of the new technique may imply the negativity of $Dln\pi_i$, and hence the divergence from π_{max}. But the convergence to the best practice technique is warranted even if $Dln\pi_i$ is constrained to be higher than a modest negative value. In general, however, this negativity is prevented by the value of k, indicating the loss for disinvestments and a precautionary factor implied by innovation. Of course, the possibility cannot be excluded that some entrepreneur may make an error of evaluation higher than k, but such an entrepreneur will be eliminated by competition. This model, however, does not embody merger and bankruptcy, but only the reduction in the activity level caused by a negative profit rate.
29 Of course, it is not realistic to presume that E_i remains unvaried notwithstanding it becomes more and more unnecessary. A progressive decay of entrepreneurship (caused by retirement and the decay of not utilized skills) will start when E_s reaches some percentage of E_i during the convergence process; such decay will push E_i toward zero sooner or later if E^e becomes equal to E_i, that is, if entrepreneurship is no more requested.
30 Some explanation of capital/output ratio is in Sylos Labini (1995).
31 More correctly, the increase in productivity should result from the increase in productivity due to innovations, weighted with the ratio between gross investment and total capital (see Fusari 2004).
32 If k > 0, the choice of π_{max} must be referred to the *adopted* new techniques, since it is not certain that the new technique will be adopted; in fact, it will not be if the cost due to disinvestments exceeds the gain in productivity. Therefore equation 3 must be substituted by 3 bis that refers only the determination of the new best practice technique to the adopted techniques, instead of to all new technologies.
33 These effects may be seen as a specification of the technological paradigm that some authors emphasize, such as the influence of some consolidated line of research on the nature of technological progress (see Dosi 1982).
34 Drucker has written on this matter: "The successful ones (entrepreneurs) I know all have, however, one thing – and only one thing – in common: they are not 'risk-takers'. They try to define the risks they have to take and to minimize them as much as possible. . . . Innovation requires much effort. It requires hard work on the part of performing, capable people – the scarcest resource in any organization" (Drucker 1985).
35 An alternative possibility is to distinguish the entrepreneurial skill concerning innovation from the remaining skill and hence also to include innovative skill in equations 10 and 11. For their part, innovative skills may be explained with the integral of successful R&D expenditure (as in Cantner and Pyka 1997) and learning due to the introduction of innovation.

36 Evolutionary theorists argue that too rapid change is prevented, in modern societies, by the rigidity of institutions, habits, routines, traditions (e.g. see Hodgson 1994). The present study suggests that some factors that prevent an explosive behavior of innovation are the rise in the variance of profit rates across firms causing endogenous uncertainty and the use of entrepreneurial skill in innovation.
37 For instance, see Haustein and Neuwirth (1982) and Silverberg and Lehnert (1993).
38 See Rosenberg (1994).
39 Some parameters used in the simulations of the adaptive model have been changed as follows: $ß_5$ is higher than in that model since uncertainty may now affect capital/output ratios through innovations; $ß_7$ is replaced by $ß_8$ for the firms that also perform innovations and hence are less alert to imitation. The autonomous part of wage variations (a_0) is lower as wages will be stimulated by higher dynamism of labor productivity. A unique g (i.e. $ß_{24}$) is considered in the equations of E_i, to reduce computation time.
40 For instance, see Romer (1990).
41 The approach suggested by Lancaster (1966) to generate or reveal latent demand curves may help in this regard.
42 A ponderous author's research on social and historical process, from primitive ages to the beginning of modern dynamic society, shows the important role played by the binomial innovation-adaptation in historical evolution (see A. Fusari, *Human Adventure: An Inquiry on the Way of People and Civilizations,* SEAM, Rome, 2000).

References

Aghion, P. & Howitt, P. (1992), *A model of growth through creative destruction,* NBER Working Paper No. 3223, January.

Blink, M. & Vale, P. (1990), *Entrepreneurship and economic change,* McGraw-Hill Book Company, London, New York.

Cantner, U. & Pyka, A. (1997), *Technological heterogeneity and its influence on the rate and direction of technological progress,* EAEPE Conference Papers, Athens.

Dosi, G. (1982), Technological paradigms and technological trajectories, *Research Policy,* vol. 11, no. 3, pp. 147–162.

Drucker, P. F. (1985), *Innovation and entrepreneurship,* Harper & Row, New York.

Fusari, A. (1992), Entrepreneurship, market process and economic development: Some theoretical and empirical insights useful for managing the transition period, in W. Owsinski, J. Stefanski & A. Straszak (eds), *Transition to advanced market economies,* The Association of Polish Operational Research Societies, Warszawa, pp. 255–268.

Fusari, A. (1996), Paths of economic development: Modelling factors of endogenous growth, *International Journal of Social Economics,* vol. 23, no. 10/11, pp. 164–191.

Fusari, A. (2004), *Some reconsiderations on the theory of the firm,* Paper Presented at the Workshop on Shifting Boundaries. Governance, Competence and Economic Organization in the Knowledge Economy. Bristol Business School.

Fusari, A. (2005), A model of the innovation-adaptation mechanism driving economic dynamics: A micro representation, *Journal of Evolutionary Economics,* vol. 15, no. 3, pp. 297–333.

Grebel, T., Hanush, H. & Pyka, A. (2001), *An evolutionary approach to the theory of entrepreneurship,* EAEPE conference of Siena.

Griliches, Z. (1990), Patent statistics as economic indicators: A survey, *Journal of Economic Literature,* vol. XXVIII, December, pp. 1661–1707.

Grossman, G. M. & Helpman, E. (1991), Quality ladders in the theory of growth, *Review of Economic Studies,* vol. 58, January, pp. 43–61.

Haustein, H. D. & Neuwirth, E. (1982), Long waves in world industrial production, energy consumption, innovations, and patents and their identification by spectral analysis, *Technological Forecasting and Social Change*, vol. 22, pp. 53–89.
Hodgson, G. M. (1994), *Economics and evolution*, Cambridge Polity Press, Cambridge.
Kaldor, N. (1960), *Essays on economic stability and growth*, Gerald Duckworth, London.
Kirzner, I. M. (1973), *Competition and entrepreneurship*, The University of Chicago Press, Chicago and London.
Kirzner, I. M. (1985), *Discovery and the capitalist process*, The University of Chicago Press, Chicago and London.
Lancaster, K. J. (1966), A new approach to consumer theory, *Journal of Political Economy*, vol. 74, pp. 132–157.
Leibenstein, H. (1978), *General x-efficiency theory & economic development*, Oxford University Press, New York.
Littlechild, S. C. & Owen, G. (1980), An Austrian model of the entrepreneurial market process, *Journal of Economic Theory*, vol. 23, pp. 361–379.
Lucas, R. E. (1988), On the mechanics of economic development, *Journal of Monetary Economics*, vol. 22, July, pp. 3–42.
Malerba, F. & Orsenigo, L. (1995), Schumpeterian patterns of innovation, *Cambridge Journal of Economics*, vol. 19, no. 1, pp. 47–65.
Mueller, D. C., et al. (1990), *The dynamics of company profits*, edited by Dennis C. Mueller. Cambridge University Press, Cambridge.
Nelson, R. R. & Winter, G. G. (1982), *An evolutionary theory of economic change*, The Belknap Press of Harvard University Press, Cambridge, MA and London.
Odagiri, H. (1994), *Growth through competition, competition through growth*, Clarendon Press, Oxford.
Pasinetti, L. L. (1981), *Structural change and economic growth: A theoretical essay on the dynamics of the wealth of nations*, Cambridge University Press, Cambridge.
Peshel, M. & Mende, W. (1986), *The predator-prey model*, Springer-Verlag, Wien and New York.
Romer, P. M. (1990), Endogenous technological change, *Journal of Political Economy*, vol. 98, no. 5, October, pp. S71–S102.
Rosenberg, N. (1994), *Exploring the black box*, Cambridge University Press, Cambridge.
Rumelt, R. P. (1982), How important is explaining profitability, UCLA working papers.
Sato, K. (1975), *Production functions and aggregation*, North Holland Publishing Company, Amsterdam, Oxford.
Schumpeter, J. A. (1934), *The theory of economic development*, Harvard University Press, Cambridge, MA.
Schumpeter, J. A. (1954), *Capitalism, socialism and democracy*, Allen & Unwin, London.
Scott, M. F. (1989), *A new view of economic growth*, Clarendon Press, Oxford.
Scott, M. F. (1992), A new theory of endogenous economic growth, *Oxford Review of Economic Policy*, vol. 8, no. 4, pp. 29–42.
Shell, K. (1967), A model of inventive activity and capital accumulation, in *Essays on the theory of optimal economic growth*, K. Shell, ed. MIT Press, Cambridge, MA, pp. 67–85.
Silverberg, G. & Lehnert, D. (1993), Growth fluctuations in an evolutionary model of creative destruction, *Structural Change and Economic Dynamics*, vol. 4, no. 1, September, pp. 9–37.
Sylos Labini, P. (1995), Technical progress, unemployment and economic dynamics, in *Structural change and economic dynamics*, vol. 1, pp. 41–55 Oxford University Press, Oxford.
Wymer, R. C. (1993), *Apredic manual*, mimeograph.

5 An analysis on the theory of the firm
Organizational forms and dimensions

5.1 Introduction

This chapter considers the problem of the firm in the perspective of general economics much more than in the perspective of schools of business administration and organization. In fact, it seems to us that a major shortcoming of the good deal of work performed by those schools is the lack of coordination with general economics.

Despite the incessant transformations of the economic background, which produce parallel changes in the organization of the firm, some basic features of this preserve substantial stability. But their meaning is obscured by various misunderstandings; some clarification is required.

A main feature of modern economies is the central and growing role that creativity and innovation play in the context of the process of dynamic competition. They generate radical uncertainty that makes entrepreneurship, decentralization and market institutions indispensable, since bureaucratic decision making is not congenial to radical uncertainty. Therefore, the treatment of the firm requires a parallel discussion of creativity, innovation and entrepreneurship and a tight theoretical interaction amongst them.

At present, economics is afflicted by a sharp division between perfect knowledge, including known probability distributions, and true or radical uncertainty, that is, incomplete knowledge and the connected notion of bounded rationality. Unfortunately, the latter unanimously supposes, as far as we know, that radical uncertainty is immeasurable by definition. We have shown that this assumption is wrong, both from theoretical and empirical perspectives; it deviates attention from the level of uncertainty and its variation. This condemns, in a state of theoretical vagueness, some important variables, such as entrepreneurship and innovation, as well as decisional criteria, and prevents a coherent formalization of the dynamic competition process, which is indispensable to encapsulating the theory of the firm in general economics.

We have also considered some way of measuring the degree of radical uncertainty and have discussed the importance of such a measure for the explanation of innovation and investment and for formation and use (hence the tension) in entrepreneurial capability. This is of great importance for the theory of the firm. Moreover, it will be restated that the refusal of optimization because it would require the unrealistic hypothesis of perfect knowledge is the consequence of the wrong assumption of immeasurability of radical uncertainty; in the presence of that measure, it is perfectly possible to arrange optimization with radical uncertainty and hence to use the consequent approach in decision making.

It is important to not forget that the firm derives its very nature of entrepreneurial agent from uncertainty. On the one side, it causes uncertainty through innovation in a more direct and insistent way than other open organizational forms; on the other side, it is obliged to meet uncertainty caused by other innovators or exogenous accidents. Profit (usually called extra profit), the main target of the firm, is the result of uncertainty, that is, of the limitations of knowledge and the connected differentials in capabilities. In the absence of exogenous shocks and innovations, the opportunities for profit would disappear.

In the perspective of general economics, the firm is the engine of the dynamic competition process, which characterizes the functioning of modern economies; that process is the result of the entrepreneurial activity of search and discovery of profit opportunities based both on innovation and arbitrage over time and space, with the aim to extract gain from the disequilibria and darkness characterizing evolutionary processes.

Our treatment will lead into a discussion of the monitoring role of the profit rate intended as an accountability (not a distributive) variable, that is, as an expression of a firm's results and hence of the success of its decision making; and some considerations on optimization, the size of the firm, the connected organizational problems and, hence, the nature of the corporation and the question of its responsibilities.

5.2 Some significant aspects of the debate on the firm

The perception of the fundamental role that uncertainty and the limitation of knowledge play has progressively entered economics. A number of theoretical approaches have grown on this perception, and they may be unified under the denomination of 'heterodox economics'.

In a seminal contribution of many years ago, E. Penrose reacted to the hypothesis of perfect knowledge, which erases entrepreneurial capabilities, through a "theory of the growth of the firm" that is founded upon the availability and evolution of its managerial capabilities and knowledge and the ability to diversify production. She says: "Thus the availability of 'inherited managers' with such experience limits the amount of expansion that can be planned and undertaken in any period of time. . . . Once a substantial increment of growth is completed, however, the managerial services devoted to it become available for further expansions".[1] A shortcoming of this development is the omission that such availability depends on the level of uncertainty, which markedly influences both the formation of entrepreneurship and the quantity of entrepreneurial knowledge used in ordinary activities and to manage the achieved expansion.

Penrose attributes great importance to versatility, which avoids that "the market for those products will restrict the firms opportunities of expansion". She adds: "a versatile title of executive service is needed if expansion requires major efforts on the part of the firm to develop new markets or entail branching out into new lines of production".[2] The author insists on depicting the firm as an administrative and planning organization. She does not consider that this kind of organization is mainly typical of bureaucratic-conservative firms. The lack of caution in this matter is an effect of the minor role she attributes to uncertainty. This one is considered as: "the entrepreneur's confidence in his estimates of expectations", that is, as a subjective and not an objective fact that influences the firm's behavior. She adds: "Risk, on the other hand, refers to the possible outcomes of action, specifically to the loss that may be incurred if a given action is taken".[3] These peculiar notions of risk and uncertainty are useful to Penrose's analytical purposes, but they are deceitful if considered in a more general sense. She is concerned about the role of information in reducing subjective uncertainty and in the resources necessary to get information, and she concludes that risk and uncertainty are final limiting factors only if managerial services are fully used. Again, she forgets to consider that the use and the need of managerial services depend on the level of uncertainty. This level is never considered; uncertainty is simply treated as a subjective entity, rather than an objective one influencing both demand and supply of entrepreneurship. A main shortcoming of Penrose's theory of the firm seems to be the marginality of the role she attributes to uncertainty.

This marginalization of uncertainty persists in all the theories of the firm that attribute a central role to capabilities; the reason for such marginalization is that the usual way to intend uncertainty makes it difficult to treat capabilities. In order to clarify this aspect, some considerations on the way economics considers uncertainty are required. As is well known, a pioneeristic treatment was provided by F. Knight. But his analysis is afflicted by two main errors:

1 The idea that uncertainty only implies some deviation from the neoclassical economics of perfect knowledge but without substantial prejudice for its teaching.
2 The idea that uncertainty is immeasurable.

Heterodox economics that, polemically with mainstream economics of perfect knowledge, underlines the importance of uncertainty plainly overcomes the first Knight's error. But it completely shares the second one. In addition, its right perception of the qualitative jump with respect to neoclassical economics that the introduction of true uncertainty in the analysis implies has strongly accentuated the consequences of the second Knight's mistake.

Neo-Austrian economics gives a clear expression of some misunderstanding caused by this equivocation. Its sharp criticism against neoclassical economics is hinged on uncertainty. But the assumption of the immeasurableness and impalpability of uncertainty has imprinted on neo-Austrian students hostility toward organization, leading them to erase the problem of the firm from the agenda of their work. More precisely, the emphasis on unknown and unintentional events has pushed their analysis, mainly in Hayek's version, toward a prejudicial preference for spontaneous order over organization and command. These are considered to be arbitrary interferences obstructing the tendency of social events toward self-adjustment. According to this school of thought, general rules, mainly market laws, are enough to allow the harmonization of spontaneous actions and unintentional events. But their emphasis on individual initiative ignores the simple fact that the limitation of skills requires organization.

Another main obstacle to a neo-Austrian theory of the firm is that this school sees entrepreneurial capability as an evanescent, immeasurable entity and, as such, not liable to rational evaluation and impossible to specify. But skills do exist, and the firm has the duty of evaluating its capabilities with a reliable degree of approximation, so as to use them properly. Neo-Austrians' analysis on market process, uncertainty, search and discovery could provide important contributions to the theory of the firm, but their prejudice against organization has deprived the analysis of the firm by those neo-Austrian deepenings.

J. A. Schumpeter made an opposite error. As we know, his attention for entrepreneurial capabilities disregarded uncertainty. This omission, which confirms the difficulty of conjugating capabilities in the usual way to consider uncertainty, induced him to emphasize, in "Capitalism, socialism and democracy",[4] the role of managerial services and to predict the end of capitalism as a consequence of bureaucratization. It is illuminating, on the importance of the consideration of uncertainty, that the Schumpeterian theoretical effort gives space, in the end, to the bureaucratic aspect at the expense of the entrepreneurial one. As a consequence, the building of a general theory of the firm has also been deprived by the support of the branch of dynamic competition process represented by creative destruction.

The effects of these misunderstandings have partially affected *evolutionary economics*, which has accomplished an interesting analysis on the micro-foundations of innovation along Schumpeterian lines. Nelson and Winter's explanatory models of technical change, search and selection within the firm have represented an interesting starting point. But an important aspect differentiates this school of thought from Schumpeter: the remark it attributes to uncertainty, mainly under the notion of bounded rationality that, as we shall see, is an ambiguous way to call up incomplete knowledge.

In a theoretical context marked by the notion of bounded rationality, the difficulty to treat entrepreneurial capabilities appears evident as a consequence of the consideration, in such a context, of uncertainty as an immeasurable, subjective, impalpable entity. In fact, evolutionary economics has performed some interesting research on capabilities that stress the power of learning and tacit knowledge for explaining the behavior, internal organization, boundaries and results of the firm. But significantly, evolutionary economics insists on the identification of capabilities through the notion of decisional routine as a partial remedy to the analytical vacuity deriving from the idea of immeasurableness and impalpability of uncertainty. This insistence is coherent with the importance that Schumpeter attributed to managerial bureaucracy and also with Penrose's insistence on capabilities separately from uncertainty. In fact, decisional routines are concerned with the bureaucratic conservative aspect of organizations. They refer to repetition much more than to entrepreneurial decision making since the latter requires versatility and the availability of skills able to face uncertainty.

5.3 Ambivalence in the theory of the firm

It must be remembered, from Chapter 1, that a fundamental ambivalence characterizes evolutionary social thought well reflected by evolutionary economics: on one side, this school of thought is inclined to disregard the problem of the firm as a consequence of a tendency to exaggerate the limits of human knowledge and hence to distrust the organization at the advantage of spontaneous behavior; but, for the other side, a branch of evolutionary social thought is greatly attracted by the evolution of institutions. In economics, this attraction is mainly concerned with the firm; the connected analysis was initially fertilized by Coase's seminal article on the nature of the firm. He wrote: "The main reason why it is profitable to establish a firm would seem to be that there is a cost of using the price mechanism. . . . It is true that contracts are not eliminated when there is a firm but they are greatly reduced".[5] Here the firm is represented as an organization that substitutes command for the price and market mechanism in the allocation of resources. This Coasian perspective has promoted useful investigations on the firm. Precisely, it has stimulated two lines of research directed toward explaining the nature and the role of the firm as an organization, at present unified as the 'contractual perspective'. One line is due to O. Williamson, who developed Coase's intuition on transaction costs and hence emphasized the distinction between markets and hierarchies; the other line is Alchian and Demsetz's approach on the 'nexus of contracts'.

Williamson writes: "The two behavioral assumptions on which transaction costs analysis relies – and without which the study of economic organization is pointless – are bounded rationality and opportunism".[6] The incompleteness of contracts due to the limits of human knowledge, in conjunction with assets' specificity (site, physical and human specificity), is said to permit opportunism in market contracting, mainly the threat of a unilateral termination of contract that will reduce the value of specific assets. This would generate costs depending on the frequency of transactions, uncertainty and the specificity of investment. So a key role of the firm, it is held, is reducing those costs by substituting a command mechanism to contracts and the market.

The consideration of transactions costs, in addition to production expenses, permits significant analytical improvement on the boundaries of the firm and its governance structure; but these boundaries mainly depend on the availability of capabilities and uncertainty, which limit the degree of understanding and hence the potential of skills. Therefore, uncertainty limits the impact of transaction costs in stimulating the size of the firm. In fact, it requires versatility, flexibility and promptness that large firms usually lack and that may only be partly stimulated by setting up a decentralized structure. However, transaction costs are not essential for explaining the firm's existence and nature, which can be referred to some more general consideration on organization, as we saw in the previous section.

Alchian and Demsetz considered the contract question from a different point of view. Their work on the firm signaled the benefits that input owners may achieve through cooperation and the monitoring of costs. This led them to argue that cooperation necessitates measuring the productive contribution of each member of the 'team' (to avoid free riding and shirking). They accordingly focused on the consequent organizational problems, mainly concerning monitoring and incentives. Probably the most important insight here is the acknowledgment that the monitoring of the monitor requires that the overseer has a residual claimant status. Actually, though, it seems inappropriate to treat the firm as a team of entrepreneurs-resource owners. The firm is a unitary structure, and its results must refer to that structure as a whole. This is the task of the person responsible for the firm's performance, the entrepreneur, who is therefore entitled to a control power, to monitor the productive contribution of every component of the organization, through incentives or otherwise, in order to improve efficiency. But to make accountability effective one needs a precise indicator of the firm's success. As we well know, this indicator can only be the profit rate, as all others are partial or misleading.

Some insights on the problem of incentives have been provided by the principal-agent approach. However, the strong insistence on the crucial role of property rights, and hence of private ownership,[7] as indispensable to the efficient use of resources and hence to long-term economic growth, appears misplaced. Monitoring based on the last-claimer principle does not require private ownership but only a clear and precise attribution of responsibility for results (profits). In small firms, with their serious problems of accountability, efficiency may require private ownership with its implicit automatic monitoring, reflecting an immediate interest in economic results. But in larger ones, efficiency does not require property rights; all that is needed is the clear and inescapable attribution of responsibility for the results (in terms of profit rate), accompanied by appropriate powers of control. This does not necessarily require the ownership of resources.

In conclusion, the contractual approach has provided important results on the internal organization of the firm. Besides, it attributes to uncertainty or incomplete knowledge an important role, mainly through the notions of transaction costs and residual claimant. But the computations it proposes express an evident ambiguity as long as uncertainty is considered an immeasurable entity. Another most serious limitation of contractarian theories is their disregard for the firm's competence and skills and, more precisely, the lack of an interest in one key task of firms: searching for and discovering profit opportunities, which are the principal driving forces of innovation and hence development and growth. On this front, the contractual theories, in both the versions sketched out here, have made no advances.

There is now a growing perception among students of the necessity to consider capabilities as key explanatory factors of the firm's boundaries, behavior and organization. N. J. Foss and R. N. Langlois have focused on this aspect. Against the dominant theory centered on contracts and incentives, they contend that "the capabilities perspective is much more conscious of the production side of the firm and represents the nature of production in a way that is potentially complementary to the transaction cost approach".[8] They also note the misunderstandings that the contractual perspective inflicts to the theory of the firm and stress the importance of revitalizing attention to production costs. An important characteristic of their approach is the insistence on the need to integrate the capability and transaction cost perspectives into a unitary approach, indispensable to the analytical revitalization of the production costs side. But the main flaw is, again, an undervaluation of uncertainty and its links with capabilities. Probably, this is mainly due to the supposed immeasurability of uncertainty, implying a theoretical vacuity that makes embarrassing the reference to this variable.

Let us insist that, in our opinion, some main, most paralyzing shortcomings of the current theories of the firm are rooted in the way the key notion of uncertainty is considered and used, and mainly in the mistaken idea that, by definition, uncertainty does not admit quantification but it is a sort of impalpable entity. The consideration of the level of uncertainty and its variation is indispensable to appropriately define entrepreneurial capabilities and conjugate innovation and adaptation (as we saw). Such a consideration is also indispensable to the specification of dynamic competition process and, through this, the coordination of the theory of the firm with general economics. The disregard in principle of the level of uncertainty and its variations precludes proper specification of the formation and use of entrepreneurial capabilities and hence the enunciation of the important notion of excess (or tension in the use) of entrepreneurial skills as well as the explanation of innovation and investment.

5.4 Optimization in the presence of true uncertainty

The controversy on optimization is important for our topic, in that it can help clarify the rather similar notions of bounded rationality, true uncertainty, limits of knowledge and other aspects of heterodox economics. As is well known, the success of the notion of bounded rationality is mainly due to its help in the criticism of the principle of rational behavior and optimization. But this critique may be misleading. Man is limited by nature; a variety of bounds are always inherent in any kind of decision. In this respect, the notion of bounded rationality is little more than a truism. Within the boundaries of his knowledge, though, man is obliged, mainly by competition, to do his best to implement the efficiency of decisions. Man and society need to act rationally; a task of science is to stimulate rationality in decision making. The critique of the postulate of rational behavior, and in particular of the optimization principle, does not take this need fully into account.

The terms *uncertainty* and *incomplete knowledge* would probably be preferable to bounded rationality. But this terminological change does not provide decisive clarification; in fact, the growing hostility to optimization and some major impediments to a stringent formalization of an alternative to the neoclassical theory of the firm spring from ambiguities in the notion of uncertainty that have precluded, as previously seen, a more satisfactory elaboration of capabilities and other theoretical advances.

The exposition of some of the main objections to the optimum principle may illuminate this subject. Kirzner writes: "The decision, in the framework of the human-action approach, is not arrived at merely by mechanical computation of the solution to the maximization problem implicit in the configuration of the given ends and means".[9]

Kirzner's reasoning is referable to the neoclassical approach, which excludes uncertainty, but it cannot be generalized. The optimum principle is a mathematical tool that may be applied to various theoretical contexts. It is mistaken to presume that it is not applicable in the presence of limited knowledge; such a mistake derives from the presumption that uncertainty cannot be measured by definition. But we know and repropose soon that the distinction of uncertainty from measurable probability does not imply the immeasurability of the degree of uncertainty. As a consequence of the absence of a measure of that degree, various authors have pretended to place uncertainty in the optimization approaches in the form of some known distribution of probabilities, which as such do not express uncertainty; however, this defect has strengthened the propensity of heterodox economists to refuse optimization.

A different and more cautious critique of the application of the optimization principle has been expressed by Nelson and Winter. They write: "Orthodoxy treats the skilful behaviour of the businessman as maximizing *choice*, and 'choice' carries connotation of 'deliberation'. We, on the other hand, emphasize the *automaticity* of skillful behaviour and the suppression of choice that this involves". And later they said: "Formal orthodox theory, on the other hand, does not rate solutions as maximizing because they are better than some other observed solutions, but because they are the best feasible solutions. It thus premises a standard of performance that is independent of the characteristics of the performers; the attribution 'skilled driver' involves no such premises".[10] This critique does not express a radical refusal of optimization in economics; it simply maintains that decision making is based on tacit knowledge and automaticity instead of deliberate choice. Nelson and Winter's reprimand of neoclassical pretension to define the best feasible solution ignoring the skills of performers is by itself unexceptionable, and it is strongly influenced by the evolutionary economics refusal of optimization.

In our opinion, even though many decisions are based on nonoptimizing methods, it is mistaken and excessively limiting to exclude optimization as a tool for improving decision making and theoretical formalization. However, the appropriate use of optimization requires a joint specification of the degree of true uncertainty and the associated entrepreneurial skill, because in the absence of uncertainty entrepreneurial skill is inconceivable. Such a specification would allow us to express entrepreneurial capabilities and the related notion of incomplete knowledge as the constraints of an optimization approach, thus removing the bounded rationality criticism to optimization. This seems to be a major challenge for the theory of the firm. But it is crucial, for that specification, to define some indicator of the lack of knowledge and to express it in quantitative terms.

At the end of a review on optimization and evolution, G. Hodgson writes: "Usefully, modern evolutionary theory immediately suggests a variety of circumstances in which the validity of the maximization idea is under strain. Only further detailed theoretical investigations can tell us more".[11] In this stage, it may be said that the perceived strain is, in large part, a result of misunderstandings. However, as far as we know, nobody has pointed out the great importance of a measure of the degree of true uncertainty that can be broken down according to firm, sector and area at global level and over time. A central purpose of our work is to demonstrate the importance, both theoretically and empirically, of such a measure. Among other things, it would enable us to formalize optimization in a realistic unorthodox way and to represent the natural inclination and interest of the firm to choose the best among different opportunities. But it must be recognized that the cost of repeated optimization is high and (by experience or guesswork) the rule-of-thumb may be a good, fast and low cost approximation.

It can be useful to set out a formal example of optimization. The prominent importance of profit both in private and public firms, as an indicator of their degree of success, suggests deriving investment from profit optimization of firms. This use of optimization intends to underline, among other things, that the hostility of limited knowledge and bounded rationality economics toward optimization (Kirzner 1973, Simon 1997) is not justified, because it is simply due to the incorrect denial of the measurability of uncertainty. Our optimization is intended as follows:

$$\underset{(Ut)}{\text{Max}} \sum_j \int_{t=0}^{\infty} \int_{s=t}^{T} [\omega_j \varepsilon_j e^{-\rho s - \lambda u j s} r_j(t,s) I_j(t,s) + \omega_2 \bar{E}_i(t,s)] d_s$$

$\bar{E}$ (the part of entrepreneurial skill depending on the firm's policy) acts as control variable in this objective function, while the letter I stands for gross investment and r is profit rate. The following integration on the life period of investment, that is, $\int_{s=t}^{T} [\omega_j \varepsilon_j e^{-\rho s - \lambda u j s} r_j(t,s) I_j(t,s) + \omega_2 \bar{E}(t,s)] d_s$, expresses expected profits as discounted by uncertainty indicated by u (that in this case may consist of a subjective evaluation operated by the firm plus an objective sectoral indicator determined, for instance, by the elaboration of the answers to a monthly survey of business conditions for a sample of firms representative of all industrial sectors and Italian geographical areas by ISAE.[12] ρ is a nominal interest rate and ε indicates the impact of other factors influencing expected profitability; ω represents weights and j indicates industry.

This objective function assumes that the firm distributes its skills and resources among sectors with the aim of exploiting, at best, the market opportunities of profit. The specification of an indicator of uncertainty allows us to overcome the present vacuous stage of the analysis of entrepreneurial capabilities. More precisely, it permits us to make endogenous both the formation and use of the firm's skills, as tightly linked to uncertainty. As is well known, these skills constitute, for the major part, a kind of tacit knowledge (in the sense of M. Polanyi) that is the result of learning by doing, watching, using and so on.

It is not correct to counter that the existence of a measure of the degree of uncertainty would imply the possibility of taking out an insurance policy against bad economic results, and hence the negation of entrepreneurship. In fact, that measure is not an estimation of risk, giving a probabilistic certainty, but just a measure of the lack of knowledge, that is, of one's distance from a state of complete knowledge. On the other hand, uncertainty implies the strong influence of entrepreneurial skills on results, and it is impossible for insurance companies to measure those skills and results from outside. Moreover, the insurance of entrepreneurial results would stimulate inconsiderate entrepreneurial decision making, thus increasing insurance costs and jeopardizing entrepreneurial role.

Many authors have pointed out that firms' decisions follow much simpler rules than profit optimization (see the pioneeristic study of Cyert and March[13]). M. Polanyi's teaching on tacit knowledge has added some powerful weapons to this argument. Nevertheless, the hypothesis that the firm optimizes the distribution of its initiative among different profit opportunities seems to express a rigorous and general interpretation of its behavior, irrespective of the various decisional routines characterizing each firm organization. In fact, it is quite natural for the firm to use its limited skills and other resources in such a way to get the maximum benefit, even more than a similar attitude is natural in consumers' spending. In fact, consumers that do not like worldly delights will disregard such maximization. Instead, the firm is obliged to maximize by competition and uncertainty on the potentialities of its rivals; otherwise, it will be defeated by optimizing firms.[14]

5.5 From individual firms to large-scale managerial firms: stimulants and boundaries to their dimensional growth

Now we consider the topic of the size of the firm, which has a great analytical importance, mainly in regard to the problem of the organizational form of the firm. In this matter, economics long accepted Cournot's solution. But it was then perceived that the hypothesis of the U costs curve, on which such a solution is based, cannot be extended to the medium term, to which the problem of the dimension of the firm refers. Consequently, a number of further hypotheses have arisen concerning the factors that depend on the size of the firm.

Some authors, following Kalecki,[15] have indicated risk (intended as uncertainty) as a limiting factor on the size of the firm, adding that the way to remove this bottleneck in the growth of the firm should be represented by 'inner capital', that is, self-financing plus shareholders' savings on dividends, which depend on the dimension of profit.

A careful meditation on the nature of profit shows that such a thesis is internally contradictory. Kalecki based his analysis on an aggregate notion of profit deduced from his theory of effective demand. However, we know that, for the entrepreneur, uncertainty is an opportunity since it allows the deriving of profit from entrepreneurial skills. This means that, in the presence of entrepreneurial skills, uncertainty does not act as a limitation to the firm's expansion but instead can stimulate expansion. With regard to the role of risk, we must also take into account the thesis of Galbraith and others, according to which the dimensional increase of the firm and the connected productive diversification would imply the reduction (instead of the increase) of risk, as a result of the tendency to compensation, in the Gaussian sense, of the effects of random events.

Another boundary identified as limiting the size of the firm is the width of the market (i.e. of the demand) of each good. It was Sraffa who initially underlined this boundary and related it to the growing sale expenditures necessary to overcome it.[16] But it is now well known that the diversification of production allows the firm to eliminate such a boundary. Other authors have emphasized the growing complexity that growth in size of the firm entails for its internal processes of coordination, control and communication. These same authors (primarily Kaldor) have underlined the limitation of the skills of direction on the hypothesis that the entrepreneurial function is indivisible by definition. But the use of computers allows an easy solution to the problems of control, coordination and communication. Moreover, Kaldor's boundary on direction makes sense only in relation to the traditional notion of the entrepreneur, not to the kind of entrepreneurship typical of the large firm. In fact, in this latter case, ability to judge the content and implications of the decisions to be taken does not depend on individual skills but rather on the quality and quantity of the organizational and managerial resources that the firm has at its disposal. This last point is central to the discussion of the size of the firm and hence deserves much attention.

In the modern large firm, the major part of entrepreneurial decision making is based on information owned by many people. J. K. Galbraith wrote: "The real achievement of modern science and technology is represented by the possibility to take normal persons, educate them accurately in a specific field and hence coordinate, through an appropriate organization, their competence with those of other specialized ordinary people".[17] This makes it possible to meet the exigencies generated by technological development and reach decisions on very complex questions by using skills that are easy to find and instruct, with the only condition being that the people endowed with the required knowledge are able to collaborate and express collective decisions. So, in the modern large firm, the entrepreneurial function is not unique and indivisible (as Kaldor supposed), but is expressed by a plurality of levels that vary according to the decisions taken over the course of time, since only he who possesses the requisite knowledge can be charged with decision. As a consequence, the limitation of the size of the firm cannot come from this side, at least not if the will and ability to make the qualitative jump from traditional to managerial organization exist. This has been clarified in the managerial literature that takes its origin from the work of E. Penrose.[18]

If the reason the firm exists is correctly treated, the true limit on the growth of its size becomes evident. The reason for the existence of the firm also contains the boundary on its growth; this reason being the necessity of committing economic and productive decisions to the competence and the knowledge of people in close contact with the changing events to which decisions refer. Such a necessity conflicts not only with centralization *tout court*, but also with an unlimited enlargement of the size of the firm, whatever its organizational form. The boundary on size resulting from the need of decentralization can only be shifted through appropriate organizational forms; it cannot be eliminated. This topic deserves attention.

148 Theoretical frame

We saw previously that an efficacious use of knowledge, in the presence of increasing technological complexity, often suggests and sometimes imposes the widening of the entrepreneurial function by entrusting managerial groups with it. Such an organizational form implies a remarkable increase in the minimal size of the firm; besides, it makes it possible to considerably increase dimension without this entailing a considerable centralization of decision making. The multidivisional organization provides further degrees of freedom in conjugating decentralization with large size, thus further amplifying the dimensional boundary. It follows that a real problem is the verification of the possibility of amplification of such a boundary through the adoption of a managerial organization. Such verification might start by considering the managerial organization that implies the maximum degree of internal decentralization, that is, group organization (but we can also refer to a unitary juridical form of multidivisional type). As is well known, at the top of the group we find a holding that controls the various operational unities constituting the group. Two cases can be differentiated:

1. The board of directors driving each unity enjoys *full administrative autonomy*, while the holding limits itself to the perception of profits. In this case, the group cannot be considered a single firm; it is a *group of firms*. In fact, the definition of the firm is based on the notion of 'autonomous' decision making, while such a definition does not give importance to the problem of the attribution of profits.
2. The holding has a unitary executive committee that resolves the conflicts among the various subgroups, bringing them back into the orbit of the general strategies of the group. In this case, the group is a single firm due to the subordination of each operational unity to the decisional powers that the holding exercises.[19]

Only the second case is of interest for our analysis of the space that the managerial organization of group (or multidivisional organization) offers to the amplification of the size of the firm. Such an analysis is facilitated by the fact that the field of decision making committed to the holding competence is usually very large, including within it all strategic choices.

Usually, the great multinational and multidivisional firms entitle the parent society to the financial management, technological research and formative services, while the branch offices administer choices of tactical character and must supply to the parent society periodical reports, must analyze the results achieved in collegial meetings of the group, and are submitted to the control visits of central inspectors.[20] This is despite the fact that the large multidivisional firms are generally the group organizations that are the most decentralized and articulated.

It is immediately evident that the links of subordination of each operative unit to the holding described remove decisional power on crucial questions from people operating on the spot. Such negative effects of this centralization of decision making grow with the dimensions of the group and the number of operative unities controlled by the holding and productive diversification, and they can be reduced only through a reduction of the decision power of the central board and top management. Such a reduction attenuates the characterization of the group as a unitary firm, ultimately tending to the complete suppression of such a character and the reduction of the parent society to the first instance described (item 1).

It must be added that the operation of a unitary group strategy does not cause only decisional inefficiency, but it also causes organizational inefficiency. Let us briefly explore the reason for this inconvenience. It is well known that, in the holding situation described in item 2, the types of investment are decided by the central direction of each society. This deprives such societies of an important component of their autonomy and generates enormous difficulties in defining the criteria of evaluation of the results achieved by them and, hence, a sharp-sighted subdivision among them of the capital to be invested. In fact, the natural parameter for such evaluation, the profit rate of the firm, becomes useless since: (a) profit is conditioned in a decisive way by the general strategy of the group, which is defined outside the operative unities; and (b) it is very difficult to define, with regard to the considered group, the firm's profits, both due to the arbitrariness of the attribution to each unit (or division) of the general costs concerning centralized services and the arbitrariness of the definition of unit prices of the goods exchanged inside the group (or inside the multidivisional firm).

We can see, therefore, that groups of firms (or the big multidivisional firms) encounter problems of decisional and organizational efficiency identical to those that, on a larger scale, are typical of centralized economies. This is not casual. In fact, we have seen that an enormous growth of dimensions determines administrative structures more similar to centralized than decentralized economic orders and also implies a substantial undermining of the main reasons for both the firm and decentralization.

It is surprising that the drawbacks caused in big firms by the need for the centralization of strategic decision making described previously have been disregarded by important students of managerial organization. E. Penrose wrote: "We have rejected the proposition that there is for every firm some optimum size beyond which it will run into diseconomies. Only for firms incapable of adapting their managerial structure to the requirements of larger operations can one postulate an optimum".[21]

According to Penrose, the adjustment of staff would allow, among other things, an increase and improvement in the quantity of available information and, hence, the skill to make decisions. But the adjustment of the staff is unable to solve either the organizational problem considered previously or to eliminate the negative implications for the efficiency of decision making that, in the presence of very large dimensions, are caused by the centralization of strategic decisions. The lack of knowledge, in the case of large dimensions, of he who takes decisions from everyday events inevitably causes some substantial extraneousness with respect to the specificity of events.

Some pages later, Penrose says: "In spite of the opportunities and pressures which lead firms into the production of a wider range of products, it seems likely that most firms still derive the bulk of their income from a relatively few closely related products".[22] Well, this circumstance that Penrose rightly underlines must be primarily attributed to the fact that the losses in decisional and organizational efficiency due to the centralization of strategic decision making are modest if goods are not numerous and, therefore, the decisions concerning them have many affinities. While a firm is expanding, its organization must change. But, up to certain dimensional levels (which vary in each case), and if the output of the firm is less diversified, these changes cause neither inefficiencies due to centralization nor substantial qualitative jumps. Some new directional powers are created, but the entrepreneurial function does not suffer dispersion.

The situation becomes more complicated if dimensions continue to grow. In this case, it becomes necessary to establish some sublevel of entrepreneurship. But these sublevels must be coordinated according to a unitary logic. As a consequence, a conflict inside the organizational managerial logics takes place; the inevitable interference of the top management within the decisional role belonging to the new sublevels of entrepreneurship causes a loss of entrepreneurial efficiency. The situation is worsened by the fact that, beyond some dimensions, a further expansion of the firm requires an increase in productive diversification, but such greater diversification raises the necessity of coordination, thus determining a further limitation on the possibility of decisional decentralization and, hence, further reducing the knowledge of problems on the part of the person who decides.

On the other hand, the dispersion of entrepreneurship throughout a variety of decisional sublevels (that operate notwithstanding the centralization of strategic decision making considered previous) is not without inconveniencies. In particular, by determining a multiplicity of subjective points of view that decision making is obliged to confront, such dispersion causes limitations in both the agility of decision making and the versatility of entrepreneurial imagination. For sure, the previous decisional technique is characterized by a greater accuracy, reflexivity and 'propensity to prepare the ground' than is the traditional entrepreneurship. But this represents an advantage only if the firm encounters an external environment that is easy to dominate and foresee. In sum, managerial organization, being well endowed with reflexivity and the power of persuasion, is more qualified to shape and influence the external world than to suffer its influence and adapt itself to it. It encounters difficulties if it needs to adapt itself more than it needs to adapt others to its exigencies, that is, if the boundaries deriving from the external environment are strong and persistent. The theorists of the giant firm have dedicated inadequate attention to the role of external boundaries. They were living in a world in which the managerial firm seemed able to subsume all by its logic, so they judged reality and theorized this process while comfortably sitting in the large stomach of the big firm. Consequently, their view is limited and one-sided. In the life of the firm with a higher incidence of external than internal boundaries, there corresponds a greater necessity to decentralize decision making; as a consequence, the obstacles that obstruct the growth of the firm rise.

From the previous considerations derives, among other things, an important explanation of the reason of the existence of the small firm, in addition to the reasons set out by the interstitial theory (Penrose, Sylos Labini) and by the theory that underlines the importance of the innovative role of the little firm (G. Berardi). The space available to the small and medium-sized firm seems due to a more general reason than those considered by these authors: these firms are, first of all, an expression of the physiological exigency of decentralization that we have underlined. This implies that their presence should be more frequent in the sectors where the necessity to decide on the spot is higher, since those sectors do not like the centralization of strategic decision making, which instead is typical of diversified large firms.

5.6 Some details on the factors counteracting the boundaries to the dimensions: the objective or institutional nature of the boundaries

We discussed, hitherto, the boundaries on the dimensions of the firm and underlined that they are much larger in managerial than traditional firms. But we have not discussed the dimension that the firm can concretely reach before the boundaries here considered become active. Now we come to do this.

The size of the firm depends on the force of the factors that counteract the previously discussed boundaries, thus promoting the enlargement of the firm. These factors are: (a) scale economies of technical, financial and managerial-organizational character; and (b) growth economies. As is well known, these economies are numerous and variegated. The problem is to see how far they are able to overcome opposition to the reduction of size deriving from the inefficiency in decision making caused by centralization, and when they are not able. Such verification can be performed only with reference to concrete cases. However, some general considerations can be stated.

The size of scale and growth economies is frequently so large as to justify the conclusion that large dimensions are obstructed, for the most part, by the qualitative jump in organization that they need much more so than by the boundaries we are discussing. Nevertheless, critical students will perceive that the theoretical relevance of such a boundary is great. If we consider the problem from the point of view of a general theory of decentralization, that is, abstracting from specific institutional forms, we must ask ourselves: what part of both scale and growth economies derives from the institutional content of the existing forms of decentralization, and what part has instead an objective character, this intended in the sense that it abstracts from the existing institutional forms? This consideration allows understanding that the boundary to the size of the firm previously underlined has a character much more restrictive and relevant (from an analytical point of view) than it appears at first sight. This point deserves further consideration.

Without any doubt, the push on the growth of size is largely due to financial factors, especially if the growth takes a conglomerate form. This happens because the organization of the group causes an increase (both through financial conjunctions and the multiplication of the levels of vertical participation) of the quantity of risk capital (present in the patrimonial estate of each firm of the group) far beyond the effective amount of capital, thus favoring both the preservation of control positions and the collection of funds in the market. But these advantages operate only if the market for capital and the financing of the firm are organized in a capitalist way.

The same can be said with regard to the economies of dimension dependent on the activity of R&D. These economies may exist only if R&D operates inside the firm. But we can suppose a decentralized economic system where such activity is largely performed outside the firm, through appropriate institutions, and where the firm only decides which of the scientific results achieved by those research institutions to utilize, as well as when and the way in which to utilize them.[23] Also market research, engineering, computation and information, as well as the assistance services needed by firms operating abroad, could be supplied, at the request of users, by specialized centers. For their part, scale economies concerning advertisement expenditures represent in the main a peculiarity of capitalist decentralization. The same is valid with regard to the dimensional growth hastened by reasons of prestige; in fact, it is possible to create a system of financing of production able to exclude those reasons from the leading criteria of distribution, among firms, of the national fund of investment.

Indeed, only a modest number of scale economies have an *objective character*, that is, are independent of the considered institutional system. Among them are those that arise due to the possibility of using, with the growth of production, superior techniques and/or from using more rationally the existing installations by specializing the phases of production. Furthermore, there are economies that arise from the fact that purchase costs and the cost of the functioning of installations are less than proportional to their dimensions. Finally, there are economies determined by the possibility of introducing, in case of larger dimensions, less expensive control systems and the possibility of reducing the unsold stocks (as an effect of the Gaussian law of larger numbers).

Further incentives to the growth of size of an objective character may depend on the tendency to consolidate, through entrance into a secondary market, the position in the main market of production; moreover, these incentives can derive from the reduction of the degree of radical uncertainty that growth allows as an effect of the connected higher control of markets and major productive diversification. For their part, growth economies that are not scale economies[24] stimulate indefinitely the dimension of the firm only if unit costs in the medium and long run remain constant; they do not do so if those costs start to rise sooner or later, due to the presence of the boundary here discussed.

On the whole, the dimension of the scale and growth economies with *objective* character (and that are, as such, unavoidable) does not seem to explain the conglomerations and industrial gigantism that we observe. After all, these economies rarely operate together so as to generate strong counter tendencies with respect to the dimensional boundary deriving from the centralization of the entrepreneur's decision making accompanying gigantism.

The analysis developed in this section shows the erroneousness of Galbraith's prediction[25] of a continuous expansion, in modern societies, of economic planning to the detriment of the market, consequent on the continuous growth of the dimensions of the firm. This means also that Galbraith's derivative prediction of the tendency of capitalism and socialism to converge toward social planning is groundless.

Our analysis also shows that in current decentralized economic systems, the firm as an institution achieves a rationalization of productive processes far below its potential; this being a consequence of the fact that gigantism proliferates well beyond objective necessities. Of course, large dimensions have (and always will have) an important role – sometimes even in stimulating 'dynamic competition' – both through their activity in the international market and also because they imply a reduction of market imperfections due to lack of information and the possible presence of a large number of separate little firms. But it does not appear that the existence and imperialism of giant firms are justified by objective reasons. Immanent and unrestrainable tendencies toward growing industrial and productive concentration do not exist.

5.7 Conclusion

It is our belief that a major deepening of the coordination between the theory of the firm and general economics is indispensable to making heterodox economics more attractive. In fact, a main reason of the survival of the neoclassical theory of the firm and its large number of followers (notwithstanding its inability to consider some crucial aspects of the economy such as innovation, entrepreneurship and uncertainty) is its perfect coordination with general economics.

The current idea of true (or radical) uncertainty as an immeasurable entity represents a main obstacle to the coordination of the heterodox theories of the firm with general economics, a coordination that, in fact, requires a specification of the notion of *dynamic competition* as representing economic process with entrepreneurship, innovation and radical uncertainty.

This chapter has presented a formulation on the firm showing some difference, with respect to usual formulations, in the explanation of capital accumulation, the role of the profit rate and technical progress. Our developments have much to do with the organizational aspect. In particular, the two final sections on the dimension of the firm lead to consideration of important organizational forms and the relative problems, mainly with regard to holdings: organization of group, managerial and multidivisional forms, and centralization versus decentralization.

Notes

1 See Penrose (1995), p. xii.
2 Ibid., p. 37.
3 Ibid., p. 56.
4 See Schumpeter (1954).
5 See Coase (1937), p. 390.
6 See Williamson (1981), p. 154.
7 See, for instance, Hart and Moore (1990). The one-sidedness of this position is well stated by Holmström and Roberts (1998, p. 92), who write: "But this approach also needs to expand its horizon and recognize that power derives from other sources than

154 *Theoretical frame*

   asset ownership and that other incentive instruments than ownership are available to deal with the joint problems of motivation and coordination".
8 See Langlois and Foss (1999), p. 202.
9 See Kirzner (1973), p. 33.
10 See Nelson and Winter (1982), p. 94.
11 See Hodgson (1999), p. 195.
12 The late Institute of Studies and Economic Analyses.
13 See Cyert and March (1963).
14 We agree with Hodgson's criticism on the idea that evolution implies maximization and on some other aspects of the optimization principle, but this author probably would not deny that, for instance, the participants in an examination for, say, a limited number of grants are induced by their ignorance of the worth of rivals to do their best to pass the examination.
15 See Kalecki (1975).
16 See Sraffa (1937).
17 See Galbraith (1968) pp. 55–56.
18 See Penrose (1995).
19 It is extremely difficult to give an empirical content to the distinctions between 1 and 2. Case 1 has an eminently theoretical character; while case 2 represents, with various degrees, the prevailing situation.
20 Often a deeper internal decentralization corresponds to the initial phase of the international expansion of the firm, but in the phase that follows a consolidation of the authority of the mother society will be practiced. In fact, the collection of financing and the use of resources are planned by the central power and the use of corporate planning is extended and strengthened, which implies the reinforcement of the interdependence among the various productive, financial and commercial administrations in the context of the global control and development strategy elaborated by the staff of the multinational firm according to a unitary logic. The adoption of refined methods to condition and train the directors warrants their behavioral uniformity, thus making easy the coordination of the activity of associated firms.
21 See Penrose (1995), p. 98.
22 Ibid., p. 150.
23 Something analogous is witnessed by the fact that a lot of innovations have been produced by small and medium-sized firms, while only excessively large firms, well endowed with financial capital and an efficient commercial organization, intervene to give full value to these innovations.
24 That is, the economies deriving from existing nonutilization of managerial resources (the services of which cannot be sold in the market) that E. Penrose has emphasized. These economies may cease with the end of the expansion that generated them; therefore, they do not imply economies of dimension.
25 See Galbraith (1968).

References

Alchian, A. A. & Demsetz, H. (1972), Production, information costs, and economic organization, *American Economic Review*, vol. 62, pp. 777–795.

Berardi, G. G. (1967), Concentrazione, conglomerate business e fusioni nell'industria nordamericana, *Rivista di Politica Economica*, Estratto fasc. XI, November, year LVII series 3, pp. 3–40.

Bolton, P. & Scharfstein, D. S. (1998), Corporate finance, the theory of the firm, and organization, *Journal of Economic Perspectives*, vol. 12, no. 4, pp. 95–114.

Cantner, U., Hanush, H. & Pyka, A. (1998), Routinized innovations: Dynamic capabilities in a simulation study, in O. Eliasson & C. Green (eds), *The microfoundations of economic growth*, University of Michigan Press, Ann Arbor, pp. 131–155.

Coase, H. (1937), The nature of the firm, *Economica*, vol. 4, pp. 386–405.
Cyert, R. M. & March, J. C. (1963), *A behavioral theory of the firm*, Prentice Hall, Englewood Cliffs, New Jersey.
Dosi, G. & Teece, D. J. (1998), Organizational competence and the boundaries of the firm, in R. A. Arena & C. Longhi (eds), *Market and organization*, Springer, Berlin, pp. 281–301.
Drucker, P. F. (1985), *Innovation and entrepreneurship*, Heinemann, London.
Foss, N. J. (1997), *Resources, firms and strategies*, Oxford University Press, Oxford.
Fusari, A. (1989), *Simulations of economic policies and strategies with a macrodynamic model of the Italian economy*, Proceedings of Beijing International Conference, Pergamon Press.
Fusari, A. (1992), Entrepreneurship, market process and economic development, some theoretical and empirical insights useful for managing the transition period, in W. Owinski, J. Stefanski & A. Straszak (eds), *Transition to advanced market economies*, The Association of Polish Operational Research Societies, Warszawa, pp. 255–268.
Fusari, A. (1996), Paths of economic development: Modeling factors of endogenous growth, *International Journal of Social Economics*, vol. 23, no. 10/11, pp. 164–191.
Fusari, A. (2005), A model of the innovation-adaptation mechanism driving economic dynamics: A micro representation, *Journal of Evolutionary Economics*, vol. 15, no. 3, pp. 297–333.
Galbraith, J. K. (1968), *The new industrial state*, Einaudi, Turin.
Grebel, T., Hanush, H. & Pyka, A. (2001), *An evolutionary approach to the theory of entrepreneurship*, EAEPE conference of Siena.
Griliches, Z. (1990), Patent statistics as economic indicators: A survey, *Journal of Economic Literature*, vol. XXVIII, December, pp. 1661–1707.
Hart, O. & Moore, J. (1990), Property rights and the nature of the firm, *Journal of Political Economy*, vol. 98, pp. 1119–1158.
Hodgson, G. M. (1999), *Evolution and institutions*, Edward Elgar, Cheltenham, UK and Northampton, MA.
Holmström, B. & Roberts, J. (1998), The boundaries of the firm, *Journal of Economic Perspective*, vol. 12, no. 4, Fall, pp. 1273–1294.
Ietto-Gillies, G. (2012), *Transnational corporations and international production: Concepts, theories and effects*, Edward Elgar, Cheltenham and Northampton.
Kaldor, N. (1934), The equilibrium of the firm, *Economic Journal*, vol. XLIV, pp. 60–71.
Kalecki, M. (1975), *Entrepreneurial capital and investments*, Einaudi, Turin.
Kirzner, I. M. (1973), *Competition and entrepreneurship*, The University of Chicago Press, Chicago and London.
Knight, F. H. (1921), *Risk, uncertainty and profit*, Houghton Mifflin, New York.
Langlois, R. N. & Foss, N. J. (1999), Capabilities and governance: The rebirth of production in the theory of economic organization, *Kyklos*, vol. 52, pp. 201–218.
Langlois, R. N. & Robertson, P. L. (1995), *Firms, markets and economic change*, Routledge, London.
Morroni, M. (2005), *Knowledge, scale and transactions in the theory of the firm*, Cambridge University Press, Cambridge.
Nelson, R. R. & Winter, S. G. (1982), *An evolutionary theory of economic change*, The Belknap Press of Harvard University Press, Cambridge, MA and London.
Penrose, E. (1995), *The theory of the growth of the firm*, Oxford University Press, Oxford.
Polanyi, M. (1966), *The tacit dimension*, Doubleday, Garden City, NY.
Richardson, G. B. (1972), The organization of industry, *The Economic Journal*, vol. 82, pp. 883–896.

Saviotti, P. P. (1996), *Technological evolution, variety and the economy*, Edward Elgar, Cheltenham.
Scandizzo, P. L. (2002), *Il mercato e l'impresa: le teorie e i fatti*, Giappichelli, Torino.
Schakle, G. L. S. (1990), *Time, expectation and uncertainty in economics: Selected essays*, edited by J. L. Ford, Edward Elgar, Aldershot.
Schumpeter, J. A. (1934), *The theory of economic development*, Harvard University Press, Cambridge, MA.
Schumpeter, J. A. (1954), *Capitalism, socialism and democracy*, George Allen and Unwin, London.
Shell, K. (1967), A model of inventive activity and capital accumulation, in *Essays on the theory of optimal economic growth*, K. Shell, ed. MIT Press, Cambridge, MA, pp. 67–85.
Scott, M. F. (1989), *A new view of economic growth*, Clarendon Press, Oxford.
Simon, H. A. (1997), *Models of bounded rationality, vol. 3: Empirically grounded economic reason*, The MIT Press, Cambridge, MA.
Sraffa, P. (1937), *Le leggi della produttività in regime di concorrenza*, UTET, Torino.
Williamson, O. E. (1981), The modern corporation: Origins, evolution, attributes, *Journal of Economic Literature*, vol. XIX, December, pp. 1537–1568.

6 Radical uncertainty, dynamic competition and a model of the business cycle

The implications of a measure and an explanation of what is supposed immeasurable and unexplainable[1]

6.1 Introduction

We have seen that a strange and elusive specter haunts economists and businessmen – the spectre of uncertainty, intended as 'true' or 'radical uncertainty', that is, uncertainty that cannot be represented by probability distributions but is the result of the limits of human knowledge and hence an expression of human ignorance. Such a specification is not always made and, indeed, general and widespread conceptual misconceptions and ambiguities concerning the definition and theoretical status of uncertainty make this phenomenon embarrassing to the theoretical economist. Radical uncertainty may be dampened by the obtaining of information, but it is likely to be stimulated by social change and innovation. Thus, the presence and influence of 'radical uncertainty' tends to grow with the increasing innovation driving the dynamism of modern economies. Indeed, one of the main implications of the Schumpeterian teaching on innovation concerns the rise of endogenous uncertainty and its effects on the economy. But as we previously saw, such an implication was almost ignored by Schumpeter and continues to be disregarded by many of his followers.

Students of the firm and the schools of business administration and organization are paying growing attention to the phenomenon of uncertainty. But widespread conceptual ambiguities persist, in particular the identification of uncertainty with known probability distributions that, as such, express probabilistic certainty.[2] On the other side, many students who emphasize the distinction between risk and uncertainty[3] have unanimously drawn, from the fact that uncertainty cannot be represented by definition through known distributions of probability, the conclusion that it cannot be measured at all. It is true that heterodox economists[4] do emphasize the limits of knowledge, radical uncertainty and the associated notion of bounded rationality, but, for the most part, they persist in considering uncertainty as a sort of vague atmosphere permeating reality that is impossible to overlook but also impossible to measure.

The resulting absence of data on and quantitative indicators of radical uncertainty represent a serious and embarrassing lacuna that entails, among other things, that students who place importance on quantitative analysis are obliged to use specifications with probability distributions as a means of quantitatively expressing uncertainty. This chapter will attempt to remedy this situation.

158 *Theoretical frame*

The plan of the chapter is as follows. Section 6.2 points out the difference between expectation and uncertainty. Section 6.3 explores the volatility of opinion, highlights the inability of the Business Tendency Surveys (BTS) data as usually computed to represent the intensity of the relationship between registered changes of opinions and actual results, and delineates some ways of calculating the degree of radical uncertainty from these surveys and some other indicator useful for the interpretation of surveys data. Section 6.4 presents some applications concerning the relationship between uncertainty and the size of the firm. In addition, this section discusses the relationship between uncertainty and the 'business confidence indicator' and carries out some econometric estimates on this matter; moreover, the section presents some other applications and corrections concerning BTS data, mainly based on the degree of permanence of the registered opinions. Section 6.5 extends the question of uncertainty to a wider theoretical perspective centered on the notion of dynamic competition; it presents a model with innovation and uncertainty and its extension to the business cycle, and it brings up the topic of an econometric test that uses a FIML (full information maximum likelihood) estimator.[5]

6.2 Clarification of notions: uncertainty versus expectations

The subject of this chapter obliges us to recall the difference between uncertainty and expectation briefly considered in Chapter 1. *Radical uncertainty* refers to uncertain events that lack an objective or subjective probability distribution. It may seem at first sight that the notion of subjective probability – that is, the degree of personal confidence that an event may happen and the connected notion of expectation – expresses a measure of uncertainty. But this is mistaken. It is important to emphasize that expectation does not represent implied uncertainty, but just an opinion. While personal degree of confidence and expectation are subjective entities expressing anticipation and hope, our research is concerned with ascertaining an objective measure of uncertainty, where uncertainty results from the limits of knowledge and is thus an expression of the degree of ignorance; such a measure is not given by people's expectations but rather by the instability and/or delusory nature of their expectations.[6]

Uncertainty expresses a disability caused by the limited reach of knowledge, and in contrast, expectation is the expression of an attempt to penetrate the fog of cognitive vagueness, that is, a reaction against uncertainty. Because they are different phenomena, the effects of uncertainty on economic variables differ from those due to expectations. The distinction between expectations and uncertainty is illustrated by our identification of changes in or the volatility of firms' opinions as indicators of uncertainty. In fact, these indicators merely express the fragility of expectations.

Another point deserves attention. It is possible to estimate the value of some proxies that provide a measure of expectations. But the *accuracy* of the estimation of such expectations is questionable. As we said, economists claim to have formulated analytical expressions of static expectations, adaptive expectations and rational expectations. These expressions substantially share the assumption of perfect knowledge. But each entrepreneur has his own proper expectations, the degree of accuracy of which will only appear *ex post*. It does not make sense to suppose some general rule of formation of expectations, especially not in the case of entrepreneurship, which is, in its very nature, action in the face of radical uncertainty.

But the key point is that, while uncertainty and expectations are measurable, uncertainty is a different thing altogether from expectation. The importance of an objective measure of uncertainty is indisputable. For instance, 'decision theory' can be substantially improved if a measure of true (or radical) uncertainty is conjoined to a subjective distribution of probability. Such a measure is also indispensable for the analysis of dynamic competition and the connected business cycle, as we shall see in Section 6.5. Nevertheless, it appears an exaggerated pretension to offer a general solution to the problem of measuring uncertainty. To grasp the spirit of this elusive variable, more than one quantitative indicator must be defined, as we shall see in the next section; and some indicator resulting from a weighted average of various indicators should be put forth.

6.3 An analytical framework for the study of survey answers and the measurement of radical uncertainty

6.3.1 Theoretical tool

A main purpose of the Business Tendency Surveys is the desire to investigate how opinions, expectations and, in sum, the considered phenomena vary over time. Indeed, these surveys are regularly repeated precisely because understanding of such variation is the goal; in the absence of change, a single survey would suffice to represent the situation once and forever. It is therefore of paramount importance to derive, from the various answers of the interviewed subjects, the largest amount and the best quality of information possible regarding changes in opinions, expectations and other relevant behaviors. But this exigency does not seem properly fulfilled by the current uses of the data provided by the European Union surveys. One (of several) consequences of this failure is that an important possibility of measuring true or radical uncertainty is obscured from view. What we shall see, in fact, is that the volatility of opinions and the difference between expectations and results as expressed by the Business Tendency Surveys and usually disregarded can be interpreted as a measure of radical uncertainty and, once noted, may facilitate the investigation of the important effects of uncertainty on entrepreneurial and economic behavior, specifically with regard to the business cycle. Such a measure would very likely prove itself to be one of the most profitable uses of the surveys, which are harmonized in all EU countries and thereby provide precious homogeneous data series.

A useful starting point of the analysis is a matrix assembling the survey results of two periods. The rows and columns of the matrix refer to the first and second

160 Theoretical frame

Table 6.1 Survey answers of two periods

Total	Y_1 (up)	Y_2 (same)	Y_3 (down)
X_1 (up)	R_{11}	R_{12}	R_{13}
X_2 (same)	R_{21}	R_{22}	R_{23}
X_3 (down)	R_{31}	R_{32}	R_{33}

periods, respectively, and express the modalities of answer (up, same, down, indicated respectively by the subscripts 1, 2, 3). The matrix is shown in Table 6.1.

X expresses the percent of each modality of answer (on total answers) in the first period, and Y expresses the same percent in the second period. R_{ij} with $i = j$, that is, the terms on the main diagonal, indicate for each modality the percentage of answers that do not change from one period to another. The remaining R_{ij} (i.e. with $i \neq j$) express the percentage of answers changing from modality i in the first period to modality j in the second period.

The current publications on the survey data show only the total by row (X) and column (Y) and the balance (up minus down), while the intermediate terms of the matrix (the transition from modality i to j) are absent. But the intermediate terms are indispensable for representing the changes in answers; in fact, the total of each modality hides changes over time by compensation.

6.3.2 Indicators of radical uncertainty

The matrix data allow the computation of some useful indicators, such as the volatility of opinions (or of results), that is, the sum of the terms of the matrix outside the main diagonal; in fact, that sum can be interpreted as an important *indicator of radical or true uncertainty*. The indicator can be formalized as follows:

$$OV = \Sigma_{t0}{}^{t1} R_{ij} \quad \text{with } i \neq j$$

OV stands for opinions' (or results') volatility.[7]

The reference to opinions and expectations stresses the need to measure their volatility. But the volatility of the answers concerning results not considered by the applications in this chapter may also be important under other respects.

To this measure of uncertainty based on the volatility of opinions, it might be objected that, by the time a new state of the world arises, this makes the change of opinion no longer a signal of uncertainty. This objection is based on a clear misunderstanding. In formulating expectations, one uses the information that one has on the state of the world; when information and/or opinions change, due to changes in the state of the world or for other reasons, new expectations will be formulated, but without the achievement of certainty – such a goal being but a chimera. It is quite natural to refer uncertainty of opinions to the volatility of opinions, that is, their variability, whatever their accuracy (and whatever the causes of their variability).

As a simple matter of fact, respondents can be very uncertain about expectations that turn out to be accurate.

We do not deny that a proxy of uncertainty based on the volatility of opinions has its limitations, as does any kind of empirical analysis. In fact, the phenomena considered by the surveys do not cover all the causes of uncertainty. To partly remedy this, a second indicator has been provided through a direct question. Specifically, starting from April 2004, and at our request, an additional question was included in the ISAE[8] quarterly business surveys: "In the last months, what proportion of your expectations on some main variables (demand and delivery orders, profit, variable costs) was confirmed?"

There exist some differences as well as analogies between the first (indirect) and the second (direct) indicators of uncertainty. While the first indicator expresses the volatility of expectations, the second expresses the effective violation of expectations. An evident linkage between the two indicators is that the nonconfirmation of expectations, expressed by the second indicator, may cause changes in expectations and hence in the first indicator.

We can identify a third indicator of uncertainty in the standard deviation of profit rates across firms. In an economy of perfect knowledge and in the absence of institutional monopolies, such deviations would be null. It is the existence of limits to knowledge (true uncertainty) that allows differentials in capabilities and the associated profits to rise. This seems to imply that the variance of profit rates across firms provides an expression of the limits of knowledge, that is, of uncertainty. As we shall see, this indicator is suitable to the representation of dynamic competition processes and business cycles.[9]

Our transition matrix of survey answers allows the derivation of some other useful indicators. It is worthwhile to dedicate some attention to what can be called a *permanence indicator*. Clearly, the answers resulting from very fragile opinions (i.e. opinions that are subject to change) are less meaningful than those resulting from less volatile opinions. This is not a question of mere reliability. The permanence of respondents' opinions (or their volatility) may be right or wrong; the point, however, is that if a respondent is, for instance, wrongly convinced of something, he operates accordingly. Conviction (in doing something) therefore represents a relevant item of information for understanding his behavior. This underlines the importance of an indicator of the degree of permanence of answers, which can be expressed as follows:

$$\text{PermUp} = R_{11}^{(t0:t1)}/\text{Up}^{(t1)}$$

This gives the proportion of the answers saying that Up does not change from period t_0 to t_1, on the percent of Up relative to period t_1. Of course, the permanence indicator for same and down must substitute in the expression 1, respectively, R_{22} and R_{33} to R_{11}, and same or down to up. These indicators can be used to weight the current percent of up, same and down, in order to obtain some new values for each modality that take into account the degree of insistence on answers; such insistence expresses any one particular marked direction of firms' expectations and opinions.

A stronger way to compute the persistence indicator is the following:

$$\text{PermUp} = (R_{11}^{(t0:t1)} + 2\, R''_{11}^{(t1:t2)})/3\text{Up}^{(t1)}$$

where R''_{11} represents the portion of the R_{11} that does not change also in the period $t_1: t_2$ or, in other words, the percentage of respondents that give the same answer in three consecutive surveys (we attribute a double weight to R''). The expression of the permanence indicator for same and down is identical, with the due changes in R and the denominator.[10]

An average of two consecutive periods may also be considered, that is:

$$\text{PermUp} = (R_{11}^{(t0:t1)} + R_{11}^{(t1:t2)})/2\text{Up}^{(t1)}$$

A different weight may be attributed to the R of the two periods.

6.4 Evidence from the business surveys

6.4.1 Uncertainty and the size of the firm

The results that follow refer to the volatility indicator OV and have been derived from the answers to the EU-ISAE monthly surveys of business tendency and conditions for a sample of firms that are representative of all industrial sectors and Italian geographical areas. The answers refer to expectations over the next three or four months, discounted by all seasonal factors and concern: delivery orders, production, prices, cost of financing and liquidity assets. These variables are defined by three modalities: modality 1, expressing 'increase' (in the rate of change of the variables); modality 2, indicating 'no change'; and modality 3, expressing 'decrease'.

The EU-ISAE Business Tendency Surveys report the number of persons employed by each firm, so the indicator of uncertainty derived from them can be distinguished according to the size of the firm. This provides for some important information. For instance, if the firm's behaviors and organization are influenced by uncertainty, then we can ask whether this uncertainty varies according to size. We have grouped firms by size into six classes. The first class (up to 15 employees) intends to show the influence of uncertainty on dimensional growth beyond the threshold that marked the effectiveness of the Italian Working People Statute. We consider here unweighted answers since the attribution of the same weight to each opinion gives a better expression of the state of opinions than answers weighted according to the size of the firm. The average (of each column) for the whole period is shown, providing a clear idea of the standard deviation (from the average) over the period considered.

The monthly data have been aggregated by year and computed starting from 1986. But the Tables 6.2 through 6.7 start from 1998, when some modifications in the survey generate a discontinuity, and terminate in 2005 for the same reason.

As we can see, uncertainty (as expressed by the indicator considered) varies inversely with the size of firms and is around 0.2 and 0.4. The high level of uncertainty of the first two classes (1–15 and 16–99 employees) means that expansion

Table 6.2 Uncertainty on production (relative change of answers based on previous month)

Years	Size of firm					
	1–15	16–99	100–249	250–324	325–499	500 and above
1998	0.385	0.345	0.325	0.342	0.334	0.292
1999	0.389	0.35	0.335	0.339	0.34	0.306
2000	0.395	0.358	0.333	0.296	0.316	0.274
2001	0.405	0.379	0.366	0.406	0.323	0.322
2002	0.373	0.35	0.343	0.38	0.33	0.274
2003	0.402	0.378	0.347	0.345	0.341	0.304
2004	0.4	0.378	0.35	0.345	0.365	0.292
2005	0.386	0.356	0.361	0.350	0.325	0.277
Average	0.391	0.362	0.345	0.350	0.334	0.293

Table 6.3 Uncertainty on delivery orders and demand (relative change of answers based on previous month)

Years	Size of firm					
	1–15	16–99	100–249	250–324	325–499	500 and above
1998	0.395	0.355	0.329	0.331	0.325	0.279
1999	0.399	0.357	0.335	0.339	0.333	0.289
2000	0.398	0.362	0.334	0.329	0.318	0.288
2001	0.412	0.388	0.374	0.405	0.353	0.332
2002	0.385	0.359	0.357	0.39	0.34	0.296
2003	0.413	0.391	0.360	0.369	0.357	0.311
2004	0.408	0.386	0.355	0.337	0.376	0.276
2005	0.4	0.367	0.353	0.378	0.351	0.265
Average	0.401	0.370	0.349	0.359	0.344	0.292

Table 6.4 Uncertainty on prices (relative change of answers based on previous month)

Years	Size of firm					
	1–15	16–99	100–249	250–324	325–499	500 and above
1998	0.186	0.209	0.211	0.261	0.242	0.229
1999	0.212	0.22	0.210	0.221	0.205	0.164
2000	0.294	0.293	0.261	0.295	0.27	0.243
2001	0.25	0.245	0.217	0.256	0.246	0.215
2002	0.181	0.186	0.196	0.151	0.239	0.181
2003	0.196	0.212	0.222	0.192	0.216	0.188
2004	0.195	0.200	0.196	0.17	0.179	0.169
2005	0.176	0.174	0.172	0.162	0.176	0.193
Average	0.211	0.217	0.210	0.213	0.221	0.198

Table 6.5 Uncertainty on cost of financing (relative change of answers based on previous month)

Years	Size of firm					
	1–15	16–99	100–249	250–324	325–499	500 and above
1998	0.317	0.306	0.301	0.317	0.316	0.229
1999	0.276	0.284	0.257	0.281	0.229	0.195
2000	0.338	0.323	0.294	0.309	0.242	0.242
2001	0.336	0.315	0.287	0.294	0.249	0.217
2002	0.271	0.260	0.246	0.235	0.225	0.191
2003	0.324	0.304	0.282	0.281	0.251	0.207
2004	0.315	0.277	0.237	0.216	0.211	0.173
2005	0.296	0.244	0.192	0.198	0.162	0.107
Average	0.309	0.289	0.262	0.266	0.235	0.195

Table 6.6 Uncertainty on liquidity assets (relative change of answers based on previous month)

Years	Size of firm					
	1–15	16–99	100–249	250–324	325–499	500 and above
1998	0.317	0.281	0.26	0.284	0.262	0.217
1999	0.31	0.274	0.232	0.22	0.277	0.205
2000	0.332	0.297	0.251	0.254	0.243	0.255
2001	0.349	0.311	0.294	0.221	0.275	0.246
2002	0.315	0.279	0.274	0.245	0.236	0.222
2003	0.351	0.314	0.262	0.261	0.282	0.241
2004	0.361	0.311	0.259	0.204	0.248	0.213
2005	0.355	0.304	0.247	0.194	0.257	0.196
Average	0.336	0.296	0.260	0.235	0.260	0.224

Table 6.7 General level of uncertainty, derived by the aggregation of the previous series (relative change of answers based on previous month)

Years	Size of firm					
	1–15	16–99	100–249	250–324	325–499	500 and above
1998	0.32	0.299	0.285	0.307	0.296	0.249
1999	0.317	0.297	0.274	0.28	0.277	0.232
2000	0.351	0.326	0.295	0.297	0.278	0.260
2001	0.35	0.328	0.307	0.317	0.289	0.267
2002	0.305	0.287	0.283	0.280	0.274	0.233
2003	0.337	0.32	0.295	0.290	0.290	0.250
2004	0.336	0.310	0.286	0.254	0.276	0.225
2005	0.323	0.289	0.265	0.256	0.254	0.208
Average	0.330	0.307	0.286	0.285	0.279	0.240

A model of the business cycle 165

over the threshold of 15 employees is discouraged, since it implies an increase in normative rigidities while uncertainty remains high.

Uncertainty decreases with increase in firms' size in the first three classes but shows some ambiguity in the two central classes and decreases substantially in the largest class. In particular, increase in size of firms significantly reduces the variability of expectations on cost of financing, and this, together with the parallel reduction of uncertainty on liquidity assets, should encourage dimensional expansion.

The uncertainty on prices is less than on other variables; it is particularly low in the largest class of firms, probably due to oligopoly, and lower than expected in the first class, probably owing to market niches.

It may be useful to add some data on the second (direct) indicator of uncertainty which, it will be recalled, expresses the effective violation of expectations. For reasons of space, we limit ourselves to a graphic comparison of the two indicators. Figures 6.1 and 6.2 refer, respectively, to the first and the second indicator.

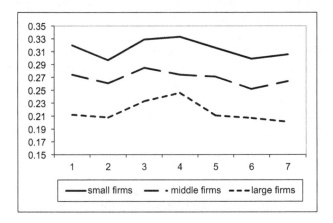

Figure 6.1 First indicator of uncertainty by classes of business size

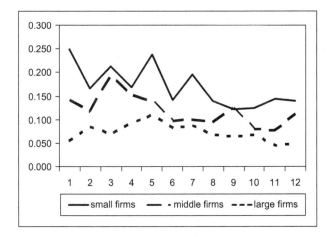

Figure 6.2 Second indicator of uncertainty by classes of business size

166 *Theoretical frame*

Figure 6.1 shows quarterly data from April 2004 to (only) October 2005 (as the computation of this indicator is disturbed in 2006 by a jump in the modality of survey). Figure 6.2 shows 12 quarterly data, from April 2004 to January 2007.

The second graph is more uneven than the first, probably due to the absence of deseasonalization (made impossible by the smaller amount of data) and to the fact that the revision of expectations is slower than their violation. Uncertainty appears to be lower in Figure 6.2, since this only considers the modality 'low confirmation' of expectations, due to the absence of weights attributed to the modalities 'high confirmation' and 'middle confirmation'. However, in both figures, uncertainty markedly decreases with increase in business size. The inverse relation between uncertainty and firms' size is thus confirmed; this is relevant for firms' transaction costs, financing and innovation, as these are greatly influenced by uncertainty.

Finally, it may be useful to provide three figures (Figure 6.3) illustrating the indirect indicator of uncertainty derived from the expectations and realizations differences of the ISAE monthly surveys. The graphs show the percentage of expectations in period t that differ from the realizations relative to one, two and three months later. Unfortunately, in recent years, the survey questions on results have been limited by ISAE to only liquidity assets and production, and this of course reduces the possibility of confrontation between expectations and results. The confrontation considered here refers to the year 2004. The six classes of size are indicated on the x axis.

This indicator of uncertainty based on the difference between expectation and realization substantially confirms the results derived from Tables 6.2, 6.4 and 6.6,

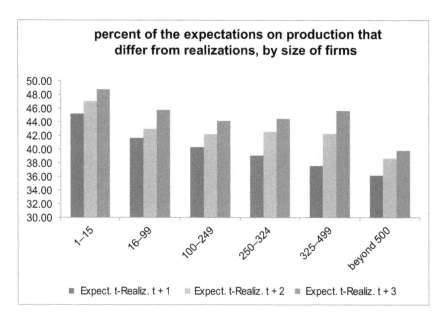

Figure 6.3 Expectations and realizations differences

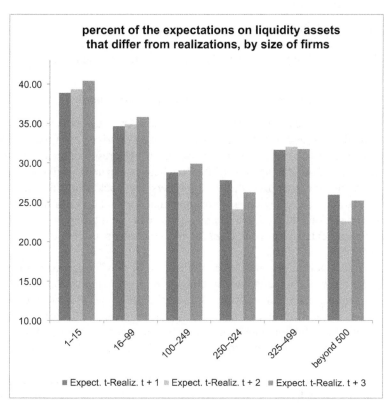
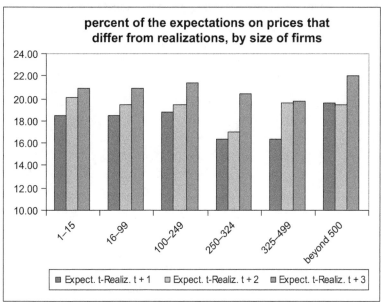

Figure 6.3 (Continued)

168 *Theoretical frame*

except that uncertainty on prices in the last class is higher than expected. It also appears that the difference between expectations and realizations grows with the time distance between the two, but with some exception for liquidity assets.

6.4.2 Business confidence indicator corrected for uncertainty

Our research on a measure of the degree of uncertainty leads us to some reflections upon the business confidence indicator currently derived from the monthly Business Tendency Surveys (BTS). This indicator is the result of an arithmetical average of the balances of answers (difference between up and down) concerning three phenomena: current overall delivery orders, the stock of finished products and expectations on production. Such computation does not consider uncertainty; in fact, expectations on production cannot be considered a proxy of uncertainty, which is rather expressed by the *volatility* of expectations, as previously seen in Section 6.3.

Of course, uncertainty influences the degree of confidence more than do any of the three phenomena usually considered in the standard computation of the business confidence indicator. It may, therefore, be interesting to compare between the current confidence indicator and our indicator of uncertainty. Both the indicators have been expressed in quarterly values, with 2000 being the year base. Figure 6.4 compares radical uncertainty to the confidence indicator.

As can be seen, the behavior of uncertainty differs markedly from that of the usual confidence indicator; it is in general higher and more uneven. This means that the possible introduction of uncertainty in the computation of the confidence

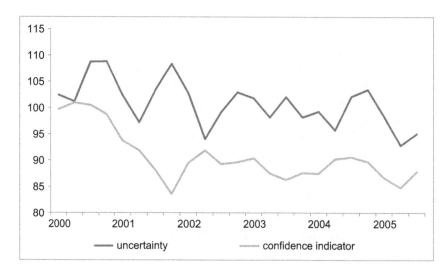

Figure 6.4 Radical uncertainty and confidence indicator

A model of the business cycle 169

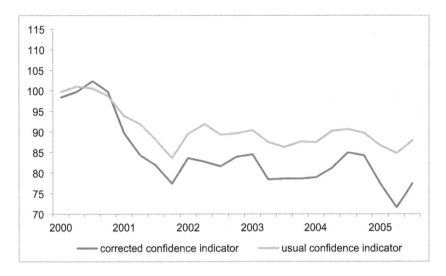

Figure 6.5 Usual confidence indicator and that corrected by radical uncertainty

indicator would lead to some remarkable changes with regard to the current computation of the indicator. This is shown in Figure 6.5. This figure compares the usual confidence indicator to an indicator that is derived by adding radical uncertainty with a weight of 0.25, and hence attributing to the usual indicator a weight of 0.75. The working hypothesis is that each one of the four components has an identical importance, although it is our actual opinion that a higher weight should be attributed to uncertainty. Of course, the influence of uncertainty on the confidence indicator is negative.

The figure shows substantial differences between the two indicators. Since in Figure 6.4 the uncertainty indicator was above the usual confidence indicator, the new confidence indicator shown in Figure 6.5 is lower than the usual one. The moderate weight of uncertainty in the computation of the new confidence indicator prevents higher differences between the time paths of the two.

It can be objected that the weight we have attributed to uncertainty in our hypothetical revision of the confidence indicator is arbitrary. But the attribution of identical weights to the three survey questions – which is used for the definition of the current confidence indicator – is also arbitrary. An approach to dealing with the question of weight attribution might be econometric testing. Here we set out some estimation of the relation between industrial production, volatility and the usual confidence indicator. The results are not completely satisfactory but nevertheless warrant some attention. They seem to suggest a deepening of the analysis on the confidence indicator and its components.

170 *Theoretical frame*

The following differential adjustment equation has been estimated:

$$DIP = \alpha\,(\hat{IP} - IP)$$
$$\hat{IP} = \beta_1 CI - \beta_2 OV$$

where:
IP = Variation of the index of industrial production
CI = Usual confidence indicator
OV = Opinions' volatility
D = Derivative with respect to time
α = Adjustment parameter

The estimate uses data concerning Italy.[11] Monthly survey data have been used from February 2000 to April 2011. Industrial production does not show a trend component and hence does not require filtering (Hodrick-Prescott or other filters) for eliminating such a trend.

The results are:

Parameters	t-values
α = 2.969	5.69
β_1 = 2.328	1.4
β_2 = 0.946	1.38
Carter–Nagar R^2 = 0.60	

All parameters show the right sign. These results consider raw IP data; CI is taken by the ISAE balances and is not deseasonalized.

In order to see the degree of significance and contribution of each component, an econometric analysis of the relations between the components of the confidence indicator and the variation of industrial production may be performed, which includes also volatility in the regression. An estimation in this regard using nondeseasonalized values has shown wrong signs, both for the current overall orders and the current stock of finished products; only expectations on production and volatility seem to have an explanatory meaning. Carter-Nagar R^2 is 0.73. This seems to show the importance of the need for a wider inquiry on the definition of the confidence indicator, that is, an inquiry that also takes into account some other survey questions.

6.4.3 *Some applications concerning the permanence indicator and the correction of up, same and down by giving a double weight to R_{ii} (the repeated answers)*[12]

The results that will follow concern three questions of the harmonized EU surveys, two of which express opinions and one expresses expectations. The questions are:

1 Do you consider current overall order to be above normal, normal for the season, below normal?

2 Do you consider your current stock of finished products to be above normal, normal for the season, below normal?
3 How do you expect your production to develop over the next three months? It will increase, remain unchanged, decrease?

The attention for those questions has been suggested by the importance that the European Commission attributes to them; they are used to provide the Industry Confidence Indicator for each state member of the European Community and the whole European Union. It seems evident that the dynamics of opinions are better expressed by unweighted survey data, as these give an identical importance to each answer and opinion.

An analogous application was performed on data for South Africa provided by Murray Pellissier and concerning four questions of the BER surveys on expectations. The results confirmed those reported here.

Figures 6.6 through 6.17 flank, to the EU survey's results, those 'modified' or corrected according to the weight attributed to R_{ii}, that is, the repeated answers. Here we give to these answers a *double weight* with respect to Up-R_{11}, that is, the remaining ones. Therefore, the expression for the corrected (or modified) up is:

$$\text{ModifiedUp} = (2R_{11} + \text{Up} - R_{11})/3, \text{ that is: } (\text{Up} + R_{11})/3$$

Of course, the correction of same and down must substitute, in the above expression, same or down to up and R_{22} or R_{33} to R_{11}.[13]

For making comparable the current percent of answers to their modified percentages, the sum of the percent of the *modified* up, same and down has been reported

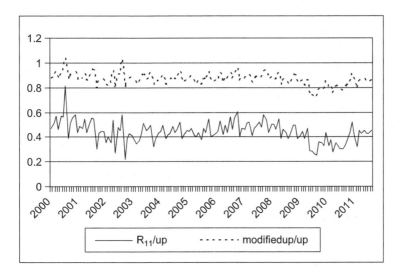

Figure 6.6 Current overall order books, up

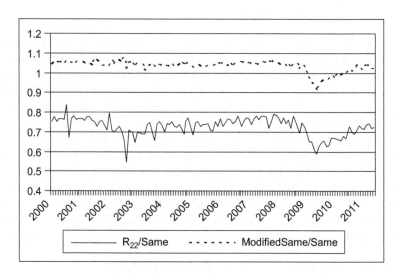

Figure 6.7 Current overall order books, same

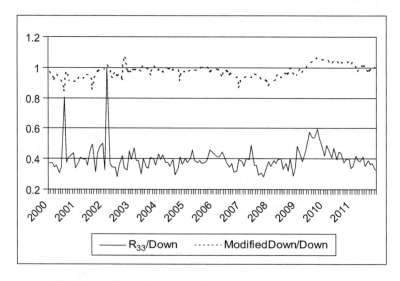

Figure 6.8 Current overall order books, down

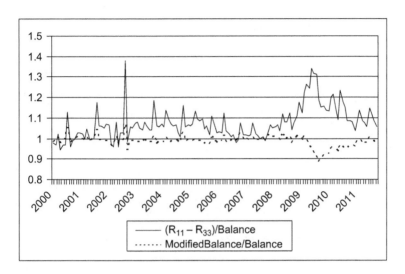

Figure 6.9 Current overall order books, balance

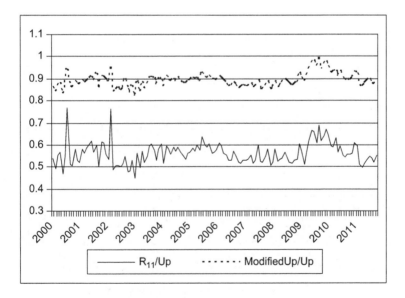

Figure 6.10 Current stock of finished products, up

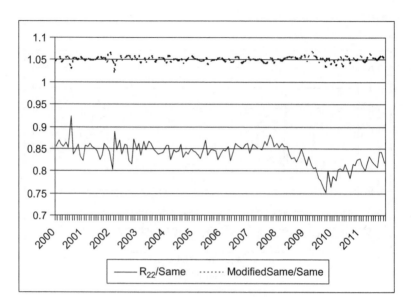

Figure 6.11 Current stock of finished products, same

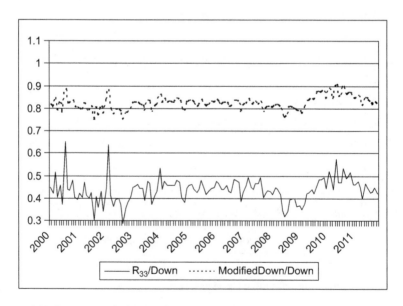

Figure 6.12 Current stock of finished products, down

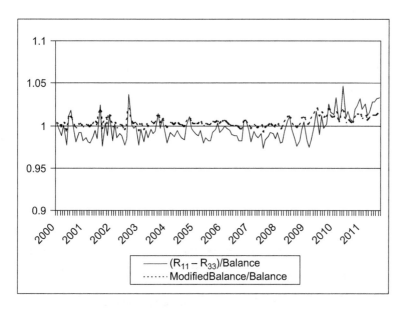

Figure 6.13 Current stock of finished products, balance

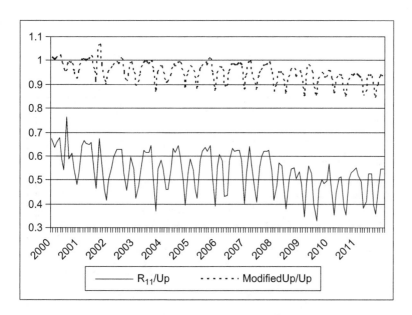

Figure 6.14 Production expectations, up

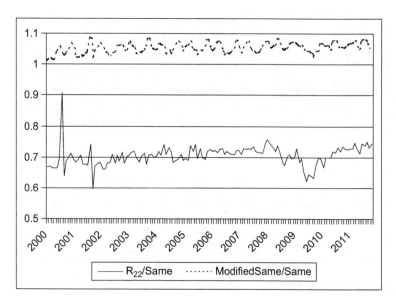

Figure 6.15 Production expectations, same

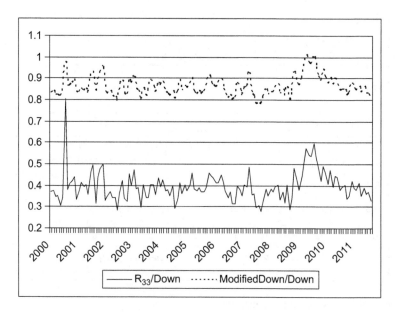

Figure 6.16 Production expectations, down

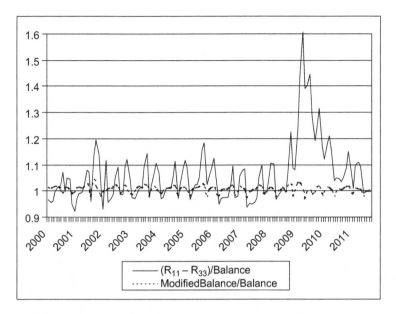

Figure 6.17 Production expectations, balance

to 100 (i.e. the sum of the *current* percent modalities of answers) simply by dividing 100 by the sum of the percent of all modified answers and multiplying by the percent of each modified answer,[14] that is, according the proportion ModifiedUp: x = modified (up + same + down)]: 100, as well as for same and down.

The figures report:

a   The permanence indicator, the first expression for PermUp (same and down) in Section 6.3, that is, a ratio the variability over time of which expresses the discrepancy between the time path of the percentage of the repeated answers (not considered by the current computations on surveys) and the total percent of the corresponding answers (up or same or down); it gives, therefore, an idea of the relevance of the correction we propose.
b   The ratio between the modified percent of answers and the usual percent of answers. The difference (positive or negative) with respect to one of this ratio expresses the *percentage of correction*, that is, the percent difference between the modified and current percentages.
c   The ratio $(R_{11}-R_{33})$/Balance, that gives the variation over time of the difference of the percent of the repeated up and down (that we use for corrections) with respect to up minus down, that is, the usual balances. This ratio gives an idea of the impact on balances of our correction. Such correction is plainly expressed by the ratio between the modified balance and the usual one: (ModifiedUp − ModifiedDown)/(Up − Down), that is, ModifiedBalance/Balance.

178 *Theoretical frame*

In the figures, variable a is indicated by the permanence indicators R_{11}/Up; R_{22}/Same; R_{33}/Down. The variable b is indicated by the ratios ModifiedUp/Up, ModifiedSame/Same; ModifiedDown/Down. The variables c are indicated, as we said, by (R_{11}–R_{33})/Balance and ModifiedBalance/Balance.

A constant of 100 has been added to R_{11}–R_{33}/Balance, and to modified balance in order to avoid negative numbers that would make meaningless the ratios under c, i.e. (R_{11}–R_{33})/Balance and ModifiedBalance/Balance.

The data concern 11 years or, more precisely, 135 monthly periods of survey, starting from February 2000.

From these figures we can see substantial differences between the UE surveys values and the modified ones (that is, attributing a double weight to the repeated answer R with respect to the remaining one, nonrepeated), but a higher weight of the repeated answers used for the rectification would imply larger differences. The percent correction (dotted lines) is lower than the oscillation of the permanence indicators and the ratio (R_{11}–R_{33})/Balance (full lines) since the first also includes the remaining (nonpermanent) answers that do not contribute to the correction.

In particular, in Figures 6.6 and 6.8 (for up and down), the correction percentage oscillates around 20%, but with a substantial dispersion as an effect of the high dispersion of R_{11}/Up and R_{33}/Down (respectively between 0.8, 0.2 and 0.8, 0.4). Figure 6.7 shows a correction percentage higher than 1 due to the higher value of R_{22}/Same than those of R_{11}/Up and R_{33}/Down. The dispersion is lower than in Figures 6.6 and 6.8 since R_{22}/Same is much less uneven than R_{11}/Up and R_{33}/Down.

Figures 6.10 to 6.13 (for current stock of finished products) and 6.14 and 6.17 (for production expectations) do not show substantial differences with respect to the behavior above.

6.5 Uncertainty, innovation and business cycle

6.5.1 Dynamic competition: the crucial role of uncertainty

The primary goal of this section is to provide further theoretical and empirical evidence of the importance of a measure of radical uncertainty.

The interaction between innovation and uncertainty is at the heart of the mechanism of growth and development and defines the process of dynamic competition in a Schumpeterian and neo-Austrian sense.[15] As we saw in Chapter 1, it is surprising that the two kinds of competition (i.e. Kirzner's market process[16] and Schumpeter's creative destruction[17]) remain separated in the literature despite their evident complementariness. Partly, this is due to the presumption that radical uncertainty cannot be measured or even defined, a presumption that we have widely criticized and challenged in the previous sections.

As we know, dynamic competition is the result of entrepreneurs' adaptive quest for profits as they search for existing profit opportunities arising from disequilibria and uncertainty (neo-Austrian market process), and as they innovatively search for new profit opportunities (Schumpeterian process). There is interaction between both the searches (i.e. adaptation and innovation), with the result depending upon the degree of uncertainty. When uncertainty grows, adaptive (neo-Austrian) competition prevails (i.e. competition directed to the discovery and obtaining of existing profit opportunities). This leads to a reduction in uncertainty and market disequilibria, which stimulates innovation, both to recreate profit opportunities and because low uncertainty makes innovation easier. But innovation stimulates uncertainty again. Once some measure of radical uncertainty becomes available, then a combination of Schumpeterian and neo-Austrian teaching on innovation and market process gains in (operative) effectiveness, and we may thereby hope to provide a more complete explanation and quantification of dynamic competition processes.[18]

In the estimation, we use, for Italy, as indicator of uncertainty, the volatility of expectations. With reference to the other three countries, we use the indicator of uncertainty represented by the standard deviation of profit rates across firms; this seems to offer a good variable for our analysis of dynamic competition and business cycles since it expresses the dimension of adaptive profit opportunities as connected to limited knowledge and market disequilibria. At the same time, for the econometric application that follows, this is sometimes the only available indicator of uncertainty.

As previously noted, innovation feeds uncertainty and the standard deviation of profit rates across firms as a consequence of the increase in market disequilibria, thus stimulating adaptive competition. But adaptive competition causes the reduction in the standard deviation of profit rates and uncertainty and hence a rise in innovation and so on, with a cyclical behavior and alternation between innovation and adaptation.

6.5.2 A formal model

The previous specification suggests the possibility of representing, at the aggregate level, the relation between innovation and disequilibria-uncertainty, as expressed by the notion of dynamic competition, through a Lotka-Volterra predator-prey system, where predation is intended only in formal (not physical) terms. Innovation acts as the prey and uncertainty as the predator, according to the following differential system:

(1) $DPA = b_1 PA - b_2 u * PA$
(2) $Du = -b_3 u + b_4 PA * u$

where:
PA = Patent applications (intended as an indicator of innovation)
u = Radical uncertainty, which may be indicated through its measure in Section 6.3 (the volatility indicator of expectations) or, alternatively, the standard deviation of profit rates across firms
D = Derivative d/d_t
The asterisk * stands for multiplication.

Equation 1 may also include a term DE for the variation of entrepreneurial skill, displaying for innovation (the prey) a propulsive role similar to that of stocking in the predator-prey models used by studies on food chains.[19]

180 Theoretical frame

The parameter b_1 is a constant exponential rate of growth of innovation, expressing the autonomous push to innovate due to entrepreneurial aggressiveness; its impact on innovation (DPA) is reduced by the degree of radical uncertainty (volatility of expectations or the standard deviation of profit rates) u that discourages (preys on) innovation (PA) according to parameter b_2. The parameter b_3 is an exponential rate of growth of radical uncertainty; the negative sign on b_3 expresses the compressing effect on radical uncertainty (and/or on the standard deviation of profit rates) arising out of adaptive competition (as stimulated by u). For its part, b_4 stimulates u according to the cross product between predator and prey, where the prey is the dimension of innovation (PA) that feeds uncertainty (volatility and/or the standard deviation of profit rates), that is, feeds the predator. Precisely, innovation is the field of pasture of radical uncertainty: in the absence of innovation, the term with b_4 would become null because of the adaptive search for profit. When innovation intensifies, u (the predator) grows, thus causing a contraction in innovation (the prey), and hence the predator, with a cyclical alternation. The system parameters give the dimension of the disequilibrating (b_1 and b_4) and equilibrating (b_2 and b_3) push expressed by dynamic competition (this being represented by the combination between innovative and adaptive competition).

It may be useful to underline in this regard that the measures of dynamic competition based on the rapidity of contraction of the standard deviation of profit rates across firms (as, for instance, in D.C. Mueller and others or H. Odagiri)[20] only consider adaptive competition or, more precisely, parameter b_3 of the previous system. They ignore the other parameters and hence give a poor approximation to the intensity of competition and economic dynamism, as dynamic competition consists both of innovation and adaptation (structural organization).

6.5.3 Econometric estimation

The following estimation refers to four main European industrial countries: Italy, the United Kingdom, France and Germany. The data on patent applications and grants are used to express innovation and derive from the Ufficio Italiano Brevetti in the case of Italy and from the United States Department of Commerce in the other cases. The data on radical uncertainty derives from the UE-ISAE Business Tendency Surveys. The data on the standard deviation of profit rates across firms for France and Germany come from D. C. Mueller and H. Odagiri[21] in the case of the United Kingdom; they refer to some samples of manufacturing firms and, respectively, to the periods 1961 to 1982, 1965 to 1982 and 1964 to 1977. It may be objected that these periods are far from the present. But the estimations are only intended to provide an example of econometric application of our theory. At any rate, for Italy, the data on patent applications and uncertainty run from April 2000 to December 2010; they have been aggregated by quarters and deseasonalized.

The data for France give pre-tax profit; those for the United Kingdom and Germany give after-tax profit. Their reliabilities are affected by their derivation from the balance sheets of some firms based on dissimilar and not well-established procedures.

The results shown must be judged in the light of the deficiencies of the appropriate data series. Nevertheless, confirmation of the theory is encouraging. But the improvement of quantitative analysis in the crucial fields of innovation and dynamic competition needs a great deal of statistical research.

A FIML estimator was used to *preserve the tight interaction* between equations 1 and 2 above, that is, innovation and uncertainty (adaptation), which is a crucial point of the research on dynamic competition presented in this section. The estimates are derived by an asymptotically exact Gaussian estimator of a differential equation system using discrete data. As there is no equivalent of a just-identified model for nonlinear systems, there is no system-wide test such as the Carter-Nagar R^2 or likelihood ratio. In order to give an idea of the efficiency of estimations, the means and standard deviations (not to be confused with the standard deviation of profit rates across firms) of the observed and estimated endogenous variables are also reported.

A system which differs from Volterra (pseudo Volterra form), in that the second equation uses only PA instead of the term PA*u in the right-hand side, has also been estimated. As a matter of fact, it may be assumed that the 'reproduction' hypothesis typical of Volterra's study on population plainly operates only in the equation of innovation in that each innovation is strongly influenced by the state of knowledge resulting from previous innovations. In the equation of u, however, it may operate only backward as large disequilibria and uncertainty stimulate adaptation. This means that in equation 2, the cross product term of Volterra, the encounter between predator and prey, may be replaced by the prey (innovation) only.

Data on patent applications have been divided by thousand, for uniformity of their scale with respect to u.

6.3.1 Italy

Table 6.8 Model in Volterra's form

	Estimate of parameters	Asymptotic standard error	t values
b_1	0.033	0.002	15.37
b_2	0.0105	0.0007	14.68
b_3	0.0458	0.0022	20.28
b_4	0.0197	0.0009	20.44

Endogenous variables	Observed		Estimated	
	Mean	Standard deviation	Mean	Standard deviation
PA_t	2.417776	0.146913	2.417424	0.148490
u_t	3.209104	0.122090	3.203985	0.137458

6.3.2 United Kingdom

Table 6.9 Model in Volterra's form

	Estimate of parameters	Asymptotic standard error	t values
b_1	0.519	0.099	5.25
b_2	0.082	0.016	5.19
b_3	1.716	0.504	3.41
b_4	0.367	0.105	3.48

Endogenous variables

	Observed		Estimated	
	Mean	Standard deviation	Mean	Standard deviation
PA_t	4.7876	0.2189	4.7925	0.2982
u_t	6.4006	0.7898	6.3773	0.9747

The model with the term PA in equation 2, instead of PA*u, does not converge.

6.3.3 France

The data series of the standard deviation of profit rates for France has two outlying observations in 1974 and 1977. The first has no justification and is probably due to inaccuracy of the data; the second is largely determined by the 1977 revaluations of the assets of mergers that consistently depressed profit rates. We have substituted for those anomalous data an interpolation from the contiguous data.[22]

Table 6.10 Model in Volterra's form

	Estimate of parameters	Asymptotic standard error	t values
b_1	0.318	0.121	2.61
b_2	0.048	0.019	2.46
b_3	0.558	0.244	2.29
b_4	0.192	0.08	2.40

Endogenous variables

	Observed		Estimated	
	Mean	Standard deviation	Mean	Standard deviation
PA_t	3.0316	0.2261	3.0295	0.2302
u_t	6.3311	0.7627	6.3183	0.8061

A model of the business cycle 183

Table 6.11 Model with the term PA in equation 2 instead of PA*u

	Estimate of parameters	*Asymptotic standard error*	*t values*
b_1	0.252	0.158	1.59
b_2	0.037	0.252	1.48
b_3	0.608	0.348	1.75
b_4	1.32	0.722	1.83

Endogenous variables

	Observed		*Estimated*	
	Mean	*Standard deviation*	*Mean*	*Standard deviation*
PA_t	3.0316	0.2261	3.0263	0.2418
u_t	6.2933	0.7637	6.3072	0.5024

6.3.4 Germany

Table 6.12 Model in Volterra's form

	Estimate of parameters	*Asymptotic standard error*	*t values*
b_1	0.316	0.115	2.74
b_2	0.09	0.037	2.45
b_3	0.089	0.177	0.50
b_4	0.128	0.023	0.56

Endogenous variables

	Observed		*Estimated*	
	Mean	*Standard deviation*	*Mean*	*Standard deviation*
PA_t	7.7933	1.4829	7.7608	1.6193
u_t	3.1622	0.3524	3.1554	0.3401

Table 6.13 Model with the term PA in equation 2 instead of PA*u

	Estimate of parameters	*Asymptotic standard error*	*t values*
b_1	0.333	0.124	2.69
b_2	0.096	0.039	2.43
b_3	0.221	0.164	1.35
b_4	0.095	0.066	1.43

(*Continued*)

Table 6.13 (Continued)

	Estimate of parameters	Asymptotic standard error	t values	
Endogenous variables				
	Observed		Estimated	
	Mean	Standard deviation	Mean	Standard deviation
PA_t	7.7933	1.4829	7.7603	1.5898
u_t	3.1622	0.3524	3.1588	0.281

For Italy, the values of parameters are much lower than in the other countries. This is mainly due to the fact that in the recent period, the rate of growth of patent applications has substantially decreased and the rate of growth of uncertainty has increased, while in the estimation periods concerning the other countries, the rate of growth of patent applications was high and uncertainty (the standard deviation of profit rates across firms) was decreasing.

For Germany, the model in Volterra's form provides a worse estimate of the equation for u (the standard deviation of profit rates across firms) than the model where the term PA is substituted for PA*u in equation 2; the contrary is the case for France and the United Kingdom. It would seem, therefore, that in Germany disequilibria do not generate disequilibria, while a self-reinforcing tendency of disequilibria appears in the United Kingdom and France, that is, u contributes to stimulate its own growth through the term PA*u.

All parameters have the correct signs, have reasonable values and, in the estimation of the model in the Volterra form for the United Kingdom and France and in the pseudo Volterra form for Germany, are significantly different from zero around the 1% level.

The models were also estimated utilizing data on patent grants instead of patent applications, but the results have not been presented as, in all cases, patent applications gave better estimates. This is not surprising since patent applications provide a better expression of the innovative propensity of firms, that is, their intention to innovate.

It may be interesting to compare the estimated parameters relative to various countries, taking it as given that parameter b_1 expresses the innovative verve, parameter b_3 the adaptive push, while parameters b_1 and b_4 represent the disequilibrating forces and parameters b_2 and b_3 express the equilibrating ones.

Italy shows a relevant innovative verve and adaptive push (b_1 and b_3), meaning a satisfactory degree of dynamic competition, while the disequilibrating and equilibrating forces are almost equivalent. The United Kingdom shows the highest innovative verve (b_1) and also the highest adaptive push (b_3), that is, the strongest dynamic competition. Germany shows a strong innovative verve and a low adaptive push while France presents an innovative verve a little lower than Germany, but a much higher adaptive push. Relative to Germany, France has a lower parameter on the term in equation 1 decelerating innovative verve and a higher parameter on the term in equation 2 decelerating adaptive push. These offsetting values of b_1 and b_3 and b_2 and b_4 tend to partly compensate for the differences in innovative verve and adaptive push, making the disequilibrating-equilibrating process closer in those two countries. The United Kingdom shows such offsetting behavior only with reference to the adaptive push (but the difference between b_3 and b_4 is large), while the parameter b_2, decelerating the innovative verve, appears higher than France and lower than Germany, implying for this aspect a widening of the disequilibrating forces relative to Germany.

6.6 Conclusion

This chapter has insisted on the possibility and importance of measuring radical uncertainty and has shown the usefulness of survey results in this regard. In particular, the study has shown that such a measure can improve both the results and use of the business surveys and the understanding of the relation between innovation and uncertainty.

The empirical applications give proof of both the solidity of our development of indicators as derived by Business Tendency Surveys and the profitableness of their use in modeling and ad hoc analyses. Moreover, the research points out the close relation between innovation and uncertainty that, as is well known, crucially influences growth and development and allows an aggregate representation of the processes of dynamic competition and its cyclical behavior.

Utilizations of other aspects of the Business Tendency Surveys could be added, such as the quantification of additional indicators and some additional correction of the current percentage of the modalities of survey answers. Regional disaggregations and some refinement of the data could be provided. The second (direct) indicator of uncertainty requires further running-in and some longer data series. However, our results seem to show the usefulness of the proposed empirical investigations.

Finally, a model of business cycle has been specified and estimated that better shows the analytical importance of our qualitative and quantitative development on radical uncertainty.

Acknowledgments

We thank M. Malgarini of ISTAT for his suggestions, particularly the additional question of the ISAE quarterly business surveys, a question providing our second indicator of uncertainty; Murray Pellissier, Bureau of Economic Research (BER), University of Stellenbosch, South Africa, who provided the results of the enquiries on business conditions for South Africa and engaged in useful discussions with the author; Angelo Reati, former official of the European Commission, who provided intensive and helpful discussion; and Clifford R. Wymer, who authored the software used for computation and estimation (WYSEA package Wymer System for Simulation and Estimation Analyses).

Notes

1. An article very similar to the content of this chapter was deposited in the RePEc archive in 2014 on behalf of and with the assent of the *International Journal of Business and Management*.
2. See Arrow (1953, 1984), Savage (1954), De Finetti (1964), Harsanyi (1967), Kahneman and Tversky (1979), Machina (1982), Pindyck (1991), Lupton (2003).
3. See Knight (1921), Hayek (1937), Keynes (1937), Kirzner (1973, 1985), Lawson (1985), Shackle (1990).
4. Nelson and Winter (1982), Davidson (1988, 1994), Dow (1995), Simon (1997), Cantner, Hanusch and Pyka (1998), Hodgson (1999), Morroni (2006), Scazzieri and Marzetti 2011).
5. Econometric estimation uses some of C. R. Wymer's programs, which form part of the WYSEA (Wymer System Estimation and Analysis) package.
6. An example of the common confusion between expectation and uncertainty can be found in Calcagnini and Saltari (1997), who use ISCO surveys but do not derive uncertainty from the volatility of expectations but rather from aggregate data on the percentage of firms expecting stability, increase or decrease of certain variables.
7. A more appropriate volatility indicator can be expressed by giving a double weight to the double jumping in the changes of answer, that is, to R_{13} and R_{31}, as follows: OV = $R_{12} + 2R_{13} + R_{21} + R_{23} + 2R_{31} + R_{32}$.
8. ISAE was charged with the execution, for Italy, of the Business Tendency Surveys harmonized at European level. But after 2010, ISAE was closed and the charge was transferred to ISTAT (Italian National Institute of Statistics).
9. Another indicator of uncertainty may consist of the specification, by way of surveys, of a min-max range of expectations, where the distance between the minimum and maximum expectation may be considered an expression of the degree of uncertainty. In addition, the standard deviation of foresights may be interpreted as a measure of uncertainty.
10. Other indicators may be derived, for instance, positive and negative disposition, that is, the variation over time of the total frequency of expected (and ex post) increases or decreases (up or down); or the ratio between the frequency of changes in a modality of answer and the total frequency of that modality, thus giving an indication of the 'turbulence' of the considered modality.
11. Some estimates for South Africa have been performed using data provided by M. Pellissier, of the Stellenbosch University, and BER (South Africa) surveys and publication, in the context of an extended collaboration on volatility of BTS answers.
12. Some other computations and graphs on relevant indicators are set out in Fusari and Pellissier (2008).
13. If the weight of the repeated answer (R_{11}) is supposed, for instance, to be 3, the expression becomes: $(Up + 2R_{11})/4$.

    If we take the numerator of the second expression for the permanence indicator (in Section 6.3) and give a weight of 2 to it, we get the following expression for correction of up: $(R_{11} + 4R"_{11} + Up)/7$. For the correction of same and down, we have to substitute in the expression, respectively, same or down to up and R_{22} or R_{33} to R_{11}.
14. In fact, [ModifiedUp/Modified(Up+Same+Down) + ModifiedSame/Modified (Up+Same+Down) + Modified Down/Modified(Up+Same+Down)]*100 = 100.
15. An extensive analysis of this interaction, along with some simulation experiments, may be found in Fusari (2005) and Ekstedt and Fusari (2010).
16. See Kirzner (1973, 1985).
17. See Schumpeter (1934).
18. This matter, indeed, goes well beyond economics. Research on social and historical processes, from primitive ages to the beginning of modern dynamic society, shows the important role played in historical evolution by binomial innovation-adaptation. See A.

Fusari, *Human Adventure: An Inquiry on the Way of People and Civilizations*, Italian edition (SEAM, Roma, 2000).
19 Alternatively, a three-equation predator-predator-prey model could be specified, with innovation that preys upon (uses) entrepreneurial skill and is preyed upon by uncertainty, that also preys upon (i.e. stimulates the use of) entrepreneurial skill.
20 See Mueller et al. (1990) and Odagiri (1994).
21 Ibid.
22 The fact that only two observations were outliers, that the model is dynamic and that there is no reason to assume that the causes, if any, of these anomalies were the same suggest that the use of a dummy variable was inappropriate.

References

Arrow, K. J. (1953), The role of securities in the optimal allocation of risk bearing, *Review of International Studies*, vol. 31.
Arrow, K. J. (1984), *The economics of information*, Collected papers of Kenneth J. Arrow, Blackwell, Oxford.
Calcagnini, G. & Saltari, E. (1997), Un'analisi del principio dell'acceleratore in condizioni di incertezza, *Rassegna dei Lavori dell'ISCO*, vol. 1, pp. 183–212.
Cantner, U., Hanusch, H. & Pyka, A. (1998), Routinized innovations: Dynamic capabilities in a simulation study, in O. Eliasson & C. Green (eds), *The microfoundations of economic growth*, University of Michigan Press, Ann Arbor, pp. 131–155.
Davidson, P. (1988), A technical definition of uncertainty and the long run non neutrality of money, *Cambridge Journal of Economics*, vol. 12, no. 3, pp. 329–338.
Davidson, P. (1994), *Post Keynesian macroeconomic theory*, Edward Elgar, Aldershot.
Davidson, P. (1995), Uncertainty in economics, in S. Dow & J. Hillard (eds), *Keynes, knowledge and uncertainty*, Edward Elgar, Aldershot, pp. 107–116.
De Finetti, B. (1964), Foresight: Its logical laws, its subjective sources, in H. E. Kyburg & H. E. Smokler (eds), *Studies in subjective probability*, John Wiley, New York, Translation in French, Annales de l'institute H. Poincaré, pp. 1–68.
Dow, S. (1995), Uncertainty about uncertainty, in S. Dow & J. Hillard (eds), *Keynes, knowledge and uncertainty*, Edward Elgar, Aldershot, pp. 117–127.
Drucker, P. F. (1985), *Innovation and entrepreneurship*, Heinemann, London.
Ekstedt, H. & Fusari, A. (2010), *Economic theory and social change, problems and revisions*, Routledge, London and New York.
Fusari, A. (1996), Paths of economic development: Modelling factors of endogenous growth, *International Journal of Social Economics*, vol. 23, no. 10/11, pp. 164–191. http://dx.doi.org/10.1108/03068299610149525.
Fusari, A. (2000), *Human adventure; an inquiry on the way of people and civilizations*, Italian edition, SEAM, Roma.
Fusari, A. (2004), *Uncertainty, competence and the theory of the firm: Some crucial omission and misunderstanding of the current debate*. Shifting Boundaries Conference, September 2–3. Bristol Business School and 2005 Second Meeting of ENEF, Erasmus University, Rotterdam, September 8–9.
Fusari, A. (2005), A model of the innovation-adaptation mechanism driving economic dynamics: A micro representation, *Journal of Evolutionary Economics*, vol. 15, no. 3, pp. 297–333. http://dx.doi.org/10.1007/s00191-005-0246-z.
Fusari, A. (2006), *Radical uncertainty indicators: Quantitative specifications and applications*, 28th CIRET Conference, Rome.

Fusari, A. (2013), Radical uncertainty, dynamic competition and a model of the business cycle: The implications of a measure and an explanation of what is supposed non-measurable and non-explainable, *International Journal of Business and Management*, vol. 8, no. 12, pp. 8–28.

Fusari, A. & Pellissier, M. (2008), *Some new indicators and procedure to get additional information from the business tendency surveys*, 29th CIRET Conference, Santiago de Chile.

Fusari, A. & Reati, A. (2013), Endogenizing technical change: A long term view of sectoral dynamics, *Structural Change and Economic Dynamics (SCED)*, vol. 24, pp. 76–100. http://dx.doi.org/10.1016/j.strueco.2012.06.004.

Galavotti, M. C., Scazzieri, R. & Suppes, P. (2008), *Reasoning, rationality and probability*, Center for the Study of Language and Information, Conference Proceedings Edition, Stanford, California.

Griliches, Z. (1990), Patent statistics as economic indicators: A survey, *Journal of Economic Literature*, vol. XXVIII, pp. 1661–1707.

Harsanyi, J. C. (1967), Games with incomplete information played by Bayesian players I-III Part. I: The basic model, *Management Science*, vol. 14, no. 5, pp. 159–182.

Hayek, F. A. (1937), Economics and knowledge, *Economica*, vol. 4, pp. 33–54.

Hirshleifer, J. (1989), *Time, uncertainty, and information*, B. Blackwell, Oxford.

Hirshleifer, J. & Rilay, J. G. (1992), *The analytics of uncertainty and information*, Cambridge University Press, Cambridge. http://dx.doi.org/10.1017/CBO9781139167635.

Hodgson, G. M. (1999), *Evolution and institutions*, Edward Elgar, Cheltenham, UK and Northampton, MA.

Kahneman, D. & Tversky, A. (1979), Prospect theory: An analysis of decision under risk, *Econometrica*, vol. 51. http://dx.doi.org/10.2307/1914185.

Keynes, J. M. (1937), The general theory of employment, *Quarterly Journal of Economics*, vol. 51. http://dx.doi.org/10.2307/1882087.

Kirzner, I. M. (1973), *Competition and entrepreneurship*, The University of Chicago Press, Chicago and London.

Kirzner, I. M. (1985), *Discovery and the capitalist process*, The University of Chicago Press, Chicago and London.

Knight, F. H. (1921), *Risk, uncertainty and profit*, Houghton Mifflin, New York.

Knight, F. H. (1950), *Risk, uncertainty and profit*, La Nuova Italia, Firenze.

Lawson, T. (1985), Uncertainty and economic analysis, *Economic Journal*, vol. 15. http://dx.doi.org/10.2307/2233256.

Lupton, D. (2003), *Risk and everyday life*, Sage Publications, Thousand Oaks, CA.

Machina, M. J. (1982), Expected utility analysis without the independence axiom, *Econometrica*, vol. 50, no. 2. http://dx.doi.org/10.2307/1912631.

Morroni, M. (2006), *Knowledge, scale and transactions in the theory of the firm*, Cambridge University Press. http://dx.doi.org/10.1017/CBO9780511617232.

Mueller, D. C., et al. (1990), *The dynamics of company profits*, Cambridge University Press. http://dx.doi.org/10.1017/CBO9780511664724.

Nelson, R. R. & Winter, S. G. (1982), *An evolutionary theory of economic change*, The Belknap Press of Harvard University Press, Cambridge, MA, London.

Odagiri, H. (1994), *Growth through competition, competition through growth*, Clarendon Press, Oxford. http://dx.doi.org/10.1093/0198288735.001.0001.

Pellissier, G. M. (2006), *Evaluating the impact of disaggregated survey panel response on business tendency survey results*, OECD Workshop, Rome.

Pellissier, G. M. (2007), *Business conditions response: Volatility versus non-volatility*, Mimeo, Bureau of Economic Research, Stellenbosch.

Peschel, M. & Mende, W. (1986), *The predator-prey model*, Springer-Verlag, Wien and New York.

Pindyck, R. S. (1991), Irreversibility, uncertainty, and investment, *Journal of Economic Literature*, vol. XXIX, no. 1, pp. 1110–1148.

Polanyi, M. (1966), *The tacit dimension*, Doubleday, Garden City, NY.

Runde, J. (1998), Clarifying Frank Knight's discussion of the meaning of risk and uncertainty, *Cambridge Journal of Economics*, vol. 22, no. 5, pp. 539–546.

Savage, L. (1954), *The foundation of statistics*, John Wiley, New York.

Saviotti, P. P. & Pyka, A. (2004), Economic development by the creation of new sectors, *Journal of Evolutionary Economics*, vol. 14. http://dx.doi.org/10.1007/s00191-003-0179-3.

Scazzieri, R. & Marzetti, S. (2011), *Fundamental uncertainty: Rationality and plausible reasoning*, Palgrave MacMillan, New York, Basingstoke.

Schumpeter, J. A. (1934), *The theory of economic development*, Harvard University Press, Cambridge, MA.

Shackle, G. L. S. (1990), *Time, expectations and uncertainty in economics: Selected essays*, editor by J. L. Ford, Edward Elgar, Aldershot.

Simon, H. A. (1997), Models of bounded rationality, in *Empirically grounded economic reason, 3*, The MIT Press, Cambridge, MA, pp. 299–318.

Ulph, A. & Ulph, D. (1994), *The irreversibility effect revisited*, Department of Economics, University of Southampton, Southampton.

Vercelli, A. (1999), The recent advances in decision theory under uncertainty: A non-technical introduction, in L. Luini (ed), *Uncertain decisions: Bridging theory and experiments*, Kluwer Academic Publishers, Boston. http://dx.doi.org/10.1007/978-1-4615-5083-9_11.

White, A. R. (1972), The propensity theory of probability, *British Journal for the Philosophy of Science*, vol. 23, no. 1. http://dx.doi.org/10.1093/bjps/23.1.35.

Wymer, C. R. (1993), *Resimul and Escona programs, manual and documentation*, Mimeo, WYSEA Systems Estimation and Analysis (computer package).

Part II
Problems of political economy
The need for reformations

7 An overview of the economic process

7.1 Premise

A clear exposition of and provision of a motivation for the economic policies and reformations suggested by the theoretical construction in Part I requires a compact treatment of the dynamic process fueled by modern economies.

The theoretical development on cycles and historical phases that follows provides a sort of leading structure for the subsequent analyses. It derives from our long-standing studies on economics and history and is part of the resultant theory on the interpretation of social and historical processes.[1] More precisely, we try to give an illuminating interpretation of history by combining, with the notion of historic ages or phases, the analysis of intermediate and long-run cycles as developed in the last section of Chapter 6 and the whole of Chapter 3. As far as we know, such a combination is absent in the literature. It provides an instructive picture as a whole of economic, social and historical processes and aids our understanding of institutional changes and other reformations needed over the course of time. In fact, our cycles are peculiar in that they result from the processes of dynamic competition; as such, they push toward the advent of new phases of development with the connected institutional changes.

The last section of this chapter completes the draft on the development process implied by our theoretical construction and concludes by tracing a 'time arrow' expressed by that process.

7.2 A fundamental misunderstanding

One of the most surprising developments of scientific thought is offered by the birth of the so-called 'queen' of the social sciences: economics; her vicissitudes provide plain evidence of the lack of scientific content afflicting social studies. Notwithstanding the fact that economics was constructed in parallel with the progressive conquest by the economy of a central position in the becoming of society and the consequent advent of its dynamic motion, such a construction disregarded dynamic motion, the most peculiar trait of the reality under consideration. The disregard continues today under the influence of dominant methodologies, in spite of the accomplishments of a succession of industrial revolutions.

Through the notion of dynamic competition and the interactions among its main agents, the chapters in Part I have highlighted throughout the nature and relevance of economic dynamics. Yet, if a naturalistic representation of the economic process is provided, that is, if this process is considered as an expression of natural laws, then both the content and implications of the decisions of the resulting political economy would be completely different than in the case that economic policies are the expression of a methodological view of organizational character and hence are a prolongation of the organizational action expressing the vicissitude and management of the economic system.

We have repeatedly underlined that the economy is a product of human action: the incisiveness of such action has undergone a growing intensity starting from the first industrial revolution. In particular, innovation has become an increasingly engaging challenge for the entrepreneur, both as a means for gaining success and due to the adjustments, imitation and restructuring to which it obliges even those who are not inclined to innovate. The backbone of competition among entrepreneurs has increasingly become engagement in innovation and structural reorganization; in the present time, the economic process is strongly characterized by the opposition and interlacement between the two moments: innovative dash followed by an entailed structural reorganization.

Economic analysis that disregards this crucial relation and opposition overlooks a decisive feature of reality and its evolution. In particular, political economy is obliged to take fully into account both the new general conditions of development generated by the succession 'innovation-structural reorganization' and the actor in the whole process, namely the entrepreneur. The resulting picture must be quite different from the content of the evolutionary approach prevailing in biology (Darwinism and neo-Darwinism). In fact, the two determinants of evolution according to Darwinism, casual genetic variations and the selection of them dictated by the necessity to survive in the struggle for existence (case and necessity), do not come close to explaining the evolutionary process at work in social reality and expressed by dynamic competition.

It may be useful to underline that Darwinism is the object of insistent criticisms even within biology. These criticisms are largely based on the observation of discontinuities in the evolutionary process, in particular, the unexplained existence of biological lacunas concerning the fossil record, pointing to the interruption of fossil continuity. Moreover, the Lamarckian idea of the hereditariness of acquired characters has recently undergone a revival in biology. The evidence of fossil lacunas has suggested to some the need to insert creativeness into the biology of evolution and, hence, to integrate into the received picture of slow Darwinian evolution some rapid evolutionary phases characterized by creative phenomena. This biological revisionism is completed by a calling for some notion of 'intelligent design' and its associated descending causality, in addition to the Darwinian ascending causality founded on genetic determinism.

Such developments are not well established in biology. Some of their adherents request the support of quantum physics, advocating its fusion with biology.[2] They also advocate some blending of physics and metaphysics and even an explicit mixture of science and religion with the aim of providing an understanding of the origin of life and the terms of intelligent design. In our opinion, this mixture of science and religion does not improve scientific understanding. On the contrary, however, and as we already know, there is clear evidence of the fruitfulness, in economic and social reality, at least in the context of the organizational view as opposed to the merely observational perspective, of the combination of creative evolutionary conceptions and the notion of intelligent design. In fact, the operation of creativeness is very evident in economics; it represents a decisive part of the competitive effort. And intelligent design is just what the organizational effort and the organizational view imply. In sum, the succession 'innovative dash and structural reorganization' expressing the evolutionary content of social reality demands a plain development of what is suggested by the somewhat contrived and forced attempts to revise biology that were just considered. Let's insist on this. The prevalence of the organizational imprint on social reality, which implies these developments, expresses a sort of deviation and escape route with respect to the naturalistic imprint of the method referable to biology.

It must be added that economic and social reality also lend importance to Lamarck's idea about the hereditariness of acquired characters, which is strongly opposed by Darwinism. In fact, the transmission of successful innovations and their fecundating role is a primary aspect of the dynamic competition process, that is, the succession 'innovation-structural reorganization'. Without such Lamarckian intercession, economic evolution would be condemned to a very slow and casual trajectory.

These clarifications and their extensions in the following section constitute an obligatory premise for the understanding of the second part of this work.

7.3 Cycles and phases of development

An analysis of the course of human societies – their motion and transformation, their falls and resurrections – is needed to allow understanding of the institutional and ethical changes indispensable to the coming economic and social world. Of course, such an analysis must pay attention to cycles, but should exclude some common notions of cycles that do not properly express cyclical motion, for instance, the so-called life cycle of man or of a product. These supposed cycles only describe parabolic curves: birth, childhood, youth, maturity, old age, death or, for new products, appearance on the market, diffusion, maturity, decay and possible elimination by the advent of new rival products. Such parables, which, moreover, may be cut short by untimely death or the rapid advent of new rival goods, do not express a cyclical vicissitude. In fact, cycles place side by side a succession of rises, decays and recoveries. As such, a cycle cannot be referred to individuals but only to social systems. Moreover, cyclical motion appears only in relatively advanced economic and social systems, that is, societies endowed with institutions, ethical conditions and, in sum, forms of civilization that favor evolutionary motion. Various primitive societies have survived in stationary conditions down to the present age. The history of human societies has known great spurts of creativity followed by (a) ruinous crises and disintegration, as is typical of pluralist, decentralized orders agitated by strong antagonism and competition but lacking organizational strength (ancient Greece being a case in point); or (b) an almost unbroken continuity of behavior across centuries, an interminable quasi-stationariness after having reached considerable levels of social and cultural development (this case is represented by the great centralized bureaucratic orders and empires, the most typical of which is the ancient Chinese empire). Both these kinds of social orders have known deep periods of growth, and have been hit and sometimes annihilated by natural disasters, military invasions or internal contradictions; thereafter, their cultural, ideological and social conquests have been partially revived and improved centuries later by other, ascending peoples.

Social processes have assumed cyclical contents only after the birth, in Western European countries, of the modern dynamic society, itself a consequence of the installation of the economy, with its mercantile and entrepreneurial action, at center stage and as the leading sector of the social system. Therefore, only by starting from such a transformation can the study of the motion of the economy and society benefit from the theory of cycles.

But the mere analysis of cycles is insufficient for the understanding of social processes. Such understanding, and the related comparison of different and subsequent cycles, requires a more general notion on which to graft cycles, namely: the notion of historical phases, which is referable to the whole of human history. Such a grafting is indispensable in order to understand the character and changeable content of the cyclical motion over time and, more generally, to arrange the process of becoming human societies, that is, from where we come and toward where we are going; this grafting is crucial, among other things, for making a comparison between the two large-scale crises of 1929 and 2008.

The problem is how to identify in a scientific way the various historical phases. Identification can be based on the character of the general conditions of development in the course of history and, more precisely, on the institutional and ethical-ideological and organizational forms at large that must be fulfilled for reasons of organizational rationality and efficiency in the presence of the given conditions of development. In Section 2.2 on method, we denominated those necessary organizational forms 'functional imperatives', while we denominated 'ontological imperatives' the institutional and ethical forms able to feed human evolutionary skills. The combination of those two notions gives the foundation of a theory of social and historic development. Precisely, functional imperatives signal the historical phase of development, that is, they concern institutional, ethical and power forms required by the existing as well as the future phases of development; whereas ontological imperatives feed the dynamical capacities of social systems and hence the possible succession of phases of development, starting from primitive times and down to the present age. With regard to the economy, entrepreneurship is the main institution (and actor) that stimulates evolutionary motion and hence the appearance of new phases of development with the functional imperatives (institutional, ethical and power forms) required by the existing as well as the future phases of development. These two notions allow us to arrive at important knowledge on the basic contents of present and coming ages and the social-historic process toward which dynamic competition pushes.

The advent of dynamic society has entailed not only the birth of the cycle of economic and social processes but also the shortening of historical ages as a consequence of the acceleration of the change of the general conditions of development. Our combination of the notions of cycle and phase of development is based on a peculiar theory and explanation of the cycle, which is almost entirely ignored by the numerous theoretical studies of the cycle, such as those founded on monetary causes: the behavior of the banking system and its instability and attitude with regard to interest rates; variations of stocks; interaction between the multiplier and the accelerator; the existence of ceilings and floors; and so on. The cycle on which we insist, mainly in Chapters 3 and 4 of this book, results from the phenomenon of dynamic competition as expressing the interaction between entrepreneurship, innovation and uncertainty. Therefore, it is strictly endogenous in nature and, moreover, more inclusive than other cycles emphasizing innovation and entrepreneurship, such as the Schumpeterian ones. As we know, it is activated by entrepreneurs' actions: precisely, the entrepreneurial search for profit opportunities through innovation that causes disequilibria and uncertainty followed by arbitrage directed to derive profits from disequilibria, thus causing the reduction of disequilibria and radical uncertainty and hence the advent of a new surge of innovations. So, uncertainty plays an important role in the whole process; uncertainty is not merely intended as a cloud of unknowing but displays an endogenous character. This cycle can concern both the medium range (intermediate cycles) and the long run (long waves), depending on the character (radical or incremental) of innovations. So, the dynamic competition process not only determines cycles but also implies the passage toward new phases of development with which those cycles are combined and from which they are influenced.

The cycle that shapes the dynamic competition process has deeply characterized, with a variable content, the history of the modern world, starting from the achievement by the economy of a leading role in medieval society. This opened the flood gates for the great creative and turbulent surge expressed by the Renaissance, which was followed by the tremendous wars and malaise that afflicted the 17th century (the 'iron century'). An age of relative and peaceful serenity cheered the 18th century and prepared the advent of the first industrial revolution, which was followed by a succession of capitalist cycles and phases of development, in particular four frequently cited long waves activated by very important innovations, and a fifth wave now in course, probably more intriguing, full of surprises and more demanding than previous waves.

7.4 On the process of social and historic development: the time arrow

Now we attempt to complete the previous analysis by tracing in draft form the implied social and historical processes. We have seen that the establishment of dynamic competition implies the advent of a marked inclination toward growth and development, even if by way of the cyclical motion inherent to the functioning of modern economies. We provide now a brief representation of the implied process as a whole and, on such a basis, we shall attempt to advance some illuminating assessments on the future behavior of the economy, assessments that extend well beyond the current ability of economics to provide information on the future and notwithstanding the strength and dimensions of unpredictable changes.

In the previous section we considered, in the context of dynamic competition, the interconnections between cyclical motions and the notion of phases of development. But this does not in itself provide a complete picture of the process. Such a complete picture requires that we also consider the requisite quality of the environment that is necessary to feed innovation and, hence, the dynamic competition process. In fact, the course of human history and the most glorious civilizations and political orders of the past have shown a strong aversion to economic and social development, with the exception of some periods of efflorescence that, nevertheless, were suffocated later by the establishment, as a result of their success, of powerful and strongly structured institutional orders.

The birth and persistent operation of dynamic motion requires a civilization characterized by the persistent operation of what we call 'ontological imperatives', that is, values and institutions that persistently stimulate the efflorescence of the dynamic potentialities of humanity. More precisely, ontological imperatives refer to the inclination of the social order to accept novelties and to be open to debate and criticism. The miracle of the appearance of a new, inherently and persistently dynamic age has its basis in the establishment, in a particular social context, of the growing and persistent dominance of economic competition under the propulsion of entrepreneurship and the parallel establishment of a scientific method able to promote inventions and to transform them into innovations. As a consequence, there came to be born a society thrown toward a 'magnificent and progressive destiny'; yet, it was not so magnificent after all in the absence of an ability to properly understand and manage such an incessant dynamic process.

So, the essential aspect of the kind of economic, social and historical development that the modern age has inaugurated, and which marks a great and ever increasing jump with respect to the past and established ways of investigating the economy and society, can be traced as follows: the presence of a civilization animated by powerful ontological imperatives in stimulating the evolutionary potential of people, that is, in stimulating the introduction of innovation and the corresponding variations of the general conditions of development, requires the construction of new functional imperatives, that is, of the corresponding institutional forms and other reorganization processes; this opens the door to the advent of new lines of development and so on. This is the evolutionary destiny of modern dynamic economies: an unavoidable destiny, indeed, which economics should study with great attention.

Social scientists dedicate relatively little attention to the direction of such a process, that is, to the so called 'time arrow'. Physicists pretend to have found an answer to the question of direction in the law of entropy, that is, in the measurement of the degree of disorder of a system; according to such a law, disorder tends to increase, thus allowing the possibility of distinguishing between past and future states. Another approach is to consider the complexity of fossils in light of the hypothesis that evolution proceeds from simple to complex forms. Other students of evolution pretend to indicate a time arrow in the supposed progressive evolution to consciousness in animal species.

Our theory of economic, social and historical development shows a quite different time arrow that consists of the change of the general conditions of development through the sedimentation of innovations and the parallel action of structural reorganization, a change that causes the advent of new ages and new historic phases. The content and evolution of the general conditions of development, expressing as it does important and enduring traits of organizational necessities, allows the possibility of perceiving the basic contents of future ages and their corresponding organizational necessities. After all, this is the very explanatory role of the notion of the time arrow, and this is what the understanding and management of a reality harassed by growing unpredictable events desperately needs.

7.5 Conclusion

We hope we have traced a useful and general representation of the dynamics of modern economies and societies, in spite of their increasingly unpredictable changeful features. This should bring economics some steps forward, in relation to both the static nature of the dominant form of economics (which is only apparently mitigated through the modeling of exogenous innovation) and to the fragmentary and often inconclusive elaborations of heterodox economics on this matter.

We proceed now to the exposition of some less general treatments founded on the experience of the phases of development and its implications propelled over the last centuries by the economic process. We also make an effort to perceive the road on which we find our modern and increasingly tormented economic and social world, and we insist on reformations in the fields of political economy, intended as a part of the organizational methodological approach on which also the economic analysis in Part I is founded.

The content of the two chapters that follow has been suggested by our experiences in the field of economic and social planning. In particular, Chapter 8 shows that Keynesian interpretations and policies become inappropriate after the transition from monopolistic capitalism to conflictual-consumeristic capitalism and the consequent emergence of growing pressures from income distribution. Chapter 9 shows, for its part, that social and territorial dualism negates the demand-led role of Keynesian policies. These clarifications underline the need for changes in policies and make evident the drive toward different phases of development. The remaining chapters underline the necessity for policies and reformations hitherto demanded in vain, both by some pathologies of capitalism and by the advent of the two last phases of development.

Notes

1 See Fusari (2000 and 2014).
2 This is a dominant trait of A. Goswami's work 'Creative Evolution' (2013).

References

Bateson, G. (1980), *Mind and nature*, Bantam, New York.
Behe, M. J. (1996), *Darwin's black box*, Simon & Schuster, New York.
Boden, M. (1990), *The creative mind*, Basic Books, New York.
Brough, J. (1958), Time and evolution, in T. S. Westoll (ed), *Studies of fossil vertebrates*, Athlone Press, London.
Capra, F. (1982), *The turning point*, Simon & Schuster, New York.
Clark, J., Freeman, C. & Soete, L. (1981), Long-waves and technological development in the 20th century, *Konjunktur, Krise, Gesellschaft*, vol. 25, no. 2, pp. 132–169.
Dennett, D. C. (1995), *Darwin's dangerous idea*, Simon & Schuster, New York.
Freeman, C. & Louçã, F. (2001), *As time goes by: From the industrial revolutions to the information revolution*, Oxford University Press, Oxford.
Fusari, A. (2000), *The human adventure: An inquiry into the ways of people and civilizations*, SEAM editions, Rome.
Fusari, A. (2014), *Methodological misconceptions in the social sciences: Rethinking social thought and social processes*, Springer, Dordrecht, Heidelberg, New York and London.
Fusari, A. & Reati, A. (2013), Endogenizing technical change: Uncertainty, profits, entrepreneurship: A long-term view of sectoral dynamics, *Structural Change and Economic Dynamics (SCED)*, vol. 24, pp. 76–100.
Goswami, A. (2013), *Evoluzione creativa: La soluzione di un fisico tra darwinismo e creazionismo*, Edizioni Mediterranee, Roma.
Jarne, G., Sánchez-Chóliz, J. & Fatás-Villafranca, F. (2005), "S-shaped" economic dynamics: The logistic and Gompertz curves generalized, *The Electronic Journal of Evolutionary Modeling and Economic Dynamics*, no. 1048. www.e-jemed.org/1048/index.php.
Mayr, E. (1963), *Animal species and evolution*, Belkap Press of Harvard University Press, Cambridge, MA.
Mayr, E. (1982), *The growth of biological thought*, Harvard University Press, Cambridge, MA.
Perez, C. (2010), Technological revolutions and techno-economic paradigms, *Cambridge Journal of Economics*, vol. 34, no. 1, January, pp. 185–202.
Prigogine, I. (1980), *From being to becoming*, Freeman, San Francisco.
Solomou, S. (1987), *Phases of economic growth, 1850–1973: Kondratieff waves and Kuznets swings*, Cambridge University Press, Cambridge.
Thom, R. (1980), *Structural stability and morphogenesis*, Einaudi, Torino.
Wesson, R. (1991), *Beyond natural selection*, MIT Press, Cambridge, MA.

8 The role of demand in contemporary economics

Theoretical and operational ambiguities and misunderstandings

8.1 Introduction

It is becoming increasingly evident that, when it comes to the problem of demand, economics encounters great interpretative and operational difficulties. These problems are sometimes due to the fact that, in the presence of bottlenecks, rigidities, dualisms and, more generally, of dearth afflicting production, the management of demand has little or, even worse, perverted effects. These equivocations are indeed not frequent. Furthermore, a large literature on underdevelopment has provided detailed evidence of such limitations and stumbling blocks, so that only an incompetent economist could ignore or fail to appreciate their nature. But these aspects of the problem are irrelevant with regard to advanced economies. The operational and theoretical mistakes concerning the role of demand are in this case, for the most part, different in nature. Indeed, their nature and implications are much more insidious.

The present analysis begins by facing some basic assumptions regarding any modeling centered on demand. The intention of this initial exercise is to clearly identify the necessary conditions for the modeling of demand to be founded on the correct interpretation of reality. We shall find that the specification of those conditions points to some inconsistency in the so-called post-Keynesian theory of distribution.

In particular, our analysis aims to make evident a great error that mars the studies of some economists into the presence of a deficiency of effective demand. Our inquiry into this mistake and its consequences is based on some considerations on the nature of investment. More generally, our inquiry leads to the conclusion that, at the present time, demand-led models are much less appropriate to the interpretation of reality than is usually supposed.

We then delineate a practical procedure aimed at remedying this misunderstanding and, hence, also the theoretical ambiguities that it generates. Our aim is to ground judgments on the conditions of demand on a more coherent logic than is usually the case – one able to take into account the real content of the analyzed situations.

Finally, some reflection is offered on the way that our analysis appears to allow some clarification of the problem of a cost-push versus demand-pull origin of inflation. The chapter thus provides some useful elements that should aid a clear understanding of the genesis of inflationary movements and, therefore, a more appropriate definition of the nature of the policies able to meet them.

8.2 Formulation of the problem

Starting from the beginning of 19th century, capitalism (in its so-called competitive character) knew a full advent of dynamic competition. The instability of the economy grew with the intensification of such a kind of competition centered on the interaction between entrepreneurship, innovation and radical uncertainty. The intensification of innovative process stimulates radical uncertainty, and this causes instability. The degree of this endogenous instability generated by the economic system largely depends on the share of saving on national product waiting to be invested. In fact, and as is well known, investment concerns the long run, and therefore it is strongly influenced by the changing expectations and hence by the level of uncertainty that negatively influences expectations.

With the advent of the age of so-called *monopolistic capitalism*, mainly through the great innovations distinguishing the second industrial revolution, the instability of the economy made a jump. Precisely, the weakness or inexistence of trade unions or, in other words, the competitive character of labor market in the presence of a high excess of labor force, kept wages down. This, and the corresponding high profits, the utilization of which was made difficult by the instability of investment, caused an acute deficiency of aggregate demand and a strong fall of production and employment: the large-scale 1929 crisis.

The economic thought of the time, deeply influenced by the so-called Say's law that production generates the demand necessary to absorb it, was unable to understand the new disconcerting situation not contemplated by current analyses and hence to provide receipts for the solution of the crisis. A great confusion dominated the scene, both among theorists and practical men.

J. M. Keynes was the economist that diagnosed more properly the nature of the crisis and the way to overcome it. He clearly saw that the crisis was a result of a marked deficiency of demand and the causes of such a deficiency. Keynes's analysis gives an outstanding example of the unification of economics and political economy; in fact, his explanation of the crisis implies, at the same time, the therapies for overcoming the crisis. He recommended the pursuit of full employment through incentives for the demand of goods, which suggested the support of poor men's incomes as poor men express high propensity to consume; deficit spending; and the edification of welfare state that has represented one of the main conquests of civilization. Western countries knew an advancement that the world had never known, a real golden age of capitalism that went on for more than 20 years and has transmitted an important inheritance to the coming generations.

The most instructive aspect of the new experience is probably represented by the advent of new and unfortunately ignored needs of transformations and new contradictions. This is what we have to examine to understand the roots of more and more serious difficulties and misconceptions that have followed up the recent 2008 large-scale crisis.

The concern of economists with the deficiency of demand is not recent; it plays a crucial role in the analyses of Malthus and Sismondi and, subsequently, in those of R. Luxemburg and Hobson; this in spite of the fact that, in the meantime, official economics had solemnly declared the groundlessness of those concerns, even if strongly challenged by Keynes.

As is well known, Keynes focused his attention on income utilization, that is, on the subdivision of income between consumption and investment. This focus is coherent with the main content of the Keynesian analysis as motivated by the degree of utilization of resources. In this regard, M. Kalecki was, in a sense, less coherent but more complete than Keynes. Kalecki considered, like Keynes, the economic problems of his time from the point of view of the degree of utilization of resources, and in fact, he anticipated fundamental aspects of Keynes's work. However, this did not deter him from the explicit introduction of the distribution side in the conceptual scheme that he used. The result of this introduction is his well-known table, which gives the description of the gross national product according to the point of view of both its distribution and utilization:

		Workers' consumptions	+
Gross profit	+	Capitalists' consumptions	+
Wages and salaries	=	Gross investment	=
Gross national product		Gross national product	

This representation of gross national product and the relations existing between the two sides of the table provide a useful starting point of our analysis.[1] In particular, and as we shall see, it allows us to make evident the important point that the presence of a deficiency of demand cannot be simply deduced from the existence of an *ex ante* excess of saving with respect to *ex ante* investment and/or from the presence of unused productive capacity. Moreover, it shows that the presence of the requisite conditions requires that the distribution of income assumes particular forms and that, in the absence of those forms, we cannot assert the existence of a deficiency of demand, even in the presence of a high degree of unused productive capacity.

8.3 The foundation of demand-led models on an important hypothesis about the labor market

It is convenient to start our analysis from the previous table, but only after a preliminary transformation of its content. By making the hypothesis that workers do not save some part of their income at all, we get from the table the following equality:

(1) Gross profit = gross investment + capitalists' consumption

Of course, this equality is simply an accounting relation and, as such, does not inform us whether profits determine investment or vice versa. Kalecki asserted that the causal direction depends on the aggregate (of the relation), which capitalists have the power to influence. He noticed that in each period capitalists are able to decide to consume more than in the previous one, but cannot decide to earn more;[2] from this it is inferred that the dimension of profits depends on capitalists' investment and consumption, not the other way around. The mechanism of such determination would be variations of the prices of consumption goods and investment goods associated with the levels and composition of demand, as represented in the right-hand side of the table.

Therefore, in Kaleki's interpretation, investment is the instrumental variable *par excellence* – a variable which is not conditioned by the level of saving since (according to the table) investment determines the saving it needs.

This interpretation depends on the hypothesis that, in principle, capitalists' decisions on investment and consumption have an exogenous character and are the fundamental a priori element in the whole process.[3] But such a hypothesis is valid only in particular conditions. It was valid in the situation that Kalecki – and also Kaldor – considered, but it is far from being valid in every case. In particular, the validity of the previous hypothesis and perspective is strictly conditional on the collateral effectiveness of the Keynesian hypothesis that trade union bargaining is able to determine only money wages but not real wages. If this is indeed the case, then the distribution of income between wages and profits is forced to adjust (by definition) to demand, thus constituting a merely residual variable (i.e. a variable consequent with respect to the level and composition of demand, mainly with respect to the level of investment). This hypothesis entails that it is sufficient to influence demand and its composition in order to influence not only production but also (due to the consequent movements of prices) the shares of income distribution. In brief, the amount of profit depends on the amount of investment, which generates the saving necessary to finance investment and the same incentive to invest. Consequently, given the conditions postulated here, the problem of demand and capitalists' decisions on the amount of consumption and investment constitute the fundamental a priori of the whole process. In other words, in this hypothesis on the labor market, the problem resides only in the right-hand side of the table but never in the left-hand side (since, let's repeat, the process of income distribution is forced to adjust to the configuration and the money levels taken by the utilization of income). Both in the table and in the equality, we move from the right to the left side, just as Kaleki supposed.

It is useful to repeat that the whole approach is based on Keynes's hypothesis about the labor market; this hypothesis assumes that real wage has a residual character (inside the limits clarified by Kaldor or within the limits of Robinson's 'inflationary barrier'). We label such an assumption the 'postulate of the residuality of real wages'.

Now we must ask ourselves: what are the indispensable conditions if this postulate is to be made effective? It is clearly evident that effectiveness requires at least one of the following three conditions:

1   Workers are completely affected by the so-called monetary illusion.
2   The productive system is coming to the end of a period of chronic stagnation and entering into a new phase of great dynamism characterized by a high rate of development or a strong 'acceleration' of the growth rate. In these conditions, the capacity of capital to pay wages can even precede as well as fully meet wage claims, thereby avoiding a real conflict over income distribution.
3   Workers' contractual power is very weak so that they are forced to submit to the bargaining power of the opposing party. Such weakness cannot be attributed to the almost unconditional control of the capitalist and the ready availability of financial resources.[4] In fact, this does not imply an unconditional control of the labor force, even if it constitutes an indispensable premise for such control. Such control requires much more: substantially, in market economies, it requires the operation, in the presence of an adequate excess of labor force, of the mechanism of demand and supply of labor and the collateral absence of the indexation of wages (or the absence of trade unions with sufficiently strong bargaining power) so as not to allow them an almost complete covering of inflation.[5]

It is easy to see that the first condition can only work for brief intervals of time and only occasionally, unless the working class is particularly ingenuous. The same is valid for the second condition, which, after all, does not represent a Keynesian condition of stagnation of demand, even if it is consistent with the Keynesian view intended in a more general sense. In sum, the effectiveness of the Keynesian postulate of residuality of real wages requires the situation under the third condition, that is, that wages depend on the availability of labor force in the presence of large-scale unemployment.[6] This was the situation that Keynes and Kalecki actually observed and that enabled them to presume a substantial residuality of real wages and, consequently, to ignore the problem of income distribution or to consider it as a consequential and secondary issue without thereby violating reality but rather perfectly interpreting its contents.

Later N. Kaldor and J. Robinson (who lived in a period increasingly concerned with the problem of income distribution) subjected the previous postulate of residuality to the constraint that real wages exceed the subsistence level. Such a correction does not undermine the substance of the considered theory,[7] but it is far from being satisfactory when (as we shall see) it comes to the interpretation of a world in which the operation of the condition of the demand and supply of labor force is increasingly and explicitly contradicted by observable facts.

It may be useful to recall, mainly for the sake of completeness, that the notions previously synthesized are at the basis of the post-Keynesian theory of distribution and development. This point requires an important specification that economists usually do not consider.

We have seen that Keynes did not explicitly consider the question of income distribution but considered only income utilization, while Kalecki explicitly included income distribution in his schemes. However, Kalecki's previously illustrated use of national accounting relations does not allow a rigorous definition of the shares of income distribution. This limitation is a consequence of the fact that, in his scheme, the degree of utilization of resources may change and the output may change for given investment, and hence the corresponding profit share may change. In order to deduce a theory of income distribution from Kalecki's theoretical scheme, it is necessary to use his notion of degree of monopoly, but he does not give a satisfactory explanation of the nature and content of this concept.

Kaldor and Robinson's theory of income distribution,[8] as well as Pasinetti's contribution on this subject,[9] suppose the full employment of resources. This hypothesis enables these three economists to provide a rigorous definition of the shares of income distribution. More precisely, their analysis concerns the long run and assumes that any situation of deficient demand has already been remedied (through Keynesian therapies).

It must be clarified that, the apparent similarities of the two notwithstanding, this hypothesis points to a great difference between the Cambridge analysis of income distribution (Kaldor and Robinson) and Kalecki's scheme. Even more important, such a hypothesis implies an incoherence that it is indispensable to underline.

Kalecki's theory is coherent (even if its validity is conditional on the operation of the three conditions considered in the previous paragraph). The postulate of the residuality of real wages, which stands at the foundation of Kalecki's theory, is possible, even if it is conditional on the operation of at least one of the three hypotheses set out previously. By contrast, the Cambridge theory of income distribution, founded on the postulate of residuality of real wages, implies an a priori denial (through the hypothesis of full employment) of the possibility that two of the previous conditions (required by that postulate) are verified: the second one, concerning the short run, and the third one, that is, the operation in the labor market of the mechanism of demand and supply of labor, in the presence of an excess of labor force and so forth. Therefore, the postulate at the basis of the post-Keynesian Cambridge theory of distribution could operate only if the first condition – concerning monetary illusion – is also operating. But unfortunately this possibility is completely unrealistic with regard to the long run. So we must conclude that the Cambridge theory of income distribution is contradictory, being based on contradictory assumptions (full employment in a long-run perspective and residuality of real wages).[10]

Of course, the Cambridge theory has some other problems as well, for instance, Kaldor's mechanism through which full employment equilibrium is achieved or the a priori assumption of Robinson and Pasinetti as to the existence of such equilibrium.[11] But, in contrast to the previous analysis, these are issues that do not concern the foundations of the theory under consideration.

8.4 Consequences and meanings, for demand models, of the nonoperation of the postulate of residuality of real wages

The success of Keynesian recipes opened the door to a new and – in terms of content – opposite phase of development that can be denominated *conflictual-consumeristic capitalism*. This new state of affairs was characterized by competition based largely on new products, the stimulation of consumption through advertisement and high wages in the most dynamic sectors, due to both the increased bargaining power of trade unions and to the interest of firms in stimulating the consumption of new goods and maintaining an unvaried mark-up margin so as to obstruct the entrance of competitors. This is a quite different world to that expressed by the phase of monopolistic capitalism, which excluded the relevance, in conflictual terms, of income distribution, even if it emphasized its contribution to demand.

In the case that the postulate of residuality of real wages does not work (i.e. that the hypotheses set out in Section 3.3.2 are not valid), the question of income distribution becomes a pressing problem, implying a substantial upsetting of the meaning of relation 1 with respect to the meaning Kalecki's scheme attributes to it. More precisely, the advent of pressures on the side of distribution will imply that profits come before investment; in fact, in this case, the decisions to invest are conditioned by their profitability, not vice versa. This means that, in the presence of the condition here supposed, interventions on demand cannot remedy the difficulties at work (on the contrary, they may worsen them, as in this condition the distributive shares cannot simply adjust to the level and composition of demand but rather follow a logic that leaves out of consideration the shaping that demand will assume and anterior to this shaping). In sum, this means that now we move from the left-hand side to the right-hand side of Kalecki's scheme and relation 1. It is important to consider this point in more detail.

Let us make the assumption that, due to the class struggle and in the absence of the operation of the postulate of residuality of real wages,[12] profits fall too low. In these conditions, investment decreases (for various reasons: due to financing, because entrepreneurs thereby hope to determine a change of distribution to their own advantage, and because profits are the main stimulus to entrepreneurship). With the decrease in investment comes also a parallel decrease of production or, in other words, a decrease in the degree of utilization of the available resources. At the same time, the increase in the labor share of income accompanying the above circumstance will cause a collateral increase in the share of consumption of total income. Probably the public deficit will also grow as a consequence of the intermediary role that public administration fulfills in the struggle for income distribution, especially if this struggle is particularly harsh. In the presence of these conditions, analysis will reveal, on the whole, quite a high level of demand (notwithstanding the reduction of investment and the underutilization of productive capacity). This high demand is due to the expansion of consumption and, probably, to the amount of the public deficit.[13] (We shall see later that, in the presence of these conditions, the demand for goods and services, with respect to their production, will be remarkable in the average). Therefore, such analysis will inform us that we are not in the presence of a deficiency of effective demand but rather in the presence of a problem concerning the composition of demand; specifically, this is a problem arising from the unsatisfactory level of one part of demand, namely, investment. As a consequence, the increase of some other component of demand will not improve the situation (as, on the contrary, would happen in the Keynesian version of this situation).

It may be objected that the low use of equipment is an obstacle to investment and that the expansion of demand constitutes, therefore, in this case, an incentive to investment. But only the premise of the previous objection is correct; the deduction is a great and very frequent error. Such a deduction would be right only on the hypothesis that the problem starts from the side of demand, and it is clearly incorrect if it originates in distribution (and when the squeeze of demand, if present, is only consequent to restrictive measures directed to control inflationary pushes caused by pressure on distribution).

Moreover, a careful analysis of the condition of demand will inform us that not even a policy of direct support of investment (this representing, in the supposed condition, the weakest component of demand) may remedy the situation. Let's set out the reason for this.

The situation can be characterized (again) in terms of an *ex ante* excess of saving with respect to *ex ante* investment, arising from the fall of investment. But investment does not represent, in the postulated conditions, the instrumental variable *par excellence,* as it does in Keynesian schemes; in fact, investment cannot be freely stimulated. More precisely, it cannot be presumed that an adequate increase of this variable is able to return the economy to motion and warrant an adequate profitability. Of course, it is, in principle, possible to increase public investment, that is, the exogenous part of investment. But this will not of itself cause an automatic increase in the performance of private investments and, hence, will not cause their increase (as would occur if the postulate of residuality of real wages were working). Therefore, private investment will continue to stagnate, due to its supposed low profitability. Moreover, from the fact that in the postulated conditions investment is in itself unable to generate profit, it can be inferred that – in contrast to what happens in Kalecki's model – this investment has not the thaumaturgic virtue of generating the saving that it needs. This implies that an increase of the public deficit aimed at financing exogenous (public) investment, instead of contributing to the stimulation of production, can further worsen the performance of the economy and simply subtract resources from private investment. The accumulation process would be stimulated only if, collaterally to the increase of exogenous investment, some decrease of consumption and public deficit and adequate transfers (mainly in the form of incentives) to firms were in operation. But such a policy is quite different from the mere stimulus of demand. Moreover, while this should provide a stimulus to the accumulation process, it will not warrant its continuation.

For the sake of maximum clarity, these considerations on investment can be put in a different and more general form. In demand-led models, the fall of investment is generated by the volatility of expectations. As is well known, the rise of demand makes expectations more optimistic, thus stimulating investment and hence determining an expansionary spiral.

However, if the fall of investment is due to distribution pressures that reduce profit (a situation less volatile than that in which expectations play the major role), the stimulus of demand is unable to stimulate investment and production. In this case, it is the struggle for income distribution that is the starting point of depression, and the rise of demand is impotent with regard to making the terms of this struggle more favorable to capital; indeed, if anything, the opposite is likely to occur.

In an open economy, the operation of the postulate of residuality of real wages is also obstructed by the fact that any increase of the prices of commodities produced by domestic entrepreneurs is opposed by the competition of foreign goods, both abroad and in the domestic market. Therefore, in this case, the conditioning arising from the side of distribution is more stringent and may cause an increase of imports, a decrease of exports and even an increase in the export of capital for reasons of profitability, thus worsening the deficit of foreign accounts. This will cause a squeeze of demand directed at reducing such a deficit. In sum, it should be clear that, in the conditions described previously, the squeeze of demand is generated by a situation that genetically has little to do with the level of demand. Of course, the situation described will be considerably exacerbated by any increases in the price of imported raw materials.

8.5 Ambiguities of the current analyses centered on demand: a scheme devoted to better considering previous arguments and some clarification on inflation

The struggle for income distribution, which is an important component of modern societies starting from the advent of conflictual-consumeristic capitalism, generates some apparent conditions of deficiency of demand that may, in turn, give rise to mistaken interpretations as to the behavior of the economy and, consequently, the suggestion of erroneous therapies. It is therefore important to set out some other clarifications on the matter.

We have seen that the conflict over income distribution causes the stagnation of investment and the underutilization of both the labor force and fixed assets – a situation exacerbated by the squeezing of demand intended to control inflation or the foreign trade deficit that arises in consequence of this conflict. But we also know that in such a case, the fall of investment and production are not due to the volatility of expectations or, in other words, we know that demand conditions do not constitute the primary cause of the observed fall but are rather a secondary and derived cause with respect to other factors preceding them. Consequently, the mere support of demand is not able to make the situation more favorable and indeed can worsen it. Such a situation cannot be considered as expressing a deficiency of effective demand, notwithstanding the presence of idle capacity or, in other words, notwithstanding the existence of a gap between potential and effective income.

This ambiguity concerning the degree of nonutilization of productive resources as an indicator of the conditions of demand raises the problem of how to avoid frequent misunderstanding on the meaning of these conditions. Well, if we exclude the operation of restrictive policies (a case in which it is easy to understand the cause of the decreasing level of demand[14]), an alternative and more appropriate method can be specified as follows.

We can, first of all, put into operation a systematic confrontation between the demand for goods (as a whole and at constant prices) and the quantity of produced goods. If the first aggregate systematically exceeds the second, this represents a partial indication of the presence of an excess of demand; if the contrary happens, we must consider the fact as a first indication of a deficiency of demand.[15]

But the confrontation described is, in itself, not sufficient to allow for the conclusion that the problem really starts from the demand side; in fact, the confrontation can show a fictitious, apparent excess or deficiency of demand (caused by the factor previously considered). Some further considerations are required in order to establish whether the origin of the problem is demand or income distribution. These additional considerations may be centered on a combined analysis of the results expressed by the comparison of the quantities of demanded goods and produced goods together with an inquiry into the degree of utilization of the productive capacity. In fact, if the above comparison shows both an excess of demand and the presence of idle productive capacity, it is extremely probable (in light of the argument set out in the previous paragraph) that the problem starts from the distribution side,[16] except in the case that the underutilizations of plant is due to bottlenecks and so forth, which testifies to the prevalence of the side of production. Of course, there may be at work a simultaneous presence of difficulties stemming from the sides both of production and distribution.

By contrast, if the comparison of produced goods with those demanded shows a weakness of demand in the presence of idle capacity, it is extremely likely that we are in the presence of a true deficiency of demand. But some further specification is indispensable on this point. In fact, if the pressure (on the available resources) coming from the side of distribution is of a modest extent, and if, at the same time, the propensity of workers to save is high, the presence of idle productive capacity will persist together with a parallel tendency of global supply to exceed global demand (in spite of the hypothetical presence of initial pressures on the side of income distribution). This means that, in the absence of a preliminary inquiry on the existence of some (improbable) pressures due to income distribution, the combined presence of an excess of the supply of goods and unused productive resources cannot be taken to mean that the problems arise only from the conditions of demand. Such an inquiry can be conducted through analysis of the nature of the class struggle or, more precisely, in the way such a struggle influences the distributive shares of income. At the same time, it is necessary to verify the possible presence of bottlenecks in production, in order to ascertain if the problem is partially generated from this side.

Finally, if the comparison between produced and demanded goods shows an excess of demand and, at the same time, a full utilization of productive capacity, this can be taken as evidence of the presence of a true excess of demand.

These three distinctions are important (and warrant some substantial elaboration). They inform us that today economic difficulties are due to the conditions of demand much less frequently than current theories seem to imply.

One particular aspect of this argument merits immediate further consideration. In general, a marked inconsistency exists between the advent of remarkable pressures coming from income distribution and the existence of a deficiency of demand. In fact, in the presence of such pressures, the reduction of investment follows (for technical reasons) with some delay the consequent decrease of the share of profits due to those pressures while, on the contrary, the increase of consumption (also due to the current public expenditure) will immediately follow the change in the shares of income distribution, so that such an increase will cause a net increase of the demand pressure. The contraction of investment that will later occur follows the reduction of the rate of growth, which will cause a higher prevalence (on the whole) of the quantity of demanded goods over their production.

The operation of pressures on the side of income distribution causes inflation. This implies that the previous analysis allows also for some clarification regarding inflation. The debate on the nature and causes of the increase of prices has always been fierce. Today, it mainly consists in the well-known controversy between Keynesian and monetarist approaches. The monetarist theories do not concern our topic and hence will not be considered here.

Keynesian economists do not have a univocal position on inflation. The main bone of contention concerns whether the primary cause of inflation lies in demand-pull or cost-push.[17] We hope that our analysis is able to provide some clarification of the controversy. The Keynesian arguments surrounding inflation arise due to a pretense that much more can be extracted from the Keynesian approach than it is actually able to say. But the controversy over cost-push and demand-pull causes of inflation cannot be resolved within the approach and, indeed, the arguments become circular, resulting in profound misunderstandings. However, if abandoning the demand-pull scheme, we approach the analysis of inflation through a more global and less unilateral approach, we can hope to obtain a useful clarification on the controversy. This point can be best understood in light of our previous discussion, as we shall now see.

So-called cost-push inflation increasingly appears to be due to pressures arising from conflict over the distribution of income;[18] such pressures constitute, at present, the single most important cause of inflation. We have seen that these pressures come together with a substantial expansion of public expenditure (due to the intermediary role that the public administration is obliged to perform in the presence of marked social conflict) and, more generally, with an excess of demand (intended as discussed in the previous point). This conflation gives to those inflationary motions the appearance of an inflation stimulated by demand, thus providing one part of the Keynesian economists' seemingly good reasons for maintaining that this is in fact the case.

But we know that the pressures surrounding income distribution are also accompanied by some degree of underutilization of resources, thus enabling other Keynesian economists, who see in this underutilization of resources a clear indication of the deficiency of demand, to maintain that inflation is due to costs. But the indication of this underutilization of productive capacity as a proof of deficiency of demand is senseless, as we know. These latter economists could properly defend the thesis that the inflation is due to costs only by abandoning the

Keynesian scheme.[19] And in fact, as soon as we do abandon such an approach, the equivocation disappears: it becomes clearly evident that it is completely mistaken to consider that this inflationary motion is due to demand and to operate interventions based on such a conviction. At the same time, we perceive the substantial appropriateness of the alternative point of view.

We consider it more appropriate to indicate the inflationary motion considered here as an inflation due to distribution, in order to capture the real nature of the inflation, and we dearly hope that such reflection throws some light on a controversy that, if not solved, will continue to generate profound theoretical and empirical misunderstanding.

8.6 Conclusion

After the 'hot autumn' of 1969 and, even more so, in the wake of the large increase of oil prices in 1973, the real nature of the situation became increasingly evident. The crucial importance of the pressure coming from income distribution has become ever clearer. But its character is not yet well understood. Above all, the reciprocal inconsistency that, mainly in conditions like those of the present, separates the points of view of demand and distribution does not seem to be acknowledged. As a consequence, the equivocation remains; that is, students continue to speak of a deficiency of demand and the necessity of stimulating this variable with erroneous consequences concerning both diagnosis and therapies. The analysis of this aspect of the problem merits a generalization.

After Keynes's work, economists' references to the level of demand became increasingly frequent. This has entailed a substitution of the Ricardian proposition that supply creates its own demand by the Keynesian proposition that demand creates supply. But the second proposition is, at the very least, no less deceitful than the first.

Economics, having increasingly ascertained the ineffectiveness of the Keynesian postulate of the residual character of real wages (on which such a proposition is based), seems to have accurately avoided the deduction of the consequences of such evidence with regard to the present effectiveness of the Keynesian approach. It has simply limited itself to substituting for the previous postulate the hypothesis of income policies[20] (mainly concerning labor income). In this way, it is supposed to have delayed the validity of Keynesian theory and even the post-Keynesian theory of distribution of income and of development. This seems to have caused a lot of ambiguities and confusions, to the point where, probably, the statement that this has become one of the most confused aspects of contemporary economics is not exaggerated.

It should be clear that the substitution of income policies for the Keynesian postulate of residuality of real wages does not allow a return to Keynesian theory. Such a substitution simply constitutes a forced pretense of extending Keynes's model to situations outside its field of application. This leads to the omission in the investigation of crucial aspects of contemporary economies, simply by way of attempts to remedy the analytical shortcomings through some mere relation of compatibility, namely, income policies.

Notes

1. The equality between the right and left sides of the table is *ex post*, the table being a relation of national accounts. Therefore, the table implies also equality between saving and investment, as is seen if we subtract from the two sides of Kalecki's representation of gross product both workers' and capitalists' consumption.

   It is possible to use a more complete representation of gross product than this, that is, one that includes also public administration (PA) and international trade:

		Workers' consumptions	+
Gross profit (excluding taxes)	+	Capitalists' consumptions	+
Wages, salaries and transfer (net of taxes)	=	Gross investment	+
		Deficit of PA	+
		Excess of exports over imports	=
Gross national product		Gross national product	

   However, while this representation does not add anything substantial to our inquiry, it would generate some additional complications.
2. See Kalecki (1975).
3. The same hypothesis characterizes Kaldor's approach. Kaldor introduces into the model the natural rate of development and hence technical progress and demographic increase; nevertheless, he attributes to investment the role of substantial and main instrumental variable.
4. Kregel wrongly emphasizes this aspect. He writes: "The possibility of creating financial means previously . . . with respect to effective production . . . allows entrepreneurs to owe real resources according to their real earnings and their wealth. . . . The possibility for capitalists to dispose some financial resources in order to buy resources to be invested confers on them the control of last instance of the proportions according to which the available resources by the system take the form of consumption and investment" and hence (we may add) of wages and profits (Kregel 1975, p. 225).
5. It is not necessary that this covering is total. In fact, if the covering of inflation through the indexation of wages is near to 1, a very high rate of inflation would be necessary to allow the profit share to rise.
6. This means that, in practice, the statement that wage bargaining is in terms of money wages but not real wages does not imply that labor market conditions do not influence real wages. In fact, the independence of real wages from the contents and the results of wage bargaining depends, after all, on the particular conditions of the labor market that Keynesian theory implicitly presumes, unless the situations under conditions 1 and 2 are verified. This is possible with reference to the short run. In fact, in this case, the postulate of residuality of real wages is operative also in the absence of condition 3.
7. Kaldor (1965) himself underlines that subsistence wages only characterize the initial stages of development.
8. See Robinson (1961).
9. The main contribution of Pasinetti in this regard is his article entitled "Rate of profit and income distribution in relation to the rate of economic growth" (1962).
10. It could be objected that the assumption of the full utilization of capital (but not labor) would make valid the post-Keynesian theory of income distribution. But such a hypothesis (scarcity of capital with respect to labor) can be considered appropriate only with

reference to underdeveloped economies, for which the Keynesian theory is not valid for different reasons, that is, due to the absence of homogeneity of the economic system, indispensable to make effective the leadership of demand.
11 In this matter, it may be useful to refer to an article by U. Marani (1976).
12 One of the last of Kalecki's articles considers the impact of class struggle on income distribution. He does this by using the interpretative model briefly outlined in the previous section and therefore arrives at the result that such struggle will determine a higher degree of utilization of productive capacity and hence a higher level of production, wages and profits, even if profits will grow less than wages. At the basis of these results there is the hypothesis that profits are consequential with respect to investment, this last being considered exogenous.

These results reawakened in the minds of many students and even trade unionists the presumption of consistency of wage claims with the needs of the economy, just when such consistency underwent a crisis. See Kalecki (1975).
13 It may be useful to underline that while a deficiency of demand can happen in this case, it can arise as a consequence of restrictive policies directed to reduce the inflationary pushes due to pressures on distribution (which remains, therefore, the fundamental a priori element of the situation).
14 Let's repeat that, in this case, it is clear that the conditions of demand do not have an autonomous character. In fact, the basic causal factor is represented by the reason why the restrictive policies have been adopted. Therefore, in this case, the genesis of the problems must not be attributed to the level of demand.
15 We limit ourselves to providing an example of the way to operate such a confrontation. Suppose that the dynamics of money incomes is, with a substantial persistence, markedly higher than that of real income and that the propensity to save is constant or decreasing. In this case, the tendency of the quantity of demanded goods to exceed the quantity of produced goods is clearly evident. Of course, it is possible that investment stagnates. But this, in the previous hypothesis, causes an increase of the demand of goods with respect to production, since such a situation causes a decrease of the dynamics of real product. A further clarification of this point will be provided in note 16.
16 We now turn again to the example set out in the previous note and suppose that the dynamics of money incomes is persistently and markedly higher than that of gross income, and also that the propensity to save is unvaried or diminishing. This means that the demand for consumption goods tends to exceed the supply of those goods. But it is possible that the dynamics of investment stagnates and is lower than that of saving. We must ask ourselves if this can be regarded as indicating a true condition of the deficiency of demand. The answer is negative (notwithstanding the possible associated underutilization of plant). In fact, if the demand for consumption goods is persistently expansionary, investment is not subjected to stagnation by the deficiency of demand. A possible reduction of this aggregate can be due to the fact that the high dynamics of money income (previously hypothesized), by influencing the costs of firms, can depress the profitability of productive processes (or the competitiveness of exports). This implies that the considered stagnation of investment must be attributed to distribution pressures.
17 On such controversy and the attempts to resolve it see, in particular, the articles by Bole and Bodkin (1972) and Weintraub (1960).
18 Inflation due to the costs of imported raw materials should also be considered as a consequence of pressures concerning the distribution of income or, more precisely, as a consequence of the redistribution of those costs among various countries. More generally, the cost increases of raw materials must be considered primarily as a consequence of the international conflict for the distribution of wealth among developed and underdeveloped countries.

19 Cost inflation would be consistent with the Keynesian scheme only if the entrepreneur were able to answer the motion of money wages with collateral increases of the prices of produced goods able to neutralize the pressure of this motion on income distribution. In fact, in this case, the postulate of residuality of real wages would operate. But this could happen only on the extremely unrealistic hypothesis that workers are plainly subject to monetary illusion and international competition is absent. In the absence of these conditions, the previous motion of wages would cause considerable pressures on income distribution and this would force the analysis outside the Keynesian approach.
20 In this regard, the conclusions of Weintraub's article (1960) are illuminating.

References

Blaug, M. (1977), *Cambridge revolution*, Liguori, Naples.
Bole, R. J. & Bodkin, R. S. (1972), A generalized Keynesian model, in R. J. Boll & P. Doyle (eds), *L'inflazione*, Franco Angeli, Milan, pp. 90–115.
Hicks, J. R. (1975), *The crisis of Keynesian economics*, Boringhieri, Turin.
Kaldor, N. (1965), Capitalist evolution in the light of Keynesian economics, in *Essays on economic stability and development*, Einaudi, Turin, pp. 263–279.
Kalecki, M. (1975), *On the dynamics of the capitalist economy*, Einaudi, Turin.
Kregel, J. A. (1975), *The post-Keynesian economics*, Laterza, Bari.
Leijonhufvud, A. (1975), *L'economia Keynesiana e l'economia di Keynes*, UTET, Turin.
Marani, U. (1976), On the post-Keynesian theory of distribution, *Rivista Internazionale di scienze sociali*, fasc. IV and V.
Pasinetti, L. L. (1962), Rate of profit and income distribution in relation to the rate of economic growth, *Review of Economic Studies*, vol. XXIX, October, pp. 267–279.
Robinson, J. (1961), *The accumulation of capital*, Edizioni di Comunità, Milan.
Weintraub, S. (1972) Two notions of inflation, in *Inflation*, Franco Angeli Editore, Milan, pp. 71–89.

9 Economic dualism
A model concerning Italy

9.1 Introduction

The problem of economic dualism has been much studied in works on developing countries, and much attention has also been dedicated to the phenomenon of backward areas within developed economies. But careful studies of advanced dualistic economies are rare. In fact, such a dualism is often analyzed on the basis of the findings of the theory of economic underdevelopment or studies on backward areas, which inevitably neglect some central peculiarities of advanced dualistic economies. The situation is highly unsatisfactory, since advanced sectors are now achieving significant dimensions in an increasing number of developing countries. Italy constitutes one of the best instances of an advanced dualistic economy and thus offers ideal material for investigating this case.

The macrodynamic model explored here focuses mainly on the impact of the dualistic character of the Italian economy on the labor market, inflation, the process of capital formation and its cyclical behavior. The model probably goes beyond the Italian experience and describes the supply and demand for goods, the distribution of income, the balance of payments on current accounts and the current account budget of the public sector. It refers to a historic period (30 years ago) during which dualism operated strongly.

Quantitative and qualitative analyses have been carried out on the model. This has been estimated as a continuous time model, using the full information maximum likelihood method (FIML). We have also analyzed its stability properties and its predictive performance and performed some experiments of sensitivity analysis.

9.2 The bitter fate of economic planning and the phenomenon of dualism

Studies into and applications of planning, at the national and regional levels and with regard also to big business, experienced a substantial flowering and diffusion throughout the Western world over the two decades around the middle of the last century. The success of planning was intimately connected to the effectiveness, for more than two decades, of Keynesian recipes suggested by the great depression that began in 1929.

As previously seen, the diffusion of oligopolies and the associated steep rises in productivity generated by the second industrial revolution, as well as low wages and the physiological volatility of entrepreneurs' expectations and, hence, investment, all combined to generate a deficiency of effective demand. The analysis of such a situation convinced J. M. Keynes to underline the importance, in stimulating demand and growth, of the management of the economy through government intervention, social and budgetary policies and, especially, the use of public expenditure. These suggestions provided fascinating topics for economic planning. Moreover, the Keynesian idea that, in the presence of a deficiency of effective demand even the waste of resources had the virtue of stimulating production, was very attractive for public operators and the political class because it allowed them to achieve electoral favor through generous gifts of public benefits and services.

In the second half of the 1960s, a new historical age was ushered in on the wings of the third industrial revolution. The phase of 'monopoly capitalism' was replaced by that of conflictual-consumeristic capitalism, a stage of development that, as sketched in Section 8.4, was characterized by a great intensification of competition founded on the supply of new goods (product innovation); a strong impetus to consumption through advertising; high wages in the dynamic sectors of the economy, aimed at stimulating affluent consumption (primarily passenger cars and household appliances) and keeping mark-up margins unvaried so as to prevent the entry of potential competitors; and the growing contractual power of trade unions and imitational increases of wages and consumption in the less dynamic sectors of the economy. All of this paved the way to acute conflicts over income distribution, which were exacerbated in the early 1970s by a large hike in oil prices. The result was growing inflation.

The advent of conflictual-consumeristic capitalism rendered traditional Keynesian-based planning inappropriate. This occurred at just the moment when Italian national planning, largely modelled on just those Keynesian recipes, started. The so-called reference tableaux (specified both at the aggregate and sectoral levels) of the two Italian five-year plans were demand-led constructions; they substantially neglected the micro level, and in particular the entrepreneurial role, which was tacitly considered an enemy of programmatic approaches. The procedures of 'programmed bargaining' with private entrepreneurs amounted to little more than a tardy imitation that, in the event, did not enjoy widespread applications.

This undervaluation of the entrepreneurial function by the planners of the mid-20th century was legitimized even by the mature teaching of J. A. Schumpeter, the father of the analysis of entrepreneurship. In his book *Capitalism, Socialism and Democracy* (1954), Schumpeter predicted the euthanasia of the entrepreneurial role in the face of the rise of big business.[1] We have already explained how these erroneous forecasts and attitudes were rooted in the undervaluation of radical uncertainty (i.e. uncertainty that cannot be estimated through objective or subjective distributions of probability), which is a fundamental attribution and the last resort reason for entrepreneurship. As a consequence of this undervaluation of the entrepreneur's role, the promotion and improvement of entrepreneurial skills were markedly disregarded. This neglect is clearly evidenced by the criteria of nomination of the managers of public firms. Such criteria did not give importance to managers' skills and success in the fulfillment of their function but instead attributed a great value to the loyalty and compliance of public managers toward the politicians that had designated them. Their firms' losses, justified by the so-called social function of those firms, were made up through the allotment of abundant endowment funds that contributed substantially to the rise of public debt. The myth of so-called *deficit spending* and, more generally, of the propulsive function of public waste (a role effective only in the presence of a genuine deficiency of demand) justified such behavior.

As we have seen, a situation characterized by strong pressure arising out of the struggle for income distribution is completely different from one distinguished by a deficiency of effective demand. A considerable and influential part of the political spectrum and of the trade unions viewed the contradictions generated by the conflict over income distribution an important means of overthrowing capitalism. Something similar to the 'income policies' started to find some applications at the beginning of the 1990s, in the wake of economic crisis and in the face of the mounting evidence of the disaster that had occurred in the countries subject to so-called real socialism.

These difficulties, acting at the world scale, were aggravated in Italy by the superimposition upon them of misunderstandings arising out of this nation's deep territorial, economic and social dualism. It is important to deepen this aspect, since (as we have seen in the introduction) it provides suggestions and learning with regard to a phenomenon (dualism) which still is largely diffused across the world.

The overcoming of Italian dualisms would have required a great programmatic effort and deep structural reformations. Unfortunately, while there was indeed an abundance of analyses and programmatic elaborations dedicated to the phenomenon of dualism and of problems specific to Southern Italy, these remained substantially separate from the framework of the plans as a whole. There was simply no real perception that the demand-led draft of economic planning was inconsistent with the marked dualistic character of the Italian economy and that the propulsive push associated with the expansion of demand, if it were to operate effectively, required structural homogeneity, functional efficiency and the absence of both bottlenecks and dualism. Let's see the effects of dualism in Italy.

Up to the early 1960s, Italian economic development for the most part followed Lewis's dualistic model, according to which migrants coming from the underdeveloped regions provide an abundant and cheap workforce for the advanced regions, thereby favoring a development of these regions that would gradually extend to the underdeveloped areas and hence give rise to the social and economic unification of the whole country. The operation of such a mechanism requires that wages are determined by the demand and supply of labor so that wages are lowered by the structural excess of the labor force until it is depleted.

In Italy, Lewis's model worked only in part. It favored the economic growth of Northern Italy and the so-called economic miracle, which was due also to the boldness and high skill levels of important public managers. But this rapid growth was accompanied by an increasing reduction of the economic activity in Southern Italy, quite different from the extension of development toward the South predicted by Lewis's model. On the one side, the economic miracle increased the contractual power of the labor force; on the other side, the promotion of consumerism induced the entrepreneurs in the advanced sectors to accede to the trade unions' demands for higher wages, so as to stimulate the consumptions of new goods, ensure social peace and avoid the entry of potential competitors. More precisely, the high wage increase in developed areas and in the sectors' productivity leaders had two main effects:

1 It stimulated migration toward the advanced areas to a degree more than required by the growing need for labor in those areas; moreover, it stimulated the collateral reductions of the productive apparatus in the backward areas. The consequent *excess of labor force* flowed into refuge sectors with low productivity (retail commerce, public administration and traditional activities).
2 All of this, in turn, stimulated high imitational wage increases in backward and refuge sectors, which were supported by the significant contractual power of trade unions that claimed, in the name of social justice, the establishment of collective labor agreements that were uniform at the national level and also the indexation of wages to the cost of living. This caused strong pressure and inconsistencies on the side of income distribution and accelerated the migration from the South and the further reduction of the productive potential of this area. Moreover, the premise for the subsequent explosion of public debt (mainly through welfare policies and refuge employment) was prepared.

So, if we consider the Italian process of development also from the side of economic and social dualism, the inappropriateness of the demand-led approach to economic planning appears even more evident. The installation in the South of big state capital intensive industries and high promotional incentives that benefited private firms (mainly petrochemical) did not produce substantial increases of employment; and, at the same time, this accelerated the demise of traditional activities. The Keynesian idea that public waste stimulates growth favored the building of almost useless infrastructures that often remained unfinished and the assignment of unmerited and pointless incentives. Almost nothing was done to promote managerial responsibility and to eliminate unearned income and the institutional monopolies that distort the ability of the market to stimulate efficiency; and almost nothing was done to promote the efficiency of nonmarket activities.

220   *Problems of political economy*

9.3   Formulation of the model[2]

The dynamic behavior of the model that will follow is significantly influenced by the sharp sectoral and territorial segmentation of the Italian economy.[3] This segmentation can be described as follows:

- An advanced sector (consisting mostly of manufacturing) characterized by high and rapidly rising productivity, consistent gains in employment, high export capacity, oligopolistic market conditions and the absence of competition in the labor market
- A backward sector (consisting mostly of agriculture) characterized by low productivity, the rate of change of which can be quite volatile, and a competitive product market
- A refuge sector (more or less covering retail trade, public administration and other services, and in some periods construction as well) characterized by low and above all nearly stagnant productivity. It should be noted that this sector is able to pass all cost increases along in higher prices.[4]

There is also a definite geographical segmentation corresponding to these sectors. The backward sector is mostly made up of agricultural zones, the advanced sector of industrial zones and the refuge sector of the large urban areas of central-southern Italy.

The role of the refuge sector remains implicit in the model; its impact is measured through the effects of the labor surplus (which it has absorbed in a more and more evident manner over time) on the cost of living, on the distribution of income, on the costs of the public administration and finally on investment.

The model is made up of 22 interdependent equations describing the supply and demand for goods, the distribution of income, the balance of payments on current account and the current account budget of the public sector.

Among the supply equations, the industrial productivity equation is of paramount importance. It is specified to be a function of the sectoral capital/employee ratio, the rate of growth in industrial investment (a summary indicator of the effects on productivity of embodied technical progress), total exports of goods and services (which affects productivity through economies of scale and the need for competitiveness dictated by foreign trade) and, with a minus sign, the share of profits (the assumption being that pressure on profits will spur innovation to boost productivity). The endogenous level of productivity (i.e. value added per employee) in industry makes it possible to calculate total industrial value added (multiplying productivity by the number of employees). Then, knowing the value added (VA) in industry, the GDP is calculated assuming a relationship of proportionality between the two variables.

The demand side is explained by three equations: an equation for industrial investment, depending on the share of profit in industry, the money supply and, with a minus sign, government's current account flow (to take into account crowding-in and crowding-out effects); an equation for total consumption, depending on GDP, the money supply (which influences liquidity conditions) and, with a minus sign, the cost of living; an equation for exports, depending on the ratio of international to domestic price for manufactures, world demand and, with a minus sign, internal demand (the assumption being that there is substitution between the latter and exports).

The equations for income distribution concern industrial wages, salaries in the remaining sectors and the share of profits.

The equation for nominal industrial wages plays a central role here. It is a function of sectoral productivity, of the ratio between currency flow and real GDP flow, and the cost of living; it is assumed, however, that the level of employment – or, more precisely, the level of the excess labor force – does not affect wage increases.[5] Through wage leadership, industrial wages determine wages in the rest of the economy. The share of profits in industry is given by an identity: the difference between one and the share of wages in value added.

In this model, the variables describing employment assume a different meaning from the one usually ascribed to them. Given marked sectoral dualism and extensive backward areas, the exodus from traditional sectors (mainly agriculture) could not avoid exceeding the needs of the other sectors of the economy. This surplus of labor force has represented a powerful cause of inflation.[6] A variety of mechanisms are at work here. First, it has stimulated early retirements and other forms of income transfer by government. Second, refuge employment (which aggravates the existing productivity gap between the refuge and the dynamic sectors) has strengthened inflationary pressures.[7] Third, there are the costs connected with the exodus from backward sectors and areas (the cost of urbanization, for one) and the bottlenecks (shortages of housing, services, etc.) created where these costs were not sustained. Finally, there was intensifying wage pressure from the employed labor force to preserve family incomes undermined by the fall in the employment rate. The previously mentioned influences have mainly concerned the cost of living.

These developments have given a vigorous impulse not only to inflation but also to public expenditure. For the private sector, this has involved the following two principal consequences which have slowed capital formation and therefore further spurred the swelling of the surplus labor force:

1 The government has borrowed increasingly in the capital markets (in competition with the private sector) to finance public sector deficits.
2 Money wages have increased rapidly, since they are driven upward by inflationary pressure owing to formal and informal indexing mechanisms. Thus, unit labor costs have increased in the more dynamic sectors, but industrial employees have not benefited greatly therefrom, since wage gains are accompanied by comparable increases in the cost of living.[8] Given acute international competition, this has driven down the profit rate in industry.

In conclusion, it seems that the profound and widespread sectoral and territorial disequilibria have provided the basic breeding ground for the unsatisfactory performance of the Italian economy. This happened principally because of the formation of an increasing structural surplus of labor which does not have an important role in regulating labor market conditions but instead, in various ways, shifts the burden of its unproductive presence to the national economy.

9.3.1 Variables of the model

Endogenous

π_1	=	Industrial labor productivity
w_{1p}	=	Money wage rate in industry
w_{rp}	=	Money wage rate in the rest of the economy
O_2	=	Employment in agriculture
CV	=	Consumer price level
P_1	=	Industrial price level
P	=	GDP price level
I_1	=	Gross industrial investment in real terms
O_1	=	Employment in industry
Y	=	Gross domestic product in real terms
C	=	Total consumption in real terms
IMP	=	Real imports of goods and services
EX	=	Real exports of goods and services
KU	=	Degree of capacity utilization in industry
M	=	Currency
U^c	=	Public sector expenditure
E^c	=	Public sector revenue
O_3	=	Employment in the rest of the economy
Y_p	=	Nominal GDP
Q_1	=	Profit share in industry
w_1	=	Industrial wage rate in real terms
Y_1	=	Real value added in industry

Exogenous

P^i	=	Exports unit value index of manufactures of main competitors (in lire)
P_a	=	Agricultural price level
Y_w	=	World real income
PIM	=	Import price level
k	=	Capital/employment ratio in industry

Other symbols

α	=	Adjustment parameter
β	=	Structural parameter
γ	=	Intercept
D	=	Differential operator
log	=	Logarithm symbol
$\wedge$	–	Indicates values of partial equilibrium

9.3.2 Equations of the model
Industrial labor productivity

(1) $\text{Dlog}\pi_1 = \alpha_1 \log(\hat{\pi}_1/\pi_1)$ where

   (1.1) $\log \hat{\pi}_1 = \beta_1 \text{DlogI}_1 - \beta_2 \log Q_1 + \beta_3 \log EX + \beta_4 \text{Dlogk} + \log \gamma_1$

Money wage rate in industry

(2) $\text{Dlogw}_{1p} = \alpha_2 \log(\hat{w}_{1p}/w_{1p})$ where

   (2.1) $\log \hat{w}_{1p} = \beta_5 \log \pi_1 + \beta_6 \log CV + \beta_7 \text{Dlog}(M/Y) + \log \gamma_2$

Money wage rate in the rest of the economy

(3) $\text{Dlog } w_{rp} = \alpha_3 \log(\hat{w}_{rp}/w_{rp})$ where

   (3.1) $\log \hat{w}_{rp} = \beta_8 \log w_{1p} + \log \gamma_3$

Employment in agriculture

(4) $\text{DlogO}_2 = \alpha_4 \log(\hat{O}_2/O_2)$ where

   (4.1) $\log \hat{O}_2 = -\beta_9 \log w_{1p} + \beta_{10} \log P_a + \log \gamma_4$

Consumer price level

(5) $\text{DlogCV} = \alpha_5 \log(\widehat{CV}/CV)$ where

   (5.1) $\log \widehat{CV} = \beta_{11} \log w_{1p} - \beta_{12} \log(O_2 + O_1) + \beta_{13} \log P^i + \log \gamma_5$

Price of industrial value added

(6) $\text{DlogP}_1 = \alpha_6 \log(\hat{P}_1/P_1)$ where

   (6.1) $\log \hat{P}_1 = \beta_{14} \log(w_{1p}/\pi_1) + \beta_{15} \log P^i + \log \gamma_6$

Price of GDP

(7) $\text{DlogP} = \alpha_7 \log(\hat{P}/P)$ where

   (7.1) $\log \hat{P} = \beta_{16} \log P_1 - \beta_{17} \log O_2 + \beta_{18} \log P_a + \log \gamma_7$

Gross investment in industry

(8) $D^2 \log I_1 = \alpha_8 \log(\hat{I}_1/I_1)$ where

   (8.1) $\log \hat{I}_1 = \beta_{19} \log Q_1 + \beta_{20} \log M - \beta_{21} \text{Dlog}(U^c/E^c) + \log \gamma_8$

Employment in industry

(9) $DlogO_1 = \alpha_9 log(\hat{O}_1/O_1)$ where

(9.1) $log\hat{O}_1 = \beta_{22}logI_1 + \beta_{23}logKU - \beta_{24}DlogK + log\gamma_9$

Real GDP

(10) $DlogY = \alpha_{10}log(\hat{Y}/Y)$ where

(10.1) $log\hat{Y} = \beta_{25}logY_1 + log\gamma_{10}$

Total real consumption

(11) $DlogC = \alpha_{11}log(\hat{C}/C)$ where

(11.1) $log\hat{C} = \beta_{26}logY - \beta_{27}logCV + \beta_{28}logM + log\gamma_{11}$

Real imports

(12) $DlogIMP = \alpha_{12}log(\widehat{IMP}/IMP)$ where

(12.1) $log\widehat{IMP} = \beta_{29}logY_1 + \beta_{30}logw_1 + \beta_{31}log(P/PIM) + log\gamma_{12}$

Real exports

(13) $DlogEX = \alpha_{13}log(\widehat{EX}/EX)$ where

(13.1) $log\widehat{EX} = -\beta_{32}log(C+I) - \beta_{33}logP_1 + \beta_{34}logP^i + \beta_{35}logY_w + log\gamma_{13}$

Degree of capacity utilization in industry

(14) $DlogKU = \alpha_{14}log(\widehat{KU}/KU)$ where

(14.1) $log\widehat{KU} = +\beta_{36}log(C+I_1+EX) + log\gamma_{14}$

Currency reaction function

(15) $D^2logM = \beta_{37}log(P^i/P_1) + \beta_{38}Dlog(P^i/P_1) + \beta_{39}log(EX/IMP) + \beta_{39}log(P^i/PIM) + log\gamma_{15}$

Public sector expenditure

(16) $DlogU^c = \alpha_{15}log(\hat{U}^c/U^c)$ where

(16.1) $log\hat{U}^c = \beta_{40}log(w_{1p}O_1) + \beta_{41}log(O_2+O_3)w_{rp} + log\gamma_{16}$

Public sector revenue

(17) $DlogE^c = \alpha_{16}log(\hat{E}^c/E^c)$ where

(17.1) $log\hat{E}^c = \beta_{42}logY_p + log\gamma_{17}$

Employment in the rest of the economy

(18) $DlogO_3 = \alpha_{17}log(\hat{O}_3/O_3)$ where

(18.1) $log\hat{O}_3 = -\beta_{43}log(O_1+O_2) + log\gamma_{18}$

Nominal GDP

(19) $\log Y_p = \log Y + \log P$

Profit share in industry

(20) $\log Q_1 = \log(1 - w_{1p} / \pi_1 P_1)$

Real wage rate in industry

(21) $\log w_1 = \log w_{1p} - \log CV$

Industrial value added

(22) $\log Y_1 = \log O_1 + \log \pi_1$

9.4 Results of estimation

The parameters of the model have been estimated by using a sample of quarterly observations which range from the first quarter of 1960 to the fourth quarter of 1981. We have used, for estimation, a FIML procedure developed by C. Wymer.[9] The nonlinear model has been linearized in the logarithms about the sample means by taking a first-order Taylor series expansion. It is worth noting that the method of estimation endogenously determines the lags (α) with which the effective

Table 9.1 Estimated adjustment parameters

Parameter	Equation number	Estimate of parameter	Asymptotic standard error	t ratio	Mean time lag (quarters)
α_1	(1)	0.551	0.089	6.13	1.815
α_2	(2)	0.715	0.118	6.03	1.398
α_3	(3)	0.868	0.135	6.44	1.152
α_4	(4)	0.190	0.050	3.82	5.263
α_5	(5)	0.090	0.019	4.77	11.111
α_6	(6)	0.542	0.094	5.73	1.845
α_7	(7)	0.317	0.050	6.29	3,154
α_8	(8)	1.345	0.223	6.03	0.743
α_9	(9)	0.061	0.007	8.11	16.393
α_{10}	(10)	1.025	0.171	6.00	0.975
α_{11}	(11)	1.460	0.199	7.33	0.680
α_{12}	(12)	1.141	0.194	5.88	0.876
α_{13}	(13)	1.245	0.175	7.12	0.803
α_{14}	(14)	0.309	0.065	4.75	3.236
α_{15}	(16)	3.701	0.706	5.24	0.270
α_{16}	(17)	2.312	0.372	6.21	0.432
α_{17}	(18)	0.352	0.109	3.22	2.840

Table 9.2 Estimated elasticities and growth rates

Parameter	Equation number	Estimate of parameter	Asymptotic standard error	t ratio
β_1	(1)	0.062	0.031	2.00
β_2	(1)	0.144	0.136	1.05
β_3	(1)	0.476	0.025	18.49
β_4	(1)	5.093	1.268	4.02
β_5	(2)	1.049	0.087	12.02
β_6	(2)	0.976	0.035	28.01
β_7	(2)	4.894	0.766	6.39
β_8	(3)	0.996	0.010	98.61
β_9	(4)	0.692	0.060	11.46
β_{10}	(4)	0.684	0.094	7.27
β_{11}	(5)	0.183	0.047	3.87
β_{12}	(5)	0.300	0.229	0.87
β_{13}	(5)	0.938	0.091	10.35
β_{14}	(6)	0.585	0.068	8.58
β_{15}	(6)	0.383	0.066	5.76
β_{16}	(7)	0.903	0.095	9.50
β_{17}	(7)	0.347	0.039	8.85
β_{18}	(7)	0.116	0.097	1.19
β_{19}	(8)	0.153	0.099	1.54
β_{20}	(8)	0.010	0.009	1.14
β_{21}	(8)	0.015	0.027	0.57
β_{22}	(9)	0.143	0.018	7.83
β_{23}	(9)	0.105	0.112	0.94
β_{24}	(9)	29.954	3.738	4.02
β_{25}	(10)	0.742	0.012	60.01
β_{26}	(11)	0.826	0.055	15.00
β_{27}	(11)	0.114	0.025	4.43
β_{28}	(11)	0.110	0.027	4.01
β_{29}	(12)	1.282	0.040	31.63
β_{30}	(12)	0.110	0.019	5.77
β_{31}	(12)	0.099	0.090	1.10
β_{32}	(13)	0.300	0.226	1.33
β_{33}	(13)	1.287	0.212	6.06
β_{34}	(13)	1.054	0.181	5.83
β_{35}	(13)	2.945	0.272	10.82
β_{36}	(14)	0.016	0.006	2.51
β_{37}	(15)	0.144	0.062	2.32
β_{38}	(15)	0.932	0.222	4.21
β_{39}	(15)	0.084	0.030	2.82
β_{40}	(16)	0.788	0.139	5.66
β_{41}	(16)	0.306	0.147	2.08
β_{42}	(17)	1.089	0.010	99.09
β_{43}	(18)	1.190	0.166	7.15

Economic dualism 227

values adjust themselves to the desired ones (which are expressed by the functional equations used to explain the phenomena under observation). Finally, this method distinguishes stock variables from flow variables and permits forecasts (or simulations) for any desired time interval (yearly, quarterly, monthly etc.). This is made possible by the fact that the parameter estimates are independent from the interval of observation of the data series. The estimation iterative procedure converges with a tolerance of 0.50%. The Carter-Nagar system R square statistic is 0.975, and the associated χ^2 statistic is 72327.2 with 74 degrees of freedom; therefore, the hypothesis that the model is not consistent with the data is rejected. See Tables 9.1 and 9.2.

On the whole, the estimation results are very satisfactory and conform with the theory presented in Section 9.2. All parameters have the correct sign and plausible values; some of the high absolute values of the parameters are due to the fact that the associated variables are rates of change and not levels. Of the 60 parameters estimated, 47 are significantly different from zero at least at the 1% level on asymptotic text and 4 are significant at the 5% level. The significance level of the remaining nine parameters is below the 5% level.[10]

9.5 Stability and sensitivity analysis

We can analyze the stability properties of the model on the basis of its characteristic roots (eigenvalues) (see Table 9.3). Asymptotic standard errors, damping periods and periods of cycles are not given for space limitations.

Table 9.3 Stability and sensitivity analysis

Eigenvalues	Partial derivatives with respect to β_{20}	Partial derivatives with respect to β_{37}	Partial derivatives with respect to β_{39}
−0.072	0.031	0.072	−0.067
−0.102	−0.817	0.259	0.103
−0.134	0.467	−0.932	−0.436
−0.188	−0.012	0.033	0.057
−0.308	−0.002	0.017	0.067
−0.310	0.020	0.005	0.021
−0.352	0.0	0.0	0.0
−0.868	0.0	0.0	0.0
−1.142	0.002	0.001	−0.017
−1.340	0.004	0.002	0.049
−2.311	0.0	0.0	0.0
−3.700	0.0	0.0	0.0
0.005 +/−0.01	0.116 +/−0.59	−0.021 +/−0.02	0.034 +/−0.04
−0.260 +/−0.56	−0.009 +/−0.01	0.223 +/−0.40	0.505 +/−1.09
−0.955 +/−1.08	0.008 +/−0.00	0.065 +/−0.29	−0.506 +/−0.37
−1.537 +/−0.24	0.003 +/−0.00	0.005 +/−0.03	0.080 +/−0.01

228 *Problems of political economy*

Table 9.3 shows that all the real eigenvalues are negative. This means that the model has a stable trend.

The complex conjugate eigenvalues describe the cyclical behavior of the model. Three of these eigenvalues have negative real part and a stable cycle (with cyclical periods of about 3 years, 1.5 years and 6.5 years). Finally, a complex conjugate eigenvalue has a positive real part, which means the system will converge to a limit cycle associated with this eigenvalue. However, asymptotic standard error shows that this positive real part appears not to be significantly different from zero, so this cause of instability is not worth much consideration.

In order to explore better the dynamic behavior of the system, we turn now to sensitivity analysis. This consists of computing the partial derivatives of eigenvalues with respect to the parameters of the model.

Sensitivity analysis does not show particularly large partial derivatives; however, increases in adjustment parameters appear, in general, to have appreciable stabilizing effects. For reasons of space, we consider here only derivatives of major significance. More precisely, in Table 9.3 we included only the partial derivatives with respect to some policy parameters, namely that of the money variable in the investment equation and that of the currency reaction function.

As we can see, an increase in β_{20} (that is in the parameter of money in the investment equation) tends to have a stabilizing effect on the trend (due to the large negative value of the partial derivative of the second eigenvalue) and a destabilizing effect on the cycle (owing to the positive value of the partial derivative with respect to the real part of the complex eigenvalue), the period of which would become longer.

Likewise, an increase of the parameter β_{37} (the ratio of domestic to international prices) in the reaction function of money will have a stabilizing effect on the trend and a destabilizing one on the cycle. Finally, an increase in β_{39} (the parameter of the balance of payments on current account) in the same equation would also have a stabilizing effect on the trend and a destabilizing one on the cycle, but this would have a longer period, since the derivative of the imaginary part of the 15th complex conjugate eigenvalue has a large positive value.

9.6 Predictive performance of the model

The analysis of the root mean square errors of the residuals allows us to consider the in-sample predictive performance of the model. Since the model is in logarithms, the root mean square error gives the average percentage error around the level of the associated endogenous variable (Table 9.4).

The root mean square errors (RMSE) included in Table 9.4 show values of more than 10% in only three cases; for about half of the endogenous variables the errors are less than 5%. These results can be considered quite satisfactory.

The in-sample predictive performance of the model might be better seen by means of the actual and forecast values of each variable and also through some policy simulations.

Table 9.4 Ex post root mean square errors of dynamic forecasts

Considered sample periods			
Variable	1976–1981 (24 quarters)	1969–1981 (48 quarters)	1960–1981 (whole sample period)
π_1	0.054	0.054	0.053
wlp deponent	0.061	0.067	0.065
wrp deponent	0.067	0.070	0.066
O_2	0.036	0.031	0.035
CV	0.035	0.051	0.039
P_1	0.038	0.037	0.039
P	0.045	0.044	0.042
DI_1	0.017	0.034	0.034
O_1	0.021	0.020	0.023
Y	0.036	0.036	0.039
C	0.026	0.030	0.043
IMP	0.098	0.094	0.098
EX	0.094	0.092	0.075
KU	0.037	0.043	0.039
DM	0.055	0.058	0.049
U^e	0.129	0.118	0.100
E^e	0.087	0.073	0.063
O_3	0.035	0.034	0.053
I	0.046	0.120	0.245
M	0.075	0.136	0.220
Y_p	0.045	0.053	0.042
Q_1	0.087	0.099	0.085
w_1	0.047	0.075	0.070
Y_1	0.042	0.047	0.053

9.7 Conclusion

Quantitative analysis confirms the peculiarities of an advanced dualistic economy like Italy; these concern principally the inflationary process, the employment equations and the wage mechanism. It also confirms their impact on capital formation, on activity levels, on the public deficit and on the balance of payments. Obviously, this implies that the adoption of the policies pursued by the principal developed countries could be quite mistaken for Italy. At least, such policies seem inadequate to check the growth-inhibiting tendencies typical of the Italian economy.

Notes

1 As previously seen, in the 1960s another influential student, J. K. Galbraith, in his book *The New Industrial State* (1967), underlined with augmented emphasis the convergence between capitalism and socialism on the wings of big business.
2 We are indebted to Dr. C. Wymer and to Dr. D. Richard of the IMF for the use of the continuous methodology and programs.
3 See, for example, Streeten (1959), Ranis and Fei (1961), Lutz (1962) and Kindleberger (1967).
4 A more satisfactory framework of analysis would require an intermediate sector between the advanced and the backward sectors. Notionally, it would consist of small business basic consumer goods and would be characterized by lower productivity than the advanced sector. It operates in competitive goods markets and partially competitive labor markets.
5 The surplus labor force in Italy has had an extremely limited influence on the process of wage formation. The fact that workers have learned how to separate the dynamics of wages from the automatic mechanism of the labor market has radically changed the way the economic system reacts to the surplus labor force.
6 In the equation of the cost of living, $O2 + O1$ intends to act as a proxy of the opposite of the excess of labor force.
7 In the model, this aspect is expressed by the functional dependence of the cost of living on industrial wages, as increases in these stimulate wage increases in the *less dynamic sectors* of the economy and then parallel increases in consumer prices.
8 Basically, the rise in unit labor costs sustained by the dynamic sectors has gone mostly to subsidize the inefficiency and parasitism of other sectors of the economy.
9 See Wymer (1976).
10 In the discussion of the results, the term *t-ratio* simply denotes the ratio of a parameter estimate to the estimate of its asymptotic standard error. In a sufficiently large sample, this ratio is significantly different from zero at the 5% level if it lies outside the interval +/–1.96 and significantly different from zero at the 1% level if it is outside the interval +/–2.58.

References

Carter, R. A. L. & Nagar, A. L. (1977), Coefficients correlation for simultaneous equation system, *Journal of Econometrics*, vol. 6, pp. 39–50.
Fei, C. H. & Ranis, G. (1964), *Development of the labour surplus economy: Theory and policy*, Richard A. Irwin, Homewood.
Fusari, A. (1986), *A development model of a dualistic economy: The Italian case*, Dynamic Modelling and Control of National Economies. Proceedings of the 5th IFAC/IFORS Conference, Budapest, Hungary, June 17–20 1986, edited by B. Martos, L. F. Pau and M. Zierman, Proceedings series, 1987, Nà 5.
Galbraith, J. K. (1967), *The new industrial state*, Houghton Mifflin Company, Boston.
Glyn, A. & Sutcliffe, B. (1975), *Sindacati e contrazione del profitto*, Laterza, Bari.
Kindleberger, C. (1967), *Europe's postwar growth: The role of labour supply*, Harvard University Press, Harvard.
Knight, M. D. & Wymer, C. R. (1978), A macrodynamic model of the United Kingdom, *Staff Paper (IMF)*, vol. 25, no. 4, pp. 742–778.
Lewis, A. W. S. (1973), Sviluppo economico con disponibilità illimitata di mano d'opera, in B. Jossa (ed), *Economia del sottosviluppo*, Il Mulino, Bologna, pp. 63–110.
Lutz, V. (1962), *Italy, a study in economic development*, Oxford University Press, London.

McIntosh, J. (1975), Growth and dualism in less developed countries, *Review of Economic Studies*, vol. 42, no. 3, pp. 421–433.
Myrdal, G. (1957), *Economic theory and underdeveloped regions*, Gerald Duckworth, London.
Phillips, A. W. (1958), The relationship between unemployment and the rate of change of money wage rate in the United Kingdom, 1861–1957, *Economica*, vol. 25, pp. 283–299.
Ranis, G. & Fei, J. C. H. (1961), A theory of economic development, *American Economic Review*, vol. 51, no. 4, pp. 533–565.
Schumpeter, J. A. (1954), *Capitalism, socialism and democracy*, Allin and Unwin, London.
Streeten, P. (1959), Unbalanced growth, *Oxford Economic Papers*, vol. X, pp. 167–190.
Sylos Labini, P. (1973), *Sindacati, Inflazione e Produttività*, Laterza, Bari.
Weintraub, S. (1960), The Keynesian theory of inflation: The two faces of Janus? *Economic Review*, vol. 1, pp. 143–159.
Wymer, C. R. (1976), *Continuous time models in macro economics: Specification and estimation*. Paper Presented at the SSRC Ford Foundation Conference on Macroeconomic Policy and Adjustment in Open Economies, Ware, England, April 28, 1976.

10 Money, interest rate and financial markets

10.1 Introduction

This chapter brings into focus some general – and indeed basic – aspects of financial markets and processes, the understanding of which is indispensable for the investigation of many penetrating questions that, notwithstanding their importance, are likely to be set aside by more specialist and sophisticated treatments of financial flows. The discussion on money and interest rate also expresses a completion of Chapter 8 on Keynes and the role of demand.

We shall start with the most typical and important of financial phenomena, money. It will be shown that the changeable role and meaning of money over time has had a strong impact upon the overall financial landscape, primarily by way of the weakening of the workings and interactions of various financial activities. This analysis makes evident both the difficulty but also the urgency of restoring the exogenous character of the money supply. We further focus upon the interest rate, underlining the nonessential role of this variable that, nevertheless, stands at the root of so many exasperating and destabilizing speculations. Finally, we face the problem of how to bring into being a financial market that does not strive for mastery over production but is rather content to work in the service of production. In this way, we face the problem of how we can foster simpler and more transparent financial markets that are able to reconcile efficiency with social justice.

10.2 A brief review on the role and operation of money from the 1930s to the present time

Both the role and the meaning of money have changed substantially over time, in parallel with some important transformations within the economic and social systems. The period between the second and third industrial revolutions witnessed the diffusion of oligopolies together with a related large increase in productivity, low wages and variable entrepreneurial expectations and investment, and hence a recurrent deficiency of effective demand and increase in liquid money. The emergent situation persuaded Keynes to emphasize the idea of liquidity preference and to base the explanation of the rate of interest on the supply and demand for money, as opposed to the earlier appeal to the quantity theory of money and related account of the interest rate in terms of the relationship of savings and investment.[1] But as is not infrequent in the history of social thought, the Keynesian view triumphed only at the moment when its own foundations began to be shaken by further social and economic development.

In the 1970s, a long and bitter controversy grew up between the Keynesian theory that (by way of liquidity preference) the quantity of money determines the interest rate and the orthodox theory, revived by Milton Friedman, that the quantity of money determines the general price level. Actually, late 20th-century socioeconomic conditions fitted neither monetarist nor Keynesian theories. Precisely, the late second half of the last century witnessed a fundamental and unprecedented change: a transition from monopoly capitalism to what we have called conflictual-consumeristic capitalism. As we have seen, the new state of affairs was characterized by competition based largely on new products, the stimulation of consumption through advertisement, high wages in the most dynamic sectors not only due to the bargaining power of trade unions menacing to cause loss of profits through strikes but also aimed at stimulating the consumption of new goods and maintaining an unvaried mark-up margin, and the imitational growth of wages and consumption in the less dynamic sectors of the economy. One consequence of this transformation has been a qualitative change in the role of money, which may primarily be expressed as the increasing importance of what may be called the 'nominal demand for money', that is, variations in the quantity of money endogenously stimulated by both price changes and as a consequence of the conflict for income distribution[2]. This demand for money is just the opposite of the Keynesian preference for liquidity associated with the deficiency (or excess) of effective demand. In fact, while the notion of demand for real money (liquidity preference) refers to the role of money as a fund of value, the demand for nominal money concerns the role of money as means of payment. More in general, this new situation, characterized as it was by the *endogenous* supply of money, differed substantially, both from the situation diagnosed by Keynes,[3] in which exogenous variations of the money supply determine the interest rate, and from the situation described by the quantity theory of money, according to which exogenous variations of the money supply determine prices.

So, the Keynesian doctrines were not equipped to react to (and govern) this consumeristic landing. Their foundation on demand induced consideration of the new situation as characterized by an excess (rather than a deficiency) of effective demand, thus suggesting the necessity of reducing such an excess through restrictive monetary policies (that is, the contrary of the expansive policies required in the presence of a deficiency of effective demand). This condemned consumeristic capitalism to the phenomenon of *stop-go* and the distinction between short- and long-period problems, with the short-run problems prevailing as more imperative over the medium and longer period structural issues constituting the backbone of programmatic designs. Precisely, structural policies were systematically postponed in the name of short-run exigencies, putting off their application until the advent of better conditions that, in the absence of any solution to the structural deficiencies, never arrived. The dominant economic thought of the day was not equipped to allow understanding that the new phase had nothing to do with the traditional theories of money, be they Keynesian or quantitative. So, Keynesianism, while initially much favoring the advent of a new age of planning, was now caught out of time – a situation that facilitated the monetarist reaction. What is worse, the old Keynesianism blocked understanding that structural action and reformation were indispensable even with regard to the control of short period depression by way of the elimination of the decay and dead ends caused by conflictual-consumeristic capitalism.

Let us examine more closely the substance and the effects of this new state of affairs. Inconvertible paper money constitutes an efficacious instrument for taking the sting out of some of the contradictions that may afflict the economy. In particular, it has the potential to diffuse the impact of the conflict over income distribution upon weak and/or ingenuous social groups. Employing a literary parallel, we may say that inconvertible money resembles don Circostanza (don Circumstance), an intriguer and an opportunist lawyer who, in defense of the people of Fontamara[4] against the plan of the mayor to deprive them of the water of the brook, proposed that each of the two conflicting parties be awarded three-quarters of the water. With this trick, he succeeds in placating a protest of the people intended to preserve more than one-half of the available water.

In conflictual-consumeristic capitalism, the money supply is stimulated, as just seen, by endogenous factors, primarily the conflict over income distribution. In some sense it reproduces don Circostanza's expediency to placate Fontamara's conflict by promising to the opposing parties more than the available water. In the presence of money illusion, a modest inflation is sufficient to make don Circostanza's strategy bear fruit. But what happens if people begin to detect the illusory quality of money wages and the object of the bargain becomes real wages? The expansion of public expenditure and public debt may become an alternative path to the elimination of the difficulties and inconsistencies that arise out of the struggle for income distribution. But it is only an apparent alternative. In the end, the financing of the public deficit stimulates the 'nominal demand for money' (the endogenous character of the last), and hence inflation.

It is precisely this 'cheeky' use of money that has opened the door to some of the main difficulties afflicting financial markets today.

10.3 The implications on financial activities of endogenous money variations

The palliative of monetary expansion in masking the inconsistencies considered previously cannot work in the long run. In the absence of monetary illusion, the cumulative rise in inflation will oblige the introduction of restrictive monetary policies that discourage growth. So in conflictual-consumeristic capitalism, inflation does not stimulate production and accumulation; rather, it primes depression, thereby generating so-called stagflation.

In the 1970s, J. Hicks provided an explanation of stagflation in terms of an extension to the long-run Keynesian goods supply curve in which, in compliance with the so-called Phillips curve, a trade-off between unemployment and inflation is postulated.[5] But in that period unemployment did not affect prices in the way predicted by this curve. Hicks pointed to the availability of primary resources as the cause of this anomaly. But, as a matter of fact, a primary cause of the stagnation in this period was restrictive policies directed to reduce the inflation caused by the intensified conflict over income distribution. The related oil price hike of those days was likewise the product of a distributional conflict, this one between oil-consuming and oil-producing countries. But the economic situation at that time was beset by more than just stagflation.

High inflation has perverse effects on the operation of financial activities. In particular, endemic inflation causes a fall in the preference for liquidity, thus demolishing the Keynesian barrier against the decline of the interest rate. Such demolition is accentuated by the fact that people with savings find it difficult, for the most part, to directly invest saved money; this induces them to accept nominal interest rates that, even if they are inferior to the inflation rate (i.e. negative real interest rates), nevertheless allow them to reduce the damage deriving from hoarding money in the presence of inflation. In other words, in the presence of endemic inflation the Keynesian liquidity trap does not operate in defense of the interest rate. In these conditions, the rate of interest ceases to depend on the demand and supply of money, not only because of the disappearance of the liquidity trap but also because, as previously seen, the money supply is not an exogenous entity but is endogenously stimulated by the factors determining the 'nominal demand of money'. In such situations, therefore, the rate of interest on savings is decided by the banking system, which is obviously inclined to dampen this rate – a decision that the monetary authority may well be inclined to allow as it provides a way for the costs of the conflict over income distribution to be passed on to defenseless savers. In effect, from the 1970s and for many years, real interest rates have frequently been negative.

The implications of all this on financial markets can be shown by a brief framing of the so-called portfolio analysis: a general equilibrium model consisting of a number of reciprocally interacting sectors and financial activities. The operation of such a model requires a satisfactory degree of communication between financial activities, in particular between the money market and the remaining financial markets. If this condition is fulfilled, portfolio analysis allows us to see the ways in which variations in the money supply directly and indirectly affect the capital market, investment and, more generally, aggregate demand. But in order for such an analysis to be meaningful, two further conditions are also required: a flexible and stable monetary system and financial operators that act with professional skill. If the money supply is endogenously driven, being forced to follow the demand for nominal money, and if the demand for real money (the preference for liquidity) is practically insensible (as previously seen) to variations in interest rates, then the result is that the interrelationships between the money market and other financial markets are obstructed. Moreover, that a large number of savers do not have professional skills hinders the interaction among the various types of financial activities (even in the presence of savers' frenzies and ingenuous speculations on shares and various bonds). So, the system of financial flows is almost deprived of some fundamental interactions. In sum, an increasing role of the demand for nominal money, by destroying the exogenous character of the money supply and causing a substantial atrophy of the demand for real money or the preference for liquidity, tends to restrict the financial structure to three poles: the banking system, the firm and the organs of the state charged with financing the public deficit. This may cause difficulties for the accumulation process and imply an unsatisfactory functioning of the economic and financial system.

However, the inflationary tendencies inherent to the endogenous character of money supply (i.e. the use of this endogenous character as a remedy in the conflict over income distribution by way of deficit spending, wages, etc.) cannot operate freely. From time to time, money restrictions to reduce inflation or, as an alternative, money depreciation will be requested.

10.4 What about the present?

The behaviors referred to previously drive (and force) the progressive restoration of the exogenous role of money – a restoration, however, that may be undermined by a heavy inheritance of public debt and inflationary potential. The situation is aggravated by the operation and strength of international financial markets in the modern global world, where speculation shifts enormous masses of capital instantaneously. There is no supranational authority able to discipline these activities and prevent the crises provoked by massive transfers of hot money.[6] The evolution of financial instruments and markets easily renders obsolete older guidelines and codes of conduct. Worldwide speculation may force monetary depreciation upon monetary authorities, resulting in inflation and a perverse impact on financial markets. In this state of affairs, the restoration of an exogenous money supply becomes a difficult, not to say impossible task, while the control of the financial market is no longer within the hands of the individual sovereign state. A new age or phase of development has started: financial capitalism.

The interest of students of economics in financial capital dates back more than a century. R. Hilferding's book, *Das Finanzkapital* (1910), captured a great deal of attention. But the dominant role, and hence the age, of *financial capitalism* began only recently, with the great acceleration of the globalization process on a world scale. The core of modern capitalism is finance and financial speculation, not productive efficiency. Production of commodities by means of commodities has been substituted by the production of money by means of money. Enormous holdings entail a combined control of important banks, industrial and commercial firms and strongly influence political power; this is an extremely fragile state of affairs, notwithstanding appearances, which strongly stimulates disequilibria and inequalities.

Chapter 5, which deals with the firm, has shown that this concentration process is not propelled, for the most part, by reasons of economic and technical efficiency. The great holdings are a degenerate phenomenon that bases both profitability and influence on mere power relations. From being a servant of production, financial capital has become master of production: a degenerate master, indeed, the agent of a truly unnatural transformation. A sort of financial theism is plagiarizing the conscience even of the masses that often engage with cupidity and supreme incompetence in ruinous financial speculations. The ghost of spread persecutes national states. The international financial market is submerged by financial by-products (hedge funds, private equities); this makes for a deceitful and extremely unstable house of cards.

At the present moment, the situation of the European community appears to be particularly confused in this regard: the restoration of the exogenous character of the money supply is obstructed by the absence of a sovereign monetary authority concerned with the new currency, the Euro. The result is an almost free terrain for international speculation that is primarily the consequence of the large economic and financial disequilibria existing between the various European economies, which condemns those countries afflicted by high public debt and some risk of insolvency both to the tyranny of the 'spread' and to the enactment of significant reductions of public expenditure, wages and hence demand, with a consequent and endemic stagnation and substantial inability to reduce public debt.

All that is well known; the problem is to find the ways to remedy this almost incredible situation. This is what we attempt to do from here to the end of this book. It is more than a question of financial institutions and their reformation that will be treated in the rest of this chapter.

We have seen that some of the main problems that have entangled the role of money with the behavior of financial markets derives from the conflict over income distribution, the mediating role of public expenditure and the consequent variation of money supply following what we have called the 'demand for nominal money'. We have further seen that the attempt to control the consequent inflation has often initiated restrictive money policies, thus generating recession or, as an alternative, money devaluation, along with the inevitable implications for financial markets. We shall see in the final chapter that one way to avoid these drawbacks is the separation of income distribution from production, with the exception of material incentives required by particularly undesirable or risky activities, thereby reducing the market to a mere mechanism for the imputation of costs and efficiency and, in this way, preventing the conflict over the distribution of income from affecting the production side. This separation seems necessary in order to meet the disorder of financial markets previously outlined.

A more complete and rigorous treatment of the matter may be found in Chapter 3 that presents and formalizes a model with all variables indispensable for the representation of a dynamic economy (in particular: endogenous innovation, radical uncertainty and entrepreneurship, noncompetitive markets, production, prices and the accumulation process). We therefore call our approach a 'necessary' model. It also includes the costs of factors as determined by their availability, but just in the mere quality of production costs, that is, excluding any implications (except material incentives, as previously noted) on income distribution, this latter being the object of policy choices. For its part, the profit rate (intended separately from interest on capital) mainly plays an accountability role or, more explicitly, is

238 *Problems of political economy*

primarily a measure of the degree of success of entrepreneurial actions and decisions, both in private and public firms. These features of our necessary model in Chapter 3 and, in particular, the implied exogenous nature of income distribution, warrant the inference that the operation of the production side is only affected by the availability of resources (and, of course, by demand) and would allow the restoration of a genuinely exogenous role of money. Here we limit ourselves to only one variable of income distribution, the interest rate, as preliminary to our proposal in Section 9.6.

10.5 The rate of interest

What we say in this section and the next may appear to have – and in a certain sense does have – a provocative content and, furthermore, is in the main a reproduction of some part of another work by the present author.[7] However, in the long run, the suggested remedies may reveal an obligatory way of overcoming some untenable behaviors of financial markets and may lead to the building of some form of social capitalism or even something better in terms of both equity and efficiency.

We have seen real interest rates moving from negative to high positive values and causing serious difficulties on such fronts as public finance, investment, production and entrepreneurship. S. Homer has given us an impressive and weighty study of the history of interest rates.[8] The first developments in banking, which occurred in medieval Italy, acted as a brake on the surge of interest rates, which indeed fell in that country to levels between 10% and 20%, while in the British Isles and Germany they shot to levels as high as 100%. In the late 14th century, Italian interest rates on commercial loans hovered around 8%, with a minimum of 5%, and in the 15th century an average of 5% prevailed in Germany. A century later, interest rates between 4% and 12% were frequent in Italy, Antwerp and Lyons. According to the historian C. Cipolla, Genoa's financial powerhouse, the Banco of San Giorgio, charged interest and discount rates of 5% in the 15th century and little above 1% a century later.[9] The wars of the 16th and 17th centuries caused a rise in the rates, but the 17th century subsequently witnessed a new fall: in the Netherlands interest rates dropped to 4% and, by the end of the century, 3%. The incessant development of the banking system was the main cause of these decreases. With the advent of the financial leadership of England in the 18th century, long-term government bond yields declined in that country toward 3%, while the usury laws reduced the maximum rate of interest to 5%. In the 19th century, Britain's long-term interest rates stabilized at around 3%, while government bond yields reached 2% by the end of the century. The wars that followed caused the rates to rise again. These various fluctuations point to an inverse correlation between prosperity and interest rates; contrary to Homer's opinion, these movements do not establish a causal direction between the two phenomena, but their association is certainly meaningful. True, low levels of interest stimulate growth, and a low level thereby often stands as an expression of prosperity. What is more important, however, is that since interest rates decrease with the development of banking, their level – and indeed their very existence – comes to depend on the characteristics of the credit system itself.

It is worthwhile to emphasize that interest basically represents a deduction from profit, and it may partially be discharged at the expense of wages, which is a sure way of exacerbating social conflict. In any case, interest stifles entrepreneurial initiative. Can such an impediment to entrepreneurship be eliminated? Can the ensuing deduction from labor income be eliminated? These are complex issues marred by a host of misconceptions.

To begin with, we have the deeply problematic challenge to the very idea of interest mounted, on the basis of the labor theory of value, by political economists and moralists from Aquinas to Marx.[10] Actually, such a challenge is senseless. But as a consequence of this challenge, the alternative justification for the rate of interest, which posits interest as just fruit (reward) of capital productivity – indispensable for the achievement of equilibrium between the supply and demand for capital – could easily gain ground (as in neoclassical and Austrian theories). But this second justification is contradicted by a simple remark: capital productivity requires technical progress; in fact, in the absence of technical progress, the process of accumulation would drive the productivity of capital toward zero; while, for its part, technical progress has almost nothing to do with financial capital. The Sraffian discovery of the phenomenon of the 're-switching of techniques' (i.e. the possibility that a rise in the rate of interest may imply an increase in the intensity of capital, instead of a decrease) and the connected controversy on capital by J. Robinson, P. Garegnani and others, undermined the thesis of Böhm-Bawerk's average period of production, finishing off once and for all the fashionable models of capital productivity built upon Robinson Crusoe's utopia.

There exists a reasoning capable of solving the debate on interest and usury at once. We ask: is interest strictly necessary for productive and organizational efficiency? If it is not, the existence (and exaction) of interest is unnecessary, and we may thus safely conclude that interest represents an arbitrary and artificial form of income pocketed by the financial cartel.

10.5.1 Is this the case?

Tily has written: "If there is no necessary limit to the volume of credit/debt that can be created then it is essentially a free good. A rate of interest is a price, and prices are paid for scarce resources. . . . Interest becomes a social construct, to be manipulated according to the mandate, principles or interests of a country's authorities".[11] We need an argument that is somewhat more stringent in this regard.

Interest has not much to do with the equilibrium between supply and demand of capital. As a matter of fact, far more than on interest, saving depends on the amount of income gained and therefore on the level of production, and the entrepreneurs' demand for capital depends on entrepreneurship and the state of business, which is mainly expressed by profit expectations.

The argument that the rate of interest is necessary in order to prevent 'overinvestment' and the concomitant waste of capital is belied by the fact that such a role is, as a rule, fulfilled not by the interest rate but by profit rate, that is, by (a) the entrepreneurial search for profit (i.e. the tendency to extract the highest rate of profit from investment), and (b) by the role of the rate of profit as a gauge of accountability.

All of the foregoing suggests that the role of interest is simply to throttle entrepreneurship and to subtract income from distribution. In principle, the share of income to be invested may be determined by the community ignoring the rate of interest; in fact, the rate of profit is sufficient to impose a judicious use of capital. This shows that it is perfectly possible and efficient to share financing among the entrepreneurs at zero interest. In sum, there are no technical impediments to the abolition of the interest rate through legal prohibition, that is, by defining as usurious a positive real interest rate. Of course, within a free international financial market, there would need to be a concerted agreement to abolish real interest everywhere across the world.

However, zero percent might encourage the tendency to hoard money, but this could be opposed through a low rate of inflation or some sort of Gesellian demurrage scheme on cash money. At any rate, nowadays the tendency to hoard seems to be almost irrelevant, since the many modern banking services manage to keep private consumption flowing in a perennial and tumultuous flow. It is indeed remarkable that on the shoulders of interest rate, a variable that is unnecessary, if not wholly pernicious, has grown an enormous, complicated and rather obscure economic body mainly devoted to speculation and entirely responsible for all the serious shocks and malfunctions of the global network.

10.6 A proposal on the organization of financial markets

Now we come to consider what suggestions may explain the combination of the cyclical motion generated by dynamic competition with the notion of phases of historical development (as discussed in Chapter 7) and their requirements in terms of functional imperatives. As we have seen, the modern phases of development are shortened by the acceleration of evolutionary processes under the pressure of dynamic competition. We shall attempt to explore the 'necessity' of transition, along this road, toward something different from capitalism. Chapters 11 and 12 will deepen and extend this important subject.

The acceleration of economic growth due to the first industrial revolution has opened the door to a succession of capitalist phases of development: competitive capitalism, monopolistic capitalism, conflictual-consumeristic capitalism and, finally, financial capitalism. Four large crises and long waves have accompanied such successions, intermingled with intermediate and short cycles.

10.6.1 What new institutional and ethical-ideological forms are required by these passages?

Here we attempt to delineate a blueprint for a financing system of production shorn of the negative and pervasive presence of interest – a blueprint capable, among other things, of clipping the wings of financial capital, stimulating entrepreneurship and contrasting the deficiency of global demand and achieving a far greater openness than exists at present toward social justice. The financial system at present is a very complicated and slippery beast; we have seen that it is also heavily subject to malfunctioning and the tricks of speculation. It seems to us that the financing of production does not need such a complicated and insidious system, and it could largely be replaced by the operation of the banking system, albeit not in its habitual features.

A discussion of the procedures required to modify the banking system in accordance with what follows is not relevant in this context; a detailed analysis of the matter may form the theme of another publication. The important point that needs to be emphasized at this juncture is the need to radically modify the central function of the banking system with regard to the funding of production. Financial capital is not at present at the service of production but, for the most, it enslaves production and exploits the toiling community into the bargain. This distortion needs to be redressed in the sense that financial institutions become the servants, not the masters, of production. Our proposal, aimed at heavily simplifying the complicated set of financial markets and activities, is presented here in as simple and transparent a fashion as possible.

Every year the community should define the share of value added to assign to consumption and to investment in selected strategic sectors. After that, care must be taken to ensure, through stimulus and instructions to the banking system, that these prescriptions are executed, as each investment is at the discretion of individual businesses. The capital required by the firms will come, in the first place, from profits. The uninvested portion of a firm's profits may be set aside for future investment. But the financing of capital must generally exceed the reinvested profits, so as to allow the formation of new firms and the financing of firms' investment plans in excess of gross profit. Such extra accumulation may be covered in part by private saving, which should yield a real interest rate of zero percent.[12] However, savers should not be allowed to buy shares directly, since the stock exchange is much worse than a gambling house. The rest of the funds required to achieve the planned rate of accumulation will be provided by a fund of common wealth (see Section 11.4). This fund should channel the necessary quota to the banking system to be distributed among firms. The banking system should also finance investment abroad, mainly in underdeveloped countries.

Each bank's application to the fund for resources should be judged on the basis of its profit rate. In fact, bankers must be obliged to operate as entrepreneurs, and their commercial tenure must depend on business results. The more successful they are, as expressed by the profit rate, the more capital will be granted by the fund of common wealth via their commercial bank. Banks' profits should derive from the prices of the services that they offer to their customers; competition should keep these prices low.

A substantial feature of such a reform would be the creation of a mechanism directed to the achievement, through the firms' investment, of the yearly rate of accumulation projected by the community, thus avoiding or reducing substantially the possibility of a deficiency of global demand. It would also act as a stimulus to entrepreneurship. A major condition for the effectiveness of the mechanism is that bankers provide sufficient credit to firms to allow them to achieve the community's projected accumulation rate. Therefore, if the banks' requests for capital do not exhaust the fund set aside for accumulation, the difference should be assigned compulsorily by the fund of common wealth to banks (say in proportion to the amount each has requested) for distribution among investing firms. This implies that, if the propensity to invest is low, banks will be forced to lower the prices for their services so that all the funds allotted to them for investment may be placed with the applicant firms. Vice versa, if the amount of capital provided by the fund of common wealth is lower than the total applications of banks based on the firms' borrowing, the negative difference will be deducted from those requests, in inverse proportion to their profit rates. This guideline of equality between the allocations for saving and investment is of crucial importance for the control of aggregate demand; in particular, it moderates the cyclical effects of entrepreneurial euphoria or pessimism. Moreover, it stimulates entrepreneurship since, when demand for credit is slack, firms may obtain inexpensive loans, as banks are required to lend funds up to the accumulation target. So banks are induced to make golden bridges to entrepreneurship.

If the propensity to invest is low, the duty of attaining the established aggregate rate of accumulation may cause heavy losses to the banking system. But this does not represent a problem for public banks, for which the profit rate is *only* an indicator of success (accountability role); in fact, the relative degree of success may also be expressed by the inverse of the rate of loss.

Such a financial system should eliminate the complications, tricks and unconstrained speculations of current financial systems, with their worldwide power over production.

10.7 Conclusion

The processes of globalization generate an increasing, and increasingly complicated, role for the financial system in the contemporary world economy. By contrast, production, even if projected on a world scale, is subjected to largely national and local constraints. Moreover, production suffers from the clear – and yet often undecipherable – hegemony of the financial side. The opposition between the urgency and the increasing difficulty of restoring the exogenous and instrumental role of the money supply represents an outstanding contradiction within the world economy – a contradiction that is aggravated by the ever-increasing aggressiveness and power of international financial markets. The present confusions and complications, as well as the fleeting adjustments and obscure maneuvers associated with international financial flows, require drastic simplification and the restructuring of what represents, so to speak, the most effective worldwide institution, that is, the financial order. This chapter has attempted to provide some ideas aimed at meeting this situation that are directed toward the construction of a national and international financial order that does not enslave but rather works in the service of production, promotes rather than brushes aside the claims of social justice, and improves rather than damages efficiency.

Notes

1 Hobson's study on imperialism preceded Keynes in underlining the explanatory role of the deficiency of effective demand, but his analysis disregarded the question of money and interest rate.
2 See Fusari (1981).
3 Some neo-Keynesians, such as N. Kaldor and J. Robinson, underlined the endogenous character of money variations. But they did not consider that this endogenous character destroys the relation between the money supply and production based on the interest rate; in fact, they ignored its reductive impact on the preference for liquidity and hence on the validity of the theory of interest rate based on the demand and supply of money. These students did indeed express doubts on the incisiveness of the relation between money supply and production, but for different reasons from those we underline, and they sometimes improperly assimilate interest rate to profit rate.
4 See Silone (1990 [1930]).
5 See Hicks (1977).
6 Significantly, Stiglitz (2002) has harshly criticized IMF policies.
7 See Chapter 8, written by A. Fusari, in Ekstedt and Fusari (2010) Routledge, Abingdon and New York.
8 See Homer (1996).
9 See Cipolla (1980).
10 In the *Tabula Exemplorum*, a manuscript of the 13th century, it is written: "All men abstain from working on Sunday days, but usurers work incessantly" (Le Goff 1987, p. 24).
11 See Tily (2004), pp. 8 and 13.
12 A real interest rate of 0% on saving would actually be a bargain for savers who, over the course of time, have generally suffered a continuous devaluation of their savings owing to inflation, fraud and robbery, which in turn are mainly caused by speculation in financial markets. Moreover, the zeroing of real interest rate would prevent the impulse to the growth in capitalism of the inequalities in income distribution due to the tendency of the rate of interest r to exceed the rate of growth g that Piketty underlines (see Piketty 2014) but without indicating a remedy.

References

Cipolla, C. M. (1980), *Economic history of preindustrial Europe*, Italian edition, Il Mulino, Bologna.
Ekstedt, H. & Fusari, A. (2010), *Economic theory and social change*, Routledge, Abingdon and New York.
Friedman, M. (2002), *Capitalism and freedom*, University of Chicago Press, Chicago.
Fusari, A. (1981), Meaning and role of money in contemporary economy: A critical revision. *Quaderni Sardi di Economia*, vol. 2/3, pp. 99–136.
Fusari, A. & Reati, A. (2013), Endogenizing technical change: Uncertainty, profits, entrepreneurship: A long-term view of sectoral dynamics, *Structural Change and Economic Dynamics (SCED)*, vol. 24, pp. 76–100.
Gandolfo, G. (1978). *Economia internazionale monetaria*. Milan: ISEDI.
Garegnani, P. (1960), *Capital in the theory of distribution*, Giuffre, Milan.
Hicks, J. R. (1974), *The crisis in Keynesian economics*, Basil Blackwell, Oxford.
Hicks, J. R. (1977), *Economic perspectives*, Oxford University Press, Oxford.
Hilferding, R. (1981), *Finance capital: A study of the latest phase of capitalist development*, edited by Tom Bottomore, Routledge & Kagan Paul, London.
Hobson, J. A. (1974), *Imperialism*, ISEDI, Milan.

Homer, S. (1996), *History of interest rates*, Rutgers University Press, New Brunswick, NJ.

Ietto-Gillies, G. (2012), *Transnational corporations and international production: Concepts, theories and effects*, Edward Elgar, Cheltenham and Northampton.

Kaldor, N. (1960), Alternative theories of distribution, in *Essays on value and distribution*, Gerald Duckworth & Co. Ltd, London and *La distribuzione del reddito nella teoria economica*, 1972, Franco Angeli, Editore: Milan, pp. 235–245.

Kaldor, N. (1970), *The new monetarism*, Lloyds Bank Review, pp. 52–63.

Keynes, J. M. (1936), *The general theory of employment, interest and money, 1973*, MacMillan, London.

Le Goff, J. (1987), *La borsa e la vita*, Laterza, Bari.

Marx, K. (1977), *Das capital*, Editori Riuniti, Rome.

Piketty, T. (2014), *Capital in the twenty first century*, Bompiani, Milan.

Robinson, J. (1953–54), The production function and the theory of capital, *Review of Economic Studies*, vol. 21, no. 2, pp. 81–106.

Robinson, J. (1965), *The accumulation of capital*, Macmillan, London.

Silone, I. (1990), *Fontamara*, Mondadori, Milan, published in 27 languages.

Sraffa, P. (1960), *Production of commodities by means of commodities*, Cambridge University Press, Cambridge.

Stiglitz, J. E. (2002), *Globalization and its discontents*, Italian edition, Einaudi, Turin.

Tily, G. (2004), *The socialization of interest*, Paper Presented at the AHE Conference, Leeds.

11 The ethical dimension
Creativity and social justice

11.1 Introduction

This chapter discusses the role and meaning of ethics in the working and organization of the economy and the relationships of this with other branches of the social system; it seems to us this is a core of the ethical question from a scientific standpoint. The discussion explores the logical possibility and, in some sense, the growing necessity to build up an economic and social system more appropriate to the modern world than the current ones. In fact, if such possibility exists and is proved, it will be carried out sooner or later.

The chapter starts from a crucial ethical question for the analysis and governance of societies and the understanding of growth process: the relations between diversity and equality and hence between creativity and social justice. It follows a brief historical perspective on outstanding civilizations and the advent of capitalism, directed to provide the analysis with depth and a wide generalization. Afterward, we concentrate on economics and its relationships with social systems.

A main purpose of the study is to show the existence, in principle, of a large autonomy of income distribution from production, except the necessity of material incentives. This implies the possibility (that will be discussed in Chapter 12) of largely subtracting production to the conditioning power of income distribution – a power that capitalism weakens through unemployment – and a large possibility to perform social justice.

These topics are strictly linked to the character of the financial system (previously discussed) and its relationships with production, mainly the paradoxical and ruinous hegemony of great finance on production, instead of being at the service of this.

11.2 Diversity and equality: a fundamental proposition

The treatment of this subject in a simple and easy-to-read way can opportunely begin with a deepening of the statement that follows: men are different from and equal to each other, different in skills and dispositions, equal in dignity. It may seem that the two terms of this statement are in opposition. On the contrary, they are strictly and positively linked to each other. The great equivocations and mystifications on the link have deeply influenced the characters and development of social systems and, in general, historic processes. The statement on diversity expresses a character of human nature that is extremely important for its implications. Mankind's skills would be very poor if men, by nature afflicted by heavy limitations, were identical to each other. So many differences in men's capacities and inclinations represent an immense patrimony of innovative and expressive skills, the main evolutionary power fueling social and economic development and, in particular, a basic propulsive force of the modern world, provided that the expression of individual skills and attitudes is stimulated.

On the contrary, the statement concerning the equality in dignity expresses an ethical principle that has a special status: it represents a necessary condition to the full expression of individuality, that is, the dissimilar men's skills and hence their evolutionary potential. This link of the moral principle on equality with the objective fact of men's diversity means that the statement on equality cannot be considered in a relativist sense and as a matter of choice, but it is an ethical principle having an objective character.

The operation of men's unlikeness, and hence of the connected evolutionary potential, has some other important ethical implications: they need tolerance, social justice, free thinking, free action and expression. These requirements subtract the mentioned ethical principles to the sphere of ethical relativism giving them an objective substance.

The equivocations on those principles, in particular the misconceptions on the relation between freedom innovation and social justice, are largely present in the various branches of economics and are, for the most part, linked to the questions of income distribution and the relationships between production and financial system. It is often disregarded that, in the presence of heavy inequalities in personal wealth and income distribution, the equality in dignity is largely jeopardized; this obstructs the improvement and use of individual skills and squeezes innovation, and hence economic and social development, mainly if production is largely dominated by great finance with its speculations. It is necessary and urgent to reconcile the terms of the initial statement, that is, diversity and equality.

We shall see that it is mistaken to think that social justice obstructs productive efficiency; if appropriately pursued (in particular without suffocating or exaggerating the role of material incentives and in the presence of a not pervasive financial system), social justice stimulates efficiency, for reasons well beyond the possible need to stimulate effective demand in the presence of a deficiency of this.

J. J. Rouseau's discourse on inequality set out, at the start of the illuminist movement, a provocative and oversimplified thesis that underlined a break between savage man who after eating is at peace with nature and is a friend of all living beings (the myth of the good savage) and socialized man, who is pushed by civilization toward great infamies. There is some truth in Rousseau's denunciation of the corruptor effects of civilizations, and it is easy to find a lot of confirmations in the course of history. But it is useless and restricting to imprecate against civilizations. The true problem is to find the ways to make civilization a friend of man instead of being a cause of affliction. A brief historic excursus on the subject, embracing different social systems, may help to deal with the theme.[1]

11.3 Equality and diversity in ancient civilizations

In the course of time, the binomial equality-diversity has caused acute contrasts among people and students and has taken various forms in the context of the relation between individuality, organization and homologation; an impressing variety indeed, mainly in primitive societies. In the most advanced civilizations of ancient times, the relation between equality and diversity was reduced to the term *equality* (ignoring diversity) by the strength of organization and homologation; in fact, those civilizations were the outcome of great centralized empires (Eastern, American and central African empires) all condemned to a stationary state both by the suffocation of criticism operated by organization and command elites and a perfidious form of equality expressed by mass poverty. But two exceptions appeared that would have a great future:

1. Ancient Greece, which privileged heterodoxy and free inquiry, with the inflamed disputes in the Agorà that pushed Greek thinking to anticipate important contributions in an impressive variety of subjects, contributions resumed (sometimes unconsciously) by the subsequent development of human thinking. The Greek world was distinguished by the prominent role of individual, but excluded consideration for personal dignity that denied to slaves, and in some sense to all foreigners, who were considered barbarians.
2. The Judaic world, where a religious message was characterized by great consideration for the individual and a strong statement of the equal dignity of all human beings as God's sons. This message sanctified in the end the absolute respect for the person.

Some centuries later, the wedding of the prominent organizational skills of ancient Rome with the Greek cultural inheritance gave birth, in the Roman empire from Augustus to Antonine's dynasty, to an outstanding political and administrative organization directed by an efficient bureaucracy of little dimensions that was complemented by the municipal self-government of the decurions and was defended by few legions. This administrative order, which was unequalled in ancient time and unfortunately has had no replications everywhere in the world, did not generate a dynamic economy for various reasons: the transgression of the principle of equal dignity of men and the associated slavery, extensive large estate and the dominating stationary idea of circular time emphasized by stoic philosophy. The malaise and contradictions caused, in the presence of such an administrative structure, by a long-lasting stationary state pushed the agile and light organization of principality toward dissolution. The disintegration of the empire was prevented, during the tormented third century, by the efficient bureaucratic and military order. This allowed the exceptional organizational skills of Romans to edify a penetrating centralized bureaucracy, the empire of dominate, that similarly to all great empires of ancient times was appropriate to have long life in (and to maintain) a stationary state, but heavily transgressing the Greek message.

Further, the Greek and Judaic teachings were recovered, in different ways, by the diffusion of Christianity. The rising church established an ambiguous relation between the role of individual and organization, which was different in the two parts of the empire. Such a relation inclined, in the Eastern Roman Empire, toward homologation (with some remarkable exceptions as expressed, for instance, by the incessant and hypercritical censorship of Mount Athos monks): the Constantinople patriarch was a substantial officer of the empire while the emperor was a kind of supreme pontiff who, indeed from the time of Constantine the Great and his heirs, had the decisive word, drawing the sword if necessary, in the resolutions of the ecumenical councils.

On the contrary, the fragility of the Western Empire, mainly due to the dominating presence of large slave-worked estates and of senatorial oligarchy (polarization aristocracy/slavery), a subsidized urban populace and the geography of state boundaries making these difficult to defend, favored the dissolution of the Roman state.

11.4 The advent of capitalism

The political and administrative fragmentation that followed the fall of Western Roman Empire and rooted, after Charlemagne, during the feudal period, started to restore the role of individual diversities but, differently from classical Greece, associated them with the message that all men are equal in dignity and are brothers, being sons of a same father. Individual diversities were exalted by Italian maritime republics and free commons and by the free towns of Flanders. The individual's role was also exalted by the new intellectual climate, mainly in monasteries and later with increasing vehemence by heretical movements. These events gave rise to capitalism that started to impress a strong push to the growth of material wealth and established the centrality of the economy.

This evolution took place through tormented spontaneous processes and in a condition of impressing administrative disintegration. Economic and social development would have been more rapid and less tormented if the great dash fueled by the explosion of entrepreneurship and the centrality of the economy had taken advantage of a light, efficient and decentralized political-administrative organization like that of the Roman empire of principality that, as previously seen, was condemned to death by the absence of a dynamic economy.

Differently from the centralized great empires, which were governed by omnipotent elites and bureaucracies endowed by great privileges and where all the remaining population was a 'protected flock' of poor men,[2] in the rising of capitalism the inequalities in wealth were the outcome of the differences in trading skills and the propensity to innovate and to adventure. This fed the dynamism of production. But the large and increasing inequalities in income distribution generated by capitalism over time, which plainly violate the principle of solidarity among men (notwithstanding cases of patronage) served by a financial establishment that in the end has subdued production, have started to cause more and more destabilizing effects and to suffocate the role of individual and hence the potential associated with the wide qualitative differences in skills that nature has abundantly endowed man.

The egalitarian reactions of last century have drawn the world from the frying pan into the fire due to a protracted darkening of diversities and the resurrection of bureaucratic centralized orders. In the end, Eastern socialist countries, defeated by the competition of the Western decentralized capitalist world, have started to converge toward a kind of capitalism much worse than the Western one in terms of inequalities in private wealth, corruption and inefficiencies. These failures of the equalitarian reaction have discredited social justice. Nowadays, global finance, with its enormous disposition power on material wealth, has in its hands the destiny of the world, and its speculations cause impressive destabilizing movements. Therefore, some important questions arise: how do we properly combine the role of organization and the ontological imperative of individuality, as required by our initial assertion on the relation between diversity and equality? Are the huge and growing inequalities in the distribution of material wealth and in power of disposition caused by capitalism inevitable and indispensable? Or the contrary is true? In order to preserve and cultivate the rhythms of innovation and development that capitalism has fed until now, is it necessary to marry decentralization and free initiative to a much more fair income distribution and bring back great finance to the service of production. Is that possible? These are central questions in the present age.

11.5 Some useful teachings: Keynes and Schumpeter

Our analysis may profitably utilize important standpoints of Schumpeter's and Keynes's contributions, notwithstanding the harsh contraposition of the two students in the course of their lives and in the interpretations of successors.

Keynes's contribution is hinged on the role of demand of goods. He underlines that, in the presence of a deficiency of effective demand, redistributive policies, deficit spending and even wasting represent some obliged way of stimulating employment and production. But what to do if production is obstructed by high costs, for example, due to social conflict or other pressures from the side of income distribution or bottlenecks in entrepreneurship? Keynes pays a little attention to the question of income equalization. Moreover, he disregards entrepreneurship and innovation that, on the contrary, are at the center of Schumpeter's teaching. Schumpeter almost disregards income distribution; he had a position similar to the neoclassical one and had a great admiration for the Walrasian model of general equilibrium, notwithstanding this approach is in plain conflict with Schumpeterian economics centered on entrepreneurship and innovation.

In particular, both Keynes and Schumpeter do not deepen the possible degree of autonomy and separation of income distribution from production (see next chapter) that imply the possible improvement of social justice without obstructing production but instead stimulating it. It may be useful and illuminating to combine some general and basic aspects of these authors' teachings. This has not been done by post-Keynesians and Schumpeter's followers. In addition, a frequent misunderstanding has caused deep contrasts not only among students but also in political and social spheres: the idea that the entrepreneur and the market are exclusively capitalist institutions.

250 *Problems of political economy*

These confusions have enabled so-called mainstream economics to easily consolidate its hegemony simply by taking care to recover and combine in surreptitious or formal ways some aspects of Keynesian and Schumpeterian teachings. However, neoclassical mainstream economics proclaims the natural character of the link between income distribution and production, through the notion of marginal productivity and so forth, a link that indeed is neither natural nor inevitable. Moreover, the neoclassical mainstream adds a notion of capital based on the Robinson Crusoe's metaphor.

11.6 Entrepreneurship, innovation and effective demand

We delineate here some congruencies between Schumpeter's and Keynes's teachings, but not according neoclassical rationalization that, as just seen, has attempted to incorporate them by erasing their real meaning. We shall consider the relations between entrepreneurship, innovation and effective demand. Those relations were extensively analyzed in Chapter 1 of this book.

The success of product innovations concerning consumer goods mainly depends on expendable income and the propensity to buy new products. If expendable income is high and continues to grow, the saturation of the demand of preexisting consumer goods will be reached. The stagnation of consumption also implies the stagnation of the demand for capital goods, and the entrepreneurs will be obliged to produce new goods to sell. The sale of new consumer goods will be facilitated if families' incomes continue to be high, which would cause a more rapid rise of the logistic curve concerning the demand of new goods, thus contributing to a shortened business cycle. But capitalism is subjected to a drawback, the stagnation of demand that causes unemployment and hence the pauperization of population, so that the consumption of new products will depend on the preferences of very rich men, that is, on income inequalities. This determines a positive correlation between the inequality in income distribution and innovation, since entrepreneurs are obliged to innovate by economic depression (innovate or perish). But such positive correlation is not unavoidable. It would be much more natural if the expendable income of masses remained high (in the presence of low inequalities); in this case, the success and diffusion of new products would be more rapid. Income inequalities are only required by the sale of expensive goods, for instance, Ferrari cars and Palladian country residences. Well, in a world with an income distribution that is not too unequal, Ferrari cars would be bought for car racing and architectural arts would be mainly promoted through public buildings, and artistic productions would not yield very high prices. People with rare qualities (e.g. managerial skills) do not have a strict need for monetary incentives to reward their use; Modigliani painted for nothing and was even tormented by hunger.

11.6.1 *What about cycle?*

Keynes's short-term analysis does not concern cycle properly. The attempts to combine, in a medium-range perspective, Keynesian and classical teachings (as in Pasinetti) take income distribution and innovation (or technical progress) as exogenous. For its part, Schumpeter's analysis on business cycles disregards the problem of the degree of autonomy of income distribution from production and the connected possibility and way to establish such autonomy through a noncapitalist system that does not refuse (and erase) the entrepreneur and the market. His work on capitalism, socialism and democracy would have had a completely different (and much more illuminating) content in the absence of such disregard and would have not asserted the inevitability of the bureaucratization of the economy through big business; this is an absurd and surprising Schumpeter's conclusion indeed, since it contradicts the substance of the main Schumpeterian teaching that concerns the role of entrepreneurship.[3]

Before Keynes an excess of Schumpeterianism was at work, and this caused a catastrophic crisis due to demand deficiency. Capitalism accepted the Keynesian recipe to avoid collapsing. An excess of Keynesianism has followed. The long-term consequences of that (public debt, etc.) now afflict Western economies and the whole modern world where a global finance is rolling in political fragmentation. Innovation and social justice, Schumpeter and Keynes, need to be combined. The welfare state has for a long time favored innovation, and not only in Scandinavian countries. This is no longer possible. In our time, a more articulated and comprehensive practice of social justice is required, flanked by a less pervasive financial system, to avoid the great and beneficial diversities in natural skills among men determining huge and unnatural inequalities in the distribution of material wealth accompanied by growing destabilizing tendencies.

11.7 Conclusion

Policy reformations and decisions involve important ethical aspects. This chapter underlines the fundamental role of social justice in stimulating creativity, this being distributed at random among individuals. Due to the limitations of human skills, the care for diversity is a central stance for increasing the total availability of skills. We have analyzed the role displayed by decentralized institutional orders, heterodoxy and later by the advancement of capitalism in mobilizing diversities and hence in mobilizing human capacities and inventiveness, at the service of economic and social systems. But such mobilization is unfortunately opposed by the parallel capitalist stimulation of social inequalities and exclusions.

We have dedicated some considerations to the two main teachings of economics on the role of creativity and social justice as expressed by Schumpeter and Keynes, and the limitations of those teachings often intended in reciprocal contraposition, by recalling the relations between entrepreneurship, innovation and effective demand as analyzed in Chapter 1. In particular, we have reproved the consideration of the entrepreneur and the market as merely capitalist institutions and underlined the importance, from an ethical and functional point of view, of the 'separation principle', that is, the separation of income distribution from the firm activity of production or, in other words, the definition of income distribution outside the firm (but not vice versa), except the needs for incentivization (what will be the main topic of the next chapter).

Many years ago G. Orwell, in the booklet *Animal Farm*, strongly criticised the failure of the Soviet Revolution with regard to the application of the ethical principle 'from everyone according to capacity to everyone according to necessity' that resulted in a condition where "all animals are equal but some animals are more equal than others" (see G. Orwell, 2008). Indeed, something much worse happened: the edification of a society unable to produce with efficiency and denying personal freedom. We hope to have shown that a high level of equality is consistent with productive efficiency, personal freedom and development.

Notes

1 What we'll say here is widely considered, with many exemplifications, in Fusari (2000). Such study starts from primitive ages and embraces the great Asian and Mediterranean empires and societies, Arab civilization, European feudal and medieval societies and the renaissance and moves through the beginning of the 18th century.
2 In the most efficient centralized society of the past, the Celestial Empire of ancient China, the Mandarin bureaucracy was selected on the basis of severe examinations devoted to make evident and reward knowledge, a culture and *forma mentis* appropriate to the administration of a stationary empire, while entrepreneurship was strongly suffocated.
3 As we know, such a surprising landing was mainly due to Schumpeter's disregard of the role and the meaning of radical uncertainty.

References

Downs, A. (1957), *An economic theory of democracy*, Harper, New York.
Fusari, A. (2000), *Human adventure: An inquiry on the way of people and civilizations*, SEAM Editions, Rome.
Hayek, F. A. (1939), *Freedom and the economic system*, University of Chicago Press, Chicago.
Keynes, J. M. (1936), *The general theory of employment, interest and money*, Macmillan, London.
Mill, J. S. (1999), *On liberty*, Il Saggiatore, Milan.
Nagel, T. (1991), *Equality and partiality*, Oxford University Press, New York.
Orwell, G. (2008), *Animal Farm. A fairy story*, Penguin Books, London.
Pasinetti, L. L. (1993), *Structural economic dynamics: A theory of the economic consequences of human learning*, Cambridge University Press, Cambridge.
Rawls, J. (1971), *A theory of justice*, The Belknap Press, Harvard University, Cambridge, MA.
Rousseau, J. J. (1962), *Essay on inequality*, Editrice La Scuola, Brescia.
Schumpeter, J. A. (1977), *Capitalism, socialism and democracy*, Universale Etas, Milan.
Sen, A. (2009), *The idea of justice*, Harvard University Press, Harvard.
Touraine, A. (1997), *Equality and diversity*, Laterza, Rome and Bari.

12 Toward a noncapitalist market system

Spontaneous order and organization

12.1 Introduction

This chapter analyzes a central question of modern society: how does one best use 'the instrument of the market' – this being a basic mechanism of organizational efficiency in dynamic economies characterized by a high degree of uncertainty – in such a way as to prevent the market itself from turning everyone and everything into expendable tools, with consequences that are ever more disastrous for equity and for human dignity?

The purpose here is to envisage the possibility and, more importantly, the necessity of economic forms adapted to human society that are *different* from those that have emerged from the spontaneous transformation of the Western world. Persisting in the denial and ignorance that such a possibility of *change* is indeed possible will inevitably lead to the (often fanatical) conviction that the capitalistic market, with all its degenerations and inefficiencies, is the unavoidable, even if bitter, outcome of institutional evolution – a necessary, teleological fruit of human exertion; in a sense, the end of history.

Students and practical people's attitudes toward social phenomena oscillate between two opposite positions: the idea that those phenomena must be considered and accepted as spontaneous events and the pretension to govern them. This chapter points out the intermingling of the two aspects in the life of each social system. As a matter of fact, the history of human societies and the logical sense confirm that spontaneous forces and their governance always operate together, even if one or the other can be largely prevalent in various cases. The suffocation of spontaneous forces obstructs creativity, thus causing stagnation. On the other hand, the ability to govern society is more and more required by the steady acceleration, via creativity, of social change. Here we shall insist on the possibility of driving market economies outside a capitalistic context (which after all is a necessity in the modern world) and the way to do that. Therefore, the aspect of *choice possibility* will be emphasized, after having insisted on the aspect of *necessity*.

To analyze this topic with the depth and the breath it deserves, we will first sketch a brief account of those institutions and forms of civilization that in the course of history have promoted the rise and spread of the market, eventually making it into an organizational necessity of modern economies. This account will be concluded by a summary of the pros and cons of the capitalistic market.

The subsequent step concentrates on the notion of *competition*, and in particular on the role of the *entrepreneur* and the significance of the rate of profit as a gauge of accountability. This is essential in order to highlight the powers of resilience of the market and to show its flexibility as an organizational tool with regard to various kinds of ideological options; for instance, we will contemplate how it may be extended to either private or public systems of ownership. In Section 12.4, we discuss how the market may be turned into a mere mechanism for the imputation of costs and efficiency, and this discussion is at the heart of the following proposal for a noncapitalist market and the merits of its social openness. This argument needs to be connected to the treatment, in Chapter 10, of a defining and fundamental component of the system, upon which all reformist propositions impinge by necessity: the nature and management of the interest rate and the attending financial system. As we saw, these are two dominating and interconnected aspects of traditional economic systems that increasingly thwart entrepreneurship and stifle production, since they are predicated on a high concentration of economic power in the hands of a social class devoted to speculation rather than production.

The goal here is to complete, after Chapters 10 and 11, a coherent reformist agenda articulated in several key points pertaining to the vital nodes of the economic system. This is just a first attempt; naturally, given the complexities of the issue, the remedies recommended are by no means exhaustive, but merely indicative of the broad path all humanist forces should undertake together in days to come.

12.2 Historical sketch of the market

In this section, which is devoted to ages in which the market was hardly the protagonist, we will identify the structural obstacles that impeded the development of market relations and the contingencies that eventually allowed those relations, in some instances, to rise gradually and spread all around.

We then consider the strong interaction between the growing influence of the market and the rapid pace of social transformation, which has brought the market to become an essential mechanism for efficiency, growth and development.

In ancient times, markets were absent or marginal because they were not necessary to the organizational efficiency of social systems; rather, as we shall see, the market obstructed efficiency. The major role played in some ancient societies by individual initiative, critical spirit and the propensity to adventure was much more a stimulus to creativity, scientific research and geographic discovery than it was to the market economy. The economy did not hold a central position[1] and did not attract the interest of students and practical men. Of course, the great empires of the ancient world devoted considerable resources to hydraulic, monumental and military works. However, these were centrally administered, authoritarian societies that suffocated individual initiative, and in particular mercantile activities. This does not mean that they could not achieve wealth, power and social sophistication;

in fact, a stationary-repetitive economy may be efficiently managed by centralized processes and bureaucracy.

Indeed, the most advanced societies of the ancient quasistationary world were bureaucratic, autocratic and centralized empires whose neatly ramified branches often afforded complete and efficient control over extensive regions, thereby avoiding dissolution and fragmentation. The crises of the two main commercial empires of the ancient world, Carthage and Athens, are good examples. Those empires were defeated by less rich but more highly structured rival powers. The organizational inconsistencies of the two empires, the avariciousness of their ruling classes and the resentment of their confederates and subjects, all represented heavy functional handicaps in the static outlook of both systems. But the best illustration of the market's unsuitability to quasistationary societies is provided by the experience of the Roman Empire from Augustus to the Antonines. That empire was governed by highly advanced institutions that were suitable to the modern world and unique in ancient times. An active and efficient body of public servants authoritatively administered justice, public order and taxation; the remaining public functions were assigned to the municipal self-government of the Decurions;[2] individual initiative was well represented and taxation was low. But the major pride of the empire, the great Greco-Roman civilization – with its central idea of circular time and the marginal role of the economy, the running of which depended on the polarization between aristocracy and slavery – hindered cumulative development and the role of the market.[3] The persistence of stationariness, hence stagnation, transformed the promising decentralized public administration of the empire into a factor of dissolution. So the great crisis of the third century and an extremely painful process of trial and error drove the Roman Empire toward the bureaucratically centralized, hierarchical society of Diocletian and Constantine the Great. In that society, as in the other great empires, the market was clearly marginalized.

The collapse of the Western Empire – which, unlike the Eastern provinces, was (as we said) socially and economically dominated by large estate slavery tenancy and a large state-subsidized urban populace – resulted in a severe regression in the general conditions of development. In this new stage of arrested growth, the social body reverted to a primitive structure governed by familial links: the quasi-familial relations of loyalty on the part of the populace to the descendants of the great senatorial landowning class, or to Germanic military chiefs, assumed a basic role. No proper state power came into being. The sovereigns of the barbaric states were for the most part do-nothing kings controlled by a military aristocracy. There was not any centralized or autocratic empire in fragmented post-imperial Europe.

Charlemagne's empire was a kind of 'shooting star'. After his death, social organization took to the feudal model: a world governed by strong and arrogant individuals, plunderers more than administrators; as Anna Comnena noticed during the transit through the Byzantine Empire of Crusaders' expeditions, these were fighters for the faith, but also for spoils and fortune, "extremely greedy for any kind of gain".[4]

In such turmoil, what became of the market? The Western European world dominated by avidity and the spirit of independence, and well disposed to adventure, favored a luxuriant efflorescence of mercantile activities. The maritime towns were clever at making huge profits from the near-eastern conquests and the growing hunger for exotic goods. The medieval communes that followed carefully created laws and institutions suited to trade and were resolved to defend and extend their independence by fraud, talent and the sword. The economy began to take on a central role; it now wielded progressively political power and came to finance troops and mastermind conquests. Innovations became more frequent, and while they might have appeared at first to be of little importance, they contributed greatly to productive efficiency. Ancient Chinese inventions were adopted; others were rediscovered in the Arab world, which had been driven into decline by Islamic theocracy, despotism and the vice and decadence, as deplored by Ibn Khaldun.[5] The figure of the so-called merchant adventurer arose, and the drive for discoveries and profit opportunities intensified.

This triumph of individualism and activism contaminated the intellectual milieu of Europe. Philosophy and scientific investigation flourished. The religious world cultivated in the monasteries, which held a monopoly of knowledge, now began to court heterodoxy. The spread of heretical groups and then the explosion of the Protestant Reformation made theocracy impossible.

The idea of linear time, which infused the perception of 'becoming' and the sense of expectation, once it became wedded to a pluralistic, decentralized social structure permeated by the individual search for material wealth, ended up fertilizing the soil of commercial spirit and economic activity. A world open to creativity and change wedges its way into history.

Nevertheless, until the 16th century, there was no such thing as the self-sustained growth of the economy. Despite the progressive build-up of this pre-modern 'dress rehearsal' for capitalism, Western Europe was still less developed than China, though it had a key advantage: entrepreneurship. In fact, the great geographical discoveries of Ming admiral Zheng-Ha in the early 15th century had no effect on the centralized Celestial Empire, hostile as it was to businessmen and inclined to isolate itself from the outside world. By contrast, the European Age of Discovery was an epochal turning point driven mainly by the impetus of merchants and adventurers. The growing dimension of the market began strongly to stimulate labor division and hence labor productivity.

Still, the immense flows of resources that accompanied those events and the appearance of manufacturers could not by themselves have averted European society's relapse into quasistationary motion (even if at a higher level of development), or even the disintegration and the extinction of creativity, as in ancient Greece. This danger was averted thanks to the immense contribution of science. Henceforth, economic competition would be based even more strongly on innovation –Schumpeter's 'creative destruction'. The era of industrial society began and capitalism was fully established, at last.

The rise of a dynamic social system made the market a crucial organizational necessity. In fact, it is impossible for bureaucracy to govern a dynamic economy, which by definition is characterized by great uncertainty and which needs a steady supply of creativity and innovation. Bureaucratic organization inevitably leads to the stationary state. Entrepreneurship, creativity and innovation need the market, which is the sole mechanism that can coordinate a large quantity of disconnected initiatives and conflicting decisions in a radical state of uncertainty and eventually ensure their overall consistency while providing adequate incentives for all activities.

The central role of the economy and the need for the market – both of which imply the ontological imperatives of individual action, creativity and inquiry – allowed the progressive destruction of the centralized, authoritarian societies that had submerged the world until modern times. The extremely peculiar causes of this turning point are well exemplified by the case of Japan, a society that, despite many affinities with European feudalism and decentralization, was unable to free itself from stationary motion but relapsed into a centralized Shogun feudalism that lasted until the Meiji revolution following the arrival in Edo Bay of the American ships of Commodore Perry, in the 19th century, and the intimation to Japan of opening to the external world. This result is starkly different from that of Western Europe and must be attributed, primarily, to the absence of the capitalist market.

12.3 The capitalist market

This section focuses on the capitalist nature of the evolutionary process previously discussed. In particular, it underlines the initial propulsive strength of the capitalist market and proceeds to single out its growing limitations, which appear to form an explosive blend of contradiction, discontent and inefficiency in the present age.

In the 18th century, Mandeville emphasized the role of selfishness and corruption in driving society to prosperity and dynamism.[6] Soon after, Adam Smith's economics celebrated the 'invisible hand,' a metaphor for the combination of the market with individual interest. Both were right as commentators of their own era. In fact, the robberies and lack of all ethical constraint on the part of merchants and entrepreneurs were crucial to primitive accumulation; they were the prerequisite for the advent of industrial society. Well-governed social orders, like the great empires or Tokugawa centralized feudalism, were unable to promote endogenous growth, which was stimulated above all by the lubricating role of the market and self-interest. However, Mandeville and Smith went too far in asserting that these phenomena represented *natural laws*.

Secularization proceeded, promoting the theory of separation of economics and politics from ethics, and thus silenced the grumbling of the moralists. Such separation represented an evident scientific error. As a matter of fact, social subsystems always interact; they cannot be separated. But the scientific mistake operated very well in practice: it eliminated the submission to some ethical rules that contradicted various organizational and functional necessities of the new, modern world. Besides, it stimulated the alluring powers of material incentives and the role of the market. This drift accelerated the completion of the great march toward the *open society*, which gradually smashed the closed and authoritarian civilizations that were still left standing.

The accumulation of financial capital represents a central aspect of dynamic economies: an acute hunger for capital has accompanied the evolution of capitalism from its first steps. In medieval times, international traders from Italy invented a peculiar institution called *collegantia* to collect the commercial capitals they needed. Loan at interest and discounting (of commercial bills) was diffused in medieval fairs. Banking systems came to know a rapid diffusion. Amsterdam, and later London, became the heart of a powerful world capital market. The domination of finance capital had just started. The management of interest rates became the crucial mechanism of the monetary system, and speculative activities gradually ousted production from center stage.

The moral impudence of market relations and standard financial maneuvers soon began to engender disgust and moral disapproval, which were strengthened by intensifying exploitation. This development gave birth, in the realm of social thought, to a great error, well expressed by K. Polanyi's analysis: namely the idea that the market is just one of various organizational possibilities and that it can therefore be discarded in favor of a different one, say, a 'redistributive' (socialist) system. Such a conception found expression in a variety of utopian designs, which were for the most part fueled by indignation over the infamies of the market and its agents and which all called for the abolition of the latter.

The aims of antimarket utopia, however, never seemed to go beyond the notion of the stationary state and the closed society, which ultimately signify regression to retarded stages of development. This was shown clearly by the most distressing of such utopias, communism, which aimed to eliminate the market but never escaped its influence, from the early period of the NEP under Lenin's tyranny up to the recent collapse of all the socialist systems. The methodological equivocations afflicting social theory obscured the fact that the market, entrepreneurship and individual initiative are simply organizational necessities in modern dynamic economies and the open society.

The only critique of the market based on scientific foundations appears to be the analysis on 'market failure', according to which the market is in some instances found incapable to act efficiently, in particular with reference to public goods, and when market demand for goods is insufficient to absorb production. As a routine, governments – colluded with business – have encouraged a large expansion of public expenditure to remedy the deficiency of demand and therefore allow the market to 'digest' less troublesomely. Yet this routine was gravely flawed from the outset: it disregarded the efficiency of the public sector and of the public administration. This oversight stimulated the birth of an alternative approach that emphasized government failure, which, coupled with the fall of 'real socialism' in the East, greatly strengthened the market fundamentalists and thus boosted the advent of the so-called *new economics*: a gospel preaching absolute free trade and a blind faith in the free market.

Meanwhile, the rapid development of communications has allowed market relations to envelop the entire planet with thousands of tentacles, transforming the open society into a *global society*. Thus the free market has become the owner of the world, with the devastating presence of the modern Four Horsemen of the Apocalypse: distributive iniquity, growing international disequilibria, social disintegration and mass unemployment. These phenomena are most acute in the underdeveloped countries, but they do not spare even the heartland of the free market. In the United States, following the trend in the concentration of wealth, the difference between the highest and lowest personal income groups has almost tripled in the last 40 years.

The earnings of a CEO are almost a thousand times those of a simple workman, while public opinion is increasingly concerned over the unspeakable abuses of corporate power. The transition in the former socialist countries has almost always taken the worst of the market economy: privatization has usually produced massive frauds and corruption.

Everywhere around the world one may see the astounding facility with which the free market makes instruments of everyone and everything. The necessity of the market favors the diffusion of so-called capitalistic 'ethics' and 'civilization', even if they are not strictly necessary to market institutions. So, an insidious kind of colonization is at work, which people accustomed to different cultural values have come to hate with a passion. As mentioned before, not even the Western world can blindly trust the sorceries of the free market.

A highly dynamic society is obliged to cultivate a diffuse solidarity and a deep sense of cooperation to defend individuals from uncertainty, precariousness, loneliness and frustrations, which rapid social change is wont to inflict on man. Here, contrary to appearance, we have a basic inconsistency of the present historical era with the idea of a spontaneous social order. Today, moreover, the virtues of public expenditure in recreating the structural consistency between production and socialization have disappeared, having the public deficit become a constraint instead of a stimulus to production.

As we shall see later, such consistency now requires the market to be a mere mechanism of imputation of costs and efficiency. This is an important new *organizational necessity* of modern social systems. The race for earnings may itself foster the worst misdeeds and has, from a moral standpoint, incredibly destructive power. We have seen that the ability on the part of market relations to furnish incentives, during the march toward the open, global society, was intensified when it came to be combined with unethical behavior. Today it is ever more indispensable to link market relations to a higher level of ethics. The global dynamic impulse of the separation of ethics from politics and economics in social thought and action is beginning to turn into an obstacle to the growth and development of human societies.

The high level now attained by the general conditions of development and the growing social maturity of the masses make the persistent phenomenon of 'power as domination' ever more indigestible, a factor of growing contradiction. The transition to 'power as responsibility' is urgent in both politics and economics.[7] One of the great merits of the market is its capacity for automatic, objective and inflexible attribution of accountability for the results of daily economic activity and decisions. But it is necessary to flank this responsibility with an equally objective and inescapable subjection to the laws governing market relations, so as to avoid,

260 *Problems of political economy*

for instance, bribery and corruption, which also undercut economic efficiency. The crucial imperative today is, again, to disengage the market from its inclination and ability to turn all of us and the world at large into its tools.

Let us provide some solution to this problem.

12.4 Some other basic organizational needs of the present and coming economic systems

Now we turn to discussion of some other important functional imperatives concerning modern economies. These are in response to some organizational needs generated by the phase of conflictual-consumeristic capitalism and have not until now been properly fulfilled. This is causing growing difficulties and contradictions in the present world that threaten to become even more serious in the future.

12.4.1 *Entrepreneurial role and profit rate: the public and private spheres within the working of the market*

In this section we will identify some precise organizational requisites for the establishment of a wholesome entrepreneurial economy. Such a careful definition will enable us to combine our revisited model with diverse ideological options.

We have seen that modern economies cannot do without entrepreneurship and market relations and that the market's automatic, objective attribution of the entrepreneurial responsibility for action and decision is a precious device. Both in private and public companies (operating for the market), the only reliable indicator of success, and hence of responsibility, is the profit rate.[8] All other significant indices refer only to particular aspects of entrepreneurial action; they are partial and may accordingly become misleading.

Various economic theories maintain that the entrepreneur is interested in total profit, not in the profit rate. But total profit is not a ratio of return; therefore, it does not represent an indicator of entrepreneurial success. The search for total profit demands that investments be ranked on the basis of their earning rate if the global activity of the firm is constrained (as it always is) by the availability of some factor of production.[9] But the profit rate is a good indicator of success only if it is obtained in a competitive market, not through monopoly, for competitive markets force the entrepreneur to engage in a ceaseless struggle for profit and thus bind him to his function and his responsibilities.

To avoid misunderstandings on this crucial matter, an important specification on the notion of competition is required. The competition based on the entrepreneur's search for profit is the one considered here. As we saw, it may also be intended as a combination of Kirzner's 'market process' and Schumpeter's 'creative destruction'.[10] This notion of competition seems to be the only appropriate one in a discursive analysis of modern dynamic economies characterized by innovation and uncertainty. But a complication arises: successful innovation causes temporary monopoly. The complication is only apparent, however; in fact, an innovator's monopoly does not cause restrictions to competition, rather it is the engine of dynamic competition. Therefore, antimonopolistic vigilance must not target this kind of monopoly, which will vanish as soon as the incumbent innovation is undermined by a superior one – and that is as soon as the benefits for the community deriving from the original innovation cease. In short, an innovator's profits express the success achieved in the performance of entrepreneurial function, not a privilege.[11]

Under this setup it will be important to prevent entrepreneurs from falsifying the accounts to show larger than actual profits in order to deceive bankers and other financiers. In public firms, such falsifications may also be triggered by the aim of avoiding blame. The greatest watchfulness is therefore required.[12]

Procedures have been devised at the EU level to facilitate monitoring and gauging of corporate profitability. Other controls on corporate results are used for tax purposes. It is important to perfect these controls. In fact, the alarming frauds reported in the press are possible only because of the 'kindness' of the authorities, which turn a blind eye; such complicity must be harshly repressed.

The basic characteristics of the market as set forth here do not, at first glance, imply any theoretical innovation. However, their strict essentiality has substantial analytical value. Our model implies the unrestricted possibility of combining the market mechanism with a large number of different institutional, ideological and relational forms. In particular, our analytical foundations allow us to deal with the problem of property free from prejudice, inhibition and mystification, making evident that private ownership may be severely limited by public firms operating in the market without damage to efficiency and with some important advantages for social justice and the control of the overall rate of accumulation, and thus of aggregate demand. For in this kind of firm, profit serves only as the indicator of entrepreneurial success, which should determine whether the managers are kept on or discharged, and not as the vehicle for personal enrichment or unconstrained speculation.

As is well known, private property is one of the institutions that has vaunted, in the course of recent centuries, the greatest merits and demerits. It has been at the same time a great source of freedom and of oppression over time. It has been the main barrier against the stifling domination of public institutions, it has stimulated pluralism, it has been an important source of individual incentive, and it has constituted an important defensive shield of personal independence. At the same time, it has greatly stimulated and inculcated greed, and it has been a formidable means for the exploitation of man by man, and for countless other abominations. Moreover, it has fostered an enormous concentration of power. How are we to separate virtues from drawbacks to preserve the former and eliminate the latter?

This problem largely coincides with the question of delimiting the appropriate sphere for private property, while guaranteeing freedom and justice for all citizens.

We can set out a general principle: private property should be preserved insofar as it promotes productive efficiency, the satisfaction of citizens and the full appreciation of their qualities and aspirations, without implying the creation of dominant positions. Both durable and nondurable consumption should be included in the sphere of private property, in particular homes, gardens and intensively cultivated plots of land. Moreover, small farms and craft and commercial enterprises, whose success is difficult to monitor and hence to control, should be privately run. For efficient performance, these firms need the dedication that comes from private ownership and private appropriation of profits. And as these firms are small, they do not imply dominant positions.

In this economic system, everyone can consume what he wishes, as the search for profit will push firms, driven by prices, to satisfy consumers' preferences. Here the question of new goods and the manipulation of demand through advertisement arise. The introduction of new goods and services is of critical importance for consumers since it broadens their range of choice.

Furthermore, in the absence of new products, consumption would be saturated and the economy would stagnate. The entrepreneur produces new goods if he thinks they will be bought. But new goods require advertisement to inform people of their existence. What must be condemned is false, misleading advertisement, not informative publicity. It is undeniable that the purpose of publicity is always to influence consumers. But the purpose of any message is always to influence the listener. The only guarantee against the risk that such influence may create a dominant position, which jeopardizes freedom, is pluralism.

12.4.2 Production and distribution within the market operating as a pure mechanism of imputation of costs and efficiency

We are about to broach the core of our reformist proposal. Its goal is to delineate the widest possible bounds of social equality in ways that are consistent with freedom, efficiency and development; in other words, we are seeking to find the preconditions guaranteeing the highest degree of social equality that modern society may achieve.[13] The pursuit of these aims requires the transformation of the market into a pure mechanism of imputation of costs and efficiency. Such a transformation needs the establishment of a special fund; therefore, some preliminary considerations are necessary to clarify the nature of this fund.

The rapport of economics and social science vis-à-vis the market is twofold: on the one hand, the market has been considered as a potent vector of immorality, instability and social precariousness, and because of this, many have called for its wholesale abolition; on the other, the market has been understood as an institution indispensable to the efficiency of production, which, at most, is allegedly thought to require the complement of social welfare to run perfectly.

We saw that the first course of action is completely senseless in modern dynamic societies, while the second perspective appears nowadays utterly insufficient.[14] We wish to offer a different model, which operates a profound transformation of the market mechanism and which is predicated, among other things, on the creation of a special fund. This fund of community wealth should enable the system to conjugate the achievement of the highest possible productive efficiency with freedom in the distribution of income. More precisely, it will be proved that this fund is crucial to the pursuit of four main aims: business efficiency, distributive justice, full employment and individual autonomy. As far as we can tell, there is no example of such a fund in the present and past ages. Let us see how our suggested model functions by starting with production.

In this model, the firm buys the goods, factors of production and services required by its productive decisions on the market, at market price, just as it does today. But it does not pay wages; instead, it pays the price of labor as computed by work offices on the basis of the demand and supply of the various types of labor.[15]

However, the firm may pay incentives to its workers and also overtime, if it deems it advantageous.

Moreover, companies will pay into the fund a penalty for any damages to the environment; conversely, they should receive contributions for any social benefits deriving from their actions. Firms are also taxed. Finally, they may have to pay into the fund a surplus over regular labor cost to assist the transfer of workers from the district of origin. The purpose of this is to stimulate capital to flow toward labor, so as to minimize the effects of uprooting, congestion and urbanization generated by migration.

At the end of the production phase, the firm will sell output at market prices. With the proceeds, it will cover constant and variables costs, including capital depreciation and costs on borrowing, as well as taxation.

The difference between revenue and costs, divided by capital employed, yields the profit rate.

In addition to incentives and overtime paid directly by the firm, workers are entitled to a portion of the fund of community wealth. The determination of this portion and its distribution among social groups will follow criteria defined outside the firms, in the political sphere and through negotiations among social groups and their representatives. The share of each occupational group in income distribution may also depend, in part, on supply and demand for each kind of labor specialization; that is, each group's share may be augmented or decreased, depending on whether demand for that type of labor is greater or less than supply. In this way, the balance between labor demand and supply will be fostered by variations of supply, not only by the reaction of demand to changes in the price of labor. Each worker will be entitled to receive, from the fund of community wealth, a compensation proportional to his working time (but not overtime work, which as noted is paid by the firm) multiplied by the hourly compensation for his skill. To reduce transactions, firms themselves may pay this compensation, deducting it from their payments to the fund of community wealth.

At the end of each year, along with the share of output to distribute to labor in the next year, the average gain in labor productivity will be calculated and the share of that increase will be allocated to labor income, and the share allocated to a reduction in working time will be set. This allocation converts technological progress into higher labor income and free time, not unemployment. People look for jobs by direct contact with firms and following the suggestions of job centers, which have the knowledge of the demand and supply conditions for various skills (because they monitor demand and supply in order to set the price of each skill that firms have to pay into the fund of community wealth). Everyone chooses the job he finds more gratifying (by the type of activity, responsibility, distance from home etc.) and, if he is satisfied, he will keep his job; otherwise he will continue to search for more satisfactory employment. In case of collective dismissals, for instance, due to a firm's closing or downsizing, the dismissed laborers will receive benefits for the time needed to find another job.

We can see that this model does not consider labor as a commodity that wage earners sell to the firm but as a service to a productive system that entitles the worker to share in income generated. To prevent people from choosing not to work, in fact, the principle must be that except for those unable to work, the condition for a person to share in the community's income is that he be employed.

In this organization of production, large-scale long-term unemployment is prevented by the perfect flexibility of the price of labor with respect to demand and supply for various skills. As the price paid by firms for the use of labor skills is determined by the job centers on the basis of supply and demand, a labor glut would drive down its price and cost, thus stimulating firms (in the search for profit) to employ more labor and adopt capital-saving technology. The opposite happens if labor is scarce. This should push labor demand and supply toward equilibrium.[16] The tendency is strengthened if the education system produces versatile workers, enabling people to find various kinds of gratifying jobs. But to move the economy toward full employment, it is also necessary to pay attention to guaranteeing the equilibrium between aggregate demand and supply, as explained in Section 10.6. This need is particularly strong in modern dynamic societies, with their continuous local and global changes and adjustments. Even more, one must consider that knowledge and its evolution come largely from experience,[17] so that people excluded from the productive process are also excluded from important channels of knowledge and will be increasingly unable to avoid marginalization and alienation.

It may be useful at this point, for a better comprehension of the proposed revision of market dynamics, to work out a more extensive critique of some important aspects of the existing economic systems and ideologies in light of this very model.

If, as in the capitalist order, the distribution of income between labor and capital is the result of the clash between wage earners and firms, unemployment cannot be eradicated. To counter unions and working people's demands, employers use the infallible weapon of unemployment. If profits are low or firms incur losses, dismissals rise to crush labor's pretensions, and in dynamic economies, firms may also try, with the help of technical progress, to save on labor where it causes rigidities. It is senseless to found protection of labor on laws, norms and rules that oppose the mobility of labor; indeed, such legislation is one of the key impediments to the increase in employment.

It seems clear that the establishment of a fully flexible labor market, which is indispensable in modern dynamic economy, requires the abolition of wages set at the company and collective bargaining levels. This is all the more urgent in that ordinary collective bargaining does cause inefficiencies in the use of labor and makes unemployment physiological. Uniformity of national wage agreements and some other rigidities swell the underground economy in the areas where labor productivity is too low for the national wage rate. These illegal activities allow a fierce exploitation of workers who have no protection whatever. And the worst of it is that this underground economy is often the only alternative to unemployment.

Trade unions must seriously consider the severe restraints on their bargaining power. They may win as long as the claims of labor lubricate the entrepreneurial system, as wages, increasing in step with productivity gains, stimulate consumption, and hence sales, and eventually lead to an improvement in the condition of the work in the name of social peace and efficiency. But as soon as profits fall, unions find it impossible to force employers to pay higher wages. In substance, the game of wage bargaining is always dominated by the employers, who are most often propelled by competition, avidity and unscrupulous behavior. It is surprising that trade unions, whose function is to defend labor, have not understood that the root of exploitation is the institution of wage labor itself. It is a misfortune that the distribution of income is so largely determined by wage earnings.

Conflict between labor and capital over wage rates is the worst possible method of income distribution, and it works as a powerful obstacle to production. The task of firms is to produce material wealth and create jobs. They should be able to do so without being plagued by the perennial conflict with labor, which may be seen as an inappropriate social conflict since it takes place in the wrong place. Income policies to remedy the conflict demonstrate the failure of the company wage approach. They are rather tortuous ways of establishing some kind of income distribution more rational than that implied by the 'labor market'. It is crucial to bring income distribution outside the firm, as far as this is possible. This is indispensable to full employment and company efficiency consistent with social justice and individual autonomy. Trade unions should oversee health and safety in the workplace. They should fight for the distribution of the fund of community wealth, but not for the company wage.

Let us also point out that the idea of the workers' self-management[18] of the firm is mistaken. And the workers' remuneration based on firms' results is a vehicle of inequalities and managerial degeneracy. Firms must be managed by entrepreneurs and must not be involved in the struggle over income distribution. Entrepreneurs' abilities in decision making and innovating must not be constrained by the decision power of incompetent persons. The entrepreneur must be responsible in terms of results, that is, profit rate, not subjected to the command of a nonentrepreneurial body. Besides, the rational organization of the economy requires that firms pay for the resources they utilize, including labor, at prices determined by supply and demand. This is a fundamental rule of efficiency, indispensable both to rational use of the resources available and to defeating unemployment. Income distribution is a totally different matter, one that concerns society as a whole. The usual forms of wage bargaining obstruct efficient utilization of resources and prevent farseeing policies of distribution of wealth. Such bargaining is the product of spontaneous evolution, a sort of 'primitive' organizational form of society. An advanced society should be able to supplant those institutions with better-thought-out organizational forms.

Moreover, the strict link between the production and distribution of income – or, more precisely, the fact that the distributive conflict affects business accounts – seriously undermines the firms' investment, as well as economic growth and employment. Aggregate investment must be determined by the community and as part of the process of income distribution. This aspect was clarified in Chapter 10 by discussing how firms should be financed.

In conclusion, it should be clear that income distribution concerns the entire society and that even production is a social entity since it depends on productive forces engendered by society, such as techniques and knowledge. Some ingenuous theories of exchange value have long maintained that there is an unbreakable connection between income production and distribution. But no such connection exists, except the part due to incentives and the fact that income distribution influences production through the propensity to consume.

In particular, it is senseless to attribute to exchange value an ethical-ideological content as, for instance, the labor-value theory does. The statement value equals labor makes some sense only in a stationary economy. In an economy based on innovation, wealth is, in large part, a result of creativity, genius and the entrepreneurial search and intuition. Price is, therefore, a completely different thing from labor value, and there is no bridge between the two. Really, exchange value displays only the mere functional price role. Precisely, it acts as an indicator of productive opportunities and relative abundance and as a means to make homogeneous a multiplicity of commodities physically different from each other; its role is thus to facilitate comparison and exchange among these goods. So the ethical and ideological flavor of the labor-value hypothesis, with its implications on income distribution, expresses not only a limiting but also a senseless formulation of the much wider ethical and ideological problem.

The organization of production, distribution and exchange as discussed here attributes a social content both to income production and to distribution. Moralists and social reformers have always considered the market a gymnasium for corruption and aggressiveness, a place of violent contrasts among men, an open space for selfishness and fraud; in brief, it has been depicted as one of the worst instruments of domination, oppression and exploitation of man by man. But we have seen that the market can be shorn of these unpleasant attributes and transformed into a mere mechanism for the imputation of costs and the stimulus to efficiency through prices, which serve to signal the availability of each commodity. We have also seen that the market mechanism, aided by competition and combined with a profit rate as an indicator of success (which, as such, allows accountability), can be a highly effective mechanism for stimulating efficient decision making and management in the absence of monopolistic privileges and under the clear and inescapable rule of law (designed to prevent bribes and other abuses). The disconnection of the market mechanism from the struggle for income distribution makes for efficiency, individual initiative and social justice, and may thus be relied upon to turn selfishness into healthy rivalry.

12.5 Conclusion

This book has shown that the growing varieties of theories and visions characterizing economic thought are mainly due to some basic misunderstandings on the changeable economic and social reality, instead of being the expressions of a sound and fecund pluralism. The misunderstandings darken, among other things, the meaning and the propulsive role of ideologies. In the absence of science, men have recourse to intuition and common sense. But this is not enough to face the growing change caused by the rapid development of knowledge on natural phenomena and technology.

This cognitive penury has heavy consequences at a world scale, the reduction of which needs a penetrating criticism of the economic system that dominates the international landscape today.

One of the chief economic problems of the West has been its increasing reliance on a strange sense of sublimated superiority, which it has erroneously imputed to the most proximate origin of its wealth: the capitalist market. The inference is mistaken in that the source of this wealth, whatever the merits and demerits of its nature and uses, lies in human ingenuity rather than in the capitalist machine, whose essentially constrictive and feudal countenance has come, fraudulently, to represent Western economy as a whole. But capitalism is not Western inventiveness as a whole; it is but a proprietary scheme that has usurped all the fruits of Western creation. And this tragic *quid pro quo* has led the West to clash violently with the rest of the world. In truth, the capitalist system is the source of so many disadvantages to the Westerners themselves: namely, social injustice, poisoned labor relations and the threat to human dignity; social and geographical disequilibria; the wideness of fluctuations; the sorceries and distortions promoted by the hegemony of financial capital; and finally the suffocation of entrepreneurship, freedom and growth.

This book has attempted to show a possible way to remedy these ills, in particular the pervasive and distorting influence of the current market and financial systems. Our aim was to devise a model that couples efficiency with social justice, structural consistency with innovation; a system able to eliminate speculation and unnecessary (if not senseless) strife while preserving the conflicts implicit in the very functioning of a dynamic society, such as the battle between innovators and conservatives. And we have shown that a proper functioning of the market is not inconsistent with man's noble propensities, and that it may very well reduce fraud and greed.

The necessary set of conditions to achieve this goal consists of: (a) the reduction of the market to a mere mechanism for imputation of costs and of efficiency, (b) an expansion of the sphere in which public firms are allowed to operate within the market and (c) a drastic reform of the banking system. More in particular, we have dwelled on the essential role of the profit rate as an instrument of accountability for all concerns (public and private); the means of rebuilding a noncapitalistic economic body with a free market; and a model of capital accumulation able to stimulate entrepreneurship and to achieve the aggregate accumulation rate – a rate to be set by the community, with a view to eliminating the tumorous growth of overhead and interest charges and the volatile disasters of finance capital.

Notes

1 In the few ancient societies based on the activities of traders, like the Phoenicians and a few other *poleis* situated on caravan routes or along the shore, trading did not engender a cumulative development. Such a failure condemned them to extinction or subordination.

2 These were the members of the councils of the urban communities who were vested with deliberative power and competence on local finance, building, public works and public utilities.
3 The enormous economic power of the Roman aristocracy grew over time as a partial compensation for the political influence subtracted to senatorial class by the emperors and their civil servants. But aristocratic culture disregarded economic productivity and influenced the culture of the merchant class, while slavery made possible the sustainability of such a culture. On the other hand, the Christian-Judaic notion of linear time was obscured by the dominating civilization.
4 See A. Comnena, *L'Alessiade* (Stamperia Andrea Molina, Milano, 1849). Cupidity was very widespread, even among true believers. The crusaders of Peter the Hermit devastated the Balkans to a surprising degree, pillaging and slaughtering. They greedily ventured into Anatolia, too impatient to wait for support, and were promptly exterminated.
5 See Khaldun (1958). He was a great Arab historian and traveler across dar al Islam that lived in the 14th century. He wrote an important and voluminous history of Arabs, Persians and Berbers in which he fashioned a peculiar theory of historical processes. Through his creative analysis, he identified the cause of the decadence of the Arab world in the excesses of absolute power, injustice, unproductive expenditure, nepotism and corruption.
6 He was persuaded that "personal vices may be made useful, by a clever government, to the worldly happiness and the greatness of the whole" (see Mandeville 2000, p. 5).
7 See A. Fusari, *Understanding the course of social reality* (Springer 2016).
8 The well-known Lange and Lerner's rules that should drive the entrepreneurial behavior in market socialism make sense only in a static economy, that is, excluding innovation and uncertainty. Therefore, they cannot be referred to reality.
9 This is made evident by the formulation of a problem of optimization under the constraint of the available entrepreneurial skills (or some other scarce factor).
10 See Schumpeter (1954) and Kirzner (1973).
11 In neoclassical economics, price competition results in allocative efficiency. However, this is a result of comparative statics as opposed to a dynamic process. This is like taking a series of pictures – the economy that results is stationary, it does not move – the process by which we go from one point to another is an illusion, just as a motion picture provides the illusion of movement. However, since the movement from one point to another is not considered, the efficiency that results is one that is based only in the moment and is, thus, a stationary efficiency. The notion of competition relevant in this context does not imply such stationary efficiency. Indeed, neoclassical competition is almost senseless; a stationary economy does not need the market.
12 In workers self-managed firms, the falsifications are stimulated by the interest of workers to increase their earnings. A way of exaggerating profits may consist of the underestimation of capital depreciation and, on the part of banks, in the concealment of the losses due to the insolvency of the financed concerns. But these manipulations (directed to hide losses) will depress profit rates of the successive years, since they will cause a fictitious growth of capital and will thus force the firms performing those tricks to feed a growing fraud over time, which would become increasingly more difficult to conceal.
13 The treatment of this topic bears some resemblance to J. Rawls' investigation (1971), but our analysis is more specific and operative than that of this author, it being specifically concentrated on the concrete management of market relationships.
14 The debate on market socialism in the years between the two wars was hinged on the hypothesis of a stationary economy, which does not need entrepreneurship, and thus made room for the formulation both of a centralized model of the economy, as elaborated by Barone (1971), and a decentralized model of market socialism, with the managers' decision making simply dictated by Lange and Lerner's and Taylor's rules (see Lange and Taylor 1938, Lerner 1938).

15 As is well known, demand and supply give, by themselves, relative prices. So, to obtain the prices of nominal labor, it is necessary to refer to some labor price expressed in money units or, taking variations, to refer to initial prices expressed in money units.
16 Sraffa's demonstration of the re-switch of techniques is not relevant in this context; it only shows the erroneousness of the notion of average period of production and of the explanation of the interest rate on the basis of capital productivity. Moreover, it makes the hypothesis that wage rate is exogenous, which disregards the relation between wage rate and the supply and demand of labor.
17 M. Polanyi's pioneering insistence on *tacit knowledge* has provided a deep and extensive illustration of this aspect.
18 Where "workers have control over the production process in the enterprise in which they work, since they have ultimate authority, one-person, one-vote, on the enterprise itself" (Schweickart 1998, p. 127).

References

Barone, E. (1971), The minister of production in the collectivist state, in G. Lunghini (ed), *Value, prices and general equilibrium*, Il Mulino, Bologna, p. 76.
Cipolla, C. M. (1980), *Economic history of preindustrial Europe*, Italian edition, Il Mulino, Bologna.
Comnena, A. (1849), *L'Alessiade*, Stamperia Andrea Molina, Milano.
Dobb, M. H. (1933), Economic theory and the problem of socialist economy, *Economic Journal*, vol. 43, pp. 588–598.
Fusari, A. (1992), Entrepreneurship, market process and economic development: Some theoretical and empirical insights useful for managing the transition period, in W. Owsinski, J. Stefanski & A. Straszak (eds), *Transition to advanced market economies*, The Association of Polish Operational Research Societies, Warszawa, pp. 255–268.
Fusari, A. (1996), Development and organization of social systems: An interpretation of historical processes, Italian edition, *Sociologia*, no. 1, pp. 125–178.
Fusari, A. (2004), A reconsideration on the method of economic and social sciences: Procedures, rules, classifications, *International Journal of Social Economics*, vol. 31, no. 5/6, pp. 501–534.
Fusari, A. (2005), Toward a non-capitalist market system: Practical suggestions for curing the ills of our economic system, *American Review of Political Economy*, vol. 3, no. 1, pp. 85–125.
Gerschenkron, A. (1952), *Economic backwardness in historical perspective*, The Belknap Press of Harvard University Press, Cambridge, MA.
Hodgson, G. M. (1988), *Economics and institutions: A manifesto for a modern institutional economics*, Polity Press, Cambridge.
Homer, S. (1996), *History of interest rates*, Rutgers University Press, New Brunswick, NJ.
Khaldun, I. (1958), *The maqaddimah (An introductory to history)*, Routledge & Kagan Paul, London.
Kirzner, I. M. (1973), *Competition and entrepreneurship*, The University of Chicago Press, Chicago and London.
Lange, O. & Taylor, F. M. (1938), *On the economic theory of socialism*, edited by B. Lippincot, Minneapolis and New York: A. M. Kelley (1970).
Lerner, A. P. (1938), Theory and practice in socialist economics, *The Review of Economic Studies*, vol. 6, pp. 71–75.
Mandeville, B. (2000), *The fable of the bees*, Italian edition, Laterza, Bari.
Marx, K. (1977), *Il capitale*, Editori Riuniti, Roma.

Mises von, L. (1946), Economic calculus in the socialist state, in F. A. Hayek (ed), *Collectivist economic planning*, The University of Chicago Press, Chicago.

Ollman, B. (Ed.). (1998), *Market socialism: The debate among socialists*, Routledge, New York and London.

Polanyi, K. (1944), *The great transformation*, Holt, Rinehart & Winston Inc, New York.

Polanyi, K. (Ed.). (1957), *Trade and market in the early empires, economies in history and theory*, The Free Press, New York.

Polanyi, M. (1966), *The tacit dimension*, Doubleday, Garden City, NY.

Rawls, J. (1971), *A theory of justice*, The Belknap Press, Harvard University, Cambridge, MA.

Rostow, W. W. (1990), *Theorists of economic growth from D. Hume to the present, with a perspective on the next century*, Oxford University Press, New York and Oxford.

Saviotti, P. P. & Metcalfe, J. S. (Eds.). (1991), *Evolutionary theories of economic and technological change*, Harwood Academic Publisher, Chur, Reading, Paris.

Schumpeter, J. A. (1954), *Capitalism, socialism and democracy*, Allen & Unwin, London.

Schweickart, D. (1998), *Market socialism*, edited by B. Ollman, Routledge, New York and London.

Smith, A. (1976), *An inquiry into the nature and causes of the wealth of nations*, Italian edition, ISEDI, Milan.

Sraffa, P. (1960), *Production of commodities by means of commodities*, Cambridge University Press, Cambridge.

Stiglitz, J. E. (2002), *Globalization and its discontents*, Italian edition, Einaudi, Turin.

Index of names

Aghion, P. 132
Alchian, A. A. 56, 141–2
Antonine's dynasty 247, 255
Aquinas, T. 239
Arrow, K. 186
Augustus emperor 247, 255

Badeau, D. 99
Barone, E. 18, 40, 268n
Becker, M. C. 30
Berardi, G. G. 151
Blink, M. 99
Bodkin, R. S. 216n
Böhm-Bawerk, E. 239
Bole, R. J. 214n

Calcagnini, G. 186
Cantillon, R. 98
Cantner, U. 106, 133–4
Carter, R. A. L. 181, 227n
Charlemagne 248, 255
Circostanza don 234
Clower, R. W. 19, 48
Coase, H. 46, 141
Commons, J. 47
Comnena, A. 25
Constantine the Great 248, 255
Cournot, A. A. 146
Cyert, R. M. 146

Darwin, C. 17
Davidson, P. 20, 100, 186n
Davis, G. B. 36, 37
De Finetti, B. 186n
Delorme, R. 48n
Demsetz, H. 141–2
Diocletian emperor 255
Dopfer, K. 48n
Dosi, G. 134

Dow, S. C. 189
Drucker, P. F. 101, 103, 134

Egidi, M. 25
Einstein, A. 12
Ekstedt, H. 16

Fei, C. H. 230n
Feyerabend, P. K. 36
Foss, N. J. 142
Friedman, M. 233
Frish, R. 48

Galbraith, J. K. 21, 43, 146–7, 152
Garegnani, P. 48, 239
Georgescu-Roegen, N. 12
Gini, C. 64
Goldstein, J. 93
Gompertz, B. 12–13
Gort, M. 61
Goswami, A. 200
Grebel, T. 133
Grossman, G. M. 56, 132

Hanusch, H. 133, 186
Harsanyi, J. C. 186n
Hart, O. 153
Haunstein, H. D. 135
Hayek, F. A. 20, 24, 42, 140, 186n
Hegel, G. W. F. 17
Helpman, E. 56, 132
Hicks, J. R. 234–5, 243n
Hilferding, R. 236
Hobson, J. A. 203, 243n
Hodgson, G. M. 135, 144, 154, 186n
Holmoström, B. 153
Homer, S. 238, 243n
Howitt, P. 56, 132
Hume, D. 37

272 *Index of names*

Ibn Kaldun 256

Johansen, L. 48

Kahneman, D. 186n
Kaldor, N. 133, 147, 205–6, 213n, 243n
Kalecki, M. 146, 203–8, 214n
Kantorovich, L. V. 23
Keynes, J. M. 15, 19, 41–2, 87, 100, 202–5, 213, 232, 239, 249–51
Kindleberger, C. 230n
Kirzner, I. M. 20–1, 23, 28, 42, 97, 133, 144, 145, 178, 260
Klepper, G. 61
Knight, F. H. 14–15, 19, 21, 46, 48, 54, 98–9, 139, 186n
Kregel, J. A. 213n

Lancaster, K. J. 135
Lange, O. 18, 40, 268n
Langlois, R. N. 40, 162
Lawson, T. 186n
Le Goff, J. 243n
Lehnert, D. 135
Leibenstein, H. 99, 101, 132n
Leontief, V. 10, 48
Lerner, A. P. 18, 40, 268n
Lewis, A. W. S. 218–19
Littlechild, S. C. 133
Lotka, A. J. 179
Lucas, R. E. 55, 132
Lupton, D. 186n
Lutz, V. 230n
Luxemburg, R. 203

Machina, M. J. 186n
Malthus, T. R. 203
Mandeville, B. 257
Marani, U. 214n
March, S. C. 146
Marx, K. 17, 19, 35, 239
Mill, J. S. 44
Minkowski, H. 12
Modigliani 250
Moore, J. 153
Morroni, M. 186n
Mueller, D. C. 180

Nagar, A. L. 181, 227n
Narduzzo, A. 25
Nelson, R. R. 24–5, 132–3, 140, 144
Neumann von, J. 10, 16, 19
Neuwirth, E. 135

Odagiri, H. 180
Oliveira Martins, J. 93
Owen, G. 133

Pareto, V. 36
Parsons, T. 48
Pasinetti, L. 33–4, 37, 39, 40–6, 47, 132, 206, 250
Patinkin, D. 19, 47
Pellissier, G. M. 171, 185, 186n
Penrose, E. 101, 132, 139, 140, 147, 149, 150, 154
Perroux, F. 63
Perry (Commodore) 257
Piketty, T. 243n
Pindyck, R. S. 186n
Polanyi, K. 258
Polanyi, M. 22, 25
Pontryagin, L. 23
Popper, K. R. 35, 37
Prigogine, I. 12
Pyka, A. 13, 56, 87, 93n, 106, 133–4, 186n

Ranis, G. 230n
Rawl, J. 268n
Reati, A. 59–1, 185
Ricardo, D. 17, 19
Richard, D. 230
Roberts, J. 153
Robinson Crusoe 239, 250
Robinson, J. 204–6, 213n, 239
Romer, P. M. 56, 132, 135
Rosenberg, N. 119
Rousseau, J. J. 246
Rumelt, R. P. 132–3

Salanti, A. 37
Saltari, E. 186
Samuelson, P. 21
Savage, P. P. 186n
Saviotti, P. 13, 56, 87, 93n
Say, J. B. 98–9
Scarpetta, S. 93
Scazzieri, R. 186n
Schumpeter, J. A. 20–1, 24, 28, 42–3, 47, 54, 87, 99, 140, 157, 178, 249–51, 256, 260
Scott, M. F. 135
Screpanti, E. 37, 48
Shackle, G. L. S. 20, 100, 186n
Shell, K. 56, 132
Silone, I. 243n
Silverberg, G. 135

Simon, H. A. 23, 145
Sismondi, J. Charles L. 203
Smith, A. 257
Solow, R. M. 46
Sraffa, P. 10, 40–1, 73, 147
Stefik, B. 60–1
Stefik, M. 60–1
Stiglitz, J. E. 243n
Streeteen, P. 230n
Sylos-Labini, P. 134, 150

Taylor, F. M. 18, 40, 268n
Tily, G. 239, 243n
Tinbergen, J. 48
Tversky, A. 186n

Ulph, A. 30
Ulph, D. 30

Vale, P. 99
van Duijn 59
Veblen, T. 47
Volterra, V. 179, 181–4

Wade, D. H. 48
Wald, A. 19
Walras, L. 40, 42, 47
Weber, M. 35
Weintraub, S. 214n, 215n
Williamson, O. E. 46, 141
Winter, S. G. 24–5, 132, 140, 144
Wymer, C. R. 78, 132–3, 185, 186n, 225, 230n

Zaghini, E. 48
Zheng-ha, (Chinese admiral) 256
Zeuthen, S. 19, 48

Subject index

adaptation process 21; adaptive competition 42; adaptive structural organization 58
aggregate accumulation rate 267; amortization 10
arbitrage 98, 197

being and doing 36, 37, 47; becoming 37
boundary values 111, 255
BTS (Business tendency surveys) 162, 168, 186
business confidence indicator 168–9

capitalism: conflictual consumeristic capitalism 199, 206, 209, 217, 233–4, 240, 260; monopolist capitalism 202, 207, 217, 233, 260
centralization of decision making 6, 99, 110, 137, 148, 149; bureaucratic centralized empire 43, 52–3, 247–9, 255; decentralized organizational forms 25, 249
civilization 39, 45, 110, 127, 195, 198, 246–7, 253; capitalist civilization 39
continuous time models 217; and FIML (full information maximum likelihood) 216
creativity 38, 245, 251, 256, 266; creative aspects and events 20, 47, 194; creative destruction 21, 42, 60, 83, 98, 127, 140, 256, 260
cycle 13; business cycle 42, 59, 119, 159, 250–1; cycle of product 13, 119; cyclical motion 195, 198, 240; cyclical phase 13; intermediate cycle 11, 193, 240; large scale crisis 203; long run cycle 193; long stagnation 63; long waves 13, 52, 59, 61–3, 78–9, 197, 200; recession 13; recovery 13

decisional routines 24–5, 28, 107, 118, 140, 146
demand: aggregate demand 208; deficiency of effective demand 42, 201–3, 207, 210–11, 214, 233, 248, 256, 258; deficit spending 202, 218; demand and supply mechanism 205–6; demand led 4, 208, 218–19; effective demand principle 36, 40; excess of effective demand 210, 233; stagnation of demand 205
development process 12, 19, 193; economic and social development 26, 246; economic growth 41; general conditions of development 5, 17, 38–9, 44, 47, 57, 196–9, 255
distribution process (of income) 44–5, 47, 207, 249, 266; conflict (and struggle) for income distribution 205, 207, 217–18, 233, 235–7, 265–6; share of income distribution 206
dualism (economic, social and territorial) 41, 199, 201; advanced dualistic economies 217, 219; advanced sectors 217, 220; backward sectors and areas 216, 219, 220–1; developing countries 216; refuge sectors 219, 221
dynamic competition 5, 9, 12, 14, 15, 17–18, 19, 21–2, 24–5, 28, 52, 56–8, 179, 198; modern dynamic society 196, 198

economic planning 213
employment: full employment 202, 263, 265; large scale unemployment 205; refuge employment 219, 221; structural excess of labor force 205, 219; unemployment 264, 265
entrepreneur 6, 10, 12, 17; adaptive entrepreneurship 2, 21, 42, 87;

Subject index 275

entrepreneurial alertness 20, 97–8; entrepreneurial arbitrage 6, 7, 15; entrepreneurial role 24, 99, 217; entrepreneurial skills 25, 97, 106, 127, 143, 218; entrepreneurship 7, 12–13, 18, 20, 24–6, 28, 43, 87, 198, 239, 249; euthanasia of the entrepreneurial role 218; excess of entrepreneurial skill 52, 58–9, 87–8, 103, 108, 114, 117–19, 123, 125, 143; innovative entrepreneurship and action 42, 54, 98, 142; routine entrepreneurship 99

equality and diversity 245, 249; diversity equality 246–7; equality in dignity 246–7; human dignity 253

ethical principles of objective character 246; ethical relativism 246; tolerance principle 246

evolution 24; evolutionary economics 24, 28, 48, 106–7, 140–1, 144; evolutionary perspective 12; evolutionary potential 38; evolutionary process 194–5; spontaneous evolutionism 25

expectations 8, 9, 23, 27, 54, 86, 88, 202; firm expectations 161; profit expectations 44; rational expectations 9, 19; volatility of expectations 209, 217

exploitation 17, 258, 261, 265

financial market 232, 234–6; finance servant of production 237; financial activities 235; financial by products 237; financial capitalism 236, 240, 267; financial flows 232; financial speculation 236; great and global finance 245–6, 249; master of production 237; tyranny of the spread 237; world capital market 258

firm, the 25, 97; adaptive firms 121–2; big business 217; boundaries of the firm 151; firm dimension 25, 141, 146; giant firm 153; holding 148; innovative firms 121–2; managerial organization 148, 150–1, 153; multidivisional organization 148–9, 152; multinational firms 154; scale and growth economies 151; theory of the firm 137; top management 150

fixed capital 10–11, 64

function of production 7, 16, 47, 54, 57, 104, 133

fund of common wealth 241–2, 263, 265

Gamma distribution 12, 56, 63, 117, 120

heterodox economics 22–5, 28, 33–4, 47, 143, 153, 199

historical ages 39, 57, 93, 196–7, 240, 217, 259

imperatives: functional imperatives 36, 38, 39, 44, 196, 198, 240, 260; ontological imperatives 38–9, 44, 196, 198, 257

incentives 142, 245, 263; promotional incentives 219

income policy 214, 218

inflation: cost push inflation 201, 211; demand pull inflation 201, 211; inflationary movements 202

innovation 18, 20, 26, 28, 251; applied innovations 115, 117–18, 120; basic innovations 115, 118–19; diffusion of innovations 41; endogenous innovations 42; exogenous innovations 199; incremental innovations 11–13, 52, 56, 87–8; innovation adaptation mechanism 6, 21–2, 28, 42, 59, 100, 119, 143, 180; innovation dash and structural organization 194, 199; process innovations 9, 33, 52, 60–1, 79, 87–8; product innovations 18, 59, 61, 79, 88, 217, 250; radical innovations 11–13, 20, 52, 56, 62, 87–8, 215; seminal effects of basic innovations 117, 119–20, 126; seminal events 117

interest rate 44, 197, 232–3, 235, 238–40, 253, 258

IS-LM 19

knowledge: incomplete knowledge 140, 143; limits and lacks of knowledge 20, 22, 24–5, 27–8, 97, 141, 142, 145; organizational knowledge 25; perfect knowledge 5, 16, 18–19, 22–3, 28; tacit knowledge 22, 26, 140, 145

law of entropy 199; law of motion 35–7; Say's law 202

learning by doing 102–3

mainstream economics 3, 17, 23, 28, 33, 36, 44, 97, 106, 139, 250

market: capitalist market 43, 257, 269; competitive market 18, 260; market failure 253; market forms 18; market laws 140; market process 98, 140; market socialism 18; monopolistic competition 63; monopoly (degree of) 18, 26; oligopoly 18, 98, 127, 136, 220

Subject index

method: abstract rationality 16–18, 34, 35, 36, 40, 46; constructivism 36; CRP-TD 39, 50; econometric estimations 27; econometrics 26–7; logic formal method 47; methodological pluralism and methodological Babel 37; non repetitiveness-repetitiveness of events 34–5, 37; observation-verification 17, 34, 36; organizational view 24, 36, 199
money supply 232–3; liquidity preference 233, 235–6; liquidity trap 235; monetarist theories 211; monetary illusion 215, 234; nominal demand for money 233–5

necessity and choice-possibility 34–5, 39, 43–5, 57, 252; natural system 34, 40, 46; necessary conditions 201; necessary institutions 57; necessary system or model 34, 456, 237; necessary variables 62; organizational necessities 198–9, 254, 256–7

open society 257, 258
optimization 14, 23–4, 28, 143–4; maximizing choice 144; optimization models 18, 26; optimization principle 24–8

paradigm 8; exchange paradigm 40; production paradigm 39
phases of development 199
polarization aristocracy-slavery 248
postulates 37; postulate of residuality of real wages 204–9, 213, 215n; realistic postulates 34, 37, 38, 40–1, 46–7; their selection 37
power as domination 259; power as responsibility 259
predator-prey system 179, 181
prices, and price system 41; classical prices of production 41; mark up margin 207, 233; natural prices 41–2, 263; prices of consumption goods 206; prices of investment goods 206
private ownership 142, 261; property rights 142
probability distributions 100; objective probability 9, 156; subjective probability 9
profit rate 13, 147, 239–40, 264; accountability role of profit rate 45; expected profit 145, 239; standard deviation of profit rates 27, 54, 161, 179–80; variance of profit rates 27, 100, 105, 114, 117–18, 120, 133–4
public debt 218; balance of the public sector 217; budgetary policies 217; public waste 218–19; welfare state and policy 202, 219, 257

rationality 18; bounded rationality 4, 22–5, 28, 137, 140, 143–4, 158; human rationality 22, 28
Ricardian 10–11; neo-Ricardian 10
routine 43; decisional routines 101

sensitivity analysis 217; predictive performance 217; stability properties 217
separation problem and principle 34, 41, 43–7, 49, 249, 251
social justice 18, 232, 240–2, 245–6, 251, 261, 265
spontaneous order 20, 24, 259; spontaneous behaviour and processes 141, 248
stagnation of consumption 250; of demand 250; stationary motion 257; stationary state 258
surveys EU-ISAE 27; BTS 185; EU surveys 159, 180
switch function 62

technological frontier 106; blueprint of techniques 106; technological progress 134
time arrow 193, 198–9; circular time 255; endogenous time 12; linear time 256, 268n
transaction costs 25, 141, 143
triggering factors 62

uncertainty 6, 8, 12, 14, 17, 19, 20, 25, 28; immeasurability of radical uncertainty 3, 14, 100; perfect knowledge 4; radical uncertainty 4, 5, 9, 12, 19, 21, 24–6, 42–4, 51, 87

volatility (of opinions) 55, 88, 159, 160–1, 179–80, 186

wages: bargaining power 233; collective labour agreements 219; indexation of wages 205; programmed bargaining 217; subsistence level 205; trade unions 202, 205, 217, 219, 233; wage leadership 221
Walrasian general equilibrium 19, 40, 42